IN SEARCH OF PROVIDENCE

TRANSNATIONAL MAYAN IDENTITIES

In Search of Providence

Transnational Mayan Identities

Patricia Foxen

Vanderbilt University Press

Nashville

© 2007 Vanderbilt University Press
All rights reserved
First Edition 2007

11 10 09 08 07   1 2 3 4 5

This book is printed on acid-free paper made
from 50% post consumer recycled paper.
Manufactured in the United States of America
Designed by Dariel Mayer

Library of Congress Cataloging-in-Publication Data

Foxen, Patricia.
 In search of providence : transnational Mayan identities / Patricia Foxen.
— 1st ed.
p. cm.
Includes bibliographical references and index.
ISBN 978-0-8265-1580-3 (cloth : alk. paper)
ISBN 978-0-8265-1581-0 (pbk. : alk. paper)
1. Quiche' Indians—Guatemala—Quiche'—Social conditions.
2. Quiche' Indians—Guatemala—Quiche'—Migrations.
3. Quiche' Indians—Relocation—Rhode Island—Providence.
4. Quiche' Indians—Rhode Island—Providence—Ethnic identity.
5. Quiche' Indians—Rhode Island—Providence—Economic conditions.
6. Quiche' (Guatemala)—Emigration and immigration.
7. Providence (R.I.)—Emigration and immigration.
I. Title.
F1465.2.Q5F69 2007
305.897'42307452—dc22   2007019252

IN MEMORY OF MARILU

CONTENTS

ACKNOWLEDGMENTS

This book has been the product of many dialogues. The voices of colleagues, teachers, institutional contacts, friends, and family have traveled with me from Canada to Guatemala to the United States and back again. At McGill University, I thank first and foremost Ellen Corin for her guidance and encouragement; she has taught me the value of creativity and rigor in the field of anthropology, and has always been so generous with her time and support. Cécile Rousseau has been a mentor whose intellect, humanism, and engagement are hugely inspiring to me and to others. I am grateful to Margaret Lock for setting the bar for excellence and always raising it higher. Many thanks to Laurence Kirmayer, Allan Young, John Galaty, Kristen Norget, Laurel Bossen, and the late Roger Keesing for their tutelage and suggested readings throughout this project. I owe much to Rose Marie Stano for her efficiency and generosity. I thank the Social Sciences Humanities Research Council of Canada (SSHRC) for a two-year grant that supported, in part, the writing of this book.

The help of many people made my fieldwork possible. Thank you warmly to George Lovell, whose advice and support throughout the project have been greatly appreciated. I am grateful to Duncan Earle for steering me in the "transnational" direction early on and for offering numerous helpful comments upon the book and the places and issues described herein. Thanks to Alain Breton for his generosity, and to Jim Handy, Irene Palma, and Linda Asturias de Barrios for sharing their knowledge of the country with me during my fieldwork in Guatemala. I appreciate the institutional support provided in Guatemala by CIRMA (Centro de Investigaciones Regionales de Mesoamérica), ASIES (Asociación de Investigación de Estudios Sociales), and AVANCSO (Asociación para el Aveance de las Ciencias Sociales en Guatemala). My work in the highlands would not have been possible without the help and accommodations provided by Anne Bourguey, Claude l'Hoiry, and Stéphane de Rengervé. Many thanks to my friends France Bégin, Pierre Chouinard, Celeste MacKenzie, and Alicia Sliwinski for their generosity and companionship throughout my fieldwork. A very special thanks to Felipe, Eustaquia, Fransisca, Josefina, and Wilma for their contributions to the data collection and translations. From my *compadres* Javier and Cristina Toj, I learned a great deal about the struggles of the past and the resiliency of the present, and I thank them warmly.

Thanks to Dan Rothenberg and Erminio Pinque for pointing me in the right direction in Providence. I am forever indebted to Grace Ashton for offering lodgings in the West End to this rather desperate anthropologist, and for being a wonderfully supportive roommate throughout my fieldwork there. A warm thanks to Denny Moers, whose friendship and humor are always a great comfort. I would like to acknowledge Bill Shuey, Karl Kruger, Mary Troger, Karen Crawford, Olga Noguera, Sandra Mora, Delia Smith, and Stan Birkirski for the valuable information they provided me during interviews in Providence. Many thanks as well to Eric Popkin, Manuel Angel Castillo, Catherine Nolin-Hanlon, Olga Odgers and Debra Rodman for sharing their expertise on Central American migrations. My colleagues from the Transcultural Psychiatry team of the Montreal Children's Hospital have been a source of kindness and support; their everyday work with victims of violence and displacement has been an inspiration for my understandings of these issues. At the University of Montreal, I thank François Crépeau and fellow researchers at the Centre de Recherche du Canada en Droit International des Migrations for providing a supportive milieu that fosters stimulating discussion and research on immigrant and refugee issues.

Portions of Chapter 5 were previously published in the article "A la recherche d'identités au Guatemala après la guerre civile: perspectives transnationales" in *Recherches Amérindiennes au Québec* 31, no. 1 (2001): 61–70. Parts of Chapter 6 were included in the article "Cacophony of Voices: a K'iche' Mayan Narrative of Remembrance and Forgetting" in *Transcultural Psychiatry* 37, no. 3 (2000): 355–81, and are reprinted here by permission of Sage Publications Ltd. Thanks to colleagues who read and commented upon those articles, including Derek Summerfield, Laëtitia Atlani, and Pierre Beaucage. I would like to acknowledge Scott Lutes, Kurt Chaboyer, María José Olivarria, and Wren Nasr for their research and computer assistance on earlier versions of this manuscript. I am grateful for the feedback provided at various times by James Cisneros, Robert Barsky, and Christina Zarowsky on portions of this book. A special acknowledgment to Dominique Behague for carefully reading and commenting on several chapters, and for her constant support; and to Kacy Silverstein, whose editing eye helped me with some finishing touches. Beth Conklin, Sergio Romero, Ted Fischer, and Tom Dillehay provided collegial support at the Vanderbilt Anthropology Department during the final write up. I greatly appreciate the very useful suggestions offered by several anonymous reviewers and extend a special thanks to my editor at Vanderbilt University Press, Michael Ames, for his invaluable writing suggestions and patience.

I would not have been able to complete this project without the love and encouragement of my parents Richard and Hilda Foxen, who have given me such tremendous opportunity and whose wisdom and world-views have always guided me. I thank my sister Theresa Timmis for her unconditional support throughout the difficult and exciting phases of this project, and I am grateful for the cheerleading of Jerry Timmis, Richard Foxen, Thomas and Cecily Foxen, Anthony and Erica Foxen, and their families, throughout this process. I also acknowledge Adela Toro, whose own transnational story has been such an important part of my life. Finally, I have an immeasurable gratitude and admiration for the K'iche' who befriended me and shared with me the lives recounted in this book; unfortunately, their names must remain hidden, but their spirit will not.

PREFACE
ONE FOOT HERE, ONE FOOT THERE

Approximately twenty-five years ago, a violence perhaps more cataclysmic than the Spanish conquest itself made its way to the Central American nation of Guatemala. At this time, the country, like several of its neighbors, was involved in a brutal civil war in which the government and its military forces were trying to extinguish what they perceived to be a significant Marxist threat in the largely indigenous highland and jungle regions of the country. Hundreds of Mayan communities were burned to the ground; tens of thousands of Indians were killed, "disappeared," tortured, widowed, and orphaned; and even larger numbers were physically displaced—a violence that was described in retrospect by the 1998 United Nations–brokered Historical Clarification Commission (CEH) as a genocide against the Mayan Indians of Guatemala.

In the face of massive economic and psychological devastation, a number of Guatemalan communities came to be lured by hopes for escape, safety, and employment in that vast landscape known broadly as *el Norte*. For the K'iche' Mayan Indians[1] of Xinxuc, an impoverished municipality located in the highland department of El Quiché,[2] the place both desired and feared, tried and tested by a few pioneer migrants following the violence's apex, was named *Providencia*. In the twenty years since this initial flight, the migratory flow between rural Xinxuc and the inner city of Providence, Rhode Island, has developed into a solid and sophisticated transnational circuit characterized, until relatively recently at least, by a regular movement of people, money, commodities, information, and ideas between these two settings. The following pages illustrate how this spiral movement between *aquí* (here) and *allá* (there) has affected Xinxuc's Mayan Indian population, raising broader questions about the notions of identity, place, and belonging in today's increasingly mobile world.

My initial acquaintance with Central American refugees began in the mid-1980s, when I worked as a volunteer for a Central American solidarity organization in Cambridge, Massachusetts, whose primary goal was to inform the American public of the role of the United States in supporting violent military regimes throughout the isthmus region. This association, which was connected to the Catholic Church's sanctuary movement, also provided shelter to those escaping oppression at home. At this time, the ideological divide between military and revolutionary groups throughout Central America was echoed in the discourses of the US government and local solidarity groups, all of whom tended to frame regional violence within the polarizing Cold War rhetoric of the time. In the years that followed, working on health projects in war-torn countries such as Colombia, Nicaragua, and El Salvador, I caught an additional glimpse of the devastation resulting from warfare and poverty. It was through these experiences that I slowly became acquainted with the complex stories of many Central Americans, stories which often fell well outside of the conflicting discourses of left and right—whether the "official stories" of governments and armies, the revolutionary language of solidarity groups, or the bureaucratic terminology of development organizations.

In the early 1990s, as I began studies in cultural and medical anthropology, I hoped to engage this interest in Central America from a perspective that could accommodate the nuances of people's war-related experiences. Seeking to avoid victimizing or pathologizing representations of "the refugee experience," I conducted a small ethnography of the Central American refugee community living in Montreal, Canada, hoping to identify the ways in which people gave meaning to past violence and their present displacement.[3] Many of the stories collected for this project (which set the stage for the approach used in this book) were striking because they contained shifting and often contradictory discourses, reflecting both real and idealized notions of home and host cultures. For example, while the poverty and violence of home were usually described as negative elements from which individuals sought to distance themselves, they were simultaneously offered up as key components of a Central American identity, linked with a sense of community or political engagement. Similarly, while the system of rights and justice in Canada was praised and contrasted to the corruption of home, it was nonetheless blamed for the familial disintegration and absence of respect found in the host culture. Situated at the margins of both home and host societies, the refugees positioned themselves within a dynamic set of cultural and moral references drawn from both "here" and "there," which enabled them to construct flexible identities within this precarious space.

By the mid-1990s, Central American nations were ostensibly on the road toward peace,[4] and I was preparing to conduct research on the psy-

chosocial consequences of war within Central America, and among Guatemalan Indians in particular. By this point, well over 10 percent of the Guatemalan population—more than one million people—had been internally
displaced, while another six hundred thousand had left to seek refuge in
Mexico and other Central American countries. Despite the imminent end
to the violence, this period proved to be particularly difficult for working
with refugees in the region. Shortly after I submitted a proposal to work
with refugees living in camps in Chiapas, Mexico, the Zapatista insurrec-
tion sprang forth, giving the Mexican government a rationale for heavily
militarizing the region, and I was strongly advised not to pursue this topic
at the time.[5] A second proposal, designed to examine issues of reintegration among Guatemala's returning refugees, was also dropped following
the massacre of Xamán, a returnee community attacked by army forces as
the country drew up peace plans.[6] I realized that working with refugees in
Guatemala would be dangerous not only for me but, more so, for anyone
with whom I would associate in the field, as many refugees (and those
who worked with them) were perceived by the Guatemalan authorities as
subversive.[7]

Immersed in the language of violence characterizing much of the literature on Guatemala, I began to question the validity—ethical, pragmatic,
and intellectual—of conducting research on these topics as an "academic"
in the current environment. Because much of the recent material on Guatemala focused on the horrific impacts of the war and since the brutality
that had swept the countryside had been documented in human rights
reports and several outstanding anthropological accounts,[8] I feared the potential "prurience" that might result from an ethnographic approach centered directly on the consequences of war (Daniel 1996). In other words,
the prospect of dredging up people's painful histories and memories in an
atmosphere of continuing fear, and with little to offer in return, seemed
increasingly unappealing.

One war-related occurrence that was receiving little attention at this
time was the growing population movement from various parts of Guatemala to the United States. By the 1990s, the earlier trickle of wartime
escapees had developed into established communities of Guatemalan labor
migrants throughout the country, many arriving from devastated highland
areas. From seasonal agricultural work in Oregon; to mushroom farms
in Colorado; to poultry-processing plants in Nebraska, North Carolina,
Tennessee, Delaware and Ohio; to landscape gardening in Long Island
and Michigan; all the way to the urban assembly lines of Chicago, New
York, and Massachusetts, Mayan Indians were finding ways to quietly fill
economic niches throughout the United States. Jobs in these areas were
becoming increasingly attractive alternatives to the saturated labor markets

and contentious immigration politics in states with large Hispanic populations such as California, Florida, and Texas.

I was surprised to discover through a casual conversation with an immigration lawyer in Boston that somewhere between ten thousand and
fifteen thousand Guatemalans, many of whom were indigenous, were also
living in Providence, Rhode Island, a city known on the outside for its
high-brow universities and relatively wealthy, white population. Most of
these migrants were working in the jewelry and textile factories and fish-
ing industries that formed an important part of the region's economy. The
majority, I was told, were undocumented or held temporary work permits,
and while they seemed to preserve strong links with their home villages,
they remained largely hidden within the host context.

At this point, what little research existed on indigenous Guatemalan
immigrants in the United States focused primarily on the border states and
tended to concentrate on people's experiences in the host context, with the
community of origin appearing primarily as a backdrop.[9] Inspired by the
recent anthropological interest in transnational migration, which encouraged research on both ends of the migratory circuit, I decided to conduct
my fieldwork with the Mayan population in Providence and a corresponding home community in Guatemala. Where to begin became an important
methodological decision. Given the delicate nature of approaching a mostly
undocumented population at a time when immigration laws in the United
States were becoming increasingly restrictive, I decided that it would be
wiser to enter the field through the context of a home community. I set
out to discover whether the Maya-Providence connection stemmed from
a particular location within Guatemala or whether its origins were more
scattered.

This ethnography is based on approximately sixteen months of fieldwork conducted in El Quiché and Rhode Island between 1996 and 1998;
the first eight months were spent in Xinxuc, followed by five months in
Providence, as well as a few month-long return visits to both communities.
This coming and going between the two places was central to my own understanding of the dynamics of transnational migration and, consequently,
to the quality of the observations upon which this work is built. These
journeys between the "hurtful beauty"[10] of the Guatemalan cornfields and
the surprising worlds of an American inner city were characterized by odd
twists of luck, moments of profound uncertainty and fear, and a constant
repositioning of my own assumptions, which in some ways parallel the
larger themes of the book.

The notion of transnational migration—what it is and how it differs
from other types of population movement—has been the subject of lively
academic debates over the past decade or so. In the 1990s, transnational-

ism became a fashionable term, referring broadly to the blurring of borders caused by accelerated globalization processes such as wide-scale shifts in manufacturing and trade and advances in transportation and communication.[11] Transnational migration was argued to be part of this process, since shifting economic trends were pushing increasing numbers of people from their jobs and land in poorer countries,[12] while simultaneously attracting them toward low-paying, unstable ones in wealthier countries.[13] In many areas of the world, large-scale migrations were also increasingly aggravated by violent military and political conflicts, thus obscuring clear-cut distinctions between refugees and economic migrants. In the particular case of Central American migrations to the United States, the host society was instrumental in instigating both "push" and "pull" factors by supporting military regimes that led people to leave devastation at home and by recruiting cheap, unskilled labor from America's "backyard." The United States' complicity in contributing to these migratory flows has not been reflected in the nation's ambiguous immigration policies toward these populations.

Over the past two or so decades, these overall patterns have led to growing numbers of people finding it difficult to construct secure bases in either their own countries or in host societies. In response to this dual vulnerability, many have felt the need to live their lives—that is, tend to their material needs, social commitments, and loyalties—in more than one place, or in the words of many transnational migrants, *con un pie aquí y otro allá* ("with one foot here and one foot there").[14] Obvious signs of this "new kind of social space" can be clearly observed throughout North American cities and in home communities, where money-transfer houses, phone parlors and cards, transnational courier services, and other transmigrant enterprises proliferate.[15] Music, fashion, family dynamics, household and community economies, and ethnic, gender, religious, class, and political formations—in short, what might be labeled cultures—are increasingly produced and consumed between "here" and "there."[16]

In the past, frameworks for studying migration tended to posit a unidirectional shift from "sending" to "receiving" communities, understood as mutually exclusive, and a corresponding temporal divide between pre- and postmigration contexts. Since the most salient aspect of transnational migration is the degree to which it involves regular and sustained contact and activities between people situated at either end of the transnational circuit, the "simultaneity" of social fields across borders has necessitated dramatically new ways of understanding this phenomenon.[17] In transnationalism, broadly speaking, notions of space and time are no longer seen to be static or linear, but reflect the multiple spaces and syncopated temporalities (the blurring of "here/there," "then/now") that influence the construction of new identities and experiences.[18] Moreover, because transnationalism defines a form of "double consciousness" whereby people remain materially and symbolically oriented to both contexts, it emphasizes the often uneven and contradictory processes through which variously situated people juggle nation-based social categories—unlike the more fixed notions of culture that have often been implicit in assimilation studies.[19]

Some of the past decade's more postmodern perspectives, which focused on the liberating potential of new transnational arrangements, have been amply criticized for downplaying the structural constraints and boundaries that continue to shape people's lives within and across borders.[20] With the growing empirical research on today's diversity of transnational movements, it has become clear that the study of this phenomenon should be firmly situated within very specific maps and histories. If transnationalism remains a somewhat nebulous concept,[21] research on transnational migration in particular has tended to focus more concretely on cross-border communities, networks, and activities, and recently scholars have proposed clarifications for studying different types and degrees of transnational contact.[22] Several broad themes have emerged from this body of research that are pertinent to an understanding of transnational identity formation in the Mayan case. First, transmigrants and their family members are often described as liminal social actors—"betwixt and between" people who tend to remain indefinitely in a transitional space.[23] Within home communities, the possibility of joining one's family members or friends abroad can become a perpetually pending life-plan, and nonmigrants are often poised to leave at any time. At the other end of the circuit, transmigrants might expect to return (or be deported) at any time but may simultaneously postpone the return home indefinitely for a number of reasons. These processes can shift through time, as a consequence of both changing structural determinants (e.g., host country immigration policy) and individual or family goals. Although this "liminality" may create an ongoing sense of possibility, it can also contribute to pronounced levels of anxiety and uncertainty about the future, particularly for those who do not have the option to migrate legally.[24]

Second, most transmigrants—those who regularly engage in cross-border activities of various types—usually seek to enhance their chances of upward socioeconomic mobility and status at home, and sometimes abroad as well. The flexibility with which these people are able to manage different social categories, such as class, ethnicity, gender, and so forth, across borders often becomes an important form of social and symbolic capital in the quest for transnational success. However, degrees of incorporation into both home and host contexts can vary widely, and some individuals and groups are clearly more successful than others at learning to juggle multiple cultural references and thus to turn their "in-betweenness" into a position of relative strength.

Third, while transnational migration is usually propelled by larger structural changes, it takes on a life of its own at the community level and becomes an integral part of local economies and the norms, value orientations, and expectations that shape community culture. The "chain reaction" built into the dynamic of transnational migration can bring about significant social changes including increased local economic inflation and class differentiation caused by remittances sent from abroad; the transformation of needs and expectations created by increased consumerism; and other changes in social values.[25] All of these processes lead people to compete in the transnational field and function to make transmigration a normative, though highly unpredictable, process.

And finally, although some authors have warned against using the concepts of "transmigrant" and "transnational migration" too loosely,[26] ethnographers have shown that it is by analyzing broader community dynamics among a range of social actors that we can fully understand the impact of this phenomenon. As Levitt et al. point out, people engage in both cross-border processes and community-bound behaviors with a fair amount of selectivity, "with considerable variation in the sectors, levels, strength and formality of their involvement" in both realms (2003: 569). In this vein, Levitt and Glick Schiller state, a distinction should be made between "ways of being in" transnational social fields and "ways of belonging to" such fields. The first pertains to the "actual social relations and practices that individuals engage in," while the second signifies an awareness of the kind of identity that action suggests, for example the "sense of belonging" of people on either end who do not retain concrete social ties but who engage with the other community through imagination, nostalgia, or memory (2004: 1010).[27] It is thus through the study of cross-border community relations, both real and imaginary, that we can observe some of the more uneven and often paradoxical changes produced by today's transnational migrations. By looking at local histories and internal struggles and by understanding the ways in which different people participate in transnational social fields, it becomes possible to highlight how the new flows (of people, money, ideas, values) meet up against older practices and identifications and to examine whether these two orientations work in harmony with, or against, each other.

While the comings and goings of transnational movement are an essential thread running through the following pages, it is the notion of Mayan Indian identity—K'iche' Mayan identity specifically—that comprises the book's core. This focus places the ethnography within a long history of ethnographic and historical literature revolving around indigenous culture in Guatemala. This fascination with the Maya is not surprising, given that the survival of Guatemalan Indians into the present has attested to a remarkable history of resistances to the threats of violence, subjugation, and assimilation imposed at first by the Europeans and then by the Guatemalan nation-state. Of Guatemala's population today (approximately 12 million), roughly 60 percent is indigenous, representing more than twice the native population encountered upon contact and ten times its population at independence (Lovell and Lutz 1994: 138). The continuation well into the twenty-first century of what has in the past been labeled Guatemala's "Indian question," transformed today into the idiom of multiculturalism and indigenous rights, indeed makes this nation unique in Central America.

Never has the subject of indigenous culture been so hotly debated in Guatemala as in the recent postwar period.[28] The struggle over Mayan Indian identity—what it consists of, who it includes, by whom it is best represented, and what it seeks to gain—has been at the forefront of peacetime efforts. A perplexing question in this period of national reconstruction, however, remains: What does it mean to be a Mayan Indian? Is it to speak one of the twenty-two Mayan languages and refer to oneself as *natural*?[29] To come from a rural *municipio* (township) of the western highlands or be settled in the northern jungles? To tend one's *milpa* (cornfield) for subsistence and migrate seasonally to the coastal plantations (or elsewhere) for cash? To weave and wear a *guipil* and *corte*[30] and make daily *tortillas*[31] if one is a woman? To serve in a community *cofradía* (religious brotherhood) and be skillful with an *azadón* (hoe) if one is a man? To believe in a Mayan cosmology of cycles of good and bad, of year bearers, *naguals* (animal spirits), and ancestors, while celebrating one's local saint each year with the help of a *marimba* band and a potent supply of *cuxa* (firewater)?

Or, can one also be a restless rural (or urban, or both) youth sporting jeans and a Walkman and well-versed in Rambo movie plots; an evangelical, teetotaler entrepreneur; an ex-Marxist guerrilla, working for a US government-sponsored development project, who has recently espoused Mayan *costumbre*;[32] an ex-soldier who has been taught to despise *la raza* (the Indian race); a cosmopolitan, multilingual university-educated anthropologist or politician struggling to promote Mayan unity; or even a factory laborer, meat packer, or fruit picker in the United States who sends monthly remittances home to monolingual[33] parents, raises American children, and, if lucky, returns home each year for the *fiesta* (patron saint's feast)?

All of these characterizations of Indianness exist today, contributing to the diversity of voices that currently constitute the Guatemalan Indian population. No longer does indigenous identity conform to the binary model that has long been the basis of racial hierarchy and state practices

in Guatemala—where the Indian, fixed in time and space, signified traditional, rural, backward, and subordinate (or subversive), while the non-
Indian, or Ladino, was seen to be modern, literate, and powerful.[34] In the
midst of the profound transformations produced by new political struggles
and rapid globalization, indigenous identity is currently understood and
represented in increasingly contested ways by the various actors involved in
its production, including Mayan activists, state organizations, the army, national and international NGOs and human rights workers, anthropologists,
and the millions of Indians living both within and outside the boundaries
of the Guatemalan nation-state.

In order to analyze the impact of transnational migration on today's
Mayan Indian communities, the following pages approach the notion of
indigenous identity from a variety of angles. To begin with, I situate Indian
culture within the much deeper history that has shaped social relations in
Guatemala since the conquest, highlighting the hybrid cultural strategies
that have long been part of indigenous responses to outside forces and that
have enabled Indian communities to endure. "Hybridity" here refers not
only to a mixture or combination of different cultural elements but also to
a range of strategies of accommodation and resistance to the nation-state,
including indigenous community practices that have balanced multiple
economic options available inside and outside of community boundaries.[35]
This particular historical approach underscores the centrality of migration
as a deeply ingrained Mayan survival strategy, and even an organizing
principle, despite the fact that indigenous identity has also been characterized by a strong attachment to land and place. I argue that newer identity
constructions emerging from Maya transnationalism must therefore be
understood not only as part of the recent (and quite radical) dislocations
produced by accelerated globalization and warfare but also in terms of the
deeper forms of historical mobility and consciousness within which they
are embedded.

A concrete illustration of these processes is offered through the case
study of Xinxuc's transnational community. The ethnography begins with
a description of the beliefs and practices through which the K'iche' have
historically forged connections to their physical and spiritual environment,
as well as the "revolving door" to the outside that has made community
boundaries fluid. The social relations and power dynamics governing
Xinxuc's own unique history and ethnic composition—and, most specifically, the ways in which these were profoundly distorted and exploited during the civil war—serve as a baseline for examining how local identities
then become reconfigured in transnationalism.

Following a discussion of the postwar exodus from Xinxuc to Providence, I examine the changing material conditions and forms of organiza-

tion ensuing from transnational movement. Life in Providence is described with special attention to new labor conditions and social activities, as well as the impact of volatile immigration laws upon transmigrants' daily lives. I then examine the ways in which K'iche's concretely balance social practices across borders in order to maintain links between home and host communities. As we shall see, changed economic relations produced by the flow of remittances and consumer goods to Xinxuc increase social cleavages, and new forms of organization, symbolic markers, and styles follow in train. Although in some ways novel to this community, these modified relations are interpreted through long-standing cultural idioms that enable the K'iche' to make sense out of the rapid material transformations produced by cross-border migration.

Transnationalism also brings with it new ways of imagining identities, communities of sentiment and belonging that integrate cultural traces from both sides of the border. I therefore go on to describe how the K'iche' self-consciously refashion notions of ethnicity and Indianness within two highly contrasting contexts—one a landscape defined by the postwar Mayan ethnopolitical movement and the other hidden, marginal spaces shared by undocumented migrants in Providence. The Mayanist project has not fully resonated in communities like Xinxuc, which remains divided and conflicted in the postwar period. In Providence, by contrast, where markers of indigenous ethnicity are muted and divisions persist, K'iche's nonetheless find surprising ways to reappropriate and affirm Indianness. Here, historically entrenched power divisions between Indians and Ladinos are transformed, and indigenous identity is linked in positive ways to the transnational migratory project.

Since the movement between Xinxuc and Providence can be characterized as both a labor migration and a response to state-sponsored warfare—two processes rooted in centuries of structural inequality—much of this book is concerned with the different types of social violence that continue to taint every aspect of life for the K'iche' people in both communities. As the following pages attest, my inclination to move away from this very topic prior to starting the research would prove to be not only impossible but also intellectually and morally undesirable. Studies of transnational migration rarely address the deeper impacts of different types of violence and their psychosocial consequences for people who remain situated between "here" and "there" (e.g., the pronounced fear, lack of trust, and fragmentation of families resulting from war, as well as the many types of social suffering resulting from exploitation, racism, criminalization, alcoholism, domestic violence, and sickness).[36] As the K'iche' case illustrates, although populations fleeing political violence may eventually establish solid transnational migration circuits, new forms of aggression at home may continue to be part of their decision to leave, while old forms still determine power dynamics in both home and host contexts.

The final chapter of the book thus focuses on how the K'iche' in Xinxuc and Providence narrate the terrible violence that spawned the migration. I examine how the psychological devastation and shattered social fabric resulting from the war is reflected in some highly ambivalent memory processes. These memories are framed within a diversity of moral frames and worldviews that enable community members at both ends of the transnational circuit to cope with the tremendous guilt and sorrow that has resulted from violence and family separation. Ultimately, memory and identity processes among the postwar Mayan Indian population are negotiated through a multitude of dialogues—between those who stay at home, those who leave, those who return, Mayanists, *mojados*, and K'iche's from different class, ethnic, religious, political, gender, and generational subgroups.

Before delving into the "roving perspective" of my own transnational journey, I offer a brief caveat to address the boundaries and limitations of this book. First, due to the difficulty of the K'iche' language and its many variants throughout municipalities, I learned only the very basics of K'iche' through a three-week course and subsequent months spent trying to absorb the language. My limited K'iche' vocabulary (in addition to fluency in Spanish) did facilitate communication and social contact, particularly with hamlet dwellers, elders, and women who did not speak any Spanish. Nonetheless, although the majority of my primary informants were bilingual and my K'iche interpreters were excellent, I would no doubt have had access to a richer set of understandings had I been able to communicate more directly in K'iche'.

Second, although this book emphasizes a historical approach to the study of identity and movement in this community, it is not meant to be read as an exhaustive historiography of Xinxuc or detailed documentation of the wartime violence and the events and actors surrounding it.[37] I do show, however, that despite the tremendous dislocations of the recent past, the K'iche' from Xinxuc have taken an active role in reshaping their own lives and identities, whether through transnational migration, participation (or nonparticipation) in various economic, cultural, and political activities, or simple human resilience. This ethnography relies heavily upon the power of my interlocutors' own words and narratives in telling the wider story (though any errors of interpretation are clearly my own), and it is my hope that it will find a place in the range of postconflict research in Guatemala by incorporating indigenous voices that often remain unheard in different literatures and institutional spaces.

Finally, the fieldwork upon which this book is based was conducted prior to the tremendous changes that occurred for immigrants in the

United States following the events of September 11, 2001. Given greatly tightened border security and increasingly punitive immigration laws, the transnational circuit has become more difficult to navigate, although far from impossible. Many of the processes described in this work remain highly relevant to the experiences of the K'iche' in Guatemala and the United States, and while this ethnography is but a snapshot in time, the voices described herein contribute to a deeper, more continuous picture of today's cross-border movements.

In Search of Providence

Transnational Mayan Identities

CHAPTER 1

ENTERING THE FIELD

In the summer of 1996, I traveled to Guatemala to discover the origins of the Maya-*Providencia* connection. Having learned that there was a growing population of Mayan Indians who had been living and working in Providence, Rhode Island, since the mid-1980s, I hoped to make some sense out of this seemingly curious migratory route. During my first week in the old colonial city of Antigua, I received my first hint rather by accident. As I got my bearings amid throngs of gringo Spanish-language students, backpackers, and locals, I was advised by geographer George Lovell that a development worker teaching indigenous school children in Joyabaj—a municipality located deep in the southern basin of El Quiché, a highland area known primarily for its very high rates of poverty and the massive violence perpetrated during the war—had several young students whose parents were living in *el Norte*.

Following this somewhat vague clue, I prepared for my trip into the mountains with some apprehension: Before leaving for Joyabaj, the national newspapers announced that a few days earlier, during that town's annual *fiesta*, three men had been doused with gasoline and burned to death in the main plaza by a crowd of villagers seeking vengeance for a *cantina* (saloon/bar) shoot-out. Judging from the violence-packed newspapers I'd been pouring over in Antigua's cafés, this type of incident was occurring with increased frequency throughout the highlands. Local frustration with corrupt police and justice systems, a dearth of economic opportunity, and the sinister residues of *la violencia*[1] were contributing to a frightening rise in lynchings, assassinations, rapes, and holdups, many of them committed by ex-military or paramilitary members.

Riding the ancient, jam-packed Canadian Bluebird school bus up the winding Quiché mountains, I was distracted for a few hours from these initial concerns. A sign at the front attesting to Canada's civic concern and firm language laws announced in French and English: THE SAFETY OF YOUR CHILDREN IS OUR PRIMARY CONCERN, though the driver's own sign, *YO MANEJO, DIOS GUIA* ("I drive, God guides") was clearly more appropriate in this setting. Processing the tremendous beauty of the green countryside, while tensing in terror at the driver's reckless swerves over endlessly deep canyons, required quite a cognitive effort—though my fellow riders, mostly K'iche' Indians returning from regional markets, seemed decidedly unruffled.[2] At the entrance to each town we passed stood large billboards for Rubios cigarettes, projecting the image of a confident Ladino *ganadero* (cattle herder/cowboy). Approaching the department's capital, Santa Cruz del Quiché, I was startled by the sight of a large army garrison, surrounded by soldiers and marking the town's entrance. These seemed to be unsubtle proclamations, to say the least, of who remained in charge in these parts. I descended the bus at the town's center in a sudden torrential downpour. Waiting for the connecting *camioneta* (bus) under the black sky for what seemed an eternity, feeling rather disoriented and discouraged by my somber surroundings, I soon noticed a number of muddy Rhode Island license plates drive by. Whether it was the work of God or the bus driver, I seemed to be in the right place!

On the bus to Joyabaj, I found a place for my backpack amid brightly colored bundles and sat surrounded by a group of rowdy young Ladinos whose loud, assured demeanor stood in stark contrast to the mostly silent Indians crowded in the front seats. After asking me where I came from, the nineteen-year-old albino at my side told me of his numerous friends and relatives living in . . . *Providencia!* His friends, teasing him mercilessly for having finally met his *canchita*[3] match, pitched into the conversation, speaking excitedly of their hopes to travel someday to *el Norte*—though not, they vehemently asserted, as *mojados.*[4]

During my first few days in Joyabaj (or Xoy, as it is known by locals) I found out that, indeed, Providence was on my side: As I had arrived on the last day of the municipality's patron saint *fiesta,* I encountered many visiting transmigrants, some of whom had risked their jobs in the United States for a chance to participate (like those who had migrated to the capital or elsewhere) in festivities, take care of domestic problems, bring home cars and consumer goods, or buy their friends rounds of drinks in the *cantina.* Many of the homes I visited proudly displayed pictures of relatives in Providence, posing seriously next to shiny cars, in front of important state buildings or large New England houses, and usually in the midst of bright autumn leaves or snow-covered landscapes. These photographs were invariably exhibited in front rooms next to televisions, refrigerators, CD players, and other symbols of consumer status and transmigrant success. I met with several people—all Ladinos from Joyabaj's *pueblo* or *cabecera*[5] (town center), who, given my limited time frame, were most accessible and eager to speak—with widely differing transnational stories.

One young man told me of his dangerous crossing by foot through Mexico, which like many had included several jail stints, and of the grueling five years spent in Providence working double shifts in building and roofing, fish-packing, dishwashing, and gardening, as well as in jewelry and plastic factories. Back in Xoy, he now owned two pickup trucks, both commissioned from Providence, with which he ran a successful business selling *leña* (firewood), construction materials, and fertilizer throughout the mountains, capitalizing on the construction boom resulting from transnational remittances. His two-story cement-and-brick dwelling, complete with balcony, running hot water, and sofas, was a veritable palace compared to the dirt-floor, adobe, or tin-roofed cornstalk huts of the surrounding hamlets.

An aging widow told me how her only two sons had left years earlier for Providence *para superar* (to excel) but had soon stopped sending money and these days sent news rarely. She, her daughter-in-law, and grandchildren made ends meet by running a tiny, run-down cafeteria in their home. They showed me mountains of pictures of the wayward men, sent soon after their departure to the United States; with a somber face and suppressed tears, the children's mother wrote down the name of her husband and pleaded with me to find him when I went next to Providence.

Walking down one of Joyabaj's three main streets, I encountered a sweet and troubled twenty-year-old strutting slowly in his baggy, low-hung trousers and "USA"-emblazoned shiny baseball jacket: "Whazzup, how ya doin'?" he greeted me in English, with perfect gangsta rap body motions. He had just returned from Providence, where he had lived with his mother and Puerto Rican stepfather since he was fourteen; after only five months, he was anxious to return. "This place is terrible, there is so much violence, so many fights, there is no way to have a good life. I don't mind workin' hard, but I don't want to make that cheap little money you make here." As I discovered, he had been planning to make the next trip *al Norte* with his cousin—one of the men caught in the week's *cantina* shoot out, who was now paralyzed in a Guatemala City hospital. Throughout my fieldwork, I would often run into him, usually quite drunk or high on marijuana, jobless and still planning to return to Providence.

While these impressionistic portraits of success stories, abandoned women, and lost or dreamy young men gave me some important preliminary insights into the significant socioeconomic and human impact of the Providence connection, other clues indicated that this town's transnational nature extended far beyond Joyabaj's *cabecera*. On a Sunday, I observed hundreds of Indian *campesinos* (peasants) descend by foot from the mountains, arriving from the township's many diffusely scattered hamlets to go to church and to buy or sell goods in the market. Many would then wait for hours to pile into the GUATEL (national telephone company) phone booths: These were the wives, parents, children, and siblings of transmigrants, who would speak for long stretches in K'iche' to their relatives *allá lejos* (far away). Along the hamlet roads, K'iche' boys with Nike baseball caps, fashionable haircuts, and earrings listened on Walkmans to the latest ranchero songs about life as an *ilegal*,[6] while their sisters and mothers, dressed in the municipal *guipil* and *corte*, balanced on their heads striped pots of water fetched from the river or well. At the express courier services scattered through town, where Ladinos and Indians mingled to send or receive packages, cassettes, photos, and letters from the United States, I saw a number of elderly and impoverished K'iche' people dictate to clerks, in broken Spanish, their brief and formal letters, marking their signatures with inked thumbprints.

My "blind search" for the home context had proved successful, so I decided, two months later, to settle in Joyabaj, hoping to compare the impact of transnationalism on K'iche' living in hamlet communities with those living in the more "urban" *cabecera*. Although I was able to make various institutional and personal contacts and participate in town activities, my anticipated research in this large municipality, which included over fifty widely dispersed hamlets, was soon frustrated by several logistical difficulties. I found that Indian transmigration from the hamlets was more diffuse than that originating from the *pueblo*, extending to Florida, the Carolinas, Alabama, Georgia, Kansas, Nebraska, Michigan, New Jersey, and Washington State, according to the courier service records. Hamlets known to have a more concentrated Providence-oriented population, moreover, tended to be scattered, some up to an eight-hour walk from the *pueblo* through rugged terrain. The fluid boundaries of transnationalism certainly seemed difficult to master in the vast mountains of El Quiché. Moreover, my visits to the hamlets accompanied by NGO and community workers, both Indian and Ladino, indicated that the level of suspicion and fear toward outsiders in outlying areas was immense. NGO workers recounted to me the tremendous difficulties of entering communities where distrust not only of outsiders but also of indigenous promoters from neighboring hamlets (whose allegiances and actions during the war were still remembered) continued to frustrate the implementation of basic health and education programs.

During this first month in Joyabaj I found that the decision to evade the theme of violence in my research would be impossible, just as I could not avoid the tremendous poverty, illiteracy, morbidity, and mortality that made life in this area so vividly harsh and that were directly related to the dynamics of both violence and mass emigration. Throughout the towns and hamlets of El Quiché, the silent weight of past fear and terror, of brutal massacres and disappearances, as well as the more conspicuous state of current "vigilante" violence, made its way into every aspect of the cultural repertoire, including the rather sinister humor through which some in Joyabaj referred to the grotesque public lynching of the *fiesta,* jokingly recalled as *la barbacoa* (the barbecue).[7] The texture of this violence felt all the more ominous in its juxtaposition to the ordinariness of life around me. Within my host family alone, largely respected throughout the community, I learned that a brother of sweet Doña Faustina, the household matriarch, had been murdered in the living room as a result of his having blown the whistle on a corrupt town mayor. During my stay, her younger brother, returning from Providence after a two-year stint, was shot at in the capital as his car left the airport, leaving his young nephew with several wounds.[8] A few months later he was assaulted by a masked gang along the road from a nearby village; while all his belongings were stolen, his fate was luckier than that of the women in the cars behind him, who, he told me, were raped. Doña Faustina, understandably, lived in perpetual fear of leaving the house or opening the door. Such stories of holdups, robberies, shootings, and other forms of social violence formed the stuff of everyday life and seemed to mock the insistent discourse on "civil society," "democracy," and "human rights" that appeared in the national papers as the country supposedly prepared for *la paz* (peace).

Frustrated by my initial difficulties in Joyabaj, I decided after a month to move my research site to a smaller *municipio,* Xinxuc. Though situated in the southern Quiché as well, Xinxuc had a distinctly different feel: In contrast to the boisterous market and more ubiquitous state presence in Joyabaj's town center (which included a prominent military outpost, a well-equipped government communications office and health center, and numerous NGOs), Xinxuc seemed oddly subdued and quiet. The lack of formal organization and institutions seemed to reinforce the rather forlorn, desolate character of the town: The municipality didn't have a covered marketplace, a local parish priest, or a police force (the police had left town during *la violencia*). The *bomberos municipales*—a group of local Ladinos working the town's volunteer fire department—performed a number of civic "duties," ranging from elementary emergency services to running (and profiting from) one of the three community phone services. My introduction to this small municipality of roughly seven thousand inhabitants came through a European NGO I shall call PLANTAS,[9] which conducted projects in the area of traditional medicine and the revitalization of Mayan culture. During a social visit with this organization (the only international NGO in the *municipio*), I discovered by talking with indigenous health promoters that the large emigration from Xinxuc over the past ten or so years, from both the *pueblo* and hamlets, had been aimed almost exclusively toward Providence. Like Joyabaj and a number of villages in the surrounding area, Xinxuc could thus be described as a transnational community—one in which a substantial proportion of the population had migrated abroad but maintained an important presence in, and had a substantial impact on, the home community. Given its small size, the relatively easy access to its hamlets, and a kind invitation by the PLANTAS director to live at the NGO's headquarters in the *pueblo*, I decided to settle in.

THE HOME COMMUNITY

Having sensed already in Joyabaj the existence of deeply rooted suspicions and factions between locals and outsiders, Ladinos and Indians, and rival religious and political groups, it became apparent that my initial positioning in Xinxuc—and the manner in which I was presented to its inhabitants—would be critical. While this might seem like common ethnographic sense, the presence of a single, female anthropologist during a highly volatile postwar period, and in an area where most foreigners had been either development workers offering *ayuda* (aid) or missionaries preaching salvation, was highly questionable. If I was offering neither material aid nor spiritual hope to these people, what, then, was I doing in their village? What was the nature of my research, and what did such an activity imply? What was my job, and who was paying me? What were the *informaciones* (information) I needed, and what would I be doing with them?

In the first place, a study of "migration," unlike, say, the local health surveys to which community members were accustomed, made little sense to many people. In a place of such tremendous poverty and need, my abstract exercise seemed both bizarre and unbelievable, and was often, therefore, viewed with suspicion. Moreover, although the signs of transnationalism were ubiquitous throughout the municipality, reflected in both absence (of people) and presence (of relative material wealth), it was not an aspect of life habitually translated into a more formal, reflective discourse, and it was certainly an odd topic to explain to a *gringa*, who after all must know more about *el Norte* than anyone here. For some, in addition, "anthropologists" were associated with the exhumations of mass graves currently conducted by forensic anthropologists throughout the region and were therefore connected with the "dangerous" postwar work of human rights organizations from which many sought to keep a distance.[10]

My association with PLANTAS, which had been able to forge a relatively neutral and respected space in Xinxuc and whose indigenous promoters had an excellent rapport within the outlying Indian communities, was critical. I hired Juanita, the young wife of one of the PLANTAS promoters, to work with me as a K'iche' translator, though the role she played would eventually extend far beyond this task, since she also served as an interlocutor who would smooth the introductions with interviewees and then assist me in clarifying and analyzing the interviews. She and her husband, like most of the PLANTAS rural promoters, had many relatives who either lived in Providence, had spouses and children there, or had returned from there. After choosing three hamlets to work in (in addition to the *pueblo*) and reviewing some interview guides, Juanita and I made a list of potential "transnational" persons and families to visit. The majority of these people, like her, were affiliated with the Catholic church; because of the tremendous social distance and tensions between Catholics, evangelicals, and traditionalists (*costumbristas*), which were closely associated with wartime factionalism, and the general suspicion surrounding outsiders, it was appropriate to employ a "snowball" methodology that began with *conocidos* (acquaintances).

In addition to the contacts I made through her, I eventually forged a few relationships of trust (*relaciones de confianza*) on my own, a product in part of my own native-level Spanish and the level of bilingualism in this community, primarily among *pueblo*-dwellers who had more contact with the Ladino world. Seeking to guide my interactions away from the quest for *informaciones,* I often introduced my work by stating that, given the large numbers who had gone so far away, I felt it was important to have stories of why so many Mayans had left Xinxuc and what impact this migration had upon the town. I sometimes voiced a concern that those people who were far from the community and their families should have some sense of their heritage. Although skeptical at first, some of the people warmed to the project, particularly older generations whose children, spouses, or grandchildren were in Providence; who had little opportunity to connect in meaningful ways with their relatives *allá*; and who placed faith in me to communicate their messages to their close ones. Others, however, were more reticent, particularly those who were themselves planning to leave.

Indeed, a second obstacle to my research was a widespread fear that I worked for *la migra* and was soliciting damaging information about undocumented immigrants.[11] Already in Joyabaj, rumors had begun quickly that the pen and paper I sometimes carried were used to jot down names of *ilegales* (illegal immigrants) for the purpose of eventually "reporting" them.[12] Though I abandoned the practice of taking notes in Xinxuc, I was advised by friends that the rumors had persisted and that I must be careful. I had no way of knowing when and to whom such rumors had spread, or who believed them, and was constantly perplexed by the shifting nature of friendliness and misgiving with which I was treated. Often, a person who had been forthcoming and open on one occasion would in another context (particularly in the presence of others who might judge him or her) seem suspicious and closed. I learned that fear in Xinxuc functioned primarily in terms of the communal gaze—that is, the anxiety of being seen by others to be allied with a "dangerous" person—a legacy of *la violencia*, when one's visible associations with the wrong person had dire consequences.

Given these difficulties, I soon realized that asking direct questions about the migration was counterproductive, often eliciting stilted, forced, and fixed responses. I eventually became more integrated into village life and began forging closer ties with people by stopping by for informal visits, accepting meals, spending hours *tortillando* (making corn tortillas), participating in special occasions and community events, and accompanying PLANTAS promoters in their work. People's stories and reflections on the phenomenon of migration began to come forth, usually at the most unexpected moments and often sparked by the mundane conversations and events of everyday life. A woman, triggered by the pained wails of a sick child, would burst in frustration toward an absent transmigrant spouse who did not send enough money home to pay for medicine; an unknown returnee would, after a few shots of *cuxa*,[13] give me a long narrative about the grueling factory life in Providence; an *aj q'ij* (shaman priest) performing a traditional ceremony in the forest would mention his children *allá* and ask the ancestors to protect them and provide work; a Ladino priest from the capital would, at a local wedding, sermonize about the evils of materialism and family disintegration caused by the urge to leave to the United States (while the wedding reception would take place in a fancy new home built with Providence money); or a K'iche' widow, pulling out a photo album of her Providence-dwelling son and joking about the effects his handsome looks would surely have on me, would suddenly burst out crying and recount the disappearance of her husband during *la violencia* that had sparked her young son's departure.

Little by little, moreover, the tremendous "transnational" gossip about others in the community—those in Xinxuc who had been abandoned and fell ill with *tristeza* (sadness) or alcoholism or had taken on new lovers, those who were *coyotes* (human smugglers), or those who had died or succumbed to other tragic circumstances *allá lejos*—reached my ears. As I became increasingly aware, gossip and rumors were a fundamental method of communicating and interpreting the uncertain world of transnationalism, though I often found myself perplexed about the seemingly outrageous, impossibly sensational, and often contradictory stories I heard. Were they true, or were they part of the "imaginary" through which people tried to comprehend the distant Providence? I consistently took note of these "data," hoping that eventually they would come to make sense.

In addition to my visits with people, I learned about the profound effects of transnationalism by engaging in ordinary activities that positioned me more directly within transmigrant culture, for example by waiting for hours with other Xinxucians for a long-distance *cita* (rendezvous) at one of the three community phones, receiving packages from the courier service, chatting with people on buses about the *péndulos* ("pendulums") who travel back and forth, and debating the possibility of mass deportations. As people grew more trusting, my everyday interactions came to include not only such abstract discussions but also requests for legal information, for the favor of transporting goods and information to and from the United States, or, more unrealistically, for procuring travel visas or taking children or grandparents with me on my next trip. People's assessments and reassessments of me (as potential friend or foe), and of the social or personal utility of being allied with me, tainted both the tone and content of their interactions.

I was able to conduct a series of long interviews in the homes of transnational families whom I got to know well and whose relatives I planned to meet in Providence. This focus on the family as a unit of study was important, both because K'iche' culture is heavily focused on kinship and family and because, as Rouse (1989) and others have shown, transnational migration engenders multiple strategies, motivations, and interpretations among different family members. Moreover, as we shall see, this deeper focus on a few extended families scattered between Xinxuc and Providence allowed me to examine the intricate connection between the effects of poverty, violence, and displacement upon familial structures and relationships as well as on the broader community.[14] Interviews conducted in K'iche' were led by Juanita, who, in addition to having memorized the general themes and questions of interest to me, often spontaneously added her own set of queries, thus greatly enriching the interview process. She was often able to solicit stories that provided details and context that would doubtlessly not have been told to this *gringa* alone. These sessions sometimes became important family events, as individuals recounted the long narratives and details of their past and present lives while others sat listening, sporadically asking for clarification or offering additional information. Juanita later revealed that she had never heard many of the stories told on these occasions, whether told by other community members or by her own relatives. While in some cases my initial interviews with transnational families gave me an "in" that permitted me to visit them on a more regular basis, in other cases more formal and lengthy interviews were conducted after a longer period of time.

The narratives, particularly those recounted in K'iche' by elders, were often told in the circular Mayan style, where time references and narrative lines rarely form a linear progression, and Juanita was careful not to interrupt the storytelling process. When my interlocutors preferred to speak in

Spanish, I would conduct the interviews myself and often bring Juanita to assist with clarifications; her presence in these instances was useful given the strong tendency toward code-switching (between Spanish and the native language) among K'iche' Indians. The interviews were all recorded and transcribed, and, if necessary, we returned at a later date with additional questions.[15] I often found, particularly with respect to migration stories, that important details, and even essential story lines, changed depending on the context, time, and persons present at the interview. By combining both formal and informal data collection strategies and by eliciting stories and information over different periods of time, I was able to analyze the many gaps, silences, and shifts that filled people's complex narratives, rather than trying to force them into a rigid interview guide.

My fieldwork took place during the critical initial phases of the official Guatemalan Peace Accords, which had a major impact on my own understanding of past violence and its ongoing repercussions for the K'iche' people both at home and abroad. The area surrounding Xinxuc turned out to be the setting for some significant postwar events, and as a privileged and ostensibly "neutral" outsider, I was able to observe some of these at close range—closer, indeed, than most locals, a factor that contributed to my ambiguous status within the community. As described in Chapter 3, the instauration of a large guerrilla demobilization camp ten minutes away from the village was rather self-consciously ignored by Xinxucians, despite the constant flow of United Nations jeeps crossing through the town on their way to the camp. The well-publicized trial of one of Xinxuc's wartime military commissioners in the nearby departmental capital, moreover, was equally hushed in spite of sensational newspaper stories concerning the trial. By integrating these events into my fieldwork (conducting interviews on the camps and attending the trial), I was able to observe the striking discrepancies between the ubiquitous "official" discourses on peace and reconciliation—those of the national and international press, MINUGUA (the United Nations Human Rights Mission), the army, and the guerrillas—and the various local interpretations verbalized, or most often expressed through veiled statements and silences, in a community that remained profoundly scarred by the war. It was through these contrasts that I pieced together bit by bit, and often by what seemed to be chance encounters, events, and utterances, the perplexing and troublesome past lurking deep below the surface tranquility of quotidian life in Xinxuc.

If Xinxuc's ostensible estrangement from the guerrilla camp and the trial indicated the lingering "culture of fear" in this community and its distance from the peace process, it also pointed to the deeply engrained "epistemic murk" (Taussig 1987) produced by past violence in this community, which made itself felt on a daily level in a myriad of indirect, intangible, and sometimes alarming ways. The ambiguous "hyperreality" of everyday life, whereby a façade of normalcy intermingled with a constant sense of fear and suspicion, nourished by rumors and innuendos, lent life in Xinxuc a profoundly destabilizing aura of uncertainty. I found myself consistently puzzled by the sense of not knowing what was real and where the truth lay. My own naive assumptions regarding the reality surrounding me were constantly questioned as I found, as most of the K'iche' believe, that "nothing is what it seems" and that all behavior, including my own friendliness toward them, could be interpreted as threatening and deceitful. Friends and foes, past and present alliances and enmities, victims and perpetrators were difficult to distinguish; as some K'iche's told me, "Cara vemos pero corazon no sabemos que piensa" (We see the face but know not what the heart is thinking). Indeed, if at first I was perplexed by the obvious suspicion and silence with which I was often initially greeted, I soon became quite wary myself of those who appeared too friendly and trusting.

The confusing reality made evident in the silences, denials, and rumors running through the community seemed in part to reflect a broader aspect of life in Guatemala, which has often been described as a blurred, distorted line between reality and fiction, creating a tension that both reflects and reinforces a long and pervasive culture of terror.[16] At a national level, the freakish twists and plots of official stories (concerning numerous events ranging from the assassinations of important political figures to child trafficking), conveyed through the media and transmitted through the oral culture of the highlands, perpetually reinforce the notion that reality is bizarre, absurd, and malleable.[17] As Zur states, this "Orwellian falsification of reality" (1998: 159) was cultivated locally by those in power both during and after the violence to intimidate and control the population. Superimposed onto indigenous culture, which is often characterized by extreme suspicion, a belief in malevolent spirits, and a fear of Otherness, such distortions sometimes become further exaggerated. Over the past few years this has been reflected both in relatively benign rumors (for example, during the time of my fieldwork many of the K'iche' became convinced that "La Pepsi da sida"—Pepsi gives AIDS—and refused to drink it)[18] and in episodes of collective brutality such as several horrific lynchings of tourists thought to be stealing Indian babies and of suspected local criminals.

Equally nefarious were the distortions caused by what Green calls "the blood on people's hands." In places where "community members denounced their neighbors as subversives to the army . . . because of interfamilial feuding and where widows saw their husbands killed or disappeared by an army in which their own sons served as soldiers" (Green 1999: 10), half secrets and past tragedies hang silently and heavily in the air, impossible to fully remember and impossible to fully forget. The cohabitation of victims, perpetrators, and victim-perpetrators has created odd, shifting (and to me, initially unfathomable) alliances and enmities in the present. Only after several months in Xinxuc did I discover that ex–civil patrol (PAC) leaders[19]—those who organized and/or conducted denunciations, tortures, and killings—turned out to include the affable Indian mayor, who enthusiastically agreed to speak to me about his children in Providence but as the interview gained depth asked uneasily how many people I had spoken with; the father of the shy indigenous *patoja* (girl) who brought me daily *tortillas,* who skillfully played marimba at the *fiesta*; and the desperately alcoholic, sad-eyed Ladino corner-store owner whose daughter wanted English lessons. An Indian widow who had told me horrific stories of her stepson's PAC activities, which included "disappearing" and turning in his own family members, made a point of being seen respectfully walking through town with him during one of his visits from Providence. Nothing, indeed, was what it seemed. Conversely, a PLANTAS promoter, with whom I spent much time and had a trusting rapport, repeatedly denied being beaten nearly to death by the PACs only four years earlier, though his siblings both in Xinxuc and Providence all confirmed this occurrence. The discrepancies between public shows of alliance and the stories I heard in private, the blending of violence-related and non-violence-related animosities between individuals and groups, and the multiple versions of both past and present events I heard from different interlocutors became a constant source of puzzlement.

My own interview questions with K'iche' people, which focused on the impact of migration, did not directly approach the issue of past violence: First, I wished neither to invade such delicate and tragic territory in a time of continuing fear, nor to be confused with those working on peacetime projects soliciting "testimonies."[20] And second, I wished to understand the place of violence (both political and social) within the broader, longer narratives and sociohistorical context of people's lives rather than as temporally limited to the time of the civil war. Indeed, people's life stories were invariably narrated in terms of the profound poverty, racism, and suffering that had characterized their lives long before *la violencia* and that clearly continued to persist: quotidian injustices at the hands of Ladinos as well as other K'iche', blatant exploitation and misery on the coastal plantations, coerced religious conversions, the loss of crops to environmental factors and the loss of land to debts, malnourished children, abused women, rampant alcoholism, and invariable stories of sickness and premature death—all formed the crux of these life stories, often encapsulated by the ubiquitous phrase: "hemos sufrido tanto" (we have suffered so much).

Nonetheless, the particularly devastating impact of the epoch of *la guerrilla* was clearly unavoidable, given not only that all families had been shattered in different ways by the war but also because the social rupture it produced was, for many, tied directly to migration. Several times, upon being asked the vague question: "Can you tell me how it was when your husband/son left for Providence?" K'iche women broke down in tears and began speaking rapidly and in hushed tones of *esos hombres* (those men), of the many deaths and disappearances at the hands of *conocidos* (acquaintances), mixing gruesome details and blatant memory gaps with the standard, safe, fixed narratives used to recount the war ("Se lo llevaron a mi marido," [They took my husband away]). In addition, because some of the worst PAC leaders were known to have left for Providence, the many rumors and postulations about their lives *allá* opened the space for people to speak of the violence in more indirect ways. Moreover, I found through these interviews that the connections made between the violence and transnational migration concerned not only concrete events and actors, but also that the two phenomena, in conjunction, contributed to the constant sense of uncertainty permeating people's lives. Just as widows were unsure whether their disappeared sons or husbands might turn up at the guerrilla camp, many were uncertain about the plight of their estranged relatives *allá*: Being "disappeared" (by the army or PACs) and disappearing on one's own (by joining the guerrillas, escaping to another region, or leaving to the United States) all formed part of the general "unknown" and of the murky culture of rumor and possibility of Xinxuc.

My own positioning during my first eight months in El Quiché was highly ambiguous, causing not only confusion and suspicion but also making people's reactions toward me difficult to grasp. For example, although I was perceived as a potentially threatening and powerful outsider with an unclear agenda, my access and ties to the "outside" (whether the guerrilla camp, the trial, or my upcoming departure to the distant Providence) were also exploited by locals, whose simultaneous distance and proximity to these "unknown" spaces gave me a useful role as a sort of quiet (and privileged) messenger. Many of the K'iche' were fascinated by the pictures I had taken of the guerrilla camp and demobilization (many wanting to buy them), as well as by the information I could give concerning the trial, and I was asked numerous questions about these forbidden places: "Is it true that the *guerrilleros* each received $500,000? That they throw degenerate parties every weekend? That they have hidden their weapons away? That the Blue Berets, like the Spanish *conquistadores,* are criminals in their countries?"

In the spring of 1997, as I prepared to leave for Providence, a state of panic swept through the country due to a series of new anti-immigration policies in the United States that threatened many Guatemalan and Salvadoran immigrants, in particular, with potential deportation orders. The

Guatemalan media sensationally spoke of the possibility of mass deportations and the profound damage this would wreak on the nation's economy,
while Rigoberta Menchú declared that the new laws could spell the ruin
of an already fragile peace process.[21] For the first time, Guatemalan politicians seemed to give stalk to the widespread phenomenon of transnational
migration (something it had previously ignored), suddenly fearful that the
tremendous amount of US dollars pumped into the national economy—
much of it arriving in the form of individual remittances to people in rural
villages like Xinxuc—would come to a halt. At the local level, as always,
rumors concerning planeloads of deportees arriving barefoot and in chains
made their way through the villages.

Despite these rumors, and the additional one that "some angry people"
in Santa Cruz were now certain I was a *migra* spy, I amassed a suitcase full
of letters, photographs, and packages filled with local medicines, spices,
clothes, jewelry, sweets, and cassettes from Xinxucians to take to their relatives in Providence. In addition, since I planned to return, I was *encargada*
(commissioned) with numerous requests for goods, many of which seemed
oddly beyond the financial means or immediate needs of those requesting
them: a computer, a Casio watch, a camera. On several occasions, K'iche's
jokingly suggested that I might be able, through the help of a magical pill,
to shrink them to fit in my *moral* (a traditional bag used by men), take
them across the border, and bring them back to size in Providence.[22] By
this time, I had been able to create some friendships and *relaciones de
confianza*, in part by simply participating in the quotidian life of the small
village and forging loyalties and in part by exposing my own vulnerabili-
ties as a sort of "transnational visitor," which gave me, in a certain respect,
a more familiar identity within transnational families. My odd questions
and tendency to get lost in the mountains, for example, came to be greeted
with laughter: "You behave here the way we must behave over there!" Thus,
eager to provide a useful "personal courier" service and knowing that the
gifts would get me a foot into people's doors in Providence, I set out to
discover the distant place and people I had heard so much about.

THE HOST COMMUNITY

Through a string of good luck and personal contacts, I found an
apartment in the middle of one of the two inner-city Providence neighborhoods inhabited by most Quichelenses (both Ladino and K'iche') as well as
by various other immigrant groups, notably Cambodians, Hmong, Dominicans, Puerto Ricans, Haitians, and Africans. The extreme contrast between
highland village life and the urban New England landscape, with its facto-

ries, large Victorian houses, and broad highways, seemed both exciting and destabilizing. In Xinxuc, where blatant poverty and injustice contribute to the harshness of everyday life—which often involves walking past random masses of pestilent garbage, *bolos* (drunks) strewn miserably on the streets, and myriad instances of daily racism and abuse—there exists nevertheless a gentler side to village social life, including the daily greetings, the rituals of marketplace, and other collective events which provide a bounded sense of community. In contrast, the neat, broad, structured space of Providence seemed at once assuaging and oddly alienating—as well as familiar. I saw hundreds of K'iche's, including women in Laundromats, English-speaking children walking to school, families on their way to Latino religious events, young men cruising coolly through the streets, and workers chatting together in the park during a break. The landscape of courier services, long-distance telephone companies, and other immigrant-oriented businesses advertised in broad Spanish letters made it clear that here, as in Xinxuc, the distant space of *allá* formed an essential part of life.

I began to call and visit people's homes, delivering letters and packages, and my initial reception was very friendly. Several K'iche's, relatives of those I had known in Xinxuc, went out of their way to enthusiastically show me around town in their cars, introducing me to the Guatemalan restaurants and *panaderías* (bakeries), inviting me to masses and dinners, and showing me the parks and downtown area. In a number of cases, I unexpectedly ran into people I had met in Xinxuc, transnational encounters that seemed to create an immediate feeling of camaraderie, a tacit recognition that we were fellow travelers between two unique places. I joined a small rosary group led by Virgilio, a catechist from Xinxuc who became a most trusted and valuable key informant and whose extended family in both places I grew to know quite well. The group, composed of a dozen K'iche' families, met every Saturday night to pray and socialize, serving traditional food and playing religious songs from home accompanied by guitars and accordions. Since many K'iche' did not speak English—most stating that their heavy workloads did not permit them to take the time—I organized an English class to fit in with their schedules. While the classes were attended by only a handful of people from the rosary group, they provided an excellent opportunity for lively discussions concerning people's everyday concerns and lives.

My connection with Xinxuc, as well as a rapidly acquired role as something of a cultural broker/interpreter, greatly facilitated my introduction into the setting. Very soon, I was asked on a daily basis to accompany people to courtrooms, schools, police stations,[23] the telephone company, hospitals, or even, in one case, the local prison, and to help fill out various English-language forms. This constant solicitation was due, no doubt, to my free provision of services: Other "translators" (Guatemalans and other Latinos), I was told, charged between US$30 and $40 per hour. But I realized soon that rather than a simple translator, I served more as a sort of mediator, a host-country representative who could afford to negotiate with authorities in their language—that is, I both literally spoke English and could also communicate and negotiate with the institutional power structure and its agents. Indeed, I was once told I was like the *guisach*[24] back home who served (particularly in past years, when there were fewer Spanish-speaking Indians) to represent monolingual Indians and negotiate legal matters with Spanish-speaking authorities, hopefully avoiding the *trampas* (traps) set forth by the authorities. Despite my informant's positive twist on the term in his explanation to me, *guisachs* in El Quiché have traditionally had a highly paradoxical role: They are perceived with ambivalence, caution, and at times hostility, as they can use their knowledge and experience either to help Indians or to take advantage of them through their own *trampas*[25]. Ironically, however, in certain matters my *guisach* abilities fell short since, despite being a *gringa,* my knowledge of Providence, its layout, and both the formal institutions and informal networks most important for undocumented transmigrants was limited. In many respects, they had much more "survival" knowledge than I did, and at times the roles shifted as I became the "new" transmigrant while my closer friends guided me. For example, when I needed to renew my expired US driver's license, one of my key informants fluently took me through the process by reminding me of the requirements and driving me to the Department of Motor Vehicles to pass the driving test, something he had clearly done many times with recent arrivals.[26] Although this paradoxical role was accepted by my closer informants and created relationships of mutual sharing and help, it also contributed to the sense of suspicion that eventually grew around me.

Given that most of the K'iche' in Providence worked twelve-plus-hour days, six days a week, I often conducted more formal interviews on weekends. During the week, I met with women who stayed home taking care of their own and others' children or those who for various reasons were not working (including a key informant who was recovering from a devastating industrial accident whereby he lost much of his hand). Given the delicate nature of the topics discussed and the fact that many K'iche' people live in crowded conditions with little privacy, many of the interviews were conducted in my apartment. On a couple of occasions, I conducted lengthy "group" interviews in homes, forming part of a mini-assembly line of women and children who pieced together jewelry and keychains, under-the-table work that provided some additional family income. In addition, I was kindly invited by different K'iche's to participate in numerous events, including Alcoholics Anonymous picnics, soccer games, birthday parties, and social outings; on one occasion I was a witness in a K'iche'–Puerto Rican wedding.[27]

One particularly useful methodological approach—which came about rather serendipitously in both Xinxuc and Providence—was the use of my extensive collection of photographs taken in both contexts, which I often gave away to informants (if they were close family members of those pictured in the photos).[28] These photos included random pictures of community members in their everyday lives and other community-related events and places (including the guerrilla camp, the *fiesta*, or various gatherings in Providence), as well as a series of posed photos that I took with the specific and declared purpose of showing to members in the "other" community. The manner in which people chose to represent themselves in posing for these "transnational" photographs, as well as the usually animated and intense discussions elicited by all these photos, became a vital part of my understanding of the dialogue between and within the two communities. While transnational K'iche's do sporadically send pictures of themselves to their immediate families, these usually entail rather formal, self-conscious poses (e.g., K'iche's in Xinxuc standing stiffly in their Sunday best, or K'iche's in Providence positioned solemnly next to a new car or radio) and serve to complement the very formal, polite, and succinct letters that usually accompany them. The photographs I presented, which were informal and showed various community members, often elicited long, deliberate examination, spontaneous stories surrounding their content, and emotional responses of surprise, sadness, criticism, and nostalgia. I also spent several afternoons in Providence with some K'iche's watching videos of the annual *fiesta* back home from previous years, discussing the various persons appearing and events taking place in the video.[29] All in all, these visual representations of the different spaces of transnationalism, and people's own participation in their production and interpretation, appeared much less threatening and more engaging than direct questions.

In Providence, I also conducted a number of interviews with informants who could fill in or contextualize my discussions with K'iche's, notably: an INS agent and a police officer; a state political representative and a Guatemalan Consulate worker; immigration lawyers, social workers, and an ESL (English as a Second Language) teacher; the director of a small Guatemalan political organization;[30] and a local television broadcaster who had visited El Quiché for a highly controversial piece on Mayans in Providence.[31] These interviews gave me a sense of the various discourses within host-context institutions regarding the rapid influx of K'iche' Indians in the area. In contrast to the rabidly anti-immigrant discourse characterizing debates in other areas of the country, I found that most spoke of the K'iche' as a timid, unobtrusive, and hardworking population, generally well-liked, if difficult to communicate with.[32] Many, indeed, were very forthcoming and interested to speak with me about this rather mysterious population that, despite its ubiquitous presence, clearly chose to hide its ethnic and cultural origins.

Despite the generally "lighter" atmosphere I encountered in Providence and the ease with which I created a role for myself, I soon found that the deep social fractures and animosities that I had sensed in Xinxuc persisted, well hidden, in the host community. Indeed, as in Xinxuc, both perpetrators and victims of past brutalities continued to live side by side, and the atmosphere of suspicion and fear (toward those both within and outside the community) rooted in past terror was compounded now by the difficult immigration situation. The stress produced by illegality and invisibility, present and future uncertainty, the ever-present web of rumors concerning deportations, the fear of being denounced by an enemy to *la migra,* and the need to remain silent about such concerns combined to create a palpable atmosphere of anxiety among most of the K'iche'. Among those who held me in *confianza* (trust), I came to represent a sympathetic, neutral ear who understood both the home and host contexts but could be trusted not to manipulate, judge, or spread the vicious gossip that many K'iche's feared from their own community members, and I thus allowed them to *desahogarse* (to unburden oneself, to speak one's mind), as I was told. In some cases, the tremendous pain, guilt, and suffering, as well as the hopes and dreams, of K'iche's separated from their home and loved ones seemed to pour out as though never before released.

However, this positive perception was not shared by all and was contradicted by an intense fear among members of the broader community concerning my motivations, particularly since I had appeared at an exceptionally tense time. In addition to the volatile immigration policies in the United States, a UN-sponsored Truth Commission was now underway back home to investigate atrocities committed during the war. Many of the K'iche' from Xinxuc seemed to have a very murky and limited knowledge of both the immigration laws and of the peace process back home (this was especially the case among those who had left before this process started), attesting to their marginalization from important structural processes in both contexts. Though at first I tried to organize meetings to discuss and provide information about these political situations, I was soon dissuaded from continuing when not a single person ventured to come, not even those who had been willing to discuss these topics with me in private—yet another example of the fear and mistrust of people who, as they told me, didn't want to "meterse en problemas" (get involved in problems).

Through Virgilio I discovered that many were either convinced, or half-doubted, that I was a *migra* spy: Had I not made this clear by speaking of *migración*? Why would I be soliciting *informaciones,* and why did I know so much about Xinxuc? Why did I speak both English and Spanish? Why, as a single woman, was I inviting people to my apartment to "talk" with them, and why now? Why was I so easily able to travel back and forth, and who was paying me? And most suspiciously, why would I be providing favors, such as classes and interpreting, for free? As it turned out, he told me, these rumors were being reinforced throughout the community by some ex–civil patrol leaders who, terrified by the prospect of deportation and judgment for wartime activities in Guatemala, were particularly prone to dislike my presence. As they had told Virgilio, they believed me to be a representative of *los Derechos Humanos* (human rights groups) who, not unlike the guerrillas back home, was trying to infiltrate the community by insinuating myself into the rosary group and would soon be returning to Guatemala to turn people into the Truth Commission. Although I knew who these ex-PAC members were, it was nonetheless impossible to know how damaging the rumors were within the broader community.

Most perplexing, however, was the fact that despite these rumors, many people—some with humble supplications and others quite aggressively—continued to solicit my help as an interpreter/accompanier, including some (though not ex-PAC leaders) whom I knew to suspect my broader identity. Slowly, I began to understand the mechanism of ingrained fear and authoritarianism that led to such contradictory behavior: As a powerful outsider, my presence was interpreted in much the same light as that of another feared authority, the army. From this perspective, like the military back home, I had asserted from the beginning who I was (*la migra*), had solicited cooperation from people whose livelihoods were being threatened, and had offered to protect and help them in return for their collaboration. And, just as one both resisted and conceded to the army, so it was that many K'iche's behaved with cautious deference, friendliness, and/or cooperation, while simultaneously striving to manipulate my perceived authority toward their own ends. In a sense, I was granted nearly the same amount of power as the civil patrol *jefes* (leaders), whose profound paranoia regarding me eventually translated into some threatening anonymous phone calls and, according to a close informant, an alleged *brujería* (witchcraft spell) against me. Expressing my concerns to Virgilio, who had been able, unlike most catechists, to escape the deadly power of the PACs back home during *la violencia,* he urged me to quietly continue my work, muttering under his breath: "If they could not intimidate us over there, they certainly will not over here."

Returning to Xinxuc the second time, now entrusted with a large package of *maniorden* (money orders), photos, and baseball caps, I was greeted to my surprise with much warmth and enthusiasm in the community and with many questions regarding life in Providence and the status and well-being of family members. The fact that I had been able to bring news, money, and photographs and to give details about life *allá* placed me on an entirely new social footing. I quickly set about creating a map and conducting a survey to obtain some quantitative data on the impacts of transnational migration (including the number of homes built with Providence remittances and the number of people who had gone or returned)—a task I was unable to implement on my first visit. However, I feared that the hostile ex–civil patrollers in Providence continued to have contacts in El Quiché, where vigilante violence was on the rise and where the Truth Commission was in full swing. Instead, I found that I was now the target of an entirely new set of rumors: I was told by friends in both Santa Cruz and Xinxuc that *los MINUGUAs* (the UN mission staff)[33] were saying that I was a CIA spy, apparently due to my earlier presence on the guerrilla camp and at the trial, my suspiciously "nonanthropological" research topic, and allegations that I had been seen with a known CIA informant in the capital.

For the first time, the false sense of safety I had allowed myself as a privileged outsider and benign anthropology student (relatively protected, I thought, by the relationships of camaraderie and friendship I had developed with the UN field staff) collapsed. Visiting the regional MINUGUA director and painstakingly trying to describe the relevance of my work on transnational migration and Mayan identity to anthropology and to the postwar period, I attempted to engage his sympathy or at least his interest by explaining the already worrisome situation with the ex–civil patrollers (his job, after all, was to monitor human rights abuses). He replied coolly, despite his friendliness in previous months, that although I may or may not be CIA ("we can never know in these places"), the rumors should cease since they might give me fuel to sue the organization for "violating my human rights." Nonetheless, several *MINUGUAs*, including some who had arrived in my absence and others who had befriended me earlier, continued to eye me suspiciously and keep a rather hostile distance. The divisive residues of violence, clearly, seemed to have penetrated even the organizations meant to redress them. A profound paranoia now overtook me, particularly in public spaces where I felt that my every move or contact might be misinterpreted, and I found myself behaving in much the same way as I had observed in other K'iche's: averting eye contact, questioning the intentions of those who solicited and spoke to me, trying to remain inconspicuous. I felt part of the postwar cast of characters described in Francisco Goldman's *The Long Night of White Chickens* (1992: 294):

> It was hard to imagine a country more justifiably saturated with paranoia. The last thirty years of violent repression—not to mention

the centuries before—had perhaps bred a new kind of human being, as if in a poisoned petri dish. Resolutely silent, suspicious [...], quick to believe the worst of anyone, guilty when guiltless, guiltless when guilty.

Surprisingly, my local Xinxuc friends did not seem perturbed by MINUGUA's dangerous rumors, which many attributed to probable *envidias* (envy) on the part of certain individuals.[34] Certainly, this is the way fear and malicious gossip function at the local level, an experience with which they were all too familiar. "Now you have lived with your own skin (*en carne propia*) what we have gone through, only you can leave at any time," several told me. Transnational migration, like any research topic in the highlands of El Quiché, was certainly not a neutral one. Once again, I assumed the privileged anthropological position, and returned home.

As this experience illustrates, one of the great strengths of conducting multisite research, particularly when studying migration issues, is that the methodology itself places the researcher within the process of movement under study. On the one hand, this shifting lens permits the anthropologist to approach and engage her subject from various angles and thus challenges the more static representations and social relationships that might be observed within a single setting (Marcus 1995; Olwig and Hastrup 1997). Through my own fieldwork, indeed, I was able to observe how K'iche's in radically different contexts shaped their lives and identities on a day-to-day basis and to hear how stories became transformed as they were recounted by people at different ends of the transnational circuit. Just as importantly, however, this type of roving fieldwork allows the anthropological "subjects" to view the ethnographer herself in different contexts. In this sense, it is the anthropologist's identity that becomes constantly renegotiated by those around her, as she becomes vested with both real and imaginary roles that then become part and parcel of the moving landscape of ideas and meanings.

An important aspect of this fieldwork thus became the issue of how various K'iche's viewed me, and how this perception changed through time and space. The rather extreme reactions evoked by my presence and the paradoxical identities I was variously assigned—*migra* infiltrator, transnational courier, *guisach,* cultural broker, CIA agent, object of *envidia*, miracle worker, *Derechos Humanos* spy, impartial confidante and supporter, and at times even simple student or friend—in part illustrate the profound confusion surrounding the intersecting fields of violence and displacement in a postwar period. In many ways, these diverse reactions also point to my own ethnographic role as a sort of communal mirror through which such a highly contested reality could be tested and narrated. In this sense, I was an "outsider/insider" who not only triangulated between different poles of identity and memory but also served as a figure through which people sought to valorize their own position—to themselves and to each other. My presence reflected people's fears and hopes in a context where most have had to remain silent and invisible to the broader world around them. Thankfully, I found that although the "questionable reality" that pervaded my fieldwork was profoundly destabilizing, it did not always work against me. My ambiguous role as both threatening and helpful, powerful and vulnerable, Latin and North American, meant that this identity was up for grabs—with some assuming the worst but others the best. The trusting friendships I was able to make in both Xinxuc and Providence provided me with the stories, and much of the insight, upon which the following chapters are based.

CHAPTER 2

MAYAN IDENTITIES THROUGH HISTORY

Esta escena se repite, se repite, se repite. . . .
Se repite en otros pueblos, en otras épocas,
en otras circunstancias. . . . Punto menos, punto más
. . . ¡Cuatro siglos y medio de lo mismo!
　　　　　　—Luis Alfredo Arango, *Discurso de Atitlán*

This scene repeats, repeats and repeats itself. . . .
It is repeated in other towns, in other ages,
In other circumstances. . . . It is more or less
. . . Four and a half centuries of the same!

Among the most remarkable aspects of Guatemala's enduring Mayan presence over the past centuries is the manner in which indigenous identity has been continuously redefined in practice and in representation, whether by Mayan Indians themselves or by outside actors seeking to exert some form of power or authority over the Indian population (Warren 1998). Today's ethnic landscape has been influenced as much by distant historical events—the colonial encounter, religious conversions, and state-building processes—as by recent ones such as the genocidal civil war and the country's attempts at reconstruction. However, if the rather fluid concept of Mayan Indian identity is to be understood in depth, it needs to be firmly situated within very particular localities, histories, and social relations. Historical pressures have rarely operated uniformly upon indigenous culture: Changes imposed from the outside have always been integrated or resisted at particular times, by particular communities, rendering highland *municipios* highly heterogeneous in ways that are often not apparent to outsiders. Thus, while ethnic identity in Guatemala has long been tied to larger issues of state power and the racial myths used to reinforce such power, the development of local Indian identities has been influenced as well by *municipio*-rooted customs and forms of social organization, and by diverse class dynamics, worldviews, and political loyalties.

The concept of Indianness has not always been perceived in such dynamic terms, however, either by scholars or by powerful actors seeking to manipulate it. The long-standing model of Eric Wolf's closed corporate community (1957) presented a rather static image of indigenous culture by focusing on how Indian peasant communities have resisted outside encroachment through enclosure, economic leveling structures, and the formation of a corporate identity.[1] Both the "essentializing" tendencies of older ethnographies, which like Wolf's model represented indigenous communities as isolated and cohesive groups whose "difference" lay in primordial traits and institutions (e.g., local speech, customs, rituals), and the Marxist perspective popular in the 1960s and 1970s, which viewed Indian ethnicity primarily as a function of capitalist oppression and exploitation,[2] have been criticized on a number of accounts, in particular for either minimizing or exaggerating the role of structural processes in shaping Indian culture. Certainly, neither approach can adequately explain the persistence of distinct local indigenous identities following many years of very intense economic and political change (Watanabe 1992; Smith 1990a; Wilson 1995).[3]

An enduring legacy of these approaches, however, has been the notion that with the increased penetration of modernity and capitalism, the loss of an authentic indigenous identity occurs through assimilation, ladinoization, or growing class differentiation. Linear notions of ladinoization have suggested not only that collective traditionalisms disintegrate through market and state pressures, but also that individual Indians who leave the rural community, its poverty, manual labor, and subsistence lifestyle become "assimilated" and lose their cultural difference.[4] This perspective has been fed by the notion that there is a binary opposition between the dominant Ladinos and the subordinate Indians, whereby the latter conduct manual labor in rural areas, are isolated, and seek prestige through service within their community, whereas the former seek status and wider influence through a broad network of personal contact and material accumulation (Warren 1998: 71–72).[5] This rather simplistic model has implied, in effect, that social change for Guatemalan Indians (that is, moving beyond poverty and marginality) can occur primarily through acculturation to the "modern" Ladino world—an assumption that has been clearly contested by the multicultural model proposed by recent Mayanists, and that is also put to rest through a deeper understanding of Guatemala's ethnic dynamics and long history of indigenous mobility.

THE COLONIAL PERIOD (1521–1821)

In 1524, Pedro de Alvarado initiated the Spanish conquest of the declining Mayan empire, a dynamic and complex society that in pre-Hispanic times had been characterized by "shifting trade patterns, changing modes of exploiting the environment, conquests, migrations, the rise and fall of states, urban growth and decline, [and] new religious cults" (Farriss 1984: 7). The Spanish conquest immediately produced a variety of demographic changes in Mayan society. As Lovell and Lutz succinctly put it, "[W]arfare, culture shock, ruthless exploitation, slavery, forced migration, and resettlement all hastened Maya demise and worked together in horrific, fatal unison" (1994: 34). As is well documented, the most destructive of the Spanish influences on the native populations were the diseases they brought with them, including smallpox, measles, typhus, and pulmonary plague—some of which continued to devastate certain areas through the nineteenth century and which, overall, caused a precipitous population decline (Lovell and Lutz 1994; Lovell 1985, 1988).

Farriss (1984) argues that the history of foreign domination persisting in the Mayans' collective cognitive repertoire allowed them, upon Spanish conquest, to erect strategies for adaptation and assimilation rather than to succumb to disintegration, in terms of both political and social systems as well as religious and symbolic beliefs. Favorable conditions for adaptation and survival nonetheless varied regionally, depending on various local factors such as the extent of Spanish encroachment on communal land, degrees of indigenous resistance to the epidemics, as well as geographical altitude (Lutz and Lovell 1990: 45). Most indigenous people in Guatemala who survived the conquest resided or took refuge in the northwestern highland communities, where the Spaniards made limited labor (or other) demands on them. These communities remained relatively isolated, less prone to outside pressure, and were thus able to preserve more of their traditional lands and systems of social and community organization.[6]

Despite being forced into an expanding capitalist world system, the colonial Mesoamerican economy remained precapitalist, running on tributes and coerced labor from the indigenous population. Grants provided by the Crown to Spanish colonists through the *encomienda* system enabled *encomenderos* to extract Indian tribute in the form of ordinary goods such as maize, poultry, produce, and woven goods, as well as more valuable ones such as cacao, salt, and cotton. These tributary demands, as well as the need for Indian labor in different sectors of the colonial economy, required Indians to migrate to various parts of the country, often on a temporary basis. Several forms of coerced migration were thus set in place by the Spaniards, including, during the first half of the sixteenth century, enslavement and *servicio personal* (unpaid forced labor), replaced later on by *servicio ordinario* (cheap labor) and *repartimiento,* whereby Indian communities had to provide approximately one-fourth of their male tributary population to work away from their communities up to twelve weeks per year for very low wages (Lutz and Lovell 1990, 2000; Lovell and Lutz 1994).

In order to centralize the availability of indigenous labor and tribute, attain greater control over Indian political organization, facilitate religious conversion, and discourage Mayan cohesion, the Spaniards spatially divided and regrouped the Mayan territories through fragmentation and the erection of administratively autonomous units, many of which were given to colonists as *encomienda* grants. Towns, villages, and hamlets were fused together through consolidation and *congregación,* processes of forced resettlement and nucleation that created the *municipio* (township), the lowest colonial administrative level liable to tribute and labor levies.[7] As early ethnographers argued (Tax 1937; LaFarge and Byers 1931), the *municipio,* with its principal town and *aldeas* (outlying hamlets), emerged as the classic form of community in the westerns highlands, a significant and lasting unit of Indian social organization.

Although the Spanish resettlement of Indians during this period engendered forced displacements, the reasons for indigenous flight and migration varied throughout the colonial era and came to include famines, epidemics, political troubles, personal conflicts, and cultural preferences. Indians also moved on a voluntary basis, both temporarily and permanently, to urban and nonurban centers of Spanish-driven economic activity, including cattle ranches, wheat farms, sugar estates (*ingenios*), indigo farms, and areas of cacao production (Lutz and Lovell 2000). "Pull factors" attracting Indians to areas outside their communities included security, better jobs, protection by a powerful *patrón* (boss), and the avoidance of tributary or labor obligations in the home community (Farriss 1984; Lutz and Lovell 1990, 2000). However, "not all migration to these estates . . . was entirely voluntary, for movement could be fueled by necessity, indebtedness, or the lure of cash advance that was given under contract, thereby requiring the debtor to travel to the place where the creditor wanted him or her to work for a specified period" (Lutz and Lovell 2000: 14). Other patterns of migration included temporary activities such as trade and religious pilgrimages, as well as longer-term or permanent movement to other communities under Spanish control or dispersal into satellite settlements in forests and mountains or (often temporarily) back to their *ejidos* (Lovell 1988).[8]

These different patterns of movement show that indigenous displacement during this period was viewed not only as a colonial imposition but also as an escape from colonial domination. Migration was an essential strategy of survival and protest among the colonial Maya and a major cause of frustration for colonial administrators and missionaries attempting to consolidate *congregaciones*. The social costs of flight were often high, however, and included weakened family and community ties and diminished mechanisms for mutual aid. Nonetheless, even the more long-term population movements did not destroy the boundaries of community or their corporate nature: The *congregación* system, in effect, turned out to be pliant enough to allow many Mayans to maintain ties to their ancestral lands and cultivate their *milpas* (Lovell 1988), thereby creating a "revolving door" for entering and leaving the community. In this vein, Farriss distinguishes between a stable core population within Maya society—which remained relatively fixed generation after generation despite temporary crises—and a more or less fluid group of migrants (Farriss 1984: 219–23). Thus, already during the early colonization period, both centripetal and centrifugal forces worked to demarcate the decidedly fuzzy boundaries of Mayan communities.

The documentation of such historical migrations counters the popular notion that Mayan communities have remained geographically nested or culturally congealed since pre-Hispanic times or since forced regroupment by the Spaniards. This perspective also debunks some of Wolf's premises concerning the colonial emergence of the closed corporate community as an adaptive response to colonial processes such as the encroaching *hacienda*[9] system and volatile markets (Wolf 1957). Indeed, since there was much regional variation in the effectiveness of *congregación* and hence in levels of flight and displacement, some communities were more "closed" or "corporate" than others (Lovell 1988; Farriss 1984).[10] Moreover, not all communities developed wealth-leveling institutions, as pre-Colombian stratification separating the native elite and commoners often persisted. Thus, rather than being isolated from economic or cultural influences, the indigenous colonial community acted more as a political instrument wielded against the state (Smith 1993).[11]

Emerging Indian communities came to be characterized by a blending of pre-Colombian and Spanish cultures. The most obvious instance of cultural blending was in the religious sphere (Warren 1978; Oakes 1951; Tedlock 1982; León-Portilla 1986). As Farriss (1984) argues, the incorporation of Christian elements and the creative process of fusion and adaptation were eased by preexisting Mayan forms of knowledge—which included metaphysical speculation and knowledge of other places—and the Mayan familiarity with accommodating new religious cults (those of previous conquering groups). As a survival mechanism, and in order to insult neither the Spaniards nor their own gods (Farriss 1984), Indians thus tended to observe public Christian religious practices and venerate saints while clandestinely adhering to their own rituals and beliefs. The religious form to which the Maya came to adhere, *costumbre,* often described as a synthesis of ancient Mayan beliefs and sixteenth-century Spanish folk Catholicism, was not an illogical jumble created by a confusion between two incompatible religions. Rather, both religions represented richly complex, multilayered systems that interacted symbiotically, and by incorporating the two Mayans were able to assert a measure of local religious and political autonomy (Farriss 1984; Warren 1978). It is through the *cofradía,* or religious brotherhood, that Mayans incorporated selected elements of Catholic religion, in particular Christian saints, as the focus of corporate identity. Indeed, one of the most tangible criteria for defining municipal boundaries became the active participation by local inhabitants in sustaining a relationship with, and honoring, the town saint. This practice, tied intrinsically to the *fiesta* system, has been an enduring element of Mayan ethnic identity through the twentieth century. Earle has argued that, overall, Mayan religious practices related to saint veneration during the colonial period—a form of "appropriating the enemy" (1990)—were "actively anticolonial in intent and effect," since this was "the one area where solidarity against cultural conquest could be exercised" (2001: 293–94).

Ethnic identities in colonial times were based on legal criteria (e.g., Indians paid tribute to and were protected by the Spanish Crown); cultural and racial differentiation between Indians and Ladinos, however, was nebulous and flexible, and the main division remained between Europeans and non-Europeans (Smith 1990a, 1990b). However, the Spaniards did bring with them, and proceeded to develop, a colonial discourse on Indians that has been transformed throughout the centuries but nonetheless sowed the seeds of cultural misunderstanding and racism in Guatemala (as throughout Latin America). The colonial "Other" was alternatively seen, on the one hand, as lazy, dishonest, dangerous, superstitious, childlike, and in need of enlightened civilization and Christianity, or conversely, on the other, as generous, gentle, peaceful, noble, humble, and at one with the land.[12] The contradiction between the burgeoning ideology of Enlightenment, natural rights, legalism, and religiosity, and the brutal means through which the conquest accomplished its exploitative goals necessitated dehumanizing and contradictory representations of the dominated peoples.[13] The racial myth of the Indian, which took form within the "epistemic murk" of the colonial imagination and resulted in an ambiguous "colonial montage of Indianness," became not only a problem of representation and epistemology, but also a "high-powered medium of domination" (Taussig 1987: 121). The seeds of terror, fear, and mistrust planted during the colonial regime have thrived through the collective history of postcolonial Guatemala; the onslaught of the conquest is not a remote historical experience but remains today a visible, tangible heritage (Galeano 1967; Lovell 1988). On the other hand, the forces of Indian resistance erected during this period paved the way for several centuries of political, economic, and cultural struggle against Ladino hegemony. As Farriss points out, political domination is not in itself a compelling force for change, since it can require one to adopt a certain behavior but cannot prevent one from investing this behavior with one's own set of meanings (1984: 392).

INDEPENDENCE AND THE PENETRATION
OF PLANTATION CAPITALISM (1821–1944)

Guatemala's independence in 1821 grew out of increased friction between *peninsulares,* people of Spanish descent born in Spain (who held ultimate colonial authority), and Creoles, those of Spanish descent born in the New World (who led the revolution). During the first two decades of independence, the Liberal rule of Mariano Galvez attempted to bring Guatemala into the modern nation-state system by establishing a direct head tax, imposing heavy demands on peasant labor for road and port building, suppressing the power of the Catholic Church, promoting private acquisition of public and communal lands, abolishing previous protections given by the Crown to Indian communities, and instituting educational programs to integrate Indians.[14] Following two decades of rather ineffectual rule by Galvez, a major popular uprising was led by Rafael Carrera, a former peasant and mestizo *caudillo,* who came to dominate the country from 1839 to 1865. Carrera's Conservative government sought to preserve many elements of the colonial ideology while restoring church institutions and their representatives. He argued for paternalistic protection for Indians whose cultural, political, and economic circumstances were different from non-Indians. Indians, for their part, supported Carrera since they viewed Liberal assimilationism as an attack on their political autonomy (Smith 1990b). Widespread Indian support for Carrera was primarily a cultural reaction to the elitist nationalism of the Liberals, who had attempted to create equal, free, culturally homogeneous citizens without regard for local cultures. The preservation of local culture, to the Indians, was crucial in staving off attacks on their property (Smith 1990b: 79).[15]

Despite Carrera's protectionist ideology, ethnic differentiation between Indians and Ladinos during the Conservative period continued to be relatively muted, as the main division was between wealthy Creoles and the colored masses. Given that the Indian-Ladino distinction remained blurred, Carrera's populist movement represented the fairly united interests of both groups as they existed in that period (Smith 1990d: 162). The class

discrepancy between Ladinos and Indians, as it exists today, was only initiated during the subsequent plantation period when the goals of capitalist
growth required a coercive state that reified ethnic divisions, privileging
Ladinos (Smith 1990d: 168).

Indeed, Guatemala's second Liberal period is generally seen as the
initiation of the greatest, and perhaps most fierce, encroachment upon
indigenous political, economic, and cultural autonomy. This period commenced in 1871, when Justo Rufino Barrios moved to reverse the policies
of the Carrera regime by launching a transition from a feudal agrarian
tradition to export-oriented capitalist production based on a plantation
economy (Woodward 1990). Barrios's aim was to "enlighten" the nation
and to integrate Guatemala into the world economy by creating a strong
and modern nation-state simulating European and American nationalist
models. Liberal ideology was grounded in notions of progress, positivism,
and capitalism, and it sought to integrate "primitive," "backward" Indians
into the national economic system (Smith 1990b; Burns 1986). Barrios
encouraged the creation of a modern infrastructure including banks, transport (roads, railways, and ports), and communication media (telegraph,
telephone) and the introduction of new machinery and foreign technicians
to facilitate the plantation economy. In their attempts to emulate Western
nationalism, the Liberals encouraged European migration in order to improve or "whiten" the racial stock (Smith 1990b), and they enacted policies
to strip the Catholic church of its political influence and wealth (Burns
1986).

Most capital for the plantation economy of the nineteenth and early
twentieth centuries was provided by foreigners, including Germans who
controlled a good deal of Guatemalan production, as well as French and
US investors who owned most of the railroads and ports (Adams 1970).
The US-owned United Fruit Company (UFCO), and its appendages the
International Railways of Central America (IRCA) and the UFCO Steam-
ship Lines, came to dominate much of the Guatemalan economy and developed powerful political clout at the national level. The consequences
of this ownership pattern were profound and long-lasting, resulting in a
plantation agriculture that remained inefficient and tied to few crops (notably coffee,[16] sugar, and cotton), in the political domination of a small
oligarchy, and in a highly centralized and rigid state apparatus developed
to assist in acquisition of capital and labor (Smith 1993: 89).[17] The spatial
segregation (between western indigenous and eastern Ladino communities) and class differentiation (between Indians and Ladinos within the
western highlands) was strengthened during the late nineteenth century
and permitted the Creole elite to maintain their power position: It guaran-

teed the labor needed for the agro-export monopoly and spawned a social hierarchy firmly rooted in the racial division between Indians and Ladinos, a division that stood in clear contradiction to the stated Liberal plan to "integrate" Indians into national culture. These basic patterns, which created a landscape of highly unequal land distribution and defined the national status of Indians primarily in terms of an exploitable and inferior population, continued to exist in Guatemala well into the twentieth century (and to a large extent still exist today).

By the end of the nineteenth century, the integration of the Guatemalan economy into the world market had profoundly transformed the national and local economies. In the first place, land reforms were developed by Barrios to ease the transfer of communal land in the highlands to private, mostly Ladino hands. Throughout this period, Indians lost influence in municipal politics as Ladinos usurped positions of power in local Indian communities. In large part, they were able to do this by taking advantage of the new plantation economy and assuming the role of local labor contractors, moneylenders, merchants, and politicians (Handy 1984; Woodward 1976; McCreery 1990, 1994; Smith 1988; Lovell 1988). By the first decade of the 1900s, it is estimated that Indian communities had lost half of the lands they traditionally claimed during the colonial period (Smith 1993: 86). In many cases, communal land, the material basis for the corporate community, was destroyed, not due to legal abolition but rather through an uneven and slow process of privatization favoring Ladinos (McCreery 1990). Many natives never gained clear legal title due to poor communication between Indian communities and government policy implementers as well as an often-unscrupulous pattern of land acquisition by Ladinos (Burns 1986; Warren 1978).

However, the process of land titling was complex and uneven, and most communities managed to hold on to some land by obtaining both individual and group titles (McCreery 1990). The variability of indigenous community response to land encroachment as well as the role of geographic location during the early plantation period have recently been highlighted by several authors (Lovell 1988; McCreery 1990; Carmack 1990). In some communities, the Liberal reforms generated some serious Indian rebellions against the authorities (e.g., in Momostenango, Santa Cruz del Quiché, the Verapaces, and Huehuetenango [Carmack 1990]). In other areas, they pitted *municipios* against each other, exacerbating intercommunity land conflicts that had resulted from unclear titles to communal land dating from colonial times. Such conflicts led individual communities to appeal to state authorities to make their claims through legal channels, sometimes increasing the chance of opportunistic intervention from Ladinos

(McCreery 1990; Lovell 1995). In any case, the state's severely repressive responses to uprisings and their involvement in land disputes made it clear to Indians that the new socioeconomic order was hegemonous.[18]

Most importantly, the Liberal revolution brought new patterns of labor migration for indigenous communities, as well as new institutions (both private and state-run) for controlling it. Barrios carried out a series of land and labor "reforms" meant to facilitate coffee production and provide cheap seasonal agricultural labor on large coastal *haciendas*. These laws, targeted toward Indians whose "duty" it was to work on plantations (Burns 1986: 18), included the legislation of *mandamiento* (forced labor requiring each Indian community to supply a specified amount of labor each year) and *habilitación* (debt servitude). In addition, the Liberals relaxed liquor laws, "making it easier to lure *indígenas* into debt servitude" (Stoll 1999: 45), thus saddling most Indians with huge debts owed to the plantations and their contractors. Compounding the cycle of debt bondage, unpaid debts were passed on to the children of laborers, who themselves continued to be tied to plantation labor. While during this period a number of *campesinos* (peasants) migrated to the coast to work as *colonos* (permanent workers, both Indians and poor Ladinos), most Indians were forced into a seasonal migratory pattern; the debt peonage system essentially classified Indian *jornaleros* (seasonal workers) as the property of coffee, sugar, and cotton *latifundistas* (plantation owners), many of whom rented out land to Indians in the highlands in exchange for plantation labor.

The encroachment of commercial agriculture into the fiber of indigenous society through mandatory seasonal migrations led to a dual Indian system of *milpa* subsistence agriculture in tandem with cash wage labor from the plantations. As Swetnam (1989) shows, labor drafts were organized along community lines, penetrating daily life in *municipios* and making use of Indians' agricultural and ritual cycles and participation in community affairs. *Contratistas* (labor contractors) as well as local Ladino *prestamistas* (moneylenders) frequently worked community *fiestas*, advancing money to (or *enganchando*, roping in) Indians during local celebrations.[19] Through this system, community and plantation economies became linked to a common calendar whereby Indians, often entire families, generally left their *milpas* for several months between August and February, returning home to harvest the maize and bean crops planted in April and May. As Swetnam states, "Indian *pueblo* and coastal *finca* became part of an interdependent economic system which shared the fruits of development unevenly" (Swetnnam 1989: 93). In addition to *finca* (plantation) work, all Indians between the ages of fourteen and thirty were required throughout the Liberal period to work for free three to six days a year constructing roads and bridges.

There is no question that plantation laboring conditions were exploitative and brutal: The plantation system had a highly detrimental effect on many indigenous communities, taking peasants away from subsistence labor, creating a dependence on seasonal migration, shrinking local economies, and offering minimal remuneration for extremely grueling, unhealthy, and hazardous work (McCreery 1983; 1990). Despite this immersion into a cash-wage economy, however, Smith (1990a, 1990b) argues that seasonally migrating Indians became a semiproletarian class and that their resistance to full proletarianism (or full immersion into a capitalist class hierarchy) during this period can be seen as a major element in the maintenance of Indian cultural identity and autonomy.

Indeed, the effects of this system were not straightforward or homogeneous, and it had rather contradictory consequences throughout the highlands. On the one hand, the devastation brought by land encroachment and forced seasonal migration led many Indian *municipios* to resist external influences through economic barriers to outside goods and influences and through the development of "a variety of mechanisms to strengthen community identification and reduce both class differentiation and the perception of class distinctions" (Handy 1994: 19). In large part this was accomplished through the elaboration of community-specific social and religious institutions, referred to as *cargo* systems. The *cargo* system can generally be described as a hierarchy of rotating civil and religious offices, or *cargos* (literally a duty, charge, responsibility or burden), whereby male individuals ascended the ranks of the civil-religious hierarchy throughout their lives, some reaching the highest level of *principal* (elder). This "gerontocracy" served to delimit community boundaries, encourage community solidarity, define status, and concentrate authority in the hands of elders. Further, those at the top of the hierarchy were also responsible for collecting money for the ritual *fiesta* system, thereby flattening socioeconomic differentiation (Wolf 1957). In addition, the religious brotherhoods, or *cofradías*, introduced during the colonial period were reinforced to provide a sense of common identity and source of prestige in return for community service and the honoring of the town saint.

These two systems comprised a model for indigenous behavior based on community participation, peace and tranquility within the family, respect for elders, and the settling of local disputes by officials of the hierarchy (Warren 1978). As Watanabe (1992) argues, however, *cargos* were not merely leveling mechanisms or symbolic expressions of solidarity but also defined access to community resources such as land. In effect, the system was used by some more than others to achieve—and monopolize—status and wealth; indeed, wealthier people tended to move through the hierarchy more rapidly, thus becoming *principales* at a younger age than others.

Although *cargo* systems virtually disappeared by the early to mid-twentieth century in some indigenous communities, in others they still endure today, coexisting (in various forms) with regional and national forms of political organization as well as with universalistic religions such as orthodox Catholicism and Protestantism.

The long-term effects of mandated seasonal migrations on local economies and power relations were variable and complex. In some communities, the plantation economy enabled certain Indians to acquire more wealth or land, thereby leading to increased class differentiation. In certain cases, indigenous elites were able to avoid labor drafts and capitalize on the absence of other community members to accumulate land; in others, Indian *caciques* became *contratistas* themselves, enriching themselves through moneylending and acquiring the land mortgaged by poorer *jornaleros* for debt payment (Handy 1994). In other communities, forced labor migrations served, instead, to inhibit (or even out) existing class hierarchies, since cash income from outside the community allowed poorer Indians to maintain plots of land, participate in the religious *fiesta* system, and perhaps even begin small businesses. Thus, although the *cargo* system, which was strengthened during this period, operated to keep any one family or individual from acquiring large amounts of cash or property, it never totally removed differences in wealth nor did it erase ambition and the desire for prestige (Tax 1953).

The relationship between seasonal migrations and local economies was thus not clear-cut. Rather than impoverishing all Indians, the plantation economy helped many to retain their land holdings and invest in measures that allowed them to produce more than before (Smith 1993: 96), thereby "evening out" access to food and consumer goods and offering young men an alternative to local patriarchal control (McCreery 1994). An additional advantageous (though contingent) effect of plantation labor was that it provided a safety valve through which unruly or antisocial members of the community could be enticed or could themselves opt to leave the community more permanently (Handy 1994). Thus, despite the clearly detrimental and disagreeable impact of coerced seasonal migrations, plantation labor was also an ambivalent endeavor for Indians: It could potentially lead to greater poverty, inequality, and dependence on Ladino *patrones*; it could strengthen individual and collective capacities for acquiring cash and preserving autonomy; or it could allow individuals to opt out of the community altogether.

In addition, despite the labor drafts, Indians during this period were involved in numerous alternative economic strategies and options, including various forms of employment that involved movement outside the community. A number of indigenous communities became highly productive during the Liberal period; Indians from Quetzaltenango to Totonicapan (Smith 1988) participated in vibrant regional market networks, and Indians from these towns chose from a variety of agricultural techniques, craft production, and other forms of trade in order to supplement threatened *milpa* subsistence. Economic interdependence both within and between *municipios* created an important, and lasting, class of local, regional, and interregional *comerciantes* (traveling merchants) who brought local goods to other municipalities or regions, often returning home with outside goods.[20] Swetnam's research on the final decade of labor coercion (the 1930s) shows older informants remembering that "the ideal was to work as a merchant until one could accumulate enough land to become agriculturally self-sufficient" (Swetnam 1989: 101); as he states, "such accounts contrast vividly with complaints of workers unable to escape from plantation labor" (102). Again, the tremendous heterogeneity of indigenous communities must be highlighted, since some have been more locked into plantation dependence than others (a pattern that continues today). Here, however, I stress the notion that already during the Liberal period, regular, periodic movement away from the community was not only associated with forced labor but also with regional commercial activities that enabled Indians to maintain a certain amount of autonomy despite their immersion in the capitalist system.

To summarize, the national economic structure created during the Liberal period resulted from a combination of the unequal social relations already established before Barrios's ascent and the opportunities provided by the world coffee market in the nineteenth century. Liberal ideology reinforced the racial myth initiated during the colonial period, which portrayed the Indian in negative terms, in order to reify and sustain class divisions between Indians and Ladinos. By the end of this period, social conditions and the relationship of exploitation and domination of Indians by the Ladino state had changed little. In the 1930s the dictator Ubico attempted to centralize political control by eliminating local elections and appointing Ladino municipal leaders. He also furthered the interests of the agricultural elite by instituting "vagrancy laws" that, while allegedly instituted to abolish *mandamiento*, forced indigenous small landholders to work 150 days per year on the plantations and national economic projects and to carry *libretos* (notebooks) containing their work and debt records; those who became "fugitives," if found, were subjected to severe punishment by the state.[21]

While Indian subalternity became clearly demarcated during this period in the eyes of the state and Ladino elites, ethnic self-categorization in the highlands remained rooted at the *municipio* level and was reinforced by institutions such as the *cargo* and *cofradía*, systems designed to resist outside encroachment. The uneven development of capitalism and land encroachment, however, meant that different regions and communities were drawn into the coffee economy at different times and under different conditions (McCreery 1990). Most communities were subject—to varying degrees—to *both* the fragmenting influences of capitalism (including increased class stratification and expanded migration patterns commanded by the plantation economy) *and* to local cultural institutions erected to resist the negative impacts of such influences. In addition, despite the fact that Ladinos during this period became the "state agents of Indian oppression" in many rural communities, others came to lose their economic monopolies as Indians increasingly claimed stakes in regional market economies (Smith 1988). Handy summarizes the diversity of indigenous communities during this period concisely: "[S]ome villages had substantial community-controlled land, while others had little or none. In some municipalities, there appeared to be little ethnic conflict, but in others, such conflict was pervasive. Significant antagonism between wealthy and poor Indians existed in some communities; in others, little was apparent" (Handy 1994: 12–13).

The link between *municipio*-level cultural systems and community ethnic identity was made explicit by anthropologists working in Guatemala during the first half of the twentieth century. Ethnographies written during that time focused on the *municipio* as the standard sociocultural unit and tended to examine "surviving" indigenous cultural traits (including language, lineage, customs, and religion), often trying to distinguish "native" (i.e., pre-Colombian) cultural patterns from Spanish ones.[22] Despite criticisms that earlier anthropologists "essentialized" Indian culture by focusing primarily on the cultural affairs of the corporate community, these ethnographers did point to some of the complexities of sociocultural and economic experience within highland communities. For example, most described the vicious circle of social decay brought about by seasonal plantation labor, disease, alcoholism, and debt, thus indicating the immersion of Indian communities into the expanding capitalist system. At the same time, some of these ethnographies also pointed to the tremendous resistances of particular communities, resistances built through a selective engagement with the state and capitalist expansion rather than in isolation from them. Sol Tax for example illustrated how the Indian defensive response to national economic encroachment was, in certain areas, a growth in local specialization, commerce, and trade. He described Panajachel Indians, for example, as penny capitalists: "[T]he Indian is perhaps above all an entrepreneur, a business man, always looking for a new means of turning a penny" (1953: 12). He argued that the impersonal marketplace and the competition of capitalism were very much part of life in communities where most foodstuff and household necessities were bought from outside markets. From this perspective, incorporation into local and national capitalist systems did not necessarily lead to the demise of indigenous community or identity, but rather galvanized adaptive economic responses that already formed part of local socioeconomic organization. Ruth Bunzel, moreover, portrayed Ladinos in Chichicastenango as having very little influence on Indian life, and she described K'iche' Indians as highly resourceful social agents. Rather than depicting Indians from this *municipio* as isolated, marginalized victims of the state, she painted the following picture:

> They are strongly organized to defend themselves against any encroachment upon what they regard as inalienable rights. They do not hesitate to take their protests to Guatemala [City] when they feel their customs threatened. . . . They are always listened to, for . . . back of the . . . Indians stands the specter of Indian solidarity in the Highlands. The threat of Indian revolt hangs over the timid heads of Guatemala's gaudy dictators, and the memory of Zapata and Obregon freezes their heart. (Bunzel 1952: 12–13)[23]

Although Panajachel and Chichicastenango are clearly not representative of all indigenous communities,[24] and while both Tax's and Bunzel's ethnographies were conducted at the tail end of the Liberal period (when labor drafts were less brutal than in the previous century), these descriptions of local community life do provide a nuanced perspective on the varied, and indirect, Indian responses to Ladino hegemony during this period.

Indeed, with the benefit of historical hindsight, McCreery argues importantly that the relative absence of a united or firm indigenous resistance to a profoundly subordinate role in the coffee economy was due to the emergence of a "colonial compact" whereby Indians accepted exploitation as legitimate as long as the "degree, extent and form of this exploitation" could be negotiated (1994: 334). As long as the state left a space for compromise (particularly at the local level), indigenous communities opted for a "peaceful, negotiated survival rather than a violent resistance" (Hale 1997: 820). As McCreery, Hale, and others (e.g., Lartigue 1983) point out, this acceptance of hierarchy and subordination within certain limits, that is, the negotiation of one's exploitation through one's own terms, has been historically constitutive of Indian consciousness, identity, and culture. Rather than being seen as conservative, it can be viewed as a powerful form of progressive resistance that recognizes the various levels, strengths, and weaknesses of both authority and subordination; as such, it has attempted to subvert and manipulate imposed structures from within, and

at the level of the community, rather than proposing a "frontal resistance."
As we shall soon see moreover, this nontotalizing view of Indian-Ladino
power relations may explain, in part, the failure of the guerrilla movement
of the 1970s and 1980s to garner a stronger and more loyal support base
throughout the Indian highlands. First, however, a description of the decades and events leading to the armed movement is in order.

THE "TEN YEARS OF SPRING" (1944–1954)
AND ITS AFTERMATH (1955–1978)

The Democratic Revolution

The decade between 1944 and 1954, or the "Ten Years of Spring,"
has been of particular interest to many authors, largely because the achievements of this period's reformist government and its demise are seen to explain much of the national and ethnic conflict of ensuing years (Schlesinger
and Kinzer 1982; Gleijesis 1991; Immerman 1982; Handy 1984, 1990, 1994;
Wasserstrom 1975; Adams 1970, 1990). This period has traditionally been
considered one of great social reform, as two democratically elected presidents together abolished all forced labor laws, introduced work codes and a
social security system, legalized unions, instituted land reform, and emphasized educational programs. However, many scholars do not believe that
this period represented a new economic or political direction, but rather
a power struggle among the national bourgeoisie, including the growing
military, whose ideology differed little from that of nineteenth-century
Liberals (Adams 1970). Some have argued, thus, that the "revolution" was
essentially a nationalist move toward instilling a more stable capitalism
based on peasant labor, with little regard for the particular cultural life
of Indian communities (Galeano 1967; Wasserstrom 1975). Within the
expanding system of export capitalism, the mutual dependence between
large *hacienda* owners and Indian laborers remained; in many parts of the
highlands, the basic pattern of seasonal migration and "land for labor" was
maintained during this "free wage" era—though the market, rather than
the state, now delivered Indian labor to the plantations.

During this period *indigenismo*, a *mestizo* humanitarian perspective
that "presented Indians as having been long exploited but of intrinsic
worth, in need of education and of being raised to their proper place in
civilization" (Adams 1990: 143), began to take root in Liberal academic and
political circles. This perspective was epitomized in Miguel Angel Asturias's
famous essay, *El problema social del indio*, which depicted Indians as children who could be made into adults through improved education, better

health and nutrition, and greater assimilation into Ladino culture. It provided a romanticized idealization of the pre-Colombian Mayas but tended to serve "as a means for political and economic elites to appropriate indigenous cultures for nation-building ideologies that end up maintaining the subaltern status of Indian people" (Field 1994: 243). *Indigenista* measures were implemented by the reform government, which increased its presence in Indian communities, largely through rural education programs designed by the Instituto Indigenista Nacional to foster patriotism and nationalism (Handy 1990). Significantly, however, the main reforms developed during this period, including emerging unions, *campesino* leagues, and political parties, did not form along specifically ethnic lines (Adams 1990).[25]

Following Juan José Arevalos's presidency (1944–1951), the government of Jacobo Arbenz Guzmán (1951–1954) moved slightly to the left, primarily by establishing the Agrarian Reform Law in 1952. This policy was designed to expropriate, with compensation, unused or underutilized land from large estates to give to individual *campesinos* and to provide *campesinos* with agricultural assistance and credit. It thus attempted to realign and confront landholding and military powers (Adams 1990) and to inspire more productive and equitable agricultural production (Handy 1990). Close to one hundred thousand peasant families received land under the reform, and agricultural production increased steadily (Handy 1994: 94–95). However, not all rural communities or indigenous sectors were pleased with land reforms, as they also included the expropriation of some municipal lands, which, in many cases, were under the control of local indigenous authorities (Handy 1994; Grandin 2000). Arbenz also sought to stimulate industry and encourage national economic production and independence, challenging the monopolies held by US interests such as UFCO and IRCA.

Several authors have argued that this period was particularly destructive to the institutions of the closed corporate Indian community (Wasserstrom 1975; Smith 1984; Lovell 1988; Adams 1970). In many villages, *cargo* systems virtually disappeared, as young Indian men fluent in Spanish and familiar with Ladino bureaucratic procedures began to take charge of local politics (Watanabe 1990, 1992). At the same time, socioeconomic differentiation and market dependence became more entrenched in local politics, causing an increased class polarization among peasants. Although highland Ladinos continued to monopolize power in some communities, in many areas *municipios* were increasingly run by an indigenous elite who now used the party system to their own advantage in local political struggles. As such, party politics often operated to strengthen individual and class positions within the community. In some areas, wealthy Indians seeking to maintain a local privileged position aligned themselves with conservative politicians desiring to halt the process of agrarian reform (Wasserstrom 1975).[26] The agrarian reform law thus produced intense conflicts and factionalism in the countryside, bringing into relief preexisting land disputes between neighboring *municipios* as well as between *aldeas* (hamlets) and their *cabeceras* (municipal capitals): The countryside was "riddled with factions which battled each other through access to secular, religious, and supernatural authorities" (Handy 1994: 112).[27]

Smith (1988) argues, however, that an examination of regional variation with regard to Indian-state relations reveals this period to be less destructive to the closed community than is often believed. First, she states, socioeconomic differentiation *among* communities was more marked than *within* communities, depending on access to commercial and artisanal occupational alternatives (Smith 1990c). For example, Indian communities close to urban centers had more access to capital and alternative occupations and were therefore better off than more peripheral communities, which remained more dependent on seasonal migrations. Second, the nineteenth-century pattern of Indian investment of *hacienda* wages into their own communities continued, with more and more Indians investing in local ventures such as trading and land improvement. Third, mass Ladino migration from the country to the capital meant that in some areas Ladino commercial monopolies, including transportation, came to be controlled exclusively by indigenous market centers. As Smith argues, these wealthier Indians did not simply replace the Ladinos' objective class position and their allegiances to the state. In fact,

> social relations in Indian communities remained coherent—
> organized by the traditional values of formal courtesy, reciprocity,
> and respect for age, hard work, and properly accumulated wealth—
> even without the *cargo* system and the other institutional devices of
> the closed corporate community. Indians in both poorer and richer
> zones maintained a steadfast stance of preserving cultural if not
> economic or political autonomy. (Smith 1993: 99)

Nonetheless, most scholars agree that the agrarian reform law did create a new more radical organization in the countryside, as local structures (promoting land and labor demands) were developed in order to more effectively represent rural populations at local and national levels. Adams suggests that the reform era, though more conservative than often depicted, promoted nonetheless a serious recognition of the rural poor and marked a sociological awakening in indigenous communities (through the emergence of educated, literate, Spanish-speaking Indians with a national and international perspective), an awakening that, in the 1960s and

1970s, would result in the emergence of an Indian ethnicity of nation-state scope (Adams 1990: 158). And Handy concludes that although this period brought a strong current of national consolidation, state penetration, and capitalist expansion, thus placing much pressure on local forms of organization, individual communities were nonetheless able to shape some of these external influences to meet their own needs and to preserve an intense sense of community identification. In this sense, Indian communities once again adapted their organizational forms to the broader structural changes by developing more responsible and nationally aware local governments with strong community orientations, rather than disappearing altogether.

Arbenz's government soon came under much pressure from large landholders, the urban middle class, the military, as well as the US State Department, which was seeking to preserve the vast interests of the United States (not least the UFCO) in Guatemala. The "revolution" was brought to the ground in 1954 by the combined forces of internal opposition and the CIA, both of whom justified the coup with a Cold War rhetoric rooted in paranoid anticommunism.[28] Following the overthrow of Arbenz by his own military (and with much encouragement from the US government and business interests), Carlos Castillo Armas took power and returned to their former owners close to 90 percent of land transferred during the reforms (Handy 1984). Although there has been excellent documentation of the critical role of the United States in staging and supporting Arbenz's overthrow (Schlesinger and Kinser 1982; Immerman 1982; Gleijesis 1991), Handy points out that it is important to understand the internal mechanisms that brought down the "revolution": The agrarian reform period had unleashed, in the countryside, a more virulent reaction than was expected, and one that did not fit into the "simplistic blueprint" designed by the national government to integrate Indians into the state (Handy 1984: 203–5).

It is clear, however, that the CIA-assisted overthrow of the elected Arbenz government and its accompanying anticommunism created an irreconcilable split between left and right in Guatemala (neither of which had thought of the Indian population as much more than backward and passive). The coup, moreover, initiated a series of dictatorships that would eventually push the left to organize an armed movement. As Stoll states, "the 1954 counterrevolution shut a mainly law-abiding left out of the electoral system and encouraged the Guatemalan élite to consider itself above the law" (Stoll 1999: 46).

The Aftermath

A major structural shift commencing in the 1950s (and continuing through the late 1970s) was Guatemala's rapid economic modernization, which, like that of most other Central American nations, occurred relatively late. Based on increased foreign investment and import substitution industrialization, and, in the 1960s, on a diversification of the export agriculture sector (which now included large cattle farms and cardamom plantations in addition to coffee estates), the modernization process led to vast changes in traditional socioeconomic structures and to numerous dislocations in the countryside. Throughout this period, many small landholders (*minifundistas*) were kicked off of their land or found themselves the owners of increasingly shrinking plots; the average size of *minifundias* decreased from 1.3 hectares per person in 1950 to less than 0.85 hectare per person in 1975 (Jonas 1991: 79). A sudden boom in population growth compounded the land problem; between 1950 and 1981, the population more than doubled in size from approximately 2,791,000 to more than 6,000,000 (Lovell 1999).

This combination of very high population growth, increased landlessness, and unemployment in rural areas resulted in an explosion of both permanent and temporary migrations from rural to urban areas, as well as to the southern coast (in particular Escuintla, Retalheleu, and Suchitepequez) (Hamilton and Chinchilla 1991: 84).[29] The growth of the urban service sector and industrial development patterns created particularly strong pull-factors toward the capital, whose population grew by 28.3 percent between 1950 and 1960. For indigenous migrants, these urban movements, like rural migrations, involved "a mix of permanent migration and circular mobility for ... short term work" (Gellert 1999: 118). However, growing numbers of rural peasants did begin to settle in the capital city, working in both formal and informal sectors of the growing urban economy, though often maintaining varying levels of contact with the home community. In addition to the internal migrations spawned in the 1950s, this period saw an intensification of cyclical movement from the western highlands to the Soconusco region across the border in Chiapas, Mexico. Though Guatemalan Indians had been working seasonally on plantations in this region since the nineteenth century (in a pattern similar to that of the coastal migrations), these cross-border movements intensified after the 1950s when Guatemalan labor came to largely replace Mexican seasonal workers (Castillo and Casillas 1988). Finally, new indigenous migratory patterns also took place in the 1960s and 1970s, spawned by a government-sponsored colonization program designed to "appear to be dealing with the land distribution crisis," but which was primarily oriented toward developing agribusiness (Nolin Hanlon 1995: 22–24). These projects re-settled highland Indians in the sparse regions of the northern rainforest areas (such as Petén and Ixcan), creating new "frontier" communities often comprised of Indians originating from different regions and *municipios*.

Despite the large dislocations of the decades following the end of agrarian reform, the 1960s, which saw the creation of the Central American Common Market and the US-sponsored Alliance for Progress (designed to contain communism), also brought new development projects, foreign investment, and new technologies to the indigenous countryside. Some Indian communities increasingly diversified their economies by importing capital goods (e.g., fertilizer, sewing machines, etc.) or planting alternative crops (other than the traditional maize and beans) to further self-sufficiency (Smith 1993; Arias 1990). The advent of fertilizer (*abono*), which became an essential agricultural necessity for Indians, had a major impact on most communities; the new dependence on fertilizer not only required larger amounts of cash but also led to an increased commodification of *milpa* products to be sold in the marketplace, thus further pushing many *campesinos* into the market economy. The creation of a vast tourism industry, moreover, led to the development of artisanal production and textile industries in parts of the highlands; new highways and communication media such as radio facilitated these economic developments. This strengthening of local indigenous economies, in combination with new forms of organizing and universalizing ideologies of resistance, would soon pose a major threat to the Guatemalan military state as well as to local Ladino powers.

One of the most profound changes during the 1960s and 1970s for Indian communities (particularly in the department of El Quiché) was the sudden influx of foreign Catholic missionaries, primarily Spaniards (followed by North Americans and Italians) of Catholic Action (Acción Católica).[30] This period coincided with the Vatican's "war against communism," and the dictator Castillo Armas welcomed the arrival of clergy committed to preventing the communist threat planted by the "ten years of spring," particularly in the poor and desperate areas of the Indian highlands.[31] The ideology of Catholic Action (CA) during this initial period was conservative and reactionary, and the missionaries set forth to convert, sometimes through intimidation and force, indigenous communities that had long been practicing *costumbre*. Catholic Action, led by the missionaries and young Indian catechists (literate, bilingual, specially trained lay leaders), took a strong foothold in the countryside, attempting to break the *costumbrista* (traditionalist) structure (including the heavy drinking and other nonorthodox practices surrounding traditional rituals and the *fiesta* system) as well as the belief in (traditional) supernatural powers (Arias 1990; Warren 1978).

Despite the conservative and hierarchical nature of the model promoted by the Vatican, the foreign missionaries arriving in the highlands in the late 1950s and early 1960s, many poorly prepared to do pastoral work and unfamiliar with the environment, eventually came to be profoundly shocked and influenced by the tremendous misery, poverty, and oppression they observed in their indigenous congregations. Most became part of the burgeoning reform Catholicism or liberation theology that comprised a critical social movement throughout Latin America in the 1960s and 1970s.[32] At the grassroots level, this new theology (now espoused by Catholic Action), which called for a "preferential option for the poor," stressed issues of social justice and equality and viewed the teaching of Catholicism as a method for mobilizing the poor against immoral social structures: CA members became involved in various development activities throughout the highlands and in northern colonization projects, including the organization of cooperatives and health and education initiatives. The base ecclesial communities (CEBs) established by priests (and led by indigenous catechists) were particularly successful in communities where religious and social organization had been dismantled and destabilized by the rapid social change of earlier years, and the CEBs, in turn, continued to erode traditional local power structures.[33]

Also during this period, a small number of Indians were given scholarships to attend universities in the capital and other large cities such as Quetzaltenango (Arias 1990; Galeano 1967). Some of these students, mastering the language of the Ladino world during their studies, then returned to their communities with clear ideas and an increased capacity to organize local development initiatives (Handy 1994). Others, however, remained in the city, creating an Indian intelligentsia that consolidated into an urban bourgeoisie whose interests, according to Arias, were quite different from those of rural organizers. For the first time ever, an Indian elite found representation in national-level politics, clinging strongly to its identity despite its nonrural, nonagricultural existence in the capital. A significant rift began to occur between this urban bourgeoisie and rural Indians, as well as between conservative and radical indigenous factions in the countryside (Arias 1990: 242). In large part, professional urban Indians saw their struggle as a cultural one against all Ladino power, whereas rural *campesino* movements tended to espouse a more popular, class-based struggle (Burgos-Debray 1983)—a split that, as we shall see, persisted in the following decades with the creation of a postwar pan-Maya movement.

The influence of Marxist ideology, which would eventually lead to the civil war between guerrillas and the Guatemalan government that devastated Indian communities in the early 1980s, also took root in the early 1960s.[34] Around 1965, a small guerrilla movement of young Ladino army officers and students was formed in eastern Guatemala, basing its hopes and ideology on the model of the Cuban revolution (Le Bot 1992). This movement—which largely ignored the Indian population—was squashed by the government, which in the process killed thousands of peasants and eliminated all active resistance in the region. During this period the political perspective of many Guatemalan academics and others interested in the *cuestión indígena* (Indian question) took on a decidedly orthodox Marxist viewpoint, shifting away from the *indigenista* model mentioned earlier. Epitomizing the "revolutionary paternalism" that characterized the Ladino guerrilla leadership of this period (and some later guerrilla leaders as well), Martínez Peláez's *La patria del criollo* (1971) argued that the "true" Maya had disappeared with the conquest, that the servile, broken Indians of the present day were mere products of colonial oppression, and that the "false consciousness" of Indian culture undermined the capacity for Indians to think and organize along political lines.[35] During much of the 1970s, survivors of the first guerrilla movement, basing their strategies on the *foquista* assumptions of the Cuban revolution,[36] focused their efforts in the capital and on the coast by infiltrating popular organizations, universities, and labor unions and by framing their message largely in terms of class struggle. While some elements of this ideology, such as the call for social awareness, struggle, and unity, began to influence the popular movements and organizing initiatives developing in the Indian highland and jungle areas during the 1970s, it was not until the late 1970s that the guerrilla leadership effectively transformed the movement into an armed struggle that went beyond a more contained urban guerrilla warfare and that sought to incorporate the Indian majority.

Arias (1990) argues that the 1960s and 1970s created profound changes in Indian culture and worldview, leading Indians to renounce "ancestral ways," to take advantage of growing educational and material tools, and to search for new meanings of identity, place, and community in this transformed environment. He contends that strongly localized ancestral bonds were gradually replaced with a more "universal" worldview and that popular organizations, formed around ethnic and class bases rather than by *municipio*, burgeoned. In addition to the various social forces described above, two events in particular galvanized the indigenous sociological "awakening" during the 1970s. First, the acute monetary crisis of the early 1970s, produced by a decline in global agricultural demand that resulted in economic stagnation and escalating inflation, led many rural indigenous community workers (such as teachers, health promoters, and young catechists) to become increasingly organized around issues of human rights and economic justice. Second, following the devastating earthquake of 1976 (which hit parts of the highlands with force and reinforced the ineffectiveness and corruption of Ladino authorities), popular organizing efforts gained momentum and coordination was consolidated between workers on the southern coast and agricultural unions (Arias 1990).

However, once again, the impact of this greater social awareness was complex and irregular, and while Indians of the new order were increasingly unified in some ways, they were also increasingly fragmented in others (Brintnall 1979). During the prewar period, many communities came to be deeply split along religious, political, generational, and class lines (due to new economic, political, and religious influences and opportunities), though such factional boundaries "cross-cut each other and shift[ed] constantly" (Watanabe 1990). Moreover, Arias's argument concerning the abandonment of traditional identities seems overstated if one examines the ethnographies of this period, which showed the highly heterogeneous nature of Indian communities at this time. As they indicate, a strong sense of local indigenous identity continued to be maintained despite class differentiation, structural changes, and new worldviews; in many communities, some elements of tradition (such as the *cargo* system) coexisted with other more modern influences and did not necessarily result in either increased ladinoization or a broader pan-ethnic identity (Colby and van den Berghe 1969; Early 1983; Smith 1977; Sexton 1981, 1985).[37] Finally, as ethnographies of the time show, the impact of the missionaries in the highland area was not universal but contingent upon factors such as preexisting political and economic divisions (Handy 1994; Falla 1978; Wilson 1995). In some towns, the increased popularity of CA led to splits between ladinoized catechists and traditional *costumbristas,* at times producing violent confrontations (Carmack 1981). In others, entire communities converted peacefully while still maintaining many aspects of their traditional beliefs and practices such as the earth cult and planting rituals (Wilson 1995: 183–88). And in yet others, *costumbristas* and catechists were able to propose a complementary dualism within which they could coexist without conflict (Tedlock 1982).

Local variances notwithstanding, the success of progressive regional projects such as cooperative movements in Indian communities became an object of great fear for the Guatemalan state. These burgeoning processes often created conflict with local as well as state Ladino powers, whose development plans and ideas behind credit provision continued to be based in capitalist expansion and national integration rather than the empowerment of Indian communities (Arias 1990). As more and more peasants focused on building and diversifying local economies (through trade and commodity production), indigenous communities were slowly achieving a greater degree of economic independence than ever before. The Guatemalan state, which had operated as an agent of development during the 1960s and 1970s, was not able to tolerate the threats to its own existing power structure generated by this very modernization and by increasing popular expectations. As Smith argues, it must have seemed to the government that the plan to incorporate Indians into the capitalist system through measures such as colonization and cooperative projects had backfired, "locking peasant labor into community projects and encouraging peasant political ambitions at a time when peasant labor was needed for grander schemes and when peasant political leadership could only mobilize resistance" (1993: 105).

Responding to these fears, the first repressive moves on the part of the army took place in 1975 in the northern part of the western highlands, a zone of potential mineral and petroleum wealth that was being claimed by high-ranking military members. By 1977 and 1978, a series of demonstrations in the capital city organized by groups such as the Comité de Unidad Campesina (CUC—Committee for Peasant Unity)[38] galvanized the optimism of organized and mostly indigenous *campesinos*. At this point, government efforts to suppress popular organization had largely involved targeted assassinations against select leaders of the progressive movement; these tactics turned toward a more generalized terror by the end of the decade, when the army effectively launched a counterinsurgency campaign designed to remove the guerrilla influence that was making its way through the Indian highland and jungle area.[39] Such conflict in turn radicalized many cooperative members and led to the strengthening of *campesino* leagues, which, along with the Catholic catechists, came to be seen as subversive and became prime targets of the military and paramilitary during the violence of the 1980s. By 1978, a full declaration of war against all progressive sectors—including those representing the rural peasantry—began to incite large numbers of Indian communities to enter the armed struggle (Smith 1993; Arias 1990). Christian-based catechists played a crucial role in generating indigenous support for the revolution: They were able to "translate the doctrine of political revolution into understandable local terms" since the notion of class consciousness was not evident to the largely illiterate indigenous peasant masses they sought to attract (Wilson 1995: 214; Le Bot 1992).[40]

THE CIVIL WAR (1978–1984)

The 1980 burning of the Spanish embassy (occupied by CUC dem-onstrators) by Guatemalan police forces is seen as the watershed event that left Indians little alternative but to join the armed struggle against the dictatorship of Lucas García.[41] Thousands of highland Indians joined the EGP (Ejercito Guerrillero de los Pobres—Guerrilla Army of the Poor) and the ORPA (Organización del Pueblo en Armas—Revolutionary Organization of people in Arms), the two main guerrilla factions operating in highland Indian communities.[42] Guerrilla leaders, in large part survivors of the failed leftist movement of the 1960s, were mostly educated Ladinos with little experience with Mayan culture or people (Smith 1991). Though ideology and strategy varied slightly among the four groups,[43] the broad aims were to instill a proletarian consciousness in the Indian population, attack the state, and replace it; as such, the decision to incorporate Indian communities in the struggle was a deliberate attempt to create a strong population base, something they had omitted in the earlier revolution (Payeras 1983).[44]

Though the significant degree of Indian participation in the war was rooted in an ideological commitment to the revolutionary agenda born in the decade's political awakening (Harbury 1994; Carmack 1988; Arias 1990), some authors have argued that the guerrillas' eventual failure to maintain a strong support base in highland communities lay in part (that is, in addition to the army's crushing counterinsurgency) in their disregard for and misunderstanding of communal Indian worldviews and visions of progress, as well as preexisting class divisions. Le Bot (1992) and Stoll (1993), whose work otherwise differs in important ways, both describe how the authoritarian, hierarchical imposition of a class-based revolutionary agenda often clashed with and misinterpreted local indigenous political behaviors, ignoring the local and heterogeneous nature of Indian communities and assuming that all Indians would identify with the revolutionary agenda.[45] Other scholars have focused, rather, on indigenous revolutionary activism throughout this period, examining the social movements that led to support for the revolution throughout the highlands and showing Mayan Indians to be active political actors within this struggle (Grandin 2004; McAllister 2000). Although the debate surrounding the popularity and support for the URNG (the Guatemalan National Revolutionary Unity, which consolidated the four guerrilla groups in 1982) throughout the different periods and spaces of the war has been contentious among some researchers (and has elicited fascinating discussions about the nature of violence, memory, historical consciousness, and postwar scholarship [see Hale 1997]), there is agreement among most that reasons for Indian participation in the movement seemed to range from ideological hopes for a

more just society (Harbury 1994; Falla 1980, 1994), to a certain millenarianism unleashed by radical liberation theologians (Le Bot 1992), to protection and self-defense against a vicious army, to a simple lack of alternatives
as a "neutral" stance became effectively barred. Often, such reasons shifted
as the war progressed, and both guerrilla and army strategies increasingly
used these communities as surrogates in their own war. By the end of the
1970s most indigenous communities, which, though they had never been
harmonious or egalitarian, had for the most part been able to avoid the
"culture of violence" so prominent in Guatemalan political culture (Le Bot
1992), were now drawn into one of the most horrific periods of political
violence seen in this century.

The army's response to the guerrilla threat was massive and disproportionate: The combination of a global Cold War rhetoric of anticommunism,
Ladino paranoia regarding the potential for a strengthened indigenous resistance, and the army's exploitation of local ethnic and class animosities all
resulted in a chaotic violence throughout much of the highlands. The hideous brutality of the army's strategies during this period has been described
in detail by many authors (Carmack 1988; Schirmer 1998; Montejo 1987,
1993; Falla 1994; Manz 1988; Burgos-Debray 1983; Harbury 1984; Lovell
1995; Sexton 1992; Le Bot 1992; Simon 1987; Stoll 1993; Wilson 1991);
by yearly reports from Amnesty International, Americas Watch, and Human Rights Watch; as well as by the subsequent Truth Commission Report
(CEH 1999) and the Historical Memory Project compiled by the Catholic
Church (ODHAG 1998b). The regime of Lucas García was followed in 1982
by the even more insidious rule of the born-again Christian General Efraín
Rios Montt, as well as his successor General Mejía Victores.

The civil war had powerful ethnic overtones and was "an explosion of
deep-seated national racism" (Wilson 1995: 217); at the same time, most
of the foot soldiers utilized in the carnage were young indigenous men forcibly recruited to serve in the army (though usually not in their own communities).[46] The rape of Indian women and the torture of anyone suspected
of being (or of knowing someone who was) subversive, the desecration of
Mayan symbols, the burning of *milpas,* and the army's appropriation of
indigenous symbolism for its own strategic ends[47] were only part of the sinister depravity unleashed by soldiers and paramilitary groups in the effort
to destroy Indian culture and replace it with a docile indoctrination. The
army used a profound racism to justify its brutality, shifting the national
rhetoric on ethnicity from one that viewed "Indians as savages" to "Indians
as communists" (Montejo 1993: 57).[48] By 1984, more than 440 Indian villages had been burned to the ground; over 42,000 civilians, mostly Indians,
were killed or "disappeared." One million were internally displaced, tens
of thousands fled the country, and over 125,000 children were orphaned.

Community health, education, and development workers, and catechists in particular—virtually anyone accused of "organizing"—were targeted.

Following its scorched earth policies in 1982, the army realized that it needed to neutralize guerrilla strategies by consolidating a more "stable" rule in the countryside, militarizing civilian life and manipulating rural communities through "civic action" programs similar to those used by the United States in Vietnam (Manz 1988; Perera 1993; Lovell 1995; Simon 1987), thus "sinking its institutional and discursive elements deeper into civil society than ever before" (Wilson 1995: 250). Ríos Montt and his minister of defense Hector Gramajo established rural programs designed ostensibly (or so the international community and the population were told) as projects of economic development, social justice, and progress in the ravaged countryside; however, "the message was clear: comply and be fed, equivocate and be killed" (Lovell 1995: 60).[49] In addition to the forced conscription of young Mayan men into the military, strategies of institutionalized violence and psychological indoctrination in the country-side included the implementation of civil defense patrols (PACs), model villages, and development poles (forced resettlement camps) and the in-stitution of special army units.[50] These civilian surveillance methods were clearly meant to inscribe state power relations, norms, and ideologies into individual bodies that could then police one another. As Schirmer (1998) argues, the military thereby sought, quite successfully in many places, to create a "sanctioned" Indian who could be used in the construction of an alternative national project (see also Nelson 1999a; Le Bot 1992).

The institution of the PACs, through which the army sought to natural-ize violence by forcibly enrolling all Indian men over the age of fifteen to surveil their communities, had particularly nefarious consequences for the social and psychological life of Indian villages. First separating, weakening, and isolating particular villages from their neighbors through repeated as-saults and killings, the army would then inform inhabitants that they must form community PACs, denounce (or eliminate) all suspected subversives, and enforce nighttime curfews. Local PAC *jefes* (leaders), as well as mili-tary commissioners, were carefully selected from among the towns' pow-erful (both Ladinos and Indians, usually with military backgrounds and connections); *orejas* (spies) were appointed; and terrorized villagers were encouraged or forced to denounce neighbors and family members. Rural confrontations became very murky, as it was difficult to establish whether the violence was instigated by the army, by guerrillas punishing villages seen to support the army, or by communities themselves seeking to "settle scores" (Lovell 1995: 64). A range of internal divisions were efficiently capi-talized upon by the army and used to promote the violence, among them economic interests; ethnic, religious, and generational antagonisms; and personal animosities and jealousies.

The PACs created a situation whereby not only did victims and perpetrators live side by side, but victims of brutality sometimes became subsequent perpetrators themselves, or, through passive complicity with the patrols, collaborated in deadly local power struggles.[51] The army and PACs became the ultimate judicial authority in many parts of the highlands; arguments over land, adultery, witchcraft accusations, and *envidias* were carried to army bases or PAC leaders (Wilson 1995). These methods were clearly designed to enter into the cultural fabric of Indian society, as the army played on indigenous notions of sin, culpability, and conformity to create (or reinforce) internal conflict and historical rivalries within and between communities, religious groups, and, most nefariously, families themselves.[52] In the process, traditional patterns of respect and authority were shattered and replaced with an endemic sense of fear, suspicion, and terror (Green 1999; Zur 1998). All of these devastating effects were compounded by the economic impacts of the war, which included a decreased demand for goods and labor, a decline in agricultural and subsistence work due to army sweeps and PAC duties, and the curtailment of intercommunity travel for commercial or cash-wage purposes.

The massive rise in Guatemala of Protestant evangelical sects, whose congregations currently comprise about 35 percent of the population, was an important component of the violence and conflict of the 1970s and 1980s (Wilson 1995).[53] The war, having torn apart the social and spiritual fabric of many highland communities, created a space for fundamentalism, a spiritual need that was not lost on the "born-again" Ríos Montt, who manipulated religious frictions in indigenous communities by inciting animosities between evangelicals and Catholics. The "capitalist" ethic of evangelicals clashed with the "social justice" worldview of Catholics, and the two groups reflected the political polarization between army and guerrilla supporters. Evangelicalism comprised an onslaught against traditional religious elements such as saint worship, *cofradía* rituals, *fiestas,* and drinking; the movement promoted instead, sobriety, a repudiation of "pagan" customs, and the espousal of "anti-*milpa*" forces such as entrepreneurship and individuality (Annis 1987). Like the Catholics, evangelicals preached an abandonment of traditional beliefs; but unlike the Catholics, their message was one of submission to authority and the acceptance of one's position in life rather than social questioning. In effect, they preached an apolitical stance, though they were clearly allied with the dominant right (Le Bot 1992). After the devastation caused by early reprisals against Indian communities and the brainwashing by the army, many Indians (including previously converted Catholics) chose to side with the evangelical churches, which operated both as a safe-conduct ticket and a relief from the tremendous psychological ambiguity and stress of the violence.[54] In many instances, conversions were pragmatic attempts to transcend the violence and remain neutral, combined with a disbelief in political solutions (Stoll 1993: 178–79).[55]

The war's massive displacement of indigenous populations added to all this destruction in the highlands; well over 10 percent of the population was uprooted through forced relocation by *la violencia* (Ferris 1993). In the departments of El Quiché, Alta Verapaz, Huehuetenango, and Chimaltenango—those targeted by the army's counterinsurgency program—more than 80 percent of the population was at least temporarily uprooted (Nolin Hanlon 1995). Displacement of individuals and populations was often used as a military strategy to cut vital links between guerrillas and their support bases (Wilson 1995; Wearne and Calvert 1989), but it also served as a survival strategy by which people in the countryside could elude the violence. The flight from communities was massive, chaotic, and variable; in some cases, entire villages were forced to flee, while in many others targeted individuals fled temporarily or permanently. All forms of displacement severely strained the fabric of Mayan communities, whether that displacement took the form of being forcibly resettled into the army's "model villages," of forming clandestine Communities of Population in Resistance (CPRs) in the jungle, or of seeking refuge in other hamlets and towns, in the mountains, on the coast, in the capital, or abroad (to refugee camps or other areas in Mexico, other Central American countries, or the United States and Canada). In addition, the forced army recruitment of young men, as well as their participation in militant guerrilla activity, led many Indians to a physical and emotional rupture with their community. Wartime displacement and resettlement of all forms exacerbated the fragmentation of community-based solidarity, breaking traditional links with subsistence fields, severing symbolic connections with the local ecology (Wilson 1995), and reinforcing the social and psychological divisions of *la violencia.*

Although the civil war has been viewed as entailing broad-scale devastation and as having led to a "generalized social and political mobilization . . . in the Guatemalan highlands" (Davis 1988: 20), a number of researchers have shown that just as Indian-state relations had varied tremendously before the eruption of war, the intensity of violence—along with resistances to and interpretations of the war—also varied throughout the highlands. Different regions and communities experienced this period in different ways, partly due to specific army strategies to divide the population and prevent solidarity, and partly due to the historically heterogeneous nature of Mayan communities and their relations to outside influences. While some were slow to join the guerrillas (due to geographic, cultural, and political isolation; local interests; or ideological opposition), others, perhaps more aware of their subordinate national position, joined "en masse" (Wilson 1995: 209). And, while in some areas political sympathies remained relatively homogeneous for a long time (for example, the CPRs [Falla 1997]), many communities and individuals shifted allegiances as the war progressed, for reasons ranging from brute coercion by the army and paramilitary to disenchantment with and a loss of trust in the guerrillas (Stoll 1993). Although many indigenous communities were overwhelmed by brutality and psychological manipulation, were completely wiped out, or experienced massive dispersal, others were able to resist, to some extent, being drawn in to the violence.[56] It is only in the past few years—after the end of the war and the opening of a political space that has enabled a collective reflection on the violence—that inquiries into how Indians experienced, interpreted, and responded to the violence have been undertaken.[57]

A "FIRM AND LASTING" PEACE?

In 1985 a civilian president was elected, and in 1987 a dialogue between the URNG and the Guatemalan government commenced under the auspices of the Esquipulas II Peace Accord in Central America.[58] However, Guatemala maintained its record as the worst human rights violator in the hemisphere during the late 1980s and early 1990s. In addition, policies of amnesty and a tangible aura of impunity meant a continued sense of unaccountability for army officers and PACs, who in some rural areas became increasingly violent; the URNG also continued to operate in some highland areas, refusing to validate the army's pretension that it had won the war against subversion.[59] It was not until 1996—after several delayed deadlines—that a "firm and lasting peace," the product of years of intensive and difficult negotiations between various sectors of society and the United Nations Verification and Human Rights Mission (MINUGUA), was signed between the URNG and Guatemalan government.

Officially established in 1994 to implement the Universal Declaration of Human Rights in Guatemala and to monitor compliance with the Peace Accords, MINUGUA's mandate, role, and activities shifted through time. Acting primarily as advisors and observers, MINUGUA staff provided training and support to a variety of national sectors and promoted international cooperation within the frame of the peace deal.[60] Institutional responsibilities extended broadly: verifying human rights denunciations; monitoring electoral reforms; reorganizing and strengthening judicial, military, police, and other institutional structures; and overseeing projects for improving schools, health care, and social services in rural areas.[61] Although much of the human rights monitoring provided by this institution echoed the work of other national and international human rights organizations—for instance, the Human Rights Office of the Archbishop (ODHA), the Guatemalan Human Rights Commission (CDHG), and organizations such as Amnesty International and Human Rights Watch—it gained authority due to its influential positioning within the Peace Accords, though it also came under much criticism at times from actors on both the left and the right.[62]

The finalization of the Peace Accords in 1996, designed to redress decades of violence and its root causes, included agreements focusing on issues ranging from indigenous rights to socioeconomic justice to constitutional reform.[63] As part of this official agreement, the UN brokered changes including the demobilization and reintegration of URNG guerrillas, the dissolution of PACs and military commissioners, the end to forced army recruitment, the reduction of military power and security forces, the institution of a National Civil Police Force, as well as series of steps outlined to incorporate the indigenous population into civil society and to negotiate socioeconomic changes.[64] The Peace Accords proposed many high-reaching objectives for postwar reconstruction and democratization, and the accords represent the largest-scale "peace-building" operation ever undertaken by the United Nations (Kinzer 2001). Their implementation, however, was far from satisfactory in most of the areas outlined, leading to a high level of frustration on the part of international actors such as the UN as well as the general population. Despite a widespread discourse on "human rights"—as well as the presence of a multitude of international and national NGOs, government organizations, and civil society sectors involved in the postconflict reconstruction—the aura of violence and corruption continue to permeate Guatemalan society to this day. Social violence in the country has soared and is often difficult to separate from the continuing political violence evidenced by assassinations, disappearances, wrongful arrests, and death threats against human rights workers, judges, lawyers, and journalists, which the army and police often ascribe to the work of delinquents.

Moreover, although there has been a quantitative decrease in human rights violations since 1996, significant levels of both social and political violence continue, as illustrated by an extremely high degree of urban violence and increased "social cleansing" in the countryside.[65] The phenomenon of *justicia por propria mano* (mob vigilante justice) has led to hundreds of public lynchings, especially in the rural highlands, motivated by property disputes or aimed toward eliminating undesirables and criminals from communities.[66] Many cases have occurred in areas where ex-PAC leaders continue to maintain a high degree of social control—they have often been found to be the main instigators—and where the local power structures of the civil war are still in place. These abhorrent acts, in which individuals have sometimes been burned alive publicly by mobs, echo the grotesque violence of the civil war and are clearly the result of an ineffectual judicial system.[67] Frustrated by mounting violence, MINUGUA has blamed government forces, unchecked military and police forces, and a weak justice system for the continuation of violence and human rights abuses. This violence has continued unabated until today, and, particularly following MINUGUA's official withdrawal from the country in 2004, the additional problems of violent gangs, narcotraffic, and prison uprisings can be added to increasingly high numbers of assassinations, kidnappings, lynchings, and other such crimes.

The effects of the war continue to be profoundly ingrained in today's indigenous communities: In addition to having destroyed many of the community and familial structures that framed people's lives, the civil war reinforced a culture of fear, authoritarianism, perceived political arbitrariness, criminality, cruelty, silence, apathy, and impunity. At the local level, long-lasting sociopolitical effects of the war include the stigmatization of victims, which creates serious obstacles to the participation of civilians in already weakened social organizations. More dangerously, the existence of an uncontrolled armed power still acting to intimidate local populations, along with the coexistence of victims and perpetrators, reproduces fear and silence in many areas (CEH 1999). A telling indicator of this culture of authoritarianism is manifested by the continued popularity of Efraín Ríos Montt (who went on to become president of the Guatemalan Congress after the war), including in some rural areas hardest hit by the violence. Indeed, in a number of highland villages, PAC members reorganized as "security committees" in the mid-1990s, and their continued allegiance to Ríos Montt was made clear (e.g., in newspaper ads in which they declared their support for the general). Within a few years, moreover, organized ex-PACs resurfaced more publicly to demand monetary compensation from the government for their participation in the armed conflict—a demand that was clearly an outrage to the many victims of the army's violence.

Ríos Montt's following and that of powerful PAC *jefes* in the highlands can in part be explained by a deeply ingrained military ideology through which many young men in the countryside were indoctrinated to value the purported discipline and hierarchy promoted by the army and which in the postwar period is justified as having enabled the military to win the war (Schirmer 1998). As Zur (1998) has pointed out, the profound respect for authority characterizing many indigenous communities became vastly distorted during *la violencia,* when conforming fully to the army became not only a matter of survival but also a way through which certain indigenous men were enabled to create powerful personal identities amid social and cultural chaos. In effect, the general's popularity in the countryside is explained by the culture of *caciquismo,* or big man leadership, resulting both locally and nationally from the structures of violence.

In addition to this devastated landscape, grueling poverty and socioeconomic inequality—the root causes of *la violencia*—also persist throughout the Indian highlands today. The continued existence of these root causes is a reminder of the cruel reality that the war was fought for naught. The Peace Accords, despite their lofty objectives (and the millions of international donor dollars they attracted), have barely made a dent in these respects. Although figures vary depending upon the source, it is estimated that around 90 percent of Guatemala's rural population lives below the poverty line. Sixty percent of Guatemalans (76 percent of the rural population and 82 percent of the indigenous population) earn less than US$2 per day (IDB 2000). Government investments in social services and human capital in Guatemala are the lowest in Latin America, and Guatemala has one of the most regressive tax systems in the hemisphere; in 1997, total public expenditures on education were 1.6 percent of the GDP, and expenditures on health were 1 percent, the lowest in the region (Gellert 1999).

Since the war, moreover, the national economy has gone through some major crises due to fluctuations in world markets, neoliberal economic policies, and a steady decline in Guatemalan agricultural production for export, all of which have reinforced the prolonged postwar depressive climate.[68] Neither the agricultural sector (in particular the coastal plantations) nor the urban industrial economy have been able to absorb rural labor, resulting in high unemployment and underemployment rates in both urban and rural areas. In addition, Guatemala continues to have the most unequal land distribution in the continent; rural families with direct access to land decreased from 61 to 49 percent in the last two decades (UNDP 2000).[69] Approximately 2.9 percent of landowners own 68 percent of the agricultural land, indicating an extreme inequality that has not changed over the past decades. Finally, high population growth rates (3.2 percent per year, the highest in Central America) and fertility rates (4.9 percent per year, 5.9 percent among the indigenous population), particularly in the countryside, continue to exacerbate pressures on land and result in further poverty. All of these problems have led many rural peasants to become squatters who occupy land (*asentamientos*) in both urban and rural areas, often eliciting violent responses from landowners.

The confluence of problematic elements described above point to the conflictive and complex nature of postwar projects, where discourses of peace and human rights often contradict local realities; indeed, they put into question the universal viability of internationally imposed reconciliation efforts in a context of continuing fear, divisiveness, social instability, and structural weakness. Despite this rather dismal picture, however, the international pressure placed by MINUGUA and international NGOs has, at the very least, checked the level of state repression. The peace process and the relentless work on the part of human rights and social justice groups has also managed to open up spaces for debate and organization that were unthinkable only a decade ago.

Two particularly important and well-documented achievements of the peace process will be discussed in more detail in following chapters. The first is the establishment of various collective memory projects, including the collection of wartime testimonies and the exhumation of graves, organized primarily by religious and human rights groups and aimed toward healing the social and psychological wounds of the war. As part of the UN-brokered Peace Accords, the implementation of the Historical Clarification Commission (CEH) in particular has sought to promote justice by documenting both the sociological roots of the violence and the subjective testimonies of its victims, thus shedding light upon a history long silenced by state terror. As we shall see, however, while the process of remembering past violence and validating the victims' suffering has been an important step toward coming to terms with the past in some indigenous communities, the notion that a collective memory can be constructed in the present remains difficult in *municipios* that remain highly fragmented and governed by continuing fear in the present.

A second major postwar achievement has been the crystallization of the pan-Maya movement, which, though rooted in a longer prewar history of ethnic organization, gained momentum in the late 1980s and has forced the nation to rethink and revise the exclusionary ethnic model that led to the violence. In order to create a broader "Mayan culture," Mayanists have sought to mobilize previously localized indigenous identities (based in municipality, language group, or region), struggling, therefore, to balance the notion of local identities with the more universalizing discourse needed to adopt self-conscious identity strategies, negotiate self-determination, and enter civil society as a political force (Fischer 2001). As such, this ethnopolitical project, which uses a sort of "strategic essentialism," has been organized in response to the nation-state and to outside forces such as international NGOs and governments from whom it receives a fair share of support and funding. As Handy (2002) argues, while the Maya movement has been very concerned with issues of locality, it has had a difficult time reconciling the "messiness" of Indian communities with the demands of the nation-state, which require a "sanitized, domesticated" version of the community. Indeed, the implementation of an "imagined community" of Mayanism is not a self-evident process in many (largely illiterate) indigenous *municipios,* traumatized by years of terror directed primarily at their culture and splintered by political, religious, and other factions. The Maya movement's difficult road toward negotiating indigenous identities points not only to the diversity of voices among today's Guatemala's indigenous population but also to the notion that cultural identity is something at once ascribed and contested within local and global arenas.

A related postwar initiative that has also been central to the peace process, and has received much attention from international organizations and academics, is the resettlement and readaptation of returning refugees and internally displaced populations. Much of this attention has focused on the roughly fifty-two thousand refugees (mostly Indians coming from areas close to the Mexican border such as Huehuetenango and Ixcan) who fled to the Mexican border during the violence and eventually settled in UNHCR-sponsored camps in the southern Mexican states of Chiapas, Campeche, and Quintana Roo (Manz 1988; AVANCSO 1992). Through an organized, highly politicized vision of their eventual return to Guatemala, and with much aid from international NGOs and UNHCR, camp refugees created new forms of organization in exile (Montejo 1993; Wilson 1995; Earle 1988, 1994; Stepputat 1995; Nolin Hanlon 1995). In a sense, exile gave these refugees the space, the tools, and the skills to examine the roots of their situation back home, interpret the political conditions of violence, and develop new forms of social and material organization.[70] The camp experience also gave official refugees—who, coming as they did from various regions and ethnic groups, were "todos revueltos" (all scrambled [Stepputat 1994, 1995])—a sense of unity and purpose for their plan to return and find a place within postwar Guatemala. Central to these new organizational forms was a revised notion of ethnicity, based around the broader pan-Mayan identity; indeed, some of the advocates and organizers of pan-Mayanism have been those exiled in Mexico during the war.

Although the complex process of postwar repatriation and negotiations for a "collective return" (Stepputat 1994) are too elaborate to discuss here, it is clear that despite the involvement of various actors and international accompaniers in supporting the highly organized Permanent Commissions of Guatemalan Refugees in Mexico (CCPPs), the returns were far from smooth.[71] Indeed, although a clear set of demands was put forth by the CCPPs to ensure their safe return (and the Guatemalan government technically agreed to these demands by signing the Basic Accord for Repatriation in 1992), returnees were confronted with numerous practical and political difficulties. In addition to the specter of army intimidation (exemplified by the 1995 Xamán massacre) and hostility from local communities in Guatemala (who either feared or resented the "subversiveness" connected with refugees), the ever-recurring problem of access to land, either in the communities of origin or in new areas of resettlement, remained highly problematic.[72] By 1997, approximately eighteen thousand official refugees had returned collectively (North and Simmons 1999), and it is only in 1999 that the final group of official refugees returned to Guatemala.[73]

There has been less attention paid to the multitude of unofficial and dispersed refugees of the war and its aftermath, scattered both inside and outside of Guatemala. As we have seen, a large proportion of rural *campesinos* coped with the violence and its economic devastation by flee-ing and concealing themselves in areas of traditional migration such as the southern coast and the capital, by traveling to other regions and munici-palities, or by crossing the border to Mexico.[74] Most researchers working with dispersed refugees (Castillo 1999; Gellert 1999; Bastos and Camus 1994; Fabri 2000) have pointed to the difficulties of finding quantitative data on these populations (both in Guatemala and outside), as they are not part of official registers and have tended to be highly mobile. While some have stayed, either permanently or for long periods, in various urban and rural areas of destination in Guatemala and Mexico, others have returned home, and some have moved on to new destinations such as the United States and Canada. Moreover, because many rural Guatemalans left their home communities for reasons that include both the violence and the eco-nomic crisis of 1980s, they are not clearly classified (either by authorities or by themselves) as political refugees or economic migrants (Earle 1994). These conditions have thus created a large number of displaced Guatema-lans within and outside the country about whom relatively little is known, though most authors emphasize the highly vulnerable and marginal po-sitions of these hidden populations who are often exposed to economic exploitation and a high level of uncertainty in their new settings (Bottinelli et al. 1990; Earle 1994; Bastos and Camus 1994; 1995; Fabri 2000).

With respect to dispersed refugees in Mexico, for example, it is esti-mated that up to two hundred thousand unofficial refugees settled in that country as a consequence of the war (Nolin Hanlon 1995).[75] Indigenous refugees who settled in rural areas were, despite their unstable status and lack of assistance or resources, able to integrate to some extent into the labor and cultural context of border areas (such as the Soconusco in Chia-pas), where, as we have seen, Guatemalan Indians have been migrating seasonally over the past century (Castillo and Casillas 1988).[76] Refugees who fled further to urban centers such as Mexico City, however, were sub-ject to highly stressful conditions including isolation, lack of access to jobs and resources, very poor living conditions, rejection from the host society, and the psychological stress associated with unresolved mourning and the inability to return home (Bottinelli et al. 1990).

Unlike camp refugees, who were "spatially concentrated, highly visible and legal" (Wolfensohn 2001: 28), dispersed refugees were vulnerable and forced to hide their identities due to their undocumented status. Plans to either stay in Mexico permanently or return home were put on hold, contributing to uncertainty; even so, despite extreme conditions of marginality and the ever-looming threat of deportation, these urban refugees were often able to create informal solidarity networks and groups of mutual support that acted to reiterate national and ethnic identities in hidden forms (Casillas and Castillo 1994; Earle 1994; Cuny, Lark, and Stein 1991). In addition, ARDIGUA (Association of Dispersed Guatemalan Refugees), the organizational body claiming to represent self-settled Guatemalan refugees in Mexico, tried to gain recognition and documentation for dispersed Guatemalans as political refugees and to organize collective returns to Guatemala (separately from the camp refugees).[77] The return objective for this organization was not very successful, however, and by 1999 only 750 members in all had gone back. This failure is attributable in part to the vulnerability of this population, which prevented effective mobilization, as well as to the Mexican government's 1999 decision to grant permanent resident status, which led many refugees to opt out of the return altogether and stay in Mexico (Wolfensohn 2001).

The situation of persons internally displaced by the war (that is, within Guatemala) has also been difficult to document, again because of the range of destinations (the northern jungles, the coast, urban areas) and because the exodus caused by the violence was transformed into longer-term searches for land and/or employment as a means of surviving the economic and political crisis of the 1980s. Aside from the CPRs, which constructed highly politicized identities through their displacement to the northern areas of Guatemala, most internally displaced populations have remained relatively anonymous in different parts of the country.[78] Bastos and Camus estimated in 1994 that there were approximately forty-five thousand indigenous *desplazados* in Guatemala City. Throughout the 1990s, despite an overall decline in urban migration rates compared to the previous decades, indigenous *campesinos* continued to move to the capital, where they often landed as squatters in urban shantytowns, or *invasiones,* in and around the capital.[79]

The past decade has thus been one of tremendous flux for Guatemalan Indians, one in which efforts toward peace and reconciliation have been juxtaposed with soaring social violence and economic dislocation. While tens of thousands of refugees returned to their homeland in the past decade, hundreds of thousands of Guatemalans left—and continue to leave—their communities in search of wages, survival, and opportunity within a national and global context that has become ever more precarious (Loucky and Moors 2000). Indeed, the fragile postwar social setting, combined with the demand for cheap labor in various sectors of the postindustrial economy in the United States, have resulted in a massive flow of Guatemalans to this country over the past two decades. By 1998, it was estimated that 1,570,000 Guatemalans (Gellert 1999: 120), roughly one-tenth of the population, lived in the United States, the majority having migrated in the 1980s and 1990s. Despite a lack of statistical evidence, existing research (Loucky and Moors 2000; Fink 2003; Popkin 1999; Chinchilla and Hamilton 1999; Hagan 1994) and media articles suggest that a large proportion of these transmigrants—including fruit pickers on the West coast, meat packers in the Midwest, and factory workers in the Northeast—are Guatemalan Indians.

SITUATING PLACE AND MOVEMENT IN HISTORY

As we have seen, while Indians have suffered greatly from the contradictions inherent in the economic and national goals of the Guatemalan elite, they have often sought to manipulate the situation to their advantage. A number of scholars argue that the resistance exemplified in historical struggles to defy the confiscation of territory and sociocultural assimilation is, in fact, the primary characteristic of Indian identity; moreover, the raw materials of indigenous culture make such resistance possible (Smith 1990a, 1990c; Watanabe 1992; Warren 1992, 1998). Many emphasize the historical flexibility and "constrained refashioning" (Wilson 1995) of symbolic boundaries, material practices, and local-level institutions through which diverse indigenous communities continually rework local structures and symbols while attempting to maintain cultural autonomy and continuity (Fischer 2001).

However, local identity processes as they have developed vis-à-vis the outside have been complex and may not be reduced to any simple power dynamic or overly determined notion of resistance. The incorporation of Mayan peasants into the Guatemalan state has been historically weak, and survival has often been a product of *municipio*-specific negotiations and relationships with various outsiders (the state, the church, other municipalities) as well as with local Ladinos. Indigenous responses to state hegemony have usually been raised as pragmatic responses to particular ill treatment during specific periods rather than against a monolithic Ladino state or race. Moreover, as Handy (2002) points out, the contradictory state project of simultaneously assimilating, protecting, and repressing the Indian population has been mirrored at the local level in a rather ambivalent indigenous response: Indian communities have at once "retreated" into cultural and economic constructs made "deliberately impenetrable in all possible ways to those from the outside" in order to preserve cultural autonomy, but they have also engaged fully with the state in numerous ways. Unlike the generalized insular resistance proposed by the notion of closed corporate community, then, local Indian identities have persisted through selective, complex, and community-specific processes that have allowed outside change to be assimilated, discarded, or negotiated depending on the community's characteristics, capabilities and, needs (Warren 1992, 1994). Indeed, the maintenance of traditions at the community level reflects much about the changing nature of contact with the outside world, while the selective incorporation of change from the outside reflects the desire to maintain community autonomy.

A second aspect of indigenous identities highlighted here is their diversity, both within and between communities. In explaining the "enduring Mayan presence," many scholars have argued that a key element of indigenous identity remains the vital importance of land, and of one's place within the boundaries and conventions of community (Earle 1986; Watanabe 1990, 1992; Hanks 1990; Wilson 1995; Tedlock 1982; Warren 1998). From this perspective, Indian identity continues to be largely rooted in a quotidian reality that emphasizes attachments to the community, to its physical landscape—including both agricultural activities as well as the sacred places wherein lie links to the ancestors, the spirit world, and the universe—and to community-level social organization. Nevertheless, as many of these authors point out, historically informed analyses of indigenous communities must also take into account various aspects of internal "difference." Local Indian identities have been defined not only in relation to the Ladino Other but also against other neighboring communities or other indigenous ethnic groups and subgroups. Important cleavages have permeated local histories, where power relations (between classes, ethnic or language groups, religions, political affiliations, generations, and genders) have produced numerous inequalities and contested identities.

In some communities, such differences have been smoothed over by strong indigenous moral codes, institutions, and social cohesion, and they have even contributed to a strengthening of community boundaries. In others, they have created various forms of conflict, alliance, and/or mutual dependence both among Indians and between Indians and local Ladinos seeking to promote particular social and economic interests and visions of community. While internal divisions have usually sharpened during particular instances of outside intervention (including greater thrusts into the capitalist state system), they have also formed part of a continuous process of internal hierarchy and negotiation. As Grandin (2000) argues, local struggles and competing interests should not necessarily be viewed as antithetical or destructive to "community," but should rather be examined as dynamic historical processes through which local identities and institutions are constantly transformed.[80] In examining the evolution of postwar community identities, thus, it becomes critical to take into account the complex webs of internal difference, opposing interests, and evolving economic relations that were already in place preceding the violence.

Finally, this chapter has emphasized the numerous forms of movement and migration that have always formed part of Indian life and that are part of the historical diversity characterizing these communities. Lutz and Lovell state, "[M]igration, in fact, is such a ubiquitous feature of Maya life that it would be possible to envision a cultural history that harnesses the theme as its principal organizing concept" (2000: 12). Throughout different historical periods government policy, shrinking land availability, high population growth, violence, and other factors have made migration, in both its permanent and cyclical forms, a "well-established survival strategy for the rural population of Guatemala" (Gellert 1999: 117).

In part, the traditional ethnographic focus on the more sedentary aspects of Indian culture might be seen as a general territorializing tendency within the field of anthropology itself to view mobility and movement as "noise" rather than as a "strong parameter in the self-definition of people" (Olwig and Hastrup 1997: 6).[81] In addition, the "fixed" nature of indigenous identity has long been opposed, in both anthropological accounts and in the state's gaze, to a more "mobile" Ladino one; indeed, the very concept of the Ladino, in the colonial period, was used to designate those Indians who had been physically driven from or had chosen to leave their communities. As described earlier, this tendency toward sedentarizing Indian culture is rooted in conceptual categories, based in national ideology, that have opposed the progressive, modern, state-integrated Ladino to the rural, community-bound Indian. At the same time, however, Indians themselves have often viewed outward mobility with a certain ambivalence and suspicion; as Nelson points out, "any indigenous person who leaves the community, the rural area, and the manual labor associated with the village is vulnerable to accusations of inauthenticity and ladinoization. *This rejection can come from village-bound indigenous people, gringos and Ladinos*" (1999a: 131; my emphasis). Indigenous mobility thus not only threatens the fixed categories often used by academics and the state, but is also part of a local, historical dialogue on identity within which movement outside the community has been viewed as necessary and potentially threatening to both individual and community identities. As such, the tensions between stability and movement, and local and outside, are connected to a broader historical ambiguity within indigenous communities whereby cultural survival has necessitated a constant negotiation between, on the one hand, strategies of individual and collective autonomy (connected to tradition and place) and, on the other, strategies of socioeconomic success and survival (connected to mobility and a selective incorporation into the broader political and economic structure).

It is important to distinguish the different patterns, motivations, and consequences of movement and migration and to situate them within particular periods and structural contexts. As we have seen, coastal migrations have been inscribed in very intricate ways in the annual agricultural and ritual patterns of many Indian *municipios,* as well as within particular forms of social organization and power relations. Here, economic debt and dependence have long been central motivators, and cyclical return to the community has usually (though not always) been the norm. The temporary mobility of regional *comerciantes*—who often are away for twenty or more days per month buying and selling in various market settings—constitutes a very different experience from the grueling work of the coastal plantations; this type of activity has usually complemented *milpa* work, allowing slightly better-off *campesinos* to maintain some economic autonomy (that is, not working for a *patrón*). Urban migration has led to new labor and social contexts that create tensions between "urban migrant" and "rural *campesino*" identities, and also create varying degrees of attachment or separation from the home community. More permanent forms of movement, such as new settlements in the north or long-term exile caused by *la violencia,* indicate more of a rupture with the "place" of home, its cycles and boundaries. Exile in other countries has (with considerable help from international organizations) fostered new "refugee" identities based around a revised ethnic identity and the concept of return; in many more cases, however, it has led to hidden and vulnerable populations whose plans to "settle," or return, are often characterized by a deep ambivalence and sense of limbo. Finally, whether movement beyond the community has been primarily a communal, familial, or individual strategy has also varied across time and place, depending both on broader structural changes as well as individual community characteristics.

All of these differences of distance, time away, and type of movement clearly have specific impacts on the ways in which migrants and refugees reconstitute themselves away from home and on whether and how they maintain connections with the home community. These particularities thus influence processes of identity production both in terms of the "imaginary" dimensions of connections with home as well as more concrete social relations maintained (or not) between those who stay home and those who

leave. Such identity production ranges from the highly politicized and crystallized pan-Mayan identifications of camp refugees to the de-ethnicization
of some urban migrants. Such transformations are based not only on the
repositioning of migrants as Others in specific places of destination but
also on revised images of and concrete links to the home community, its
past, and its importance for the future.

It is equally important, however, to examine the continuities between
different forms of mobility and the ways in which they have interacted historically with the more localizing aspects of identity, that is, both the ways
in which groups and individuals have strategically organized themselves
materially around different types of movement and the more symbolic
forms through which mobility has been incorporated into collective meanings. Indeed, since we will soon be examining new forms of cross-border
movement, we can hypothesize that the very notion of displacement—its
historical meaning for the individual and collectivity—will be reworked
and incorporated as a key dimension of identity through which transnational displaced Mayans reterritorialize identities. Thus, it is not only those
collective and individual identity markers that organize a "sense of belonging" which will be transformed through transmigration, but those that
organize a "sense of movement" will be refashioned as well. This variable
reworking of historical displacement is suggested in some of the literature
on recent Mayan displacements. Montejo (1993), for example, shows how
camp refugees in Mexico likened their forced exile to the displacements of
the Spanish Conquest; this distant past was perceived to be echoed in the
Maya movement, which viewed forced displacement as an example of historical indigenous oppression that must be resisted and redressed through
a revised ethic identity and a return to a newly (imagined) "civil" society.
Bastos and Camus (1994: 86), on the other hand, have shown how some Indians displaced to the capital (also by the war) have compared their inser-
tion into the urban informal economy to the traditional *comerciante* activities that have always complemented the *campesino* identity—thus viewing
it as an extension of the *independencia campesina* (peasant independence)
that characterizes indigenous relationships to the external economy. Here,
movement is viewed as a positive, dynamic indigenous attribute that has
long enabled Indians to survive and maintain their autonomy.[82] In each
case, however, a revised memory of migration and movement has enabled
displaced Mayans to make sense of and cope with their uprootedness.

How does the new transnational migration, characterized by a vastly
increased spatial and temporal distance as well as the entirely new "host"
context of America, compare to and differ from previous patterns of migration? How are the various forms of both fragmentation and "reterritoriali-
zation" created, on the one hand, by *la violencia* and its ensuing postwar

reconstruction and, on the other hand, by transnational migration, reflected at the level of individual communities? How do indigenous individuals and communities give meaning to these changes, and how have they been worked into local conceptions of identity? In order to answer some of these questions, we shall now turn to the particular case of Xinxuc.

Chapter 3

The K'iche' of Xinxuc

Xinxuc is a municipality situated in the lower basin of the department of El Quiché, at approximately two thousand meters above sea level in a vast highland topography of hills and ravines, rich wooded areas, and splendid natural vegetation. At the time of this fieldwork, the town's population reached approximately seven thousand inhabitants.[1] Xinxuc's town center (*pueblo*) is surrounded by fifteen rural hamlets (*aldeas*), most of which are accessible only by rugged dirt roads. The latter assemble approximately 70 percent of the *muncipio*'s population and range from small hamlets comprised of one hundred to two hundred inhabitants to larger ones housing six hundred to eight hundred people. Seventy-two percent of Xinxuc's population is indigenous, belonging to the K'iche' ethnic group, which itself includes a diverse population whose broad range of dialects, customs, and local histories vary by region and municipality.

The richness of the landscape in this area is contrasted by the tremendous harshness of life. Poverty rates in El Quiché are very high: Approximately 70 percent of the Quiché population is considered to live in conditions of extreme poverty, a figure that largely encompasses the predominant indigenous population. Xinxuc is no exception in this regard, and the town has been ranked within the ten poorest of the department's twenty-one municipalities. Thirty percent of Xinxucians do not have access to potable water, and 56 percent do not have electricity, making firewood (*leña*) the predominant resource for heating and cooking. Sanitation is a major problem; 69 percent of homes do not have latrines, and the drainage system is extremely poor, contributing to high rates of infectious disease. Garbage disposal is virtually nonexistent, so waste is often burned, buried, or left to pile up and rot in areas immediately adjacent to or within the *pueblo*. Xinxuc's infant mortality rate is 64 per 1,000, and less than 50 percent of children under the age of one have had standard vaccinations. As in the rest of El Quiché, half (52%) of children are malnourished. A rudimentary health center, which covers only 21 percent of the population, is staffed by one doctor, who also operates a private clinic. For serious problems, Xinxucians are referred to the hospital in the department's capital, which reports high maternal mortality and morbidity rates for the region. In 1997, alcohol-related illness had been the primary cause of adult mortality for three years in a row (followed by chronic malnutrition, dehydration, and broncopulmonary disease). Xinxuc is famous throughout the region for its *cuxa* production; there are approximately twenty *fábricas de cuxa* throughout the hamlets, almost all Ladino-run and totally unregulated; *cuxa* thus forms a crucial part in understanding the local informal economy, power dynamics, and health.[2]

The town of Xinxuc is underdeveloped, attesting to the minimal amount of government investment in this isolated *municipio,* as well as to the ravages of the war. The *pueblo* has one preschool and one high school, and although primary schools exist in each hamlet, these are usually one-room classes incorporating children from seven to twelve years old, and only 55 percent of children in this age range attend school. While the figures have improved with the past generation, most Indians, particularly rural ones, have little more than a third-grade education, and many K'iche' adults have no formal education at all. Fifty percent of Xinxuc's adult population (over age fifteen) is illiterate. A small minority of Xinxucians, mostly Ladinos, make it to *ciclo básico,* which is equivalent to three years of high school and allows for specializations in technical, business, and teaching professions. In 1998, the *pueblo* had three pharmacies, approximately twenty *tiendas* (small stores), two *comedores* (cafeterias), four *cantinas,* three community telephones, and a *salon municipal* for important community activities or festivities.

A handful of local Ladinos run five public-sector institutions (dealing with health, education, communications, and agricultural services), and only three private NGOs (including PLANTAS) and a couple of Peace Corps workers operate in Xinxuc (which differentiates the town from others nearby, such as Joyabaj or the department capital, that benefit from a stronger international presence). Development projects in Xinxuc are organized around several *comites,* local organizations created during *la violencia* as part of the government's so-called development initiative, including the *Comite de Pro-Mejoramiento* (Community Improvement Committee) and others, which organize community access to water and electricity, all of which must be authorized by the department or municipality.[3] Many Indians deplore the racism and exclusion of the Ladino-run *comites,* some of which have made access to services in primarily indigenous hamlets an uphill battle.

There is, however, no shortage of churches and religions in this small town. In addition to the Catholic Church and rural *parroquias,* the municipality is dotted with Evangelical churches including Adventists, Mormons, Jehovah's Witnesses, Seventh Day Baptists, and Pentecostalists. Some of these arrived after the 1976 earthquake to help with reconstruction, though most of their converts joined during the civil war. There are also two charismatic churches in the hamlets. While officially aligned with the Catholic Church, the charismatic movement has been likened to Pentecostalism and rejects the political leanings of Catholic Action; like the evangelicals, most charismatics converted during the war.[4] There are also many *costumbristas* in Xinxuc, some of whom belong to the Catholic Church. Although these different religious groups are generally clustered in particular *aldeas,* members of the different religions are also scattered throughout the community. Moreover, many of the K'iche' people have changed religion more than once (sometimes reverting back to their old religion, sometimes converting to a new one), and families often include members of different persuasions. Since the signing of the peace, a group of "new traditionalists," sparked by the Maya movement and aided primarily by PLANTAS, has formed in Xinxuc. This group, comprised of persons of various religious backgrounds and ages, seeks to promote the Mayan religion, conducting Maya ceremonies, revitalizing traditional healing practices, and training select community members to become *aj q'ijab'* (shaman priests).[5] As in many other indigenous villages, the profusion of religions in Xinxuc is visually and aurally striking: The sounds of various evangelical preachers shouting and singing salvation songs through loudspeakers often mingle with church bells, as *costumbristas,* hidden in the mountains, perform their quiet ceremonies invoking the ancestors with incense and gifts.

LOCAL K'ICHE' ORGANIZATION

Land, Milpa, and Family

In Xinxuc, as in most other indigenous communities, quotidian life revolves around an intimate connection to the physical landscape: The spatial boundaries of house, hamlet, town, fields, mountains, and the "outside" are circumscribed by particular daily practices, routines, and habits that give each space a meaningful connection to land and to the morality and values that make one *"natural,"* or indigenous (Watanabe 1992; Earle 1986; Fischer 2001). Most of the K'iche' engage in *milpa* cultivation, primarily of maize and beans, a risky enterprise often compromised by drought, heavy rain, wind, and pests. Over the past thirty years the use of chemical fertilizers and pesticides has had an important impact on *milpa* cultivation, permitting greater yields, on the one hand, but contributing to an erosion of natural soil fertility due to a dependence on the chemicals, on the other.[6] The *milpa* agricultural cycle revolves around climate changes, comprised of rainy and dry seasons: The weather is cool and clear between November and April, the first rains begin around May, followed by heavy rain, colder weather, and fog between August and October. The K'iche' usually plant their *milpas* around April or May, just after the first rainfall; by September, the *milpa* has been weeded (*limpia*) several times and fertilized, and the harvest usually takes place between October and December. Between January and April, the soil is turned and dried maize and cornstalks are burned. Maize is the staple food of the K'iche', used primarily to make *tortillas*, *tamales*, and *atol* (a traditional corn drink). Beans, as well as vegetables such as *ayote* and *chilacayote* squashes, *guisquil*, and other vegetables usually bought in the market are also used to prepare meals. Eggs, homegrown chickens, and sometimes meat from domesticated pigs and cattle are also consumed, though not often. Among poorer *campesinos*—and in difficult times—*tortillas* and *hierbas* (greens) are sometimes the only food available.

Subsistence production and household economies among the K'iche' are ideally guided by traditional notions of complementarity and balance, whereby a gendered division of labor and knowledge is meant to produce harmonious relations within the household and with the land (Barrios 1987; Earle 1986). As such, activities related to the production of corn—preparing, tending, and planting the field—as well as labor and commercial activities outside the community, are generally considered man's work. The transformation of maize into food is a female activity and includes shelling, preparing, grinding, and cooking corn to produce *tortillas*. Women also perform other domestic activities such washing, cleaning, raising domestic livestock, and buying food at the local market. While women are also involved in some agricultural activities such as secondary crops (beans and vegetable gardens), it has traditionally been considered shameful for them to assist in most phases of *milpa* maintenance.[7]

K'iche' morality places high importance on marriage and kinship; a person is not complete until married or *unido* (united, though not officially married), and the union of male and female is also seen as an extension of the broader duality that governs the universe. Traditionally, marriage involved *pedidas*, a series of visits whereby the groom's parents sought out the bride's parents with gifts (bread, chocolate, liquor) to fix the matrimony. During the marriage ceremony, older people from both lineages offered advice to the newlyweds concerning the values of honor, hard work, and the rules, rights, and obligations of matrimony. Often, an elder intermediary or *pedidor* served to bring the family together and, subsequent to the marriage, acted as an authority who resolved marital disputes. A less costly ritual has been the *robo*, whereby the couple simply eloped. Although these customs still exist and are practiced by Catholics, *costumbristas*, and evangelicals, today's young people often simply agree to get married or cohabitate, sometimes to the great disapproval of their parents. Usually, the couple starts their married life in the groom's parents' home. The young wife must prove herself to her in-laws by working hard and respecting family customs; after a few years the couple starts their own home, ideally on a plot of land inherited through the groom's father.

K'iche' identity is thus ideally based in the family as a unit of social organization, production, and consumption, usually in the form of exogamous patrilineal clans; essential to this conception are the ideals of economic cooperation and solidarity, inheritance and patrimony, and various forms of knowledge passed down through the generations. K'iche' women are often quite secluded; they are the conservers of tradition and, unlike men, are often "protected" from contact with Ladino culture and people. They tend to be monolingual, they always wear *traje,* and they are in charge of the primary socialization of children (based on non-Ladino concepts of family, household, and community). Younger women today, in particular those with some education or urban experience (for example, some who live in town centers), are more worldly, fluent in Spanish, and sometimes wear T-shirts over their *cortes.* Women socialize girls into household chores such as sweeping, washing, cooking, collecting herbs, pasturing, and producing *tortillas,* while men teach boys the use of the *azadón* (hoe) in agricultural production. Children are frequently responsible for herding animals and for collecting and carrying large amounts of *leña* (firewood), which they usually carry on their backs. Children often attend school sporadically or for only a couple of years, particularly in the *aldeas,* because their parents cannot afford the materials required (e.g., books, uniforms) and they cannot spare the labor time that they would lose by sending children to school. Children inherit the principal means of production, including land, house, agricultural tools, and animals. As important as the inheritance of land is the inheritance of *la experiencia* (experience), which can only be reached through age and which ideally gives older people power and respect at the family and communal level; children are thus socialized to respect authority, elders, and hard work from a young age. Such socialization often occurs at a tacit, unspoken level, and it is in imitating their parents and other older relatives that children absorb the habitus and "culturally received norms" that make them distinctly Indian (Fischer 2001: 145–46; Watanabe 1992; Barrios 1987).

In the *aldeas,* a typical Indian household is constructed out of adobe, reeds, and/or sheet metal, with a dirt floor. The conception of the K'iche' family as a unit of cooperation is reflected in the architecture of hamlet homes: One room is usually divided into different areas to sleep, cook, store grains, and gather around the fire; a second more formal room is used during transcendental life moments such as deaths, weddings, and vigils; and an outside adobe *temascal* or *tuj* (steam bath) is employed for bathing and sacred rituals attended by a *comadrona* (traditional birth attendant). Large families often sleep on one or two mattresses, or *petajes* (straw mats), which provide little protection from the cold. This physical layout is designed to reinforce many of the indigenous values described above—division of labor, hard work, respect for elders, and for the obligations of matrimony—values that are kept in check through the extended family: "[A] man who fails to tend his fields properly or to contribute enough money for weekly household expenses (*gastos*) is admonished by his parents and family elders; a woman who does not complete her wifely duties within the household may be similarly cautioned or accused of laziness" (Zur 1998: 57).

Although the majority of the K'iche' are rural *campesinos,* increasing numbers of Indians have moved from the hamlets to the "urban" *pueblo* area over the past thirty years, initially drawn there due to the "push" of land pressures and the "pull" of economic opportunities and better services (water and electricity) in the 1970s, and subsequently due to the violence, which was much more severe in Xinxuc's hamlets. Unlike most hamlet Indians, urbanized K'iche's live in Ladino-type homes (often made out of cement or brick). However, they usually maintain *milpa* land in the hamlets or close to town, and this land is tended either by family members or, increasingly, by hired *mozos.* Urban K'iche's have, in the past, primarily consisted of store and transportation owners, as well as butchers, bakers, carpenters, tailors, and other urban *comerciantes,* many of whom gained their initial wealth through commerce or outside wage labor. The class division between K'iche's living in the rural *aldeas* and those living in the *pueblo* has led to a general discourse, reinforced by the army during *la violencia,* that characterizes the hamlets as somewhat backward, archaic, and suspicious places, as compared to the town center where more upwardly mobile Indians and Ladinos reside.[8]

Social Complementarity and Conformity

Zur, echoing other anthropologists who have worked in this region (Tedlock 1982; Earle 1986), states that a "relentless ideology of complementarity" (1998: 192) and balance not only informs ideal notions of family and household, but more broadly forms a prime characteristic of K'iche morality and social organization, linking people to the community and to ideal values of respect, conformity, and acceptance within the natural and supernatural realms. Many K'iche' believe that spiritual and material entities inhabiting the universe in general and the community in particular—

gods, saints, ancestors, earth, humans—possess both positive and negative qualities that must continually be kept in check. K'iche's must therefore strive to avoid social transgression, must not offend ancestral spirits, and must respect the natural order of the universe.

This concept of reciprocal balance between the physical and metaphysical realm has played a central role in Mayan cosmology since the precolonial period and has been documented by ethnographers throughout Mesoamerica (Tedlock 1982; Gossen 1986; Earle 1986; Monaghan 1995; Watanabe 1992). Traditionally, this complementarity was ideally translated to all levels of social and symbolic reality, expressed in communal political, economic, and familial forms of organization (e.g., *cofradía* and *cargo* systems); agricultural and other rituals led by *aj q'ijab'* (in which the ancestors and local landmarks are venerated);[9] and beliefs about illness, health, and healing.[10] These forms of organization and belief have been watered down over the past decades, particularly through outside impositions such as Catholic Action and evangelicalism, the advent of political parties, and Western medicine. The practice of *costumbre* was abandoned by many K'iche' people around mid-century, though others have maintained *costumbre* rituals, albeit in more hidden forms, and others yet have abandoned the practice, but not necessarily the beliefs, associated with traditional religion (Watanabe 1992).[11]

Since many of today's K'iche' and their parents or grandparents have converted to new religions and worldviews, and since traditionalists both today and in previous years did not always successfully incorporate complementarity into a balanced social or economic reality (Watanabe 1992), I, unlike some Mayanists, do not argue here that the harmonious spiritual foundations of *costumbre* are or even have been essential to local indigenous identity. However, as both Zur (1998) and Bourgey (1997) illustrate, despite the encroachment of numerous social influences that have diluted traditionalist beliefs and practices in the past decades, the social consequences of the ideology of complementarity do continue to be manifested and echoed in local social relations, and therefore this complementarity is, to some extent, an integral part of K'iche' collective identities. In particular, the fear of disrupting social harmony and balance continues to be expressed through the strong emphasis among the K'iche' on social conformity, whereby displaying "difference" or violating strict moral codes is seen to cause an imbalance in existing power relations, to provoke retribution, and therefore to connote danger. As such, complementarity is also related to another salient aspect of K'iche' identity, namely, a marked respect and obedience for the established authority.

Of course, these aspects of K'iche' identity cannot be generalized or exaggerated, and they should be viewed in terms of particular contexts, times, and changing social relations. For example, the fact that thousands of K'iche' Indians throughout this region joined Catholic Action, the CUC, and eventually the EGP before and during the war (often at great risk to local social cohesion) shows that social forces stronger than the push toward conformity and harmony were compelling in many communities. However, as discussed below, the unique history of ethnic and power relations in Xinxuc (between Indians and Ladinos, and between different groups of K'iche's) have strongly reinforced the need for both social conformity and tolerance of Ladino control. An understanding of these processes is important for examining both the war and the impact of transmigration in this particular town.

At an obvious level, conformity and the "façade" of social harmony among the K'iche' are governed by strict cultural bounds of politeness that command a very reserved posture in public. The K'iche's tend to place a high degree of importance on shared interpersonal constraint, sensibility, and respect, and to place a negative value on public, conspicuous expressions of emotion (such as stubbornness or anger) or pretentiousness. At a more covert level, social conformity affirms a moral affinity, and accountability for one's actions is enforced through a variety of mechanisms that incorporate fear of both social and supernatural punishment for those who transgress social norms. K'iche' social behavior is thus constantly under the close scrutiny of both the wider community and the spirits and witches inhabiting the boundaries of the community. Succumbing to antisocial behavior by, for example, expressing anger or impatience (which disrupts psychological and physical harmony), falling prey to adultery (which disrupts familial harmony), or, most grievously, displaying ostentatious behavior economically and socially (which disrupts communal harmony and the balance of needs) are believed to cause misfortune. They invite *chismes* (malicious gossip, which contain oblique messages of social disapproval), *envidia* (envy), *brujería* (witchcraft), and *castigo* (ancestral punishment), all of which comprise explanatory categories for misfortune, illness, and death and which therefore function as strong preventive mechanisms to reinforce conformity to social values (Zur 1998).

The negative value placed on "difference" among the K'iche' (displays of wealth, prestige, popularity, or any form of Otherness) is manifested through the omnipresent discourse on *envidia*, described as "the desire to acquire something possessed by another person" (Foster 1972: 168), or "bad feelings which one has for not being equal to another" (Zur 1988: 234). The *envidia* economy stems from the notion of "limited good" (Foster 1965, 1972), whereby the good fortune of one is seen to come from the misfortune of someone else.[12] In this sense, a person who achieves some success is perceived to have appropriated it through illicit or harmful means such as witchcraft or ancestral retribution; by the same token, a person experiencing misfortune often assumes that someone had *envidia* for him, and the person might seek restitution through supernatural punishment. Both good and bad fortune are thus often suspected of being brought on by one's own antisocial behavior or "difference"; a "good" person as described by the K'iche'—one who does not attract such evil—is "someone who is satisfied with his lot and lacks ambition" (Zur 1998: 34). Maintaining a low profile and remaining *humilde* (humble) avoids both *envidias* and witchcraft, both of which are believed to bring disastrous and life-threatening consequences.

At the same time, the notion of *suerte* (fate), a characteristic that determines one's basic personality and life course, offers an alternative explanatory model for individual behavior, for fortune or misfortune (one's own or another's). Zur argues that among the K'iche', for whom the world is highly mysterious, uncertain, and (particularly in recent times) terrifying, the notion of *suerte* provides people with "a self protective mechanism against too much introspection." As such, it "can be seen as a process whereby the imagination manufactures the idea of fate in order to protect itself against the ravages of random circumstance" (Zur 1998: 231), ranging, for example, from a failed *milpa* crop to having one's entire family massacred. Unlike *envidia*, which generates communal fear and conformity, *suerte* allows a certain individual flexibility within the social realm. While *suerte*, among *costumbristas*, is connected to one's day of birth and *nagual* (animal spirit) and has predictive value, many K'iche' also refer to *suerte* as an explanatory category for life events that are attributed to outside agency; in this second sense, *suerte* refers more to a sense of luck, which is impermanent. In either case, *suerte* does not, like *envidia*, imply evil intent or retribution by another person.

All of these "ideal" conceptions of economic cooperation, family solidarity, social conformity, and balance were influenced by profound social changes in the years preceding and during the violence, as described below. Moreover, even in the absence of rapid social change, individual and collective behaviors and practices can obviously deviate from expected norms, though this does not necessarily invalidate the imperative of social and moral codes (Fischer 2001).[13] The beliefs and practices described above thus do not represent "essential" elements of K'iche' identity but rather serve as blueprints for social behavior that have been influenced by various degrees of transformation and retention in the distant and recent past. As such, they represent creative and flexible responses to changing colonial and postcolonial conditions.

The "Revolving Door": Movement beyond the Community

Most anthropological accounts have viewed Indian migration as a phenomenon external to the workings of community identity, imposed by a history of forced resettlement, labor exploitation, land encroachment, and state-sponsored terror. Because of this history of oppression, outward movement has largely been viewed (by academics and development workers alike) in terms of its negative and divisive impacts. However, as we have seen previously, various types of movement have also been incorporated in numerous advantageous ways into local patterns of community organization and identity.

Most K'iche' communities in the southern basin of El Quiché employ a range of migratory strategies, accumulated through time, to enhance familial and communal prosperity. Xinxuc has relatively fertile land compared to some neighboring towns, so coastal migrations have not been quite as strong as in some nearby *municipios* (including Joyabaj). The extent of seasonal migration to the coast nonetheless does vary from hamlet to hamlet in Xinxuc, depending on factors such as the productivity of land, hamlet-specific histories, and opportunities to engage in commercial activities. Xinxuc's poorest *campesinos* tend to work as *jornaleros,* or regular seasonal workers; these are usually hamlet Indians with minimal property (*microfundistas*) or landless peasants with little technological specialization or capital with which to exploit their own land or conduct other commercial activities (Flores Alvarado 1995). Over the past few decades, new agricultural tools and better transportation and roads have improved plantation labor conditions for *jornaleros,* if only because they can return home more often during seasonal work.[14] Since workers are now paid by the amount that they gather rather than by daily wages, plantation owners increasingly seek highly productive laborers, usually young men and heads of families, for the physically exhausting work. Seasonal migration has thus become more of an individual or family strategy rather than a collective enterprise as it was in previous years.

A number of comparisons, nonetheless, can still be drawn with the earlier labor drafts described in the previous chapter. Coffee, sugar, cotton, and cardamom plantations continue to employ *contratistas* (contractors) who recruit groups of *cuadrilleros* (*jornaleros*) during particular periods, often indebting laborers through money advances and packing them onto coast-bound *camionetas* (buses) for a determined number of *jornales.*[15] Remuneration remains extremely low; for instance, in 1994, a *jornalero's* wages amounted to approximately Q360 per month (US$60) (Flores Alvarado 1995: 33).[16] As with earlier migrations, poor conditions on plantations contribute to outbreaks of malaria, cholera, tuberculosis, and intestinal and pulmonary diseases; seasonal migrations also engender a high level of school absenteeism and illiteracy among migrant children. Clearly, Indian *jornaleros* continue to be among the most marginalized and oppressed members of Guatemalan society (Flores Alvarado 1995).

Those K'iche' people with a bit more land and economic choice, however, consider coastal migration as one of a number of different options and therefore migrate not for lack of land or corn but in order to buy fertilizer and thereby increase their *milpa* output. For them, coastal wage labor is not only a source of cash income but an extension of a broader range of economic interests and endeavors, which may include *comerciante* or even urban economic activities (Watanabe 1992; Flores Alvarado 1995). As such, seasonal migration connotes an element of choice and agency that enables both survival and independence.

Some of Xinxuc's hamlets are known as *aldeas de comerciantes* (trader's hamlets), containing *comerciantes* who specialize in raising and selling *coches* (pigs), produce, and small livestock or in making crafts. *Comerciantes* usually return home every fifteen days or so, after making their way through the bustling regional markets of the department and in the capital. A fair number of youth, also, work as *ayudantes* (assistants) on buses or for lumber and *cuxa* merchants (usually Ladinos), jobs that often take them outside of the community on a daily, weekly, or longer-term basis. Finally, urban migration (both temporary and long-term), which leads to the distinctly different work and living environment of, in most cases, the capital city, has been an important part of Xinxuc's "revolving door" over the past thirty years. Despite their integration into urban settings, many urban Indians continue to identify with their rural community and with their *campesino* identity. The type and extent of contact with home may vary from frequent visits to maintain the *milpa* and family, to sporadic returns (i.e., for the annual *fiesta),* to a permanent return. These migrants often assume a sort of "double identity" that allows them to hide or reveal their Indianness depending on the context (*municipio*/city, private/public), to move between the different spaces, and to view urban and rural identities as complementary rather than contradictory (Bastos and Camus 1995).

As large-scale migration studies have shown, migratory patterns often follow a sort of "step migration" whereby one type of migration becomes replaced (by individuals or by the community) with another that is more lucrative and less oppressive. To some extent this has occurred in Xinxuc, where urban migrations supplant seasonal ones and where transnational migrations replace various internal movements, contributing to greater social cleavages. Particularly in the past thirty years, this has spawned a local status hierarchy within the Indian population, with increased differentiation between landless *mozos, jornaleros, comerciantes,* urban migrants, and wealthier *pueblo* merchants. It is not only the local rural/urban divide, but also chosen migratory strategies, that have contributed to such social cleavages, whereby *los del monte* (hamlet Indians), landless peasants, and *jornaleros* are situated at the bottom, and *pueblo* Indians (including some successful *comerciantes* and urban migrants) are at the top.

What is particularly striking in communities such as Xinxuc, however, is the variety of, and overlap between, different types of outward mobility. Here, an absent community or family member may be in one of several places: on the coast picking coffee (returning home within a month, with wages); in the capital working as a domestic, merchant, or worker (sending money home to the family, returning periodically or permanently, such as after a stint or a marriage proposal from home); in another *municipio* selling firewood, animals, or agricultural products (returning once or twice a month for business and domestic activities); and, increasingly, *allá lejos* (in the United States), sending US dollars home on a regular basis. In addition, an absent person may have left during the war and now has a whole new life elsewhere, even as he is awaited by family members back home. These different migratory strategies exist at the community level but are present as well within families, such that different family members may chose between (or be assigned to) these options at different times. What's more, individuals as well may shift between the varying strategies of movement depending on a variety of factors ranging from job availability to personal choice.

This pursuit of multiple migration strategies and economic alternatives is, indeed, critical to marginalized people and families for whom any one option is highly susceptible to failure. In a context where one's *milpa* may be wiped out by a draught, where one's small animal business may fail, or where one's informal urban-sector job may suddenly end, maintaining a variety of options and possible strategies becomes a crucial means of preserving some stability and may even lead to the accumulation of some wealth. Such stability has tended to revolve around material and social attachments to the home community and family, which serve to anchor identities despite habitual movement (Hanks 1990). At the same time, all types of movement beyond the community produce variable levels of separation from family and community, and migrants run the risk of a more permanent detachment. Given this multiplicity of types of migration and return, it is useful to think of migratory patterns in terms of a continuum of identities and attachments that might include persons who have not left the community, migrants for whom the home village remains the primary home, those who reside outside but travel home at intervals, those for whom the "home" village is primarily a place of nostalgic attachment, those who leave for good and cease contact, and those who return permanently (Ferguson 1992; Poerregaard 1997).

For the K'iche', then, the specter of movement beyond the community forms part of the multiplicity of strategies that have enabled communities to survive and maintain autonomous identities. The "revolving door" through which Indians have historically come and gone from the community might be seen then as a fundamental dimension of K'iche' identity, one that has contributed to an appreciation of various orientations and practices that connect "community" with the outside. François Lartigue lyrically captures this notion as follows:

> The people of El Quiché share this inclination toward hazardous travel and activity with all indigenous peoples of this region for whom the feeling of being rooted in an ancestral territory does not seem to have ever excluded either the desire to fly from summit to summit, or the habit of engaging in commerce and maintaining multiple allegiances. This ability to benefit from the ecological mosaic, whose outlines change with the rhythm of volcanic activity and the intemperate tropical climate, this familiar understanding of geographical diversity are the heavy fragments of an enduring human experience, one that is expressed within a particularly rich cultural constellation. . . . It is therefore inappropriate to insist upon the notion of an indigenous identity that restricts its experience to the local community, bounded by the constraints of impermeable borders. (Lartigue 1991: 280–81; my translation)[17]

In order to situate all of the aforementioned cultural beliefs and practices within the context of reorganization produced by transnational migration, it is useful to first provide a brief history of the social relations in this particular town, including the events that sparked the movement to Providence.

XINXUC'S UNIQUE HISTORY

Xinxuc's history within the region differentiates it somewhat from its surrounding towns; its evolving social structure and ethnic relations explain much about the town's more recent dynamics, in particular those set in place before and during the civil war. During the colonial period, Xinxuc's fertile soil and warm climate made it an attractive setting for agriculture and animal husbandry (cattle and sheep raising) by the Spaniards, and subsequently by Ladinos. Xinxuc was converted by the Spaniards into a large cattle *hacienda,* and its sparse indigenous population was expected to provide food for the *hacienda* owners with little in return. Unlike church-owned lands surrounding Xinxuc, which were returned to Indian ownership by the end of the colonial period, Xinxuc remained firmly in the hands of Ladinos. It was not until 1872 that Xinxuc was declared a formal *municipio.*

Unlike many other *municipios,* Xinxuc's indigenous population is comprised largely of settlers and migrants from other municipalities who arrived during various historical periods, starting with the turbulent indigenous territorial disputes of the 1800s. Already in the late 1700s, Indian migrants had begun arriving from the area of Totonicapán, in particular from Santa Maria Chiquimúla, where Indians were experiencing massive land shortages. Indians from Chichicastenango (Max K'iche') also began to take the eastern route, and a few Max families settled in some of Xinxuc's hamlets. Carmack (1981) has shown that conflicts between Nimab K'iche' (which include those originally from Xinxuc and Santa Cruz) and Max K'iche' around this time were rooted in older territorial conflicts, and tensions between these two groups—whose female members still wear *trajes* from their original townships—have continued to the present day despite their long cohabitation in Xinxuc.[18] Indian migrants who arrived in Xinxuc in the nineteenth and twentieth centuries affiliated themselves with Ladino landowners, who rented them small *milpas* in exchange for temporary seasonal labor on the coastal *haciendas* or sometimes for local labor on highland *fincas.* This settlement pattern led to a relationship of protectionism between Ladino *patrones* and Indians, the latter preferring the stability and safety of this economic arrangement over the sometimes aggressive land disputes taking place between Indians, and between Indians and Ladinos, in other municipalities (Earle 1982).

At the beginning of the twentieth century the cheap labor provided by Indians resulted in an economic boom evident in the town center, leading to the construction of houses, *cantinas,* stores, and a school. Seasonal migrations also brought capital into the rural areas and led to a general expansion in agricultural and market activity over the next decades. Indian settlement in Xinxuc, meanwhile, continued apace well into the Barrios regime: In 1944, for example, the government granted a prominent Ladino family a large *finca* in a hamlet close to town (in return for political allegiance) under the condition that landless Indian peasants from other areas could reside on the property. Eventually, increasing numbers of rural Ladinos began to move to the town center, either selling their lands or employing others to administer them, and reinforcing Xinxuc's reputation as a "Ladino-run *pueblo.*" The town's prosperity, however, soon resulted in a rather antagonistic split between hamlet and *pueblo* Ladinos, leading many of the latter and their children to migrate permanently—in search of better educational or career opportunities—to larger regional towns or to the capital (Earle 1982: 185).

The decades between the 1950s and 1970s were, throughout the southern Quiché area, characterized by numerous events that had a profound impact upon the organization of *municipios* and intergroup relations, but, as pointed out in the previous chapter, also varied from place to place. One of the most important regional changes was the initiation of development projects (usually by foreign missionaries) centered around a cooperative system that provided new avenues for credit and savings for the indigenous population, new products including fertilizer and pesticides, and increased organization to set fair prices. Through popular initiatives organized around health, education, community, and economic development, as well as Bible study groups promoting *concientización* (the awakening of a greater social consciousness), Catholic Action came to fill an important social space throughout the indigenous Quiché region. The conversion to Catholic-based communities was especially appealing to young men who could now circumvent the elders' control over sacred knowledge as well as avoid the financially crippling and time-consuming *cofradías* (Wilson 1995). In addition, it "offered access to things often enjoyed by Ladinos . . . such as literacy, goods, and control of transportation, as well as introduction through the priests to more profitable ways of managing agriculture, craft production and marketing" (Earle 2001: 294–95).

By the 1970s, these changing dynamics in the countryside began to contribute to a tense atmosphere in a number of *municipios* as political parties became aligned with religious factions, both of which were increasingly polarized. Throughout the region, the DCG (Democracia Cristiana Guatemalteca), which since the 1950s had forged a strong relationship with Catholic Action, gained power, increasingly allying itself with the Indian population (and with CA catechists in particular), organizing indigenous municipal candidates in different townships including Xinxuc. At the same time, conservative *costumbristas* were also being increasingly drawn into municipal politics, usually courted by the fiercely anticommunist MLN (Movimiento de Liberación Nacional), which sought to attract the indigenous commercial middle class. These political divisions, like religious ones, were crosscut by the generational factor since older Indians, who often felt they were losing their traditional control to the outspoken youthful CA catechists, frequently opted to join the MLN while the younger generation increasingly rooted for the DCG (Remijnse 2002).

While situated in the midst of this wave of change, Xinxuc was relatively slow to catch on in a substantial way to the more radical forms of organizational change happening in surrounding towns, perhaps because of the less cohesive nature of the *municipio*'s Indians, and Xinxuc's tendency toward entrenched patron-client relationships with powerful local Ladinos. In contrast to some neighboring indigenous communities that were quick to join the "progressive" movement of Catholic Action and its energetic impetus toward socioeconomic development, many Xinxucians describe the town in the three decades preceding the 1970s as being quite undeveloped and isolated (the asphalt road connecting Xinxuc to other municipalities was only built in the late 1970s, and the town did not have a health center until 1974). By the mid-1970s, however, some important changes did begin to take place, contributing to a shifting balance of power within the community and to increased divisions. First, Ladino outward movement resumed in these years, this time sparked by the competition created by booming markets in nearby indigenous towns, which diminished the economic edge of both urban and rural Ladinos, as well as their ability to compete with larger coastal plantation wages and therefore attract Indian laborers to work their land (Earle 1982). At the same time, a few commercially oriented Indians in Xinxuc started moving into the *pueblo,* and like the Ladinos before them began buying houses and opening stores and businesses, often to the consternation of remaining urban Ladinos, who nevertheless seemed to accept the change.

Economic differentiation among Indians also grew quite rapidly during this period, as opportunities for wage labor outside the community became more diverse.[19] The impact of increased wage dependence on individual households, family structures, and relations to the land was significant. The growing commodification of the indigenous economy tended to disrupt the traditional balance of power between men and women and to erode the social networks that had comprised the collective economic enterprise of family and community (Smith 1977; Bossen 1984). Frequent and extended absences and separations (usually of male kin) for wage labor in other places, in addition to poverty, debts, and illness, often worked against the ideal of harmony and balance within K'iche' families. Zur argues that male urban migration often allowed married K'iche' men to evade local obligations, leaving them free to assume a second identity in the city while their wives remained under the supervision and control of in-laws. Economic dependence often forced women to put up with infidelity, domestic abuse, and poverty, clearly upsetting the balance of mutual needs and marriage practices in K'iche' families and removing men from quotidian obligations related to *milpa* production (Zur 1998: 56).

Despite Xinxuc's somewhat conservative nature, by the mid- to late 1970s a number of local young *indígenas* had joined Catholic Action and embraced its progressive worldview, some also becoming increasingly politicized through their party affiliation with the DCG. Like other left-leaning Indians throughout the Quiché region (as well a few Ladino *campesinos*), some also began to have various levels of involvement with the Comité de Unidad Campesina (CUC—Committee for Peasant Unity), an agrarian organization based in Santa Cruz del Quiché and founded by Indian catechists seeking to organize migratory labor from the highlands to the plantations.[20] By the end of the 1970s, a fairly hostile division within this *municipio* had developed between the "outward-looking" indigenous Catholic Action members (who espoused social, economic, and cultural progress, organized community development projects, and were connected to a nationwide movement for social change) and the conservative *costumbristas,* who viewed the change-oriented message of the *catequistas* as a form of intolerance and arrogance. The conflation of religious, political, and generational tensions, combined with growing class differentiation among both Indians and Ladinos, thus contributed to a fragmented though still relatively calm social climate by the last years of the decade.

Viewing these local processes in terms of culture change rather than in anticipation of the genocidal state violence that was to come, several anthropologists working in the southern Quiché area in the 1970s were concerned with the "deculturation" of Indians by the forces of modernization and capitalist integration; as Carmack stated, "[M]any natives have acculturated to [the Ladino] way of life, taking on Latin language, dress, and economic modes" (1981: 347). In the 1970s, Earle forecast a fairly calm future for the town, predicting that, "[b]arring unforeseeable events, the urbanized Ladino population will continue to leave the town center, and commercially oriented Indians will slowly replace them. . . . Those [Ladinos] who remain will have to compete more equally with the *indigena* population that is becoming more westernized." (1982: 187).

Instead, however, by 1980 *la violencia,* whose cataclysmic proportions were indeed unforeseeable, hit Xinxuc, as it did most of this area, with a devastating force. Unleashing its brutal counterinsurgency strategy for the area, the army bombed and burned villages throughout El Quiché; schools, cooperatives, clinics, and churches were destroyed; and Indians were killed en masse. The department's Catholic diocese in Santa Cruz was closed down and all priests ordered to leave. Between 1981 and 1982, thousands of Indians joined the armed struggle, and the EGP soon appeared to have gained control of the area, blowing up government buildings and roads and attacking the military base in Santa Cruz; the army retaliated with force, heavily militarizing the entire region.[21]

In Xinxuc, however, unlike in a number of surrounding towns that maintained a strong EGP base, the time of the *itzel winak,* or the "bad men" (as this period is referred to among many K'iche'),[22] is often remembered as having little to do with guerrillas (whom most told me they had not seen), though this did not diminish the amount of death and destruction in the village. As several Xinxucians have recounted, the EGP formally entered the community once, placed some revolutionary graffiti in the town center, and never reappeared; what significant guerrilla support did exist in the *municipio* is said to have been concentrated in two outlying hamlets that were later razed in their entirety by the army. While it appears from my interviews with CA families that some *catequistas* collaborated with the CUC and EGP during this period while others did not, most CA leaders were promptly "disappeared" (killed), regardless, at the beginning of the violence. The gray zones of allegiance and ideology that shaped people's choices during this terrifying time are illustrated in the cases of Virgilio and Dionisio, two of my key interlocutors in Providence, who had been active CA *catequistas*. They both told me that although they had been solicited to join the armed movement, neither had agreed with the EGP's message and tactics and declined to participate (under pressure as well, clearly, from the military's threats)—a life choice that would force them into the army camp and eventually have horrific, though very different, consequences for each man, as we shall see further on.[23] Although it is difficult to know the exact extent of guerrilla support in Xinxuc, the early wiping out of the progressive segment of the population certainly crystallized local power relations, as the *municipio* was quickly placed under the control of a particularly ruthless and infamous Ladino civil patrol *jefe* (leader) and *comisionado militar* (military commissioner) selected and supported by the army for this community. Xinxuc's PACs rapidly came to be known as some of the most brutal in the country—and the only ones in the region to fully resist the guerrillas.

Indeed, by 1982 the opportunity to kill and ravage with impunity had unleashed furious responses on the part of some local Ladinos, who clearly did not wish to "compete more equally" with the Indians and who came to lead the municipal civil patrols. The patrol leaders, not only angered by the Indians' social and economic usurpation of their place within the preceding decades but also motivated by the increasingly lucrative lumber business—a resource amply provided in the fertile mountain terrain and which they could sell in the capital—led them to a full reign of terror within the community.[24] In Xinxuc, the lust for lumber and power, combined with a profound racism toward Indians now justified through the army's discourse (Indian=Subversive=Enemy), led both PAC leaders and military commissioners to become prime implementers of the army's psychological warfare against Indians, gaining riches and status at the same time. As a deliberate strategy, the army and *jefes*—capitalizing on the pronounced guardedness against outsiders among many K'iche', an orientation that incorporates both a belief in malevolent spirits and the association of "stranger" with "danger" (Zur 1998)—portrayed the elusive guerrillas as cruel and evil spirits able to change their appearance and lead double lives, perhaps as one's neighbor or kin (Carmack 1988; Zur 1998; Warren 1998; Earle 2001). By comparison, they pronounced themselves protectors and saviors who would rid the town of "subversives"—that is, anyone who did not show them full allegiance and compliance.[25]

In this way, the PACs were able to kill, rape, and loot in the country-side; intimidate the population into letting them take lumber, corn, or any other goods; transform Xinxuc's Justice of Peace building into a torture and killing chamber; force Indians to denounce each other; and remove them from their land.[26] The religious hostilities preexisting the war in Xinxuc were exploited by the army and its local collaborators, who now pitted *costumbristas* against *catequistas,* urging the former to denounce the latter and promising security to those who converted to the evangelical churches. One rural Ladino recounted to me, moreover, how the civil patrols would stage a guerrilla presence in the hamlets by planting flyers and sounding shots so that they could then come in with an excuse to terrorize and kill. Each of the hamlets, moreover, came to have its own PACs, whose *jefes* were handpicked and under the control of the brutal urban PACs. Not only were nearly all the town's catechists killed, but so were a number of *aj q'ijab'* and elders, since their powers in the community were feared. Two hamlets were completely razed, and two others suffered massacres; approximately eighty-eight houses were burned down; many people were disappeared, and clandestine cemeteries currently exist in six hamlets. Some of the more notorious Ladino *jefes, conocidos* (acquaintances) and neighbors to their Indian victims, would often kill select persons from a hamlet or even family, yet warn the others to leave, thus brainwashing survivors into a distorted sense of allegiance to their "saviors."

While some of the K'iche' left Xinxuc during this period, hiding on the coast or in the capital, others temporarily fled into the mountains or to nearby hamlets and neighboring *municipios.*[27] Leaving the terror was viewed by the PACs as an admission of guilt (or at least, the latter used this logic to further their tyranny), and because remaining family members were often threatened for their supposed connection to "subversives," those who escaped sometimes felt compelled to return. Virgilio, for example, who had been the town's leading *catequista* and had been appointed as the president of the parish, was accused by some locals of harboring *guer-rilleros* in the church, to which he held the keys (an accusation he has vehemently denied). He decided in early 1982 to leave to the coast, despite having only recently married his wife, Ramona. Virgilio soon received a letter from his brother Nicolas advising him that the situation at home had taken a turn for the worse: The PACs had come to their home looking for Virgilio and, not finding him, had killed his father and youngest brother. Virgilio decided to return to Xinxuc, where he had to join the civil patrollers, like so many others, in order to stay alive and prevent more deaths in the family. During this time, his brother Gonzalo (who like Virgilio eventually left to Providence) had been forcibly recruited by the army and was sent to fight the war in other communities.

A very large number of Xinxuc Indians sought *posada* (shelter) in the *pueblo,* some staying in the homes of relatives and *compadres,*[28] others living in the homes of absent urban Ladinos. Indeed, some wealthier Ladinos, fearful of the guerrillas and well-connected in other areas of the country, chose to flee to other parts of Guatemala. A large proportion of Indians converted to evangelical churches, which was seen to be a clear antiguerrilla statement. Either converting to Protestantism or moving to the *pueblo* thus offered some degree of protection against the intimidation and death in the rural areas, and it demonstrated a show of loyalty to Ladino *jefes.* While some of the K'iche' eventually returned to their hamlets (often finding them either destroyed or inhabited by others), a number of Indians remained in the *pueblo* following the violence, thus greatly accelerating both the urbanization process and the divisions between rural and urban populations. Some Indian families and widows from neighboring *municipios,* many of them Max, also came to Xinxuc seeking refuge during the violence.[29]

The terror and confusion created by these events, and the twisted psychology through which the *jefes* reinforced their power, are captured in the following narrative told to me by a K'iche' widow living in a hamlet:

> When the killings in my hamlet started, I told my husband that we must leave because many people were going. But he said no, because this is where we are from. The patrollers were tearing down trees, to prevent the cars from passing. First they killed my uncle and his son, and we became frightened. I heard noises close to the road, and my husband told me to go see what was happening. When I tried to go see, I saw that our house was already surrounded by the patrollers. I told this to my husband and he went outside with a machete. They took him away. Before this we had heard some shots—they say that they killed my brother-in-law when he was sleeping, but they let his wife go. He was wounded and they left him there, they tore out his tongue and left him in a tree. There were so many patrollers and soldiers.... When they took my husband, I quickly went to the neighbors to tell them. Our neighbor said do not worry, he said that the soldiers would return with my husband.

But they didn't, and only my daughter appeared, crying, saying that they had killed my husband. She had been looking for her father, her husband and her brother-in-law, she was very brave. And some people told her that they had seen them all, dead. Another woman arrived saying that they had killed her husband and son. Her husband was my godfather. When I found out that my husband was dead I asked for shelter in a neighbor's house, and they agreed, but when I arrived that night they were gone, they had escaped to the *pueblo.*

My daughter went to the *pueblo* to ask the *jefe* if he had seen the bodies, without knowing that it was he who had done the killings. My son-in-law was not dead yet, but had only his underwear on—they had tried to kill him. He was asking for water but nobody wanted to help him, because otherwise they might be mistaken for one of them [the guerrillas]. His aunt went to give him some water, but when she heard someone coming she hid. A man came with a gun and shot my son-in-law.

After three days we went to look for the bodies of all our relatives. First we went to get the permission of the *jefe.* My husband had left some money, so we were able to by a box, we dug a tomb, and there we buried the five of them: son-in-law, husband, son, and some other *conocidos.* We had to do this alone because nobody would help us, it was too dangerous, because they might be asked why they are out on the road. It was only women and children, we did it alone. We ran into two men on the road and they started to laugh at us because we had all died. They made fun of us. My daughter and daughter-in-law came to the *pueblo* because they no longer had husbands. Everybody left the hamlet, not one remained.

I went to a hamlet in the next *municipio,* and after six months the soldiers came and told us that we could return, but we were very scared thinking that they would kill us. When we came back we were surprised because there were cows, horses, children playing, and people living in my house. I said, "Who gave you permission to be here?" And they said, "Why did you leave your home?" as though we had been the killers and for that reason had escaped. . . . And then some men came and told us that before we could return to our home we had to ask for permission from the *jefe* and his son. I said, "But it is my house," but they insisted that they were the ones in charge now. And when I went to see him the *jefe* said: "Aah, I am happy you came, this is your home, but why did you leave tell me, did you do something wrong?" I said, "No, it is because they killed my husband that I had to leave."

He said that I could stay in his house, but on the condition that I go find my oldest son who had stayed in the other *municipio*. I sent for my son, and I told the *jefe* when he would arrive. He said we would go to meet him. But when we went, they put my son in another car, they took him to Quiché to make declarations.[30] He was there for a week, they asked him the whole time why he had killed people. He said, "I did not kill anyone." They asked him who are his bosses, his people, and he said, "I have no bosses." During that time I came every day to the *pueblo* to ask the *jefe* why he had not returned my son. I brought him chickens every day for the information and he said, "Many thanks," but he did not tell me anything.

The subservience of the Xinxuc K'iche' to the army, *jefes*, and Ladinos during *la violencia* might be explained in several ways. Clearly, the sheer panic unleashed during this period led many of the K'iche' into a sort of mental paralysis. Not only the arbitrary use of direct violence, but also other terror tactics—disinformation, rumors, and even the distortion and manipulation of language—resulted in compliance. Playing on the poor Spanish-language skills of many K'iche', the PACs virtually banned certain words and, eventually, thoughts. As Zur notes, in a context where simply acknowledging that one's family member was missing could signify danger and death, highly ambiguous terms and phrases—a sort of "discourse of denial"—came to be used by the K'iche' to refer to evil deeds that occurred during the violence (1998: 75).

In the midst of chaos and madness, many Indians felt they had nowhere to turn and no one to believe in but their own oppressors and killers. In addition, the entrenched cultural value of obedience and subordination to authority, combined with Xinxuc's particular historical relations between Indians and Ladinos, reinforced their submission: As one Xinxucian K'iche' states, "We think the Ladino is the one who knows, who studies, and we must not harm him. So they did what the army told them to do." Moreover, the lack of a longer history of communal solidarity based in a common provenance meant that the K'iche' in Xinxuc, unlike those in many other communities, appealed less to a common identity in order to resist Ladino violence, allowing instead their internal divisions to contribute to the chaos. Finally (and this is a point rarely mentioned), though local Ladinos, like K'iche's, sided with the PACs (partly in order to survive, partly due to racism, and partly because they believed the antisubversive rhetoric), a number also helped K'iche's during this time: Either out of kindness or out of a fear of losing their *mozos,* some Ladinos warned K'iche's in advance or sheltered them in their homes. Indeed, in Xinxuc the PACs held the entire village in terror—both Indians and Ladinos—threatening its overall disappearance if the community as a whole did not obey them.

The army's violence shattered both individual and collective identities among the K'iche', specifically targeting those core elements of identity identified previously. The war engendered a profound disintegration of the family, which despite years of social change had long been the main unit of solidarity. Children, spouses, and siblings were encouraged to inform on each other, leading to an extreme mistrust and fear even within families. Because many elders were killed during the violence (since the army wished to replace all existing authority), connections with the past and with the ancestors were also destroyed. Gender relations, moreover, changed dramatically during the war, particularly in areas such as El Quiché where *la violencia* produced thousands of widows. Many widows had to assume the role of sole caretakers while coping alone with both the psychological and social consequences of their husband's deaths, which both decreased their economic support and made them vulnerable to negative gossip and social isolation (Green 1999). The very fact of being "unattached," moreover, made these women obvious symbols of victimhood, who thus needed to be controlled and silenced by the PACs (González 2000). In addition, indigenous men became "increasingly influenced by the patriarchal norms of the ladino military" and espoused a *macho* sexual identity during the war, no longer viewing women as complementary partners but rather as subordinate and "legitimate targets of abuse" (Zur 1998: 156). Finally, the displacement of many K'iche' families and individuals both within and outside the community, in addition to the time spent patrolling, negatively impacted economic strategies related to both *milpa* production and cash earnings. All of these factors contributed to a breakdown of familial structures and the destruction of bonds of respect, which, in turn, reinforced submission to the army and *jefes*.

Attesting to the army's astute manipulation of indigenous culture, Indian allegiance to the army and PACs in Xinxuc was largely facilitated by simultaneous chronic factionalism among the K'iche', on the one hand, and their extreme emphasis on social conformity, on the other (Zur 1998). In the first place, the mechanisms traditionally used to encourage conformity in the face of division and social change—*envidia*, gossip, and witchcraft—became profoundly distorted during the violence, as these were now converted into deadly forms of vengeance: *Chismes* and *envidias* became transformed into false accusations to the army or civil patrollers in the form of *denuncias* (denunciations) and *calumnias* (betrayals), which often came to replace the slower vengeance of witchcraft. Through these means, victims of brutality sometimes became perpetrators or through passive complicity with the patrols collaborated in deadly local power struggles.

As we have seen, the notion of social conformity was already being tested by socioeconomic and religious differentiation in Indian communities before the violence. The antagonism felt to be provoked by *catequistas* prior to the war, for example, stemmed precisely from the perception that they wished to stand out, and disrupt the balance of power, and they were therefore considered belligerent and arrogant—often accused of wanting to act like Ladinos—by more conservative community members who eventually turned against them. During the war, however, the army's discourse brought new meaning to traditional notions of Otherness and conformity, and many K'iche' people came to greatly fear (and sometimes denounce) community members who might be perceived as "different" in any way. Both extreme fear, as well as ingrained cultural values emphasizing suspicion of Otherness and respect for authority, led many to demonstrate a concerted allegiance to the patrols and army. Now, displaying difference of any sort (leaving for too long, being a widow, making too much money, being a health or development worker, or simply being seen with any such people) was enough to make others suspect that one was collaborating with the "blue-eyed devils," whom most had never seen (Zur 1998; Earle 2001; Bastos and Camus 1995). Under these conditions, maintaining a façade of total conformity and normalcy despite madness became a critical survival tactic.

K'iche's internalized this distorted reality to different degrees, some seeking to avoid it as much as possible through strategies of silence and concealment, some becoming either passive or active participants in the terror, and some engaging in "dramatic demonstrations that they had never been on the enemy's' side" (Zur 1998: 105). A few, moreover, became fierce and vicious civil patrol *jefes* themselves, denouncing, killing, humiliating, and demanding labor, services, and deference from villagers—in essence, treating fellow Indians as *peor que animales* (worse than animals).[31] Steeped in an internalized racism reinforced by the army and "freed from traditional restraints," these men could now assert themselves by identifying with the omnipotent Ladino *jefes* (Zur 1998). Some of them, like Cipriano, were known to be *brujos,* who now doubled their power through their sanctioned criminality. Others, "aware that the job [was] fundamentally despicable, [clung] to the advantages of the appointment because it confer[ed] the most authority within the new social structure" (Zur 1998: 107). While the majority of Indians, however, were clearly victims of both Ladino and Indian deprivation and co-optation, their complicity in the violence—whether passive or active, forced or willful—has led to a tremendous amount of guilt and confusion following the war, as shall be explored in Chapter 6.

Thus, many of the elements of identity characterizing K'iche' culture, already in the process of change before the war, came to be totally fractured and distorted during the violence: Attachment to land, bonds of respect and authority, familial solidarity, norms of social conformity, and even traditional supernatural beliefs (the very elements that facilitated community cohesiveness and survival despite rapid change) were manipulated and shattered. While racism and inequality were then, as now, a well-entrenched aspect of life in the highlands, the destructive opportunities created by the war led both Ladinos and Indians to act out, in often virulent ways, decades of hostility within a vacuum of traditional morality, power, and structure.

The violence left people psychologically scarred, not only by the deaths and destruction of the war but also, perhaps even more nefariously, by the new structure of fear and authority that came to be internalized by many K'iche's. Indeed, Xinxuc's civil patrollers continued to maintain control of the community well after the worst part of *la violencia* (that is, into the 1990s), and they exerted their power in numerous ways, including physical intimidation and economic coercion. Attesting to the PACs' local hegemony, for example, K'iche's who were eventually allowed to resume various types of outward movement (whether seasonally migrating to the coast or leaving to the United States) were forced by patrol *jefes* to either find a substitute during their absence or, more often, pay off the *patrulleros* with a "fine" for each day missed. Xinxuc's PACs were not officially disbanded until 1994, when the notorious *jefe*, rumored to have been kidnapped and all but left for dead by the *guerrilleros*, finally fled to Providence (as other patrollers had done before him).

By the time I found myself in Xinxuc at the end of 1996, most evidence of this dreadful past seemed, to my outsider's eye, to be nonexistent: The town felt like a tranquil, if not sleepy, village, with a characteristically suspicious and guarded indigenous population. Slowly, as I took into account Xinxucians' conspicuous show of oblivion toward some rather important postwar events taking place in the immediate vicinity, I began to piece together the extent of continued fear and isolation that permeated life in this town:

Field Notes, El Quiché, December 29, 1996
Today the peace was signed, and it has certainly brought a lot of fanfare: an odd layer of excitement and grand declarations eerily juxtaposed to the deep cynicism, fear, and silences expressed by

most locals. Throughout the country, massive banners for Pepsi-Cola—official sponsors of the peace!—decorate town centers and government buildings. At the entrance to each municipio, a banner proclaims: "Let us stretch out our hands and join our hearts because the peace has arrived to our country: Peace is Opportunity."

In Quiché, a large crowd gathered for a morning mass in front of the cathedral. Popular human rights, ethnic, and widows' organizations such as CUC, CERJ, and CONAVIGUA held activities in the plaza throughout the day.[32] Under banners which spoke of "la lucha del pueblo" (the fight of the people) and "el derecho de los marginados y oprimidos" (the rights of the marginalized and oppressed), they read through painful, lengthy lists of persons killed and disappeared, villages razed and churches burned throughout El Quiché. In the evening, people waited in the central plaza, abundantly decorated with blue and white balloons, for a large-screen broadcast from the Palacio Nacional. After televised speeches by President Arzú and UN Secretary General Boutros-Ghali, some local politicians, the director of MINUGUA–El Quiché, and several army generals in full uniform stood at the podium to make lengthy pronouncements. One particularly vehement general, after reinforcing a clear message to forget about the past violence, finished by quoting Jesus: "I give you peace, my peace I leave you!" he barked, as the balloons were liberated into the sky and a loud string of *cuetes* (firecrackers), sounding like an explosion of gunfire, was let off.

In Xinxuc, by contrast, I attended Christmas mass a few days ago during which the Spanish priest solemnly explained *la paz* as a time to forgive past wrongs and abandon the urge for revenge. Around me, impassive K'iche' faces stared ahead, displaying neither appreciation nor emotion, as rabid-looking *chuchos* (dogs) staggered through the pews and the usual faltering electricity plunged the congregation into temporary darkness. On my way home, I struck up a conversation with a *campesino* who asked me whether they would also be signing the peace in Canada; he seemed stunned to find out that neither Canada, nor the rest of the world, had been at war. Most K'iche's here, if asked about the peace, either hasten away or in slow, measured tones tell me with the usual vagueness: "pues, saber[33] ... hay que ver lo que hacen esos hombres" (who knows ... we'll have to see what those men will do).

Three months later, as part of the official demobilization phase of the peace process, the guerrillas of the EGP descended the mountains by foot, uniformed, armed, and in single-file formation. They passed through

Xinxuc and neighboring communities toward a demobilization camp (one of six in the country) situated only ten minutes from Xinxuc.

Field Notes, Xinxuc, March 14, 1997

The guerrillas arrived today under a blazing sun, colliding in the plaza with the weekly pig market and intercepting a pre–*semana santa* (Holy Week) religious procession. Amidst the confusion that followed, the large purple-robed, cross-bearing Christ figure was shuffled away, as wide-eyed school children, market-goers, and *guerrilleros* chaotically filled the plaza. Before their arrival, small URNG flags had been mysteriously distributed through town, though many Xinxucians appeared to be consciously ignoring the tremendous significance of this event. People eyed the ex-rebels with veiled expressions that variously suggested curiosity, regret, admiration, or hatred: as usual, impossible to discern.

After a brief and unconvincing welcome by the town's mayor and a polite general applause, the guerrillas were whisked off by the Blue Berets to continue their journey. On the way out of town I commented to a diminutive elderly K'iche' woman, "¿Que bueno, no?" (It's good, no?); she put her arm around me and answered, "¡Si, que bueno que se hayan arepentido, que se han dado cuenta, que se acaba esto!" (Yes, how good that they have repented, that they have realized their mistakes, and that this is over with!). Further on I encountered Doña Josefa, who only last week told me the devastating story of her catechist father's and brother's disappearance during the war, carrying a URNG flag. When I asked her about this, she quickly concealed the flag and told me that she had not understood the letters on the flag, since she cannot read.

The guerrilla camp, funded by foreign organizations such as the International Red Cross and USAID, housed the guerrillas during a two-month period meant to facilitate their reintegration into civil society. The camp's atmosphere was a mixture of media fanfare, emotional reunions, festivity, and a clear continuation of URNG affirmation. I visited the camp on a number of occasions to conduct interviews with ex-combatants who, unlike the stereotypical thuglike "guerrilla" images disseminated in the media, mirrored the social composition of indigenous communities: They included elderly, toothless peasants; breast-feeding women in *guipiles* and camouflage pants; and adolescents eager to be photographed posing Rambo-like with their rifles. Each day, amid soccer tournaments and visits from hundreds of family members from surrounding villages, armed guerrillas conducted military drills, adamantly chanting slogans and carrying banners displaying the names of the EGP fronts that had fought in these areas. Social activities included weekend dances where solemn, intense indigenous *guerrilleros,* rifles slung over their shoulders, danced side-by-side with cheerful foreign aid and UN workers. Despite the tremendous national and international attention received by the guerrilla camp (including a visit from then–US Secretary of State Madeleine Albright) and the camp's proximity to Xinxuc, life in the village remained peculiarly removed from these events. While a couple of widows confided to me that they had surreptitiously visited the camp in the hopes that they might find their long-disappeared husbands or sons, and though one village Ladino (who, I eventually heard, had been a vicious civil patrol leader during the war) offered his services as a mechanic to the Blue Berets, most villagers seemed to both ignore and fear the goings-on next door. On several occasions, as I conducted interviews in the hamlets, URNG bombs being exploded on the camp by the Blue Berets could be heard in the distance; amazingly, I found myself explaining to panicked *campesinos* that this was part of *la paz.*

An additional "postwar" event that, like Xinxucians' silence regarding the guerrilla camp, clued me into the profound fear lingering in the community despite the national rhetoric of peace and human rights, was the trial of an ex-military commissioner from the village, who had been accused by a group of K'iche's from a neighboring municipality of dozens of human rights violations, massacres, and extrajudicial killings during *la violencia.* I found out about the trial through the newspaper (not a word about it was mentioned in the village) and decided to attend the week-long hearing after which, despite ample forensic evidence, the accused was dismissed on grounds of contradictory testimony.[34] Again, in spite of the wider national significance of this unique event,[35] Xinxucians (including those whose own relatives were killed by the army and civil patrols) were clearly ill at ease discussing the case, many claiming that they did not know the accused, an established Ladino *ganadero* from the community, and some even defending him.

As we've seen in this chapter, Xinxuc's pre–civil war history is characterized by a relatively late establishment of municipal boundaries and identity, a strong but eroding Ladino hegemony, and an Indian population divided by its various ethnic, religious, and geographical origins. This history differentiates Xinxuc somewhat from many highland towns, such as the more cohesive *municipios* derived from the *pueblos de indios,* which contained from the outset of colonization a majority indigenous population and a local authority structure of Indian elites. In addition, in the years immediately preceding the violence and sparked by the exodus of Ladinos, growing class cleavages and new worldviews, authority structures, and economic options among the Xinxuc's K'iche' were all transforming traditional ideals of harmonious social and family relations. The extreme fear and social disintegration produced by the war in Xinxuc must be taken into account when examining the cultural and psychological impacts of subsequent cross-border movements on the lives of K'iche' Xinxucians. These processes are an especially important backdrop to the following chapter, which describes the exodus to Providence following *la violencia* and the development of transnational social organization within and between Xinxuc and Providence in the current era.

CHAPTER 4

LA COSTA DEL NORTE
TRANSNATIONAL
SOCIAL PRACTICES

Each month, Inocente Morales sends a US$200 money order to his twice-widowed mother (Doña Isidra) in Xinxuc through Gigante Express, one of several transnational courier businesses operating between the inner city of Providence, Rhode Island, and the rural highland villages of El Quiché. Inocente works ten-hour days at a recycling mill in Providence and lives in a small apartment with his K'iche' wife Magdalena, his two American children, his sister Estela, and her small daughter Carmen. Over the past ten years, Inocente's salary has supported two households. In Providence he pays for rent, telephone and electricity bills, food, medicines, car repairs, and the other costs of maintaining a family in urban America; the remainder goes toward all daily *gastos* (expenses)—mainly clothes and food—as well the education of his half-sister Cati, in Xinxuc.

His sister Estela, who works in a jewelry factory, also sends home a large portion of her paycheck; her share contributes toward the fertilizer, seeds, and the salaries of *mozos* (day workers) hired to tend the small family *milpa* (cornfield) in the absence of Inocente, the only adult male family member. Estela also pays for the maintenance and education of her son, Cristian, who has lived with Doña Isidra since he was a baby; his mother was forced to take the *viaje* (cross-border trip) to Providence in search of her husband, who had left her pregnant without money and had never returned. Although she moved in with her husband in Providence and had a second child, she eventually left him due to his repeated physical abuse. Back home, Cristian speaks K'iche' with his grandmother; without a father to raise him, he has never learned to use an *azadón* (hoe) but knows that he can rely on his mother's support. His sister Carmen speaks, reads, and writes fluent English; she has never met her brother or grandmother but talks with them on the phone a few times a year.

Inocente's savings over the years have enabled him to buy a plot of land

and a house in Xinxuc's *pueblo*, in addition to a small piece of property near Guatemala City, which he rents out to some Xinxucians working in the capital. His remittances have enabled Doña Isidra and her family to make the move from landless rural peasants to urban dwellers who can afford the luxuries of a sturdy home, potable water, electricity, and new clothes. Inocente's Providence neighbor, Dionisio, has likewise bought a house in Xinxuc's *pueblo*; however, while this house stands as an emblem of Dionisio's transnational success, his wife and children have preferred to remain living on the rural *milpa* while Dionisio has continued to labor in Providence. Dionisio often dreams of the day his family will be reunited in the empty house.

Inocente, Estela, and Dionisio's achievements have some important personal costs. In addition to the prolonged separation from their family, land, and home, and the grueling factory life in Providence, they must be constantly aware of the potential *envidias* (envy), criticisms, witchcraft, and malicious gossip that are often targeted toward successful transmigrants such as themselves—and which can lead to disaster and downfall. At the same time, they are proud to be able to send money home to contribute to the yearly *fiesta*, thereby achieving some social recognition in their home community. Both Inocente and Estela, who live with a constant fear of being deported from the United States, plan to return to Xinxuc permanently to reunite with their family; each year, however, with their children growing in the United States and decreased economic opportunities in Xinxuc, the decision becomes postponed.

How did Inocente and Estela arrive at this situation, and how do their success stories compare to the trajectories of other transmigrant K'iche's? How do K'iche's like these maintain links with their home community, and what has been their impact on Xinxuc? As we shall now see, although the divisions and antagonisms exacerbated by the war in Guatemala have clearly produced a fractured and mistrusting transnational community, K'iche' labor migration to Providence has also been able to flourish through solid cross-border social and economic networks—a legacy, to some extent, of previous migratory strategies that have allowed the K'iche' to survive.

THE EXODUS: LEAVING XINXUC

Around 1984, a handful of Ladinos and Indians from Xinxuc's *pueblo* made their way to Providence, Rhode Island. The initial migration was clearly related to the effects of *la violencia*: Some community members left largely out of fear of vengeance, while others left, or sent their children, as a protection measure against the residuals of the war or in order to escape the army draft. Given that some civil patrol leaders were able to capitalize on *la violencia* financially, it is not surprising that a number of initial migrants from Xinxuc to Providence—those who could afford the trip—were from this group. At this time, New England was becoming an attractive destination for recent Central American immigrants and refugees due to its distance from the *migra*-heavy southern states, as well as the substantial demand for cheap unskilled labor that had been opened by the upward and outward movement of previous immigrant groups (e.g., Italian, Portuguese). Within a couple of years, it became clear that pioneer migrants had not only been able to find work *allá lejos* (far away) but were also sending home large sums of money. Although at first many K'iche's were dubious about the distant place called Providence, they slowly became part of a growing chain of migrants moving between Xinxuc (and a few of its neighboring *municipios*) and the host community.

Several factors contributed to the massive surge in cross-border migration in the late 1980s and 1990s. First, Xinxucians, like other Guatemalans, were able to "piggyback" on the transnational patterns and networks already in place due to growing cross-border movements from other Central American countries, and Mexico in particular, to the United States. Secondly, the quetzal's dollar value increased dramatically following the war, making US dollar remittances an extremely sought-after currency: While in 1982 the quetzal was on par with the US dollar, by 1986 it had risen to Q3 to the dollar, and the quetzal continued rising through the 1990s (approximately Q6 to the dollar in 1996). Third, the large sums of US dollars sent home via newly sprouted transnational courier services resulted in tremendous local inflation, causing land and property prices to climb and thus furthering the impetus to migrate.[1] And finally, the web of language, rumor, and myth concerning these voyages up north and the people who make them, which became incorporated into popular lore and the collective imagination, soon gave *Providencia* an intriguing and ubiquitous space in everyday life—and placed it within new patterns of economic survival, social values, and expectations.

Organizing to Leave

As the population of Providence-bound migrants has increased through the years, important networks and strategies have been established by K'iche's to facilitate the trip to Providence. As many authors have shown, transnational migrant networks tend to perpetuate cross-border movement by "lowering the costs, raising the benefits, and mitigating the risks of international movement" (Massey et al. 1994: 728). At one level, transnational K'iche' migration follows older migratory organizational patterns and discourses surrounding the departure of community members. Leaving the community temporarily or seasonally has long been a normative aspect of life in Xinxuc that, though having changed through time, remains part of long-standing social and familial networks. Today, people often leave to the coast or capital quite spontaneously, without lengthy preparations or good-byes, and it is often expected and planned that the person will return within a given time frame. At another level, transnational movement clearly entails radical new forms of organizing and envisioning the migrant project; preparing for the arduous, risky border crossing, leaving toward an unfamiliar setting and language, ensuring contacts in Providence, and coping with the risk and uncertainty of being undocumented differentiate the new migration from internal movements in important ways.

The trip across borders is a highly perilous one requiring undocumented migrants to travel through Guatemala, Mexico, and a variety of cross-border pathways (e.g., through rivers, across the desert, as stowaways in transport vehicles) into the United States. The passage through Mexico is particularly difficult and uncertain: Being caught and deported is a common occurrence, and several attempts are often necessary.[2] Numerous human rights violations by Mexican Immigration and Judicial Police officials (illegal detentions, physical and sexual abuse, bribes, and robbery) have been documented; illiterate K'iche's with poor Spanish-language skills are particularly susceptible to mistreatment from both officials and gangs of thugs who prey on them. The trip across the border between Mexico and the United States is physically exhausting and often dangerous: *Mojados* (wetbacks), or *pollos* (chickens), are dependent on sometimes unscrupulous *coyotes* (smugglers) who are known to demand sexual favors from women or steal from their clients and abandon their charges. K'iche' women are especially vulnerable, as the possibility of sexual "misconduct" (or rape) during the border crossing can subsequently be used as an excuse for abandonment or physical abuse by their husbands. Because the United States dramatically tightened its border patrols in the 1990s, *coyotes* have searched for new (and more dangerous) routes and have hiked up cross-border fares substantially. Sensational reports of border crossers dying of dehydration in the desert, drowning in rivers, and found asphyxiated in the back of trucks have consistently been reported in the news on both sides of the border.[3]

As migrant networks have matured through time, however, border crossing has also become an increasingly well-organized, sophisticated, and lucrative local endeavor. Local *coyotes*—people (both Ladino and K'iche') from the region who have learned the various routes, methods, material, and other necessities of border crossing—organize groups of migrants for departure, often preparing them beforehand with a quick course on Mexicanisms,[4] survival skills, and behaviors to assume or avoid (i.e., anything that will distinguish one as being Guatemalan) during the journey. Typically, one *coyote* orients the group through Guatemala and Mexico while another takes the migrants to the United States. Among some of the K'iche', the role of *coyotes* is seen in light of previous coastal labor migrations. Not only do *campesinos* refer to Providence as *la costa del Norte* (the coast of the North), they also compare local *coyotes* to the *contratistas* (labor contractors) who send *cuadrillas* (groups) of workers to particular plantations. As one woman states, "[T]he *coyote* is the same as the *contratista* on the coast: he should know when there is work over there, and should not be sending people if there is no work." When asked why people had chosen Providence as a destination, many say they went there because that is where the *coyotes* sent them. Over time, however, and given the large demand, *coyotes* have become more specialized. In some cases I heard of, K'iche' *coyotes* arranged for an *aj q'ij* to conduct a ceremony before the trip and ask the ancestors to help the group pass *sin novedad* (without problems); in another case, a female transmigrant told me she had traveled with an evangelical *coyote* because they are more respectful. As more K'iche's have made the trip more than once, moreover, border crossers increasingly find a friend or relative to take them across safely and at a lesser fee. Finding a *conocido* (acquaintance) to whom one can *pegarse* (attach oneself) more closely parallels recent strategies for internal migration, such as from Xinxuc to the capital.

Taking the *viaje* to Providence costs approximately $US3,000 to 4,000, most of which goes toward *coyote* fees and airfare from a border city in the United States to Providence.[5] Often, the plane fare is sent by a contact in Providence who agrees to advance the funds. The K'iche' use various strategies to raise the remaining money locally. Most borrow money from lenders (*usureros*), usually local Ladinos who have traditionally advanced money to Indians at high interest rates and now capitalize on the transnational exodus.[6] Many transmigrants also mortgage their land and property (and sometimes their animals), thus leaving their remaining family in a highly precarious situation and fearing that they will be expulsed from their land if the debt is not repaid in time. Some K'iche's have used bank credit acquired for agricultural loans toward financing their *viaje*;[7] landless K'iche's are less likely to travel as they lack the collateral needed to obtain loans, though a few find ways to borrow the full amount.

Clearly, then, the trip to Providence is a highly risky endeavor; the chance of *fracaso* (failure, disaster) is substantial, and both arriving and repaying one's *deuda* (debt), that is, finding a job in Providence as soon as possible, become crucial; otherwise, one may lose one's land, render one's family homeless, and be forced to return with no resources left at all. Most transmigrants try to secure a family member or friend in Providence who promises to provide *ayuda* (help) by fetching the person at the airport, providing an initial place to stay, and helping to find work. These plans must be made before the trip and are usually arranged over the telephone; this is a slow process because of the lack of telephones in Xinxuc and the work schedules of most of the K'iche' in Providence, which combine to make the telephone *cita* (rendezvous) a hit-or-miss task.

In spite of the obviously substantial preparation and networking necessary to *viajar*, departures to Providence are often both highly secretive and swift: Many K'iche's do not want others to know that they are leaving, most likely to avoid the *envidias* that may result from such knowledge and thus to maximize the possibility of a smooth crossing. Some young men recount their trip as a sudden decision to embark on an adventure, usually at the suggestion of a friend who tells them he will be leaving soon. Others leave without their wives' approval, sometimes without bidding even close family members farewell. Still others, particularly women, take more measured decisions, making arrangements with their families for childcare or to raise money for the trip.

A pronounced feature of many narratives regarding the decision of K'iche's to leave is that it is often recounted as a question of *suerte*—a sudden occurrence, encounter, or opportunity that rendered the trip auspicious—which again appears to contradict the actual planning required. As we shall see, the idiom of *suerte* becomes extremely important at every stage of transnational migration, where uncertainty—failing to cross the border, being deported, being laid off, or falling sick—are constant possibilities that may lead to ruin. Referring to *suerte* from the onset enables transmigrants, on the one hand, to pinpoint a compelling force governing their decision to leave and, on the other, to avoid accusations of abandonment. It also allows them to explain and avoid criticism for subsequent "failures": "Se le acabo la suerte" (his luck ended) is often said with reference to those who are deported, lose their jobs, or have to return home earlier than planned.[8] These attitudes do not apply as much to transmigrants who travel back and forth between the two communities more regularly. The latter establish a useful position within the transnational circuit, bringing money, letters, consumer goods (such as refrigerators, stereo equipment, etc.), as well as cars to the home community, and sometimes taking people along with them on the way back to Providence—and charging quite substantially for both services.[9] Along with *coyotes* and moneylenders, they are perceived as part of the local transnational business enterprise that facilitates the flow of things and information across the border.

Not only do many K'iche' appear to *viajar* (travel to the United States) from one day to the next,[10] but their family members at home often state that they expect them to return *ya mero* (soon enough, any day), even if they have been absent for several years. Indeed, most K'iche's, having heard that a best-case scenario permits one to pass and repay one's *deuda* within a few months, calculate that they will make enough money to return with substantial capital to invest at home within two or three years. As we shall soon see, however, a number of factors in Providence usually prolong the process of a permanent return, often resulting in very lengthy separations or in relatives joining their family members in the United States. In a sense, the contradictions in the home community between the rather flippant discourse on absence and *viajar,* on the one hand, and the actual prolonged absences and complex strategies necessitated by transnational migration, on the other, might be explained as a way of warding off the tremendous anxiety and uncertainty associated with leaving—for both the migrant and those who stay behind. It also seems to place the migration toward *allá lejos* (an often-used phrase that does not acknowledge national boundaries) within existing community norms and discourses surrounding departure and the expectation of return.

Reasons for Leaving

Motivations for leaving among the K'iche' have varied not only through time but also according to individual circumstance. Like other transmigrant populations, the majority of the K'iche' who leave are single or married men of "working age" (roughly fifteen to forty-five years old); recently, however, the disruption of a gender balance at home caused by the large male migration has led increasing numbers of indigenous women, both single and married, to follow their husbands or siblings to Providence. Given the establishment of lending schemes and border-crossing networks, transnational movement has also become an option for K'iche's of varying socioeconomic status. Among poor *campesinos*—who have primarily subsisted through coastal migrations and small *comerciante* activities—economic reasons are usually given as prime motivators for the cross-border movement. Most state that they left out of *pura necesidad* (pure necessity), usually associated with the combination of unemployment, decreased land availability, and accrued debts. K'iche' youth often say that they left out of *pura obligación*—a familial duty inscribed in the traditional division of labor whereby children are expected, often by migrating elsewhere, to help the family with *gastos* and survival at home. A large number of K'iche' transmigrants, particularly young men and women in their twenties and thirties, have already worked for varying periods of time in the capital; for them, Providence is seen as a step above and beyond urban migration at home.

We even see interest in Providence among more educated young K'iche's such as *maestros* (schoolteachers), who decide to make the journey because of lack of employment opportunities in Guatemala and lengthy waits before being placed in a position. They don't act out of *pura necesidad* but out of what is called *pura ambición* (pure ambition), or *para superar* (to succeed or excel). More recently, as more and more Xinxucians have migrated to Providence and returned with tales of life *allá*, youth also state that they leave for *aventura* (adventure) or *para conocer otra cosa* (to know something else), a rather ambiguous terminology reflecting at once the imaginary appeal of Providence, the sense of challenge and adventure given to border crossing, as well as the uncertainty associated with the transmigrant project.

The decision to migrate is sometimes made by the family, though many K'iche's also leave against the wishes of their parents or spouses. Transmigrant K'iche's often state that they did not have particular economic goals before they left for Providence. Those who return for second or third "stints," however, usually have clearer objectives in mind, such as buying a particular plot of land. Dionisio (in Providence) summarizes his own and others' decisions to migrate as follows:

> I started to think, when I saw that people were sending money, they could send $100 and that was Q380, and I saw that they were doing well here. So I just told my family that I am going to try this, but nobody told me to do this. I didn't have any big plan to buy a house, to buy land, but I wanted to see what it is to earn and send $100. There had been people who brought back trucks, cars, they built a nice house, they bought land, and one is over there admiring them, seeing and hearing those people, and knowing that those who went to the United States were able to do this, but before they couldn't.
>
> At first it was the people with money who left, those who could mobilize themselves, who had experience already, it was not the hamlet people who are always working and working. But with time, and with that desire that everyone started to have, everyone such as myself wanted to try. When I came anyone could do it, it just took a bit of money and someone to take you, and there you go. . . . I think that now there are more Indian people here, and they are the poorer Indians, those from the *monte* (hamlets), not those with money, not the *negociantes* (merchants) who already have something over there, although sometimes their children come too.

Many K'iche's also have left for reasons associated with the tremendous social pressures, criticisms, and divisions of the hometown. Both good and bad fortune among the K'iche' tend to generate much social criticism and negative gossip; in a sense, transnationalism offers not only an escape for those who have bad luck or feel undervalued or attacked at home, but also a way to vastly improve their lot as a response to such criticism. While Virgilio, for example, left in order to repay a large debt he had incurred in his efforts to create a community cooperative, it was the social blame and ostracism this unfortunate endeavor produced, and its effect on his personal life, that was the catalyst for his leaving. Women in particular tend to cite both personal problems (e.g., abusive or delinquent spouses or in-laws) and social pressures as primary reasons for migrating. Those who have been abandoned by their Providence-bound husbands, moreover, are often criticized by the community or in-laws for not being good wives. Unable to make a living alone at home, they leave precisely to escape such reproaches as well as to seek a livelihood. Young men who had spent grueling childhoods on the coast or in the capital often describe their reasons for leaving as a combination of duty, economic initiative, and resentment and anger toward their parents for being unable to find a better life for them back home, which forced them to find *su vida* (livelihood, life) elsewhere. Although economic need as well as a sense of adventure and competition seem to form the bases of most people's reasons for migrating, Virgilio (in Providence) summarizes the core issue when he says what is often left unsaid: "Aquí, todos han venido huyendo" (Here, everyone has come to escape).

Most of the reasons given for migrating are situated within older idioms surrounding migration and absence. Montejo (1999) has described (among Jakalteko communities) traditional indigenous meanings, moral and social assignations given to different types of outward movement of the past and present. The first category of migrants is the *porisal,* which refers to "the voluntary, individual decision to abandon one's community for the sake of adventure or to wander without a fixed goal or destination," is often reserved for antisocial or immoral men who desire to leave or are driven from their communities. The main protagonists of *porisal* stories are tricksters and adventurers who are often associated with ladinoized men. A second category is the *yinh smeb'ail,* which usually refers to men who migrate as merchants or in search of work; unlike the *porisal,* these men are described as having to leave the community due to poverty, and their return is anticipated and prayed for by community members. Finally, the *elilal* is a "massive, violent dislocation of entire communities as a result of violence and warfare"; these are refugees exiled in a place distant from the homeland (Montejo 1999: 191–94).

Among the Xinxuc K'iche', Montejo's first two categories are roughly akin to the difference between those seen to leave *por aventura* or *am-*

bición and those seen to leave *por necesidad* or *obligación*.[11] As Don Mingo explains:

> Before, I worked all the time on the *fincas* (plantations) to make some *centavos* for my children, because if I had not struggled on the *fincas* I would not have been able to feed them and they would have starved. My sons in the US, it is out of *pura necesidad*, because we had debts for corn and chemical fertilizer, and also the weekly *gastos*. We had Q25,000 in debts, and that is why they went, to pay those debts. They went out of a lot of necessity, because we lacked money. Not like the people who go, they have money, they have land, animals, cows, and they sell them to go. For me that is not *necesidad*. Not us, we went *por pura necesidad*.

These categories become quite blurred once transmigrants leave the community, even if people continue to refer to such reasons (sometimes interchangeably) in discussing their own or others' reasons for having left. Indeed, as we shall soon see, the gaze of the home community and family (their expectations, judgments, and needs) remain crucial to K'iche's abroad, often generating massive contradictions in their strategies, goals, and very raison d'être as transmigrants.

THE DRUDGERY OF PROVIDENCE

In Providence, the majority of K'iche's reside in two bordering inner-city neighborhoods also inhabited by Dominican immigrants, Cambodian and Laotian (Hmong) refugees, African American and Puerto Rican residents, as well as Ladinos from both El Quiché and the eastern departments of Guatemala. The Latino presence in inner-city Providence has grown substantially in the past few decades, evidenced by the landscape of Hispanic supermarkets, *tiendas* (small stores), discotheques, business offices, country-specific festivities, and the ubiquitous sounds of Spanish language and Latino music. Between ten thousand and fifteen thousand Guatemalans were estimated to reside in the city at the time of this research.[12] The Guatemalan presence, though less obvious at the level of businesses and institutions than that of other Hispanic groups, has nonetheless made a mark: Several restaurants, a couple of *panaderías* (bakeries),[13] a Guatemalan weekly newspaper, courier and travel companies advertising trips and communications to Guatemala—all owned and operated by Ladinos—are interspersed through the multicultural enclave. Although Providence has its share of inner-city problems (poverty, overcrowding, crime, gangs, and drugs), its environment is far less violent and anti-immigrant and racial frictions are much less pronounced than many other cities with high immigrant populations (e.g., Los Angeles).[14] Most of the K'iche' nonetheless live secluded and marginalized lives in Providence, due to a number of barriers—linguistic, cultural, and legal—that not only impede access to mainstream American institutions and services, but also often place them at the bottom of the Latino social hierarchy.

At the same time, the K'iche' community (like the broader Guatemalan one) in Providence is both heterogeneous and in the process of change, two factors that make it difficult to generalize about the impact of transnational migration on the collectivity. The shattering of social positions generated by *la violencia* and other disruptions in the Guatemalan context before the migratory movement has influenced current social and economic strategies along the transnational circuit. Moreover, like most other transmigrant communities, the K'iche' become integrated into the host context at various paces and in different ways, all of which impact their visions of the future and plans to return, stay, or maintain different options in both home and host contexts.

In addition to the general reasons given for migrating (as described above), a variety of specific familial strategies define the goals and roles of transmigrants in the United States. Some K'iche's are male heads of families who have left behind wives and children. Among these, some have returned temporarily to Xinxuc, while others have spent years in Providence, sending monthly remittances; maintaining contact through the telephone, letters[15] and packages; and perhaps eventually sponsoring one or several of their children to join them. Some are women who came to Providence with their husbands; others arrived after their husbands. A number of female transmigrants have been widowed at a young age by the war, illness, or accident, and have remarried (officially or unofficially)[16] in Xinxuc or Providence. Many K'iche's have left their young children to be raised on the *milpa* by their parents or in-laws, some have brought their children with them, and others have had children in the United States; these options do not exclude each other, however, and K'iche's often have children on both sides of the border who depend on their wages.

Other K'iche' migrants are single (usually male) children of aging parents; they have come to Providence, or rather have been sent, out of *pura obligación*; some of these send regular money orders back home to support their families, though others do so only sporadically or not at all. While some K'iche's have not gone back to Xinxuc for years, many others have returned to their hometown to buy land, build a house, start a business, participate in the yearly *fiesta,* or perhaps just drink the time away; still others travel back and forth, transporting cars, consumer goods, mail, and the latest news or rumors. Finally, some are American citizens, children born and/or raised in the United States, English-speaking public school students well versed in the latest Latino rap, whose acquaintance with their own K'iche' siblings and grandparents back home comes only from photos and hearsay. Given this diversity and the continual movement between home and host communities, it is impossible to pinpoint clear, time- or space-bound migrant categories.

Although most transmigrants come to Providence with the idea that they will return (or be deported) sooner or later, many describe their integration into the United States as a reason for not returning permanently, or not just yet: Perhaps they have married in Providence, or they have become accustomed to the luxuries of America, such as running water, paychecks, medical care, proper nutrition, and consumer goods. Those who have children born in Providence, in particular, become integrated into various systems and institutions, health and social welfare for example, and come to rely on American programs such as food stamps and prenatal and other health care. It becomes increasingly difficult for them to imagine returning with their children to Xinxuc, where such basics as nutrition, health care, and education are lacking. A number of transmigrants have gone home at some point with the full intention of staying, and some have indeed remained; many, however, decide within a few months or years to return to Providence, finding it difficult to maintain a secure economic position, fulfill their goals, or simply *hallarse* (feel at home) following their experience in Providence. A few unattached K'iche's have found a balance between working half of the year in Providence's factories and returning home to work on the *milpa,* though this strategy is difficult to sustain for practical reasons. Most transmigrants in the host setting describe their situation as having "un pie aquí y otro allá" (one foot here and one foot there) or, in a more negative assessment, as being "ni de aquí ni de allá" (neither from here nor there).

Herein lies a major contradiction experienced by K'iche' transmigrants. Several factors contribute, on the one hand, to a very strong ideology of return. First, the Mayan attachment to birthplace and land as a "part of their being" (Nolin Hanlon 1995), and as critical to their cultural identity (both past and future), remains an important part of the worldview of many K'iche's'. For many, an eventual return is not only assumed but comprises the very reason for their Providence existence. Indeed, given the fact that the main goal of the transmigrant project is to improve one's family's status at home, it is logically expected that people will, indeed, come back to rejoin their wives, children, or parents and enjoy that status. Moreover, the K'iche's have a profound fear of dying in the United States since having a proper burial in the ancestor's land is critical. Therefore, it is usually taken for granted that one must return to one's land and community before dying. Finally, the tremendous guilt of having left one's wife alone or of having left one's children to be raised by others or of having left behind aging parents often wears on K'iche's, who dream of reuniting their families. At the same time, however, because one's very success as a transmigrant might come to a halt if one goes home, many postpone the return indefinitely despite always stating that they will, indeed, return, *ya mero* (soon), *el próximo año* (next year), or *cuando nos sacan* (when they get rid of us). K'iche's who have children in the United States, moreover, find themselves in an ambiguous predicament: "[O]ur children are from here, they are American, but we are from there, and we must return." As we shall see, this state of limbo within which the K'iche' find themselves—the push and pull between the expectation of return and the need or desire to stay in Providence—is reinforced by their legal situation, which has a profound impact on both their lives in Providence as well as the economic and familial linkages through which they maintain an absent "presence" in Xinxuc.

The Present: A Life of Work and Struggle

For K'iche's, the organization and practice of everyday life in this urban center marks a radical change from home; as for many other Central American transmigrant groups in American cities, life revolves largely around strenuous industrial work schedules and coping with the uncertainty and marginality associated with a temporary or undocumented legal status (Popkin 1999; Chavez 1998; Chinchilla and Hamilton 1999; Loucky and Moors 2000). K'iche's summarize the precariousness and liminality of both situations with the phrase *aquí, somos prestados* (here, we are just borrowed [labor]). The majority of K'iche's work in jewelry and textile factories, and some in fish packing plants, restaurants, and gardens (though these are often considered less desirable and lucrative). Many have changed jobs several times, in part because of the instability of low-wage work, in part because of the unattractiveness of certain jobs, and in part because they constantly seek higher wages. Although a few women stay home to take care of their own and other K'iche' children, most also work in the factories; as Magdalena says, "The *gastos* (daily expenses) are too high here, and if the man only makes $200 a week, he cannot pay the rent, the *biles* (bills), the children, clothes, food, and the money we send home, so the woman must work also." Unlike Mayan women in some other cities (Hagan 1994), K'iche' women do not opt to work as domestics; factory work provides better wages, offers more flexibility, and does not require English fluency; furthermore, most K'iche's never venture to the wealthier (and whiter) side of town, where they fear they will stand out and invite problems.

During their initial years, most K'iche's acquire jobs through *oficinas* or *agencias*—Hispanic-run temp agencies—which recruit workers for temporary jobs in the industrial sector and assume the legal risk of hiring undocumented immigrants. These agencies siphon off a portion of the worker's salary, do not provide any benefits such as health care or vacation days, and offer little stability. Eventually, K'iche's are able to find work directly through the factories if they have acquired experience, are able to present work papers, and have a contact or *conocido* to vouch for them. Though most start out at minimum wage, some are eventually promoted as they learn to use more complex machinery, and a few have even become floor managers. A large portion of the K'iche' (most men, and nearly all women) are employed in assembling and polishing jewelry, a major industry in this area. Although this work is less volatile than most, it is also governed by seasonal demand, and many fear being laid off temporarily or permanently after the main season (Christmastime) or in times of economic downturn. While keeping a job, like everything, is a question of *suerte,* those who have stayed with the same employer for many years have also made concerted efforts to cultivate good relations with their American *patrones* (bosses).

Industries in Providence have welcomed the inexpensive, hard-working, and relatively docile labor force provided by K'iche's; like other Mayan immigrant groups, the Providence K'iche' have acquired the reputation for being hard, modest, and respectful workers (Popkin 1999, Wellmeier 1998). Many work overtime, often double shifts, and usually six days per week; a sixty- to eighty-hour workweek is considered desirable, and many become highly anxious when job availability decreases their hours, when they are laid off, or even when a national holiday prevents them from working. Due to the new time-space relations involved in industrial work—and, in some cases, the lack of safety measures in certain factories—a number of K'iche's have been involved in work accidents, some more serious and debilitating than others. During my fieldwork, a key informant had his entire hand nearly torn off by machinery in a textile factory; another K'iche' was crushed to death by a metal tank used to mix fish guts. The news of such devastating accidents, like the dangers of border crossing, creates tremendous anxiety among all transmigrant family members back home.

Many K'iche's are frustrated by the high cost of living in the United States; paying for the monthly rent, water, electricity and phone *biles,* food, transportation, and other costs usually adds up to far more than what they had anticipated, and the expenses prolong the amount of time needed to save money. In order to lower their costs, the K'iche' often live in very crowded living conditions; both single people and family members tend to share cramped living quarters, alleviating the crowding by working alternate shifts that allow some to sleep while others work. Free time is rare and is usually spent washing clothes, grocery shopping and cooking, and going to mass (or *culto* for evangelicals). Carrying out domestic tasks is particularly difficult for men who are accustomed to having women perform such work. K'iche' women, for their part, often assume the double burden of factory and domestic work, though some share home duties with their husbands or other family members. Strenuous work schedules constrain other forms of social organization not centered around work and kinship. For most, social activities are limited to religious functions, as well as the weekend soccer tournaments where K'iche' and Ladino players (organized around hometown teams or by department) compete against other teams made up of players that are Guatemalan, Latino, African, or from other groups. Some K'iche' youth begin to take on more Latino-type social activities such as frequenting discotheques, often with the disapproval of older community members.

A fair number of K'iche' men in Providence have had one or several run-ins with the police, usually involving driving without car insurance or a driver's license.[17] Arriving from a setting where there is little or no enforcement of the law and where Indians have always been vulnerable to abuse and arbitrary behavior on the part of authorities, many of the K'iche', initially at least, find it difficult to adapt to the rules and regulations of the United States. Moreover, the notion of trust in a broader system organized for the benefit of both individual and collectivity—the idea behind car insurance, for example—does not resonate for people who have rarely benefited from such long-term planning by outside organizations or the state.[18] In addition, because having a car in Providence is both a necessity and a prime indicator of status, something entirely inaccessible for most K'iche's back home, some have fallen prey to a Guatemalan-run car-theft ring operating in the city, from whom they have unsuspectingly bought stolen cars off the street for relatively cheap prices. This is but one of many ways in which K'iche' transmigrants—especially those who are illiterate and ignorant of legal norms in the States—are being "screwed by their own people" (as described by one Providence police detective).

In addition to these instances, other legal problems for the K'iche' have centered around DUI (driving under the influence) cases and domestic violence, which is also usually associated with heavy drinking. Indeed, loneliness, frustration, and marginality can lead to an exaggeration of reckless and violent behaviors; the desperation and rage provoked by the many cruelties of life in Providence—being laid off and unable to find work, hearing that a family member back home is sick or has died, or becoming a helpless victim of malicious gossip or of an assault—sometimes lead K'iche' men to binge drinking. As in Xinxuc, drinking is not considered a social activity that brings people together but rather a vice through which people bury and forget their sorrow and rage. While at home, heavy drinking and its consequences are somewhat kept in check by parents, in-laws, and the community (though it is doubtful that its prevalence is any lower there, as borne out by health indicators), in Providence it is the American legal system that becomes the arbitrator, at a great cost to K'iche's who may end up in jail (or, if they are even less lucky, killed in street accidents). At the same time, such problems do connect some people with the state's social service system, which seeks to orient K'iche's toward rehabilitation programs (such as Alcoholics Anonymous) and domestic abuse counseling, with varying levels of success.

The problem of domestic abuse has led some K'iche' women to separate from their husbands, something that occurs more rarely back home. In Xinxuc most couples live with or near the husband's family; women are under the close scrutiny of their in-laws but also tend to have their parents nearby. Although domestic abuse clearly exists back home, interference by the family or community elders, the *ley de la comunidad* (community law), is meant to resolve disputes and keep such abuse in check. Without this structure in Providence, women can become extremely vulnerable, as Estela recounts:

> When [my husband] came here he changed a lot, he was thinking of another woman. . . . But when I arrived he came to fetch me, told me how good to see you, and to move in with him. But then he started with his questions, his doubts about the *coyote*—whether he had taken advantage of me—and then he started beating me, he treated me terribly. And I kept leaving him and returning, and he would go out into the street drinking, and come home to beat me. I worked to pay the rent, the bills, and when I came home tired to cook, he would beat me more! And because Inocente was working at night I was at home alone, he would beat me too much, and I could not accuse him in front of the law because I was scared, because I thought the police were the *migra*, and me without papers.

After a particularly horrific beating that sent her to the hospital, Estela, with the guidance and encouragement of a social worker, eventually left her husband and obtained a divorce. Her situation is far from typical, however. Josefa, for example, was so badly beaten by her husband one night that she called the police; he was sent to jail for fourteen months (he was also violating a previous DUI parole). At the age of twenty-six, Josefa has four children back home (by her first husband, who was killed in a car accident on a return visit from Providence) and a fifth in Providence by a man who violated her during her border crossing and then left. When her new husband was sent to jail, Josefa felt guilty and desperate, asking me to accompany her to the justice building to see what could be done: As she told me, "Who will help me pay for the rent now, and how will I send enough for *gastos* and to feed my children?" Her situation, moreover, left her wide open for abuse by other men and for malicious gossip and social ostracism. The costs of being alone—both financial and social—for many K'iche' women are thus felt to be much higher than those of tolerating domestic violence.

Given all the potential problems outlined above, many of the K'iche' feel that they must restrict outside activities as much as possible *para no meterse en problemas* (to avoid getting into trouble); many often repeat, almost mantra-like, that they go from home to work and back again, and avoid hanging around in the street. Indeed, since life outside of home and work can include a whole range of real or imagined risks—getting stopped by the police or *la migra*,[19] being seduced by alcohol or women (which involves not only misspending one's money but also inviting malicious gossip), falling in with a bad crowd, being assaulted, and so on—one's best bet is simply to avoid much of the outside world. As a result, some of the most common complaints regarding life in Providence are represented in the following recurring phrases: *Aquí, uno viene a encerrarse* (here we are always locked in). "Over there, one has one's own work, you can go where you want, when you want. Here it is only work and money, it is madness." Or, "Here, our children cannot *respirar como allá*" (breathe [the fresh air] like back home).

The separation from land and family—two elements that in Xinxuc are intimately connected with work, subsistence, and identity—is very difficult for many transmigrant K'iche's to cope with. Being *prestado* so far away impedes involvement in the (at least partial) subsistence and autonomy that *milpa* labor affords: The *independencia campesina* (peasant independence) that provided a certain flexibility and agency for the rural K'iche' at home no longer exists in Providence. As Kearney states, transnational labor migration "heightens the capitalist alienation of labor by geographically separating the site of the purchase and expenditure of that labor from the sites of its reproduction, such that the loci of production and reproduction lie in two different countries" (Kearney 1998: 125). One of the most difficult aspects of toiling in this faraway place is that the fruits of one's labor, the money invested in improving the lot of one's family back home, remain largely unseen and abstract, often engendering a strong sense of alienation and marking a rupture from previous forms of short- and long-term migration within Guatemala. In addition, the focus on work, remaining hidden, and being *encerrados* transforms the very concept of time for K'iche' transmigrants; unlike back home, where many say *hay más tiempo que vida* (there is more time than life), Providence time is instead consumed with the duties and hardships of earning that life.

The Long Term: A Life of Limbo

> I am ready to be punished, I know I have been *abusivo* (abusive) coming here illegal, as a *mojado*, that it is an abuse, but I did it out of necessity. . . . And now I cannot take it anymore, I cannot live like this, always lying, never knowing, always with fear. . . . I would like to meet the director of immigration, tell him the whole truth the way it is, and that he would just give me a punishment, a fine and I will sell my car, he can put me in jail for a while, punish me and then either give me my papers or send me back once and for all. . . . If I were alone, I would return to my country, but here I have my children, and I do not want them to suffer the way I suffered, I am here for my children. (K'iche' man, Providence)

DeGenova (2002) argues that "illegality," like citizenship, requires a relation to the state—a consent to surveillance, discipline, and control—and also serves to stigmatize particular populations, factors which then come to be integrated and internalized into individual and collective identity processes. The legal situation of Guatemalans in the United States since the war has been highly volatile and complex, and has produced a tremendous amount of anxiety and uncertainty among the K'iche'. Barring marriage to a US citizen,[20] it is virtually impossible for the majority of poorer Guatemalans—like most immigrants who lack "special skills" and capital resources—to obtain permanent residency through standard immigration processes. Inconsistent immigration policies put forth by several US administrations have forced many into a life of limbo and fear that impedes the ability to plan for their future or the future of their children. This section describes some of the structural contradictions governing the lives of K'iche' transmigrants in the host context: At once criminalized as "illegal aliens," desired as cheap (and disposable) labor, and, at times, recognized as victims of a devastating political violence, many embody the profound paradoxes, conflicts, and ambivalences surrounding current immigration debates in the United States.

The initial reception of Central Americans in the early 1980s—particularly of Guatemalans and Salvadorans, whose military governments the United States was supporting—was hostile; given its Cold War political stance, the Reagan government systematically refused to accept asylum applications from these populations. In 1986, the Immigration Reform and Control Act (IRCA), designed to halt the growing flow of undocumented cross-border movement, legislated sanctions against businesses that hired "illegal aliens" and legalized approximately three million undocumented immigrants who had arrived before 1982. Many Guatemalans, including most of the K'iche' in Providence, were too poorly informed, fearful, and traumatized to apply for the "amnesty," or they had arrived after the specified date. It has been widely recognized that IRCA stemmed neither the flow nor the hiring of undocumented immigrants, whose numbers soared in the late 1980s and 1990s.

In 1990, the American Baptist Church (ABC) won a five-year suit against the INS for its unlawful denial of asylum applications for Guatemalans and Salvadorans. Hundreds of thousands of undocumented Central Americans were able to submit asylum applications and were given temporary work permits (renewable on a yearly basis) allowing them to remain in the United States until a hearing could be arranged. The INS became virtually swamped with such claims, since anyone could now apply for asylum and obtain a temporary work permit. At this time, the cheap labor provided by disenfranchised workers—who could eventually be deported—was welcomed in the United States, as they were filling vacant low-wage industrial and service-sector jobs. By the mid-1990s, however, economic tensions in certain areas had produced a rabid anti-immigrant backlash and led undocumented immigrants to become "the scapegoats for job losses and deteriorating wages" in the United States (Chinchilla and Hamilton 1999: 10).[21] The anti-immigrant climate became particularly strained in 1996, leading the Clinton administration to double the INS budget, greatly increase the size of the Border Patrols and the sophistication of their "security" enforcement, and pass the Illegal Immigration Reform and Immigrant Responsibility Act (IIRIRA). The act introduced measures to facilitate the deportation of new (undocumented) arrivals and made it extremely difficult for those who had been working in the United States for years with temporary permits to request a suspension of deportation when called in for a hearing.[22]

As Mahler has described, these confusing shifts in immigration legislation created a "lucrative, liminal law" that has left many Central Americans—in particular those such as the K'iche' whose knowledge of legal concepts and of English is very limited—particularly open to manipulation from numerous sources and largely uninformed about either their legal status or options. The passage of IRCA "fostered unbridled opportunities of profiteering off the illegals' plight" (Mahler 1995: 184). In Providence as in many other places, some K'iche' transmigrants have paid large sums to local brokers for counterfeit documents (*papeles chuecos*); many, however, have been deceived and manipulated by a "pseudo-legal" industry claiming to procure legal papers—that is, promising work authorizations—for undocumented immigrants.

In what Mahler calls the "political asylum trap," many K'iche's who arrived before 1995 were told by *notarios* (often fellow Guatemalan or Hispanic notaries, of dubious credentials) that, for anywhere between $500 and $2,000, they would procure their *permiso* (work papers). Under the ABC law, the *notario* would then fill in asylum applications—often with bogus information that K'iche's could not read and without explaining the political asylum concept to their client—and deliver temporary work permits, knowing that a lengthy time lag would ensue until the person's hearing, which in most cases would lead to deportation procedures.[23] Most K'iche's I met who had procured *permisos* had no idea what asylum meant or what sort of information they would be expected to give during their hearing; had they known, I suspect that, like the Salvadorans in Mahler's study, they would have been far too fearful to even entertain the notion of requesting political asylum and revisiting the painful and dangerous past. The total confusion surrounding understandings about the legality and illegality of different types of documentation is illustrated by the reference that K'iche's both back home and in Providence sometimes make to the possibility of obtaining *papeles legalmente falsificados* (legally falsified documents).

In 1997 and 1998 (during the time of fieldwork) many of the back-logged ABC asylum cases were reopened.[24] Given that peace had been declared back home and with the new legislation in place, Guatemalans with temporary permits feared that they would now be deported, causing many to avoid their hearings altogether and/or to change their addresses, thus forcing them further into a hidden and fearful existence.[25] In addition, since work authorization papers were no longer immediately given to those applying for asylum after 1995, Guatemalans who had arrived after this period increasingly resorted to purchasing illegal work documents. Thus, rather than discouraging people from coming or forcing them to leave, these new immigration policies barred most people from becoming legal, made them increasingly vulnerable to outside manipulation, and forced them further into a life of uncertainty.

Shifting national policies have led many K'iche's into an unstable and contradictory relation with both institutions and employers in Providence. On the one hand, many are terrified of dealing with host country institutions for fear of being detected, avoiding them as much as possible and leading "shadowed lives" (Chavez 1998). Many who fall ill, for example, wait until their situation is advanced before they seek hospital help. Sensational rumors of INS factory raids during which undocumented immigrants are rounded up cause a high degree of anxiety on a daily basis. K'iche's involved in even minor traffic accidents often "run"—even when they are the victim—rather than being caught by the police. In addition to this constant stress, undocumented status often leaves K'iche's open to assault and robbery: Because they cannot open bank accounts and sometimes carry around large quantities of cash, most K'iche's have been victims of street violence. A K'iche' woman explains:

> Our poor men here are always abused by blacks and Dominicans.
> ... They know that we cash our checks at the liquor store, and they
> wait for us, and those without a car they follow them and take all
> their money.... It is because they know that we are humble people,
> and that we are *dejado* (careless), that they will let people do this.
> Everyone knows that most Guatemalans can't, well they have no
> papers and for this reason they abuse them, they know they cannot
> defend themselves. How could we go to the law when we are too
> afraid?

Paradoxically, host institutions in Providence simultaneously "turn a blind eye" to the undocumented status of K'iche's—and, indeed, sometimes knowingly help them: *Agencias* and industries continue to hire undocumented workers;[26] unless they are convicted of serious crimes, the police do not report K'iche's stopped for misdemeanors to the INS; the Department of Motor Vehicles grants driver's licenses without proof of residency; schools are often aware that their students' parents do not have documents; and social and health care workers sometimes go out of their way to help those in need of special assistance.[27] Several of my informants became seriously ill in Providence, and they had to be hospitalized and required expensive treatment, costs that were absorbed by the state hospital. In many respects, despite their undocumented or temporarily documented status, Providence has offered more social assistance to the K'iche' than the Guatemalan state has ever been able or willing to.

The K'iche', thus, embody the tremendous ambivalence of current US policies toward undocumented Central American immigrants. As Kearney describes:

> The contradiction in US immigration policy ... is inscribed on the
> social person so constructed, the "alien." This "alien" is desired as a
> body, or more specifically as labor power which is embodied in this
> person, by employers and indirectly by all who benefit economically

and socially from this cheaply bought "foreign" labor. But this alien as a legal person who might possess rights and prerogatives of a national, of a citizen of the nation, is the dimension of personhood that is denied. The ambiguity of the alien results from policy and policing which inscribe both of these identities—worker and alien—onto his person simultaneously. (1988: 128)

Indeed, Guatemalans have been in the "eye of the storm" of intense ideological conflicts characterizing US discourses and policies surrounding immigration, citizenship, and national identity in the post–Cold War period. K'iche's belong to the host nation's fastest growing ethnic group—thirty-five million Americans of Hispanic origin—to whom businesses increasingly target their marketing strategies and whom politicians seek to court. At the same time, they also belong to the soaring numbers of undocumented immigrants (somewhere between nine and eleven million) currently at the center of highly polarized deliberations. Public debates between "nativists" who wish to curb or stop immigration and pro-immigrant advocates take place daily in national and local news, evoking a sort of "noble-savage" dichotomy: The former group warns against the social and economic "threat" posed by masses of poor, uneducated (and usually dark-skinned, Spanish-speaking) undocumented immigrants, while the latter summons the economic and cultural benefits immigrants bring to the nation and the long history of America's openness toward the "poor and huddled masses."[28] The undocumented Central American or Mexican Other, in the public eye, is alternatively criminal parasite or hard-working victim.

Despite these discourses, the primacy of economic concerns is clearly what has guided the fluctuating and ambivalent immigration policies of the United States throughout the 1990s and into the new century, as it has in the past. Indeed, by the end of the 1990s and with the US economy on an upswing—that is, only a few years after the harsh IIRIRA laws—an odd coalition of interest groups, some of whom had previously maintained a relatively hostile stance toward the influx of undocumented immigrants (including the AFL-CIO and some conservative Republicans), began to advocate aggressively for a national "amnesty" for this population. In both public and policy sectors, the debate surrounding undocumented immigration has intensified in the present decade, now connected by anti-immigrant advocates to post-9/11 questions of national security. While most of the K'iche' quite desperately hope to become fully legalized eventually, this desire is based in the wish to end the tremendous insecurity and fear associated with being illegal (or the frustrating uncertainty of temporary status), to facilitate border-crossing, and to plan for a cohesive future with their children. Although it is probable that legalization would facilitate the integration of K'iche's in the United States, it is unlikely that such a policy would put an end to the transnational connections and goals through which they remain linked to the home community. Indeed, most told me that, on the contrary, legalization would allow them to return home more often and preserve stronger links with their land and family. For the moment, however, the ambivalence of these policies has the effect of reinforcing fear, marginality, and exposure to manipulation, as well as furthering the tremendous divisiveness and mistrust that, as we shall now see, exists among the K'iche' in Providence.

The Contradictions of Social Organization in Providence

Literature on transnational migration often analyzes the manners in which transmigrants reproduce and transform social and political structures of the home context in the host community (Basch et al. 1994; Levitt 2001). The type and extent of social organization among Guatemalans in the United States has varied widely depending on the time period, geographic location, and characteristics of the communities of departure. During the 1980s, some Guatemalans in the United States (generally those who had been politically active at home) joined progressive solidarity and social justice organizations to oppose American policies in Central America. Today, various organizations still maintain a focus on political conditions at home by dispersing knowledge concerning human rights abuses and by sponsoring delegations of church groups and politicians to the home country (Chinchilla and Hamilton 1999).

Over the past two decades, Guatemalan communities in the United States have created hundreds of cultural, athletic, commercial, political, and social organizations, in some cases to improve conditions in the host country (and facilitate assimilation) and in others to strengthen ties to Guatemala (and facilitate the transnational flow of money and people).[29] In some places, undocumented Guatemalans—both Indian and Ladino—have joined host country organizations that seek to modify US immigration and refugee policy by sponsoring demonstrations and legal advocacy; some immigrants have participated in class-action suits protesting the treatment and legal status of undocumented immigrants. Compared to some other transmigrant communities (e.g., Haitians, Filipinos, Mexicans), Guatemalans have had relatively little success obtaining cooperation from their home government in these endeavors. Indeed, it was only in 1997 that local consulates began making an effort to focus on the legal situation of many of its conationals and to provide information concerning immigration laws.[30]

Existing research on Mayan transmigrant populations in the United States shows that many such groups have organized collectively in the host context around home-based ethnic and/or municipal identities. Popkin (1999) has shown how Kanjobal Maya in Los Angeles have formed hometown associations or *fraternidades* that raise funds for development projects in their respective home communities (including, in the case of Santa Eulalia, a doctor's salary, an innovative medical insurance program [Buchner 1997], and the construction of religious edifices). The *fraternidades* also fund projects in the host community (e.g., collecting money to send the recently deceased home or sponsoring events in the United States such as *fiestas* and soccer games). As such organizations have developed, they have usually connected with other immigrant advocacy organizations in order both to facilitate transnational connections with the hometown as well as to improve the status of migrants in the host context. Other authors (Burns 1993; Wellmeier 1998; Hagan 1994; Earle 1994) have shown how Mayan communities in Indiantown (Florida), Houston (Texas), and Los Angeles have formed ethnic or neighborhood associations that create a sense of solidarity—and often incorporate Mayans from a variety of home *municipios,* regions, and language groups—around a broader pan-Mayan identity. Fink (2003), moreover, has described the labor struggles of different Mayan Indian groups who have drawn on previous organizational skills to enter into unionization drives in Morgantown, North Carolina, poultry plants. While all of these authors have pointed to areas of contestation and conflict within these groups, the fact that the latter attempt to organize at all around a home-based identity (whether identifying with the actual home *municipio* or a more abstract ethnic and national identity) differentiates them from the K'iche' described here.

What is striking about the K'iche' community in Providence is its lack of formal or structured organization. Indeed, most types of visible Guatemalan social organization in Providence—whether they involve the creation of businesses, the organization of community "cultural" events (e.g., celebrating Guatemala's independence day), or in some cases political organization to protest immigration laws—have been organized by educated Ladinos.[31] The main umbrella organization, Guatemalan Americans of Rhode Island (GARI), run entirely by Ladinos, seeks primarily to carve out a place for the Guatemalan community within the broader Latino environment, improve the image of Guatemalans in Providence, and facilitate economic and social links with Guatemala. Most of the events sponsored by them have not been attended by the majority of K'iche's, though the symbols of indigenous identity are utilized in the effort to promote the "Guatemalan culture."[32] A second smaller organization, Guatemaltecos Unidos (United Guatemalans), has organized sporadically around changing immigration laws since the early 1980s but has never been able to incorporate the indigenous population into its advocacy and organizational efforts.

Most people familiar with the K'iche' in Providence (immigration lawyers, language teachers, community workers, Ladino and Latino activists, and often the K'iche' themselves) agree that two of the main characteristics of the Providence K'iche' are that (1) they often seek to hide their origins, avoiding any discussion of their homeland, and (2) most efforts to organize—whether around legal or social issues, or around ethnic or municipal identities—have resulted in failure. Ironically, then, while in other settings (such as those discussed above) Indians from different regions have fostered organizations based in a common Mayan identity, the K'iche' in Providence—all originating from the same few municipalities—do not wish to organize around the home identity. This difference speaks to the impossibility of generalizing about a Mayan refugee or immigrant "experience" in the United States, as well as to the persisting impact of fragmentation and violence, which is much stronger in some home communities than in others and which leads to diverse collective strategies in the host context.

The lack of visible K'iche' organization is, indeed, largely related to the divisive impact of the violence in Xinxuc, though it also results from other factors. In the first place, most of the political, religious, and ethnic cleavages existing in Xinxuc persist in Providence; as K'iche's often state, "Siempre hemos estado divididos" (we have always been divided). Divisions and suspicions become even more exaggerated in Providence, where new kinds of threats loom: One never knows who might report one to *la migra,* who will spread rumors about oneself back home, or who is a criminal or has a sordid past. Even extended family members and in-laws, with whom one might have a past history of disputes and mistreatment at home, might shun one upon arrival. In this context, it is best to maintain the façade of social harmony (remain polite and appear humble) but narrow one's contact with others to harmless or obviously pragmatic and necessary activities.

Most K'iche's in both Xinxuc and Providence live in tremendous fear of the mere connotations of *organizarse* (organizing), which was considered a dangerous and subversive activity during the violence. As the Truth Commission has reported, "[S]tate terror was applied to make it clear that those who attempted to assert their rights, and even their relatives, ran the risk of death by the most hideous means. The objective was to intimidate and silence society as a whole, in order to destroy the will for transformation, both short and long term" (CEH 1999). Moreover (as I found out when I tried to organize English classes and discussions regarding immigration laws), K'iche's not only fear participation but are often profoundly suspicious of those who try to *aconsejar* (counsel) them, suspecting them of having ulterior motives.[33] Given the authoritarianism of the home political culture, whereby the advantages of democratic participation at any level are not ingrained, many continue to lack any confidence in their ability to participate in formal organizations with a social, cultural, or political mandate. The K'iche', thus, do not tend to view organizing as potentially beneficial; on the contrary, given the devastation resulting from past efforts to organize at home, the best strategy is to remain marginal: *Mañana veremos* (we'll see what happens tomorrow).

The need to remain invisible due to precarious legal status further impedes formal organizing. Since K'iche' transmigrant lives are characterized largely by ambivalence and uncertainty regarding the future, a sense of liminality and instability constrains the creation and investment in a solid community organization in Providence. Moreover, the divisions between transmigrants who remain committed to their family and land at home, cognizant that they are here temporarily, and those who hope to assimilate more permanently to American culture create divided and sometimes contentious loyalties and visions of the future.

Finally, practical issues also contribute to the lack of organization and solidarity. Given the constant time pressures of unstable and exhausting work schedules, the basic structure of everyday life makes it very difficult for most K'iche's to maintain any involvement in organizations. Because many are illiterate, moreover, their connections to any institutions or media, such as the weekly newspaper put forth by GARI, which might permit participation in a broader community, are highly limited.[34]

Given all these facts of life in the host context—being *encerrados* at work and home, living in constant legal limbo, and fearing participation in most forms of social organization—many K'iche's in Providence feel tremendously isolated not only from the society surrounding them but from their own community members. The daily spatial and temporal structure that permitted at least some sense of shared community at home, as fragmented as it was by the war, cannot be reproduced in Providence. As one man states:

> I do not feel that there is a community because now we are all separated, now there is no communication, we do not say hello in the street, we do not meet in the plaza, we don't see each other in a meeting. And sometimes, if we do see each other at mass for example, we don't talk about what is happening, what shall we do about this problem. . . . Over there yes, we visit each other and get together, we tell each other problems, we try to help each other.

> Here it is hard to help someone in trouble, partly because of fear
> and partly because there is no time. So I don't feel that there is a
> community, just some acquaintances here.

Despite this fracturing, it is important to point out that many K'iche's
do, nonetheless, recreate important social bonds in Providence that enable them to both maintain a connection to home and survive in the new
context. As other authors (Casillas 1995; Chavez 1998) have pointed out,
being a transmigrant requires creating bonds of dependence and solidarity
with others upon whom one must rely for a multitude of needs, including
financial support, finding a job, locating a home, and learning the "ropes"
of survival in the new context: "[M]igrants create new relations of exchange
with those around them based on values, norms and practical knowledge
about daily life" (Casillas 1995: 38–39). For most groups, such relations are
usually imbedded in both old and new social support systems based on
trust, dependence, and solidarity.

One of the great contradictions among the K'iche' in Providence is that,
despite their tremendous divisions and mistrust, a sort of tacit "migrant
solidarity" is developed whereby both asking for and providing information and assistance regarding the actual *viaje* and the many challenges that
face the migrant upon arrival becomes part of a system of shared knowledge and expectation, without which the entire transmigrant project could
not exist, either for individuals or the collectivity. Depending on others for
help in the new context and also relying on others to facilitate connections
with the home community become necessary aspects of the transmigrant
life: It is clear to all that, given their difficult situation as *mojados,* most
will need help at one point or another. In one sense, such informal bonds
of mutual aid and support are inscribed in older communal patterns of
organization, whereby solidarity and networking have always facilitated the
search for jobs and opportunity in other places. This connection between
past and present types of organizations often comes through in K'iche'
narratives. For example, when I asked one K'iche' man, during the course
of an interview, how his Max grandparents had come to settle in Xinxuc,
he told me:

> They went from X municipality, then to a *finca,* and then, because
> they had no more land they went to the hamlet in Xinxuc. It was
> just like we do here in the United States, we talk with each other and
> find out where to go, where there is work and it is good.

At the same time, however, the profound power distortions, fears, and
competition created by the confluence of violence and transnationalism

are in constant tension with this need for social support and communication. This point is best illustrated in the case of Don Cipriano, Inocente's stepbrother and one of Xinxuc's most violent K'iche' ex–civil patrollers, who has obtained residency in the United States. Cipriano has achieved a dominant position over other K'iche' transmigrants through his ability to provide initial shelter to recent arrivals, whom he nonetheless resents and abuses. So persistent are his mistreatments that stories abound in both Xinxuc and Providence regarding his evil deeds. He has strived to maintain power through various forms of intimidation, including creating financial and other forms of debt, threatening to turn people into *la migra,* attempting to sexually coerce indigenous women, and pressuring other Mayans to convert to the evangelical sect he joined following his migration. He is also known for introducing newly arrived indigenous men to the novelties of strip clubs, thus creating a further mass of sinners to convert and manipulate. Cipriano's ability to return home regularly enables him to circulate and capitalize on information and rumors in both communities, reinforcing his power over those who cannot afford to move between the two spaces. His reputation for practicing *brujería,* moreover, makes him even more notorious and dangerous. As Inocente recounts, Cipriano has recreated the relationship of dependency and mistreatment that he had with other K'iche' in Xinxuc within the new atmosphere of Providence.

> When I came here I went to live in Cipriano's place, they called it the White House. Almost all the [Indian] *mojados* go there when they arrive, it was very sad because we were about nine people living there, in a very small apartment like this one, but it was divided in two and we had just a little room with a small bathroom and kitchen, and in that little hole we would crouch in each corner. . . . Cipriano started to mistreat me, he said why did you come here, you are an imbecile, that when I went to the capital it was only with his help, because his father had married my mother, that my mother was a prostitute, and he continued to insult me until he hit me. . . . There were many fights in that house, between him and the others, and a few times the police came. . . .
>
> He used a notebook, like the one you have, and each time I took even a glass of water he would write it down, to charge me. He charged me $300 just for arriving, those $300 were like a tip for him. He told me he would not help me find work, and he would drink a lot and would say: "You thought it would be easy here, you thought it is just picking up dollars here, well you are screwed. . . . In Guatemala you took my business, you made me compete in the business, but you cannot get anywhere without me, because without

me you are nothing, and if I open a business you do the same, and if I come here, you come too, and if I eat shit, you will too. . . ."

One Saturday night I came back from church—I had to ask God to help me—and Cipriano was very drunk, and he beat me up until he split my forehead, and thanks to some black people who called an ambulance I went to the hospital. . . . I did not return to Cipriano's, I went to live with some other people, they lent me clothes and things, and I worked on a farm for a few days, until I met another friend who told me to come and live with his family. That's good, I said, I am looking for somewhere to go and this opportunity came from the sky.

Although Cipriano is renowned for being uniquely cruel and power hungry among the K'iche', the story above shows the extent to which the social consequences of *la violencia* and local power structures at home, continue to affect the social reality of the K'iche' in the transnational context. It also hints at the increased competition and *envidia* that have both led to and have been reinforced by transnationalism.

The life of K'iche' transmigrants in Providence can thus be largely described as one of liminality and limbo, situated somewhere between a hollow absence (whereby the migrant no longer belongs to either the home or host community) and the anticipation of a more stable future (either through a better life at home or further integration into the host context). Many K'iche's cope with this liminality by focusing exclusively on day-to-day activities such as work, child rearing, and saving money. One youth says:

These days I don't have time for anything. Sometimes I tell myself, for what purpose am I working so hard, no? But I think a lot about the future, at least this year I do not have a problem. But what happens if next year they say you can no longer work here, we will not give you a permit. Well, without having worked hard, how can one return home, no? So I am trying now to work as much as I can, to save the *centavitos*, because one doesn't know, right, from one minute to the next they change the laws, and because we are not here legally, well, we cannot say that we will stay because we do not belong to this country, no?

This limbo, characterized by the possibility of deportation and *fracaso*, leads many K'iche's to envision a range of future plans, although the uncertainty of all such plans continuously reorients many to the present and

to the concrete aspects of life in Providence, as this twenty-eight-year-old
man states:

> It is good to have different plans, because we cannot be sure of
> anything. . . . I have three plans now. I would like to stay in this
> country, to get a visa, perhaps to go home and try to get a visa there,
> or maybe get married here. The other plan is to go home, to Xinxuc,
> I would build my house, it would have to be close to my parents'
> house, or maybe somewhere where there is water and electricity. If
> I don't build my own I will build one for them. [P: Would you stay
> there or return here again?] Return here, that is the idea. [P: Why do
> you want a house there if you will return here?] Well, that is why I
> have not done it, otherwise I already would have. It's because if there
> is a problem, if I cannot live here, it would be logical to return to
> my country. And to be ahead a little, I would have a house already.
> To return and live a tranquil life, to look for work there. [P: What
> would you do?] There's lots of . . . that's what I don't know! That is
> something that, I don't know how I will work, because I do not want
> to work as I did before, from sunrise to sunset, I slept two hours,
> no. . . . So yes, yes, someday I would like to have my wife there,
> to have a home for her, so that she does not have to go through
> that. . . . My other plan is to go to Canada, to go see something else,
> and I have a friend there. . . . But if I have to make a decision now,
> because many of my past plans have failed (*fracasado*), many, so
> now I think it is best to live for today, to not think about tomorrow,
> tomorrow I will think about the next day, but at the same time one
> has to think of what might happen.

In this extended present and uncertain future, the passage and very concept
of time—whereby the projected two-year stint is lengthened on a yearly
basis—seems to become qualitatively transformed. Echoing statements by
many other K'iche's, Antonio says:

> I told my father that I would go for two years, but now seven have
> gone by. And I don't feel it, I don't know how they went by, they
> went by so quickly that I don't feel anything, it is as though I had
> just arrived! The time goes so fast!

At the same time, however, due to the diversity of strategies, circumstances, and legal situations, the K'iche' experience this "limbo" in different ways: Some purposefully leave their entire family at home, with

definite plans to return and build their lives in Xinxuc, using Providence as a temporary cash-wage destination. Others change their earlier strategy, hoping to stay in Providence for a longer, indefinite period of time while making periodic home visits. Most, however, continue to be extremely torn between the two contexts, devising a multiplicity of present and future options—which might include returning temporarily, permanently, or not at all—in order to cope with the uncertainty of their situation.

TRANSNATIONAL SOCIAL FIELDS

Transnational migrants are, nonetheless, able to maintain important economic and familial links with the home community, as illustrated at the beginning of this chapter. The huge inflow of money, consumer goods, and new styles resulting from such contact has in many ways altered traditional values and expectations. On the one hand, the impact of transnationalism is continuous with some social changes that were already occurring prior to the exodus and is situated within older discourses surrounding the potential dangers and advantages of movement beyond the community. On the other hand, transnationalism has also brought with it an entirely new set of social and personal benefits, costs, and contradictions, some of which are connected to the accelerated incorporation of global consumer society and its values. These rapid changes, and the meanings given to them by the K'iche' in both home and host communities, form an important dimension of emerging postwar identities in transnational communities such as Xinxuc.

As most studies of transnational migration have pointed out, one of the main projects of transmigrants is to send enough money home to substantially improve their economic stability and class position back home (Rouse 1992; Basch et al. 1994; Georges 1990). The quest for an enhanced social status in the home community may, in fact, be perceived by transmigrants as the only possibility for upward mobility and thus for coping with marginality. Paradoxically, this project can only be made possible by the continual struggle for wages in the host country and, hence, by staying abroad (Bretell 1982). Social and class mobility is thus a complex affair for transmigrants, who juxtapose past memories of the poverty and marginal class position that led them to migrate, their present situation of relative poverty and proletarian labor in the host country, and, finally, future visions of (real or imagined) projects toward upward social mobility, prestige, ownership, and success "back home" (Rouse 1989). Obliged to live in a transnational world and to combine quite different forms of experience, transmigrants thus broaden their repertoire of attitudes and standards, becoming "skilled exponents of a cultural bifocality that defies reduction to a singular order" (Rouse 1992: 15). Rather than forming a syncretic blend of cultural or class systems, however, transnational circuits engender several distinct ways of life that are "chronically maintained in awkward juxtaposition" (Rouse 1989: 147). These "incompatibilities [are] often hidden but always capable of coming to the surface in the course of events" (1989: 32).

For K'iche' transmigrants and their relatives at home, these "awkward juxtapositions" are quite pronounced. As alluded to above (and discussed in further chapters), the K'iche' in Providence seek to distance themselves from the pain, poverty, and shame of "home." At the same time, most maintain important connections with the home community and family—some by going home temporarily or permanently, others by using a variety of strategies to maintain their presence—and indicate success despite their actual absence. Just as those at home rely on relatives in Providence for both sustenance and for helping to make the trip *al Norte*, the entire success of transmigrants in the host community—the ability to *superar* at home—depends on maintaining links with one's family, land, and heritage in Xinxuc.

Although the "present absence" of transmigrants is somewhat reflected at a more symbolic and collective level within the broader *municipio* during particular social events, the material benefits of transnationalism are not targeted toward broader community improvement, a factor related to the tremendous amount of factionalism in both home and host communities that impedes a strong sense of organization. The most significant and obvious connections maintained with the home community are, rather, through family-based organizational and material practices. Sending money and consumer goods, building houses or buying land, and leaving certain family members for the maintenance of *milpas*, child-rearing, and preserving land inheritance all form the crux of K'iche' transnationalism. What are the impacts of these new flows on K'iche's in both home and host communities, and how is the mobilization of resources, strategies, and connections across borders situated within a context of broader cultural and symbolic meanings?

Remittances

Clearly, the most important impact of transnationalism has been the massive amount of money that has been sent home in a relatively short period of time. Throughout Guatemala, US dollar remittances have become a major source of national revenue over the past two decades, having surpassed tourism and coming in second only to Guatemala's main export, coffee.[35] As House and Lovell state, "[T]he Guatemalan economy as a whole is increasingly subsidized by foreign remittances," which are estimated to total US$500 million per year (House and Lovell 1999; Jonas 1995). It is impossible to calculate exact figures for remittances received in rural towns such as Xinxuc, however. Most K'iche's send US dollar money orders through courier companies or with *conocidos* who return home; family members almost always exchange these for local currency with individuals (often influential persons such as the mayor) who can provide better rates than the banks and who then sell the dollars in the capital at a profit.

From November 1996 to November 1997, Xinxuc's main courier office reported approximately US$460,000 received; a second office reported US$58,000 for this time period. Given that Xinxuc has one more courier office (which would not provide access to their records) and that a number of money orders are sent to offices in other towns or through personal contacts, it can be estimated that somewhere between US$600,000 and US$1,000,000 are sent annually to this small town. Most K'iche's state that they try to send home an average of US$200 a month, roughly four times the amount (Q300, or US$50) one currently makes in that time on a coastal plantation.

How are these remittances spent? As numerous economic studies of transnational remittances have shown, large inflows of cash from abroad can result in a variety of changes in local patterns of investment, income generation, and consumption (see Massey et al. 1994 for an overview). At a very visible level, successful Xinxucian transmigrants (both Ladino and Indian) have invested their resources by buying property and building houses (including two-story homes made out of cement or bricks) in the *pueblo,* as evidenced by the construction boom that has occurred since the beginning of the exodus. The growth of transmigrant housing is also evident in some of the *aldeas* close to town (which some now refer to as the *suburbios*), which have become attractive because of their proximity to town, the availability of water and electricity, and the slightly lower land values.

A survey conducted by myself and two assistants at the end of 1997 indicated that, at that time, 100 *pueblo* houses (74 Ladino, 26 Indian) had been constructed (or were under construction) with dollar remittances from Providence.[36] More broadly, 144 *pueblo* households (between one-fourth and one-third of all households) included at least one family member who had gone to Providence (whether or not they had returned). Overall, approximately 250 people (153 Ladinos and 97 Indians)—close to 20 percent of the town's population—had left at some point for Providence.[37] Counting and classifying transmigrant households in the outlying Indian *aldeas,* however, was a more difficult task.[38] Some people had left and returned permanently (and of these, some had built a house in the *pueblo*, others moved to another *aldea*, and still others stayed in the hamlet); others had left and returned but then had left again. In the three hamlets observed, between 10 and 30 percent of the hamlet population was estimated to have left to Providence at some point.[39]

A declared goal for many K'iche' transmigrants (though achieved only by some, given the soaring costs of urban property) is to send enough money to build a *pueblo* house, which is considered to be a major indicator of upward mobility for rural *campesinos*. Ironically, however, these new homes often remain vacant, as transmigrants continue to labor in the United States while families (e.g., wives, parents, and/or children) in Xinxuc sometimes prefer to stay on the rural *milpa*. These houses, built by transmigrants themselves on return visits or by hired workers, stand as silent emblems of absent community members who, despite their situation as mere *mojados* in the United States, can nonetheless achieve and maintain social status for their families in absentia. In the case of Gonzalo and Petrona, moreover, their *pueblo* house is rented out to a Ladino family, to whom they have effectively become absentee landlords, a reversal of the usual ethnic power dynamic that would have been highly unlikely without transnationalism. The "present absence" maintained through the purchase of a *pueblo* home and the notion of juggling two class positions and "homes" are described by Estela in Providence:

> Thank God we are in this country, because if we weren't we would never have been able to progress. We wouldn't live in the *pueblo* the way that we do, to have a house there. . . . So if we had not come here, we would not have arrived at this, to have a house and live in the *pueblo*, we would probably be like before. But because we are here, and we work hard, then we have been able to do something. But we would like to go, to return permanently (*de una vez*) there.

For many of the impoverished rural K'iche', however, remittance money is spent on survival and the alleviation of poverty rather than on such obvious success symbols as urban dwellings. In *el monte* (the mountains), relatives anxiously await monthly *maniorden* (money orders), which are often spent on daily *gastos*, debt repayment, clothes, food, medicine, and fertilizer. This money lessens the likelihood of being kicked off of one's land, having to drag one's children to the coastal plantations, or going hungry. Courier office records show that remittance amounts increase quite substantially around April and May, when the costs of *milpa* maintenance go up; at this time, money must be sent to pay for fertilizer, seeds, and perhaps *mozos* who take charge of planting, preparing, and weeding the *milpa* in the absence of the male transmigrant labor. Around November, remittances again increase as cash is needed to pay *mozos* for cutting, gathering, transporting, and peeling the *milpa* corn that will, hopefully, enable the family to subsist for the remaining year. Transmigrants in Providence thus remain connected to the agricultural cycle at home through the (often desperate) phone calls and letters from relatives requesting more money during these periods.

With time (and *suerte*), however, many transmigrant *campesinos* do try to save enough money to buy additional *milpa* land and even livestock. Over the last few decades land has become scarcer, so the size of inherited plots shrink with each generation. Some young Indian men, who out of *pura obligación* send money home for their parents' *gastos,* try to save enough money to buy a plot of land and perhaps even a house to which they will (ideally) return when they establish a family. Transmigrant heads of family or married couples, for their part, often try to buy more land to pass on to their children (who may or may not nonetheless join them in Providence). Although newly bought land is sometimes used as a *milpa* (that is, for the subsistence of the remaining family), in some cases it remains uncultivated as there are not enough men to tend it and the cost of hiring *mozos* exceeds the remaining family's subsistence needs. Like empty *pueblo* homes, then, this unused land seems to embody the "liminal" transmigrant project, the anticipation of an undefined future whereby certain family members will be able to enjoy the fruits of transmigrant labor at home.

In addition, land acquired by transmigrants—whether those from the *pueblo* or hamlets—is increasingly bought in places removed from their homes, for example in other *aldeas.* Traditional land inheritance patterns, already undergoing changes due to land pressures prior to the war and distorted by the many dislocations of *la violencia,* are thus being further transformed through the availability of transnational remittances. While enabling some transmigrant families to purchase more land (or a *pueblo* home) rather than being pushed off of shrinking plots, the cash inflow also leads, in some respects, to a greater spatial fragmentation of the immediate and extended family within the boundaries of the *municipio.*

Economic studies point to the positive and negative effects of remittances, both of which can effect a potentially radical change on the socioeconomic context of the home community (Massey et al. 1994). Transnational remittances may have an equalizing effect on local economies by allowing poorer members to "leapfrog" their way up the socioeconomic ladder, as has been the case for some *aldea* K'iche's. In communities where remittances are spent on productive enterprises and income-producing activities, transmigrant families may not only further improve their local status and assets but create further employment (e.g., for *mozos* and other laborers). The positive effect of productive activities may be further reinforced where skills, knowledge, education, and expertise acquired in the host context are transferred back to the home community (House and Lovell 1999). In Xinxuc, only a few successful transmigrants, primarily Ladinos but including some K'iche's, have returned and invested their savings in the local economy (e.g., by buying a truck to start a lumber business, opening a shop, or providing construction equipment to build other transmigrant homes). The transference of skills from Providence, moreover, is limited, since most transmigrants work in the unskilled industrial sector. A minority of K'iche's (mostly urban dwellers) have allocated part of their remittance money to the education of their children or younger siblings, pointing to long-term strategies for family status enhancement. For the most part, however, K'iche' remittances have largely been spent on land, housing, and everyday consumption.

On the other hand, the inflow of remittance money has also been shown in many studies to have an "unequalizing" effect by creating increased class cleavages, uneven income and property distribution, and feelings of relative deprivation (among nontransmigrant families), thereby encouraging further migration among those who strive to "catch up" (Massey et al. 1994). Due to the inflation of land prices usually caused by transnationalism, moreover, land ownership often becomes concentrated in the hands of a few successful transmigrants, rendering subsequent transmigration increasingly competitive. In addition, transmigrant families whose relatives *allá lejos* terminate or greatly reduce their remitting lose not only the advantage of receiving US dollars (becoming unable to compete with other transmigrant families) but also often find themselves without male household labor, their main source of income and of *milpa* sustenance. Such is the case of some K'iche' women, for example, who find themselves with few economic options other than joining the transnational circuit.

Although some studies have shown that with time the unequalizing tendencies of transnational migration subside as a majority of households come to include transmigrants (Georges 1990), Xinxuc has not (yet) reached this "critical mass." Given the constantly changing and volatile nature of undocumented cross-border migration, moreover, remittance strategies are rarely fixed, but rather shift over time. Due to circumstance or choice, not all transmigrants are able to send remittances at the same rate. Indeed, the amount and allocation of remittance money in individual households may depend on a host of factors, including the transmigrant's household economic status prior to departure, the length of time spent in Providence, access to a stable job, the number of family members sending remittances, a sudden illness, changes in US policy, and so forth. Although one transmigrant may, as planned, be able to save enough to return permanently within a given time, another might, with the arrival of a new baby in Providence, have to reduce the amount of cash sent home; yet a third may choose to accelerate the remitting process by "sending for" a son or other relative. Thus, although transnational migration in Xinxuc has increasingly become a normative part of life, fostering various systems and networks of mutual support, it is also a highly uneven process, contributing to an increasingly competitive economic milieu and enhancing class differences.

Another negative economic impact of transnationalism noted in the literature, evident in Xinxuc, is increased economic dependence on outside income, particularly when families abandon local economic activities to subsist on remittances (Pessar 1988). Migration to *la costa del Norte* has almost fully replaced coastal migrations in some hamlets and is often seen as a logical step "up" from urban migration. Despite its apparent volatility, it is also perceived (and hoped) by many to be both more lucrative and more stable than productive local endeavors such as *comerciante* activities. Dependence on transnational income is particularly evident in the case of numerous transmigrants who return home with plans to stay but, in the absence of local jobs and income, eventually return to Providence for another indefinite stint. As one Xinxucian states, "Over there they work a few years, then they return. They go around with their cars and things, up and down the streets, but after a while there is nothing left, they are here with arms crossed and have to go back." While some transmigrant households use remittances to supplement local income sources provided by remaining family members, others become totally dependent upon cash inflows from the United States. Such dependence may even lead to the abandonment of subsistence activities (*milpa* cultivation) as children of transmigrants no longer wish to work with an *azadón*, preferring to subsist on parental remittances and, perhaps, planning to migrate eventually themselves. These changes are caused not only by the receipt of monthly remittances but also by the long-term familial separations whereby, in the absence of their parents, children no longer learn, nor wish to learn, the skills needed for *milpa* maintenance (often to the great chagrin of their grandparents).

The fact that outward migration brings with it both potential economic benefits (the ability for the poor to *superar*) and dangers (increased class cleavages and the possibility of greater poverty) is not new to most Indians. These tendencies were already present in the previous century's coastal migrations, and the large migrations (both rural and urban) taking place in the three decades preceding the violence were enhancing class differentiation at an accelerated pace in communities such as Xinxuc. What the new transnational migration has done, however, is greatly exaggerate both the potential for success and the risk of failure associated with outside movement. In a community already divided and fragmented by religious, class, ethnic, and wartime factions, thus, transnationalism has added one more divisive dimension, in spite of the networks and connections set up to facilitate the movement *al Norte*. The sheer amount of money sent by Providence transmigrants, moreover, has not only heightened economic competition between households in the home community but has set in place new expectations and values that both clash with and are adapted to older social relations defining community norms and identities.

Symbolic Markers of Success

The public display of wealth and status in home (and sometimes in host) communities takes on prime importance for transmigrants and their families, particularly since the desire to validate or enhance class status can only be achieved by accepting low-status, marginal positions in the host country. Increased access to and evidence of host context resources such as consumer goods, new styles, and current fashions become intimately related to the perceived social status of transmigrants and their families, and are thus integral to the manner in which they represent themselves to their communities and to themselves (Thomas-Hope 1985).

Projecting an image of success at home is thus critical to transmigrant K'iche's, who do not want to be perceived as having wasted their time or as having accomplished nothing during their time abroad. This image is also an indication of belonging to the select group who have been *listo* (clever) enough to cross two borders, survive in distant Providence, and send home the goods to prove it. As Ibañez (2001) states, "[A]ccess to certain material goods, the consumption of certain commodities, may . . . become a means of access to an imagined group represented by those goods; it may become a form of looking for recognition. Material things make one belong or rather, give one the feeling of belonging to a desired community." Regardless of their abilities to save enough money for larger investments, certain symbolic markers of belonging (directly or indirectly) to the "desired community" of Providence (whether as a return transmigrant, an absent transmigrant, or a transmigrant relative) often adorn homes in Xinxuc. Consumer goods such as televisions, stereo systems, and/or refrigerators (either sent from Providence or bought with Providence remittances), which sometimes stand in odd contrast to the poverty of the home setting, are prominently displayed in front rooms along with posters of US flags and images of American consumerism and success (e.g., expensive race cars). At their side, numerous snapshots of the K'iche' transmigrant, standing proudly next to a newly purchased car on a Providence street, are common.

Symbolic displays of transnationalism are particularly evident in the style and dress of those who return *para dar una vuelta* (for a visit). Returning transmigrants, in particular young men, often indicate the fact that they have been *allá lejos* and can afford a consumer lifestyle through new styles of clothing that include expensive brand names and fashionable styles. The (often dirty) secondhand trousers, T-shirts, sandals, straw hats, and *moral* (traditional bag) worn by male *campesinos* are replaced with the global consumer aesthetic of new baggy jeans, Nike baseball caps and shoes, and perhaps even a gold chain or earring. Women are far less likely to return only temporarily, given the many dangers associated with the cross-border trip; those who do come home always return to wearing *traje,* though they may now show that they can afford an expensive new *guipil* or leather shoes.

The desire to show one's "difference" upon such visits is illustrated in the case of Petrona, who returned to Xinxuc after nearly seven years in Providence in order to fetch her two teenage daughters, one of whom was threatening to get married against her will. Before her trip, Petrona had her mother buy her an expensive new *traje* in Xinxuc; in Providence, she had her hair permed and new gold caps placed on her teeth (a sign of wealth). She also brought with her a prized stylish leather coat, an item of clothing unseen on K'iche' women (particularly hamlet women) at home. Knowing that she would be unable to carry the coat back with her on her return trip as a *mojado,* she asked me, already in Providence (knowing about my upcoming trip to Xinxuc), to bring it back on my return flight to the United States. This sort of "conspicuous consumption" is much less marked among long-term or permanent returnees, who not only lose access to US dollars but also become aware of the tremendous criticisms and envies elicited by such behavior (as discussed below).

Some Indian men show off their transnationalism through a relationship with a *gringa* (who is often, though not always, Dominican or Puerto Rican). While marrying an American has its pragmatic purposes, it also seems to form part of the imaginary of the "American Dream": Even before leaving, young men often state that they hope to acquire a *gringa* girlfriend if they go to Providence. As Virgilio says, "For a young man it is like having another world, like having something better!" Some young men send home pictures of themselves with these girlfriends, and a couple have brought them to Xinxuc during the *fiesta*.[40] For K'iche' women, on the other hand, the idea of marrying a non-K'iche' is not even entertained, either in Xinxuc or Providence. As preservers of tradition, such a move would be entirely unacceptable to the family and community. Women tend to view the coupling of indigenous men with American women quite scornfully. One K'iche' woman in Providence expresses this disdain: "I've seen some Guatemalans here, such little Indians (*aaii, pero bien indiecitos, indiecitos*) but they can take these American women who are fat and white! And sometimes they leave their wives back home."

Xinxuc's most obvious and celebrated expression of local community identity, as in all other municipalities, is the yearly *fiesta*. Transmigrants who go home *para dar una vuelta* (for a visit) almost always plan their return around *fiesta* week,[41] and Xinxucians who have migrated within Guatemala (e.g., to the capital) also take the opportunity to return home. Both Ladinos and Indians participate in the long-planned event, which takes place primarily in the *pueblo*. Despite the fact that the community as a whole celebrates the same town saint, the *fiesta* is largely divided along ethnic lines, although in recent years this division has become based more strongly on class since wealthier Indians participate in some of the Ladino events. Xinxuc's indigenous *fiesta* has not retained the same degree of tradition as have the *fiestas* of many other towns in El Quiché. Although the connection between *costumbre, cofradía,* and the *fiesta* cycle remains strong in its main *costumbrista* hamlet, the two town *cofradías,* run by wealthy K'iche' families, focus mostly on garnering financial support and organizing festivities for the *fiesta*. Indians elect a *reina indígena* (an indigenous beauty queen, usually a young girl from the hamlets) who must demonstrate indigenous values such as knowledge of K'iche' language and dance. Indian religious processions travel from the hamlets to the *pueblo*'s church and *calvario,* praying for an auspicious year and agricultural cycle. The town *cofradías* also hold several *zarabandas* (dances), raucous and long-lasting events that often involve much heavy *cuxa* drinking, live music, and dancing.

The Ladino-run *pueblo* holds its own set of louder, more expensive *fiesta* events. During the town's beauty pageant, the (usually) Ladina *reina* wears the indigenous *traje típico* as well as fancy evening wear. Festivities include three *convites* (parades) during which pairs of Xinxucians, wearing elaborate and colorful costumes ranging from Spanish Conquistadors and North American Indians to pop culture icons such as the Flintstones and punk rockers (and, in 1997, a smirking Bill Clinton and a seductive Hillary), dance their way through the town all day, revealing their identities only at night. Only wealthier townspeople (those who can afford to pay for the costume) participate in the *convites*. In addition, the *pueblo* puts on a formal *baile,* or ball, in the *salon municipal* (municipal hall), attended almost exclusively by Ladinos.

Although the K'iche' in Providence do not reproduce the *fiesta* in the host context (for reasons that will become clearer in the following chapter), they do nonetheless organize contributions for the event.[42] Some of the children of the main *cofradía* families, themselves transmigrant youth, collect money from Providence K'iche's (those who can afford it) and return to Xinxuc to participate in the *fiesta* and deliver the donations.[43] During one of the main *fiesta* events, US transmigrant donors (as well as local ones) are individually thanked, by name, over a loudspeaker. These same youths arrange to have the *fiesta* events videotaped (including the *convites, zarabandas,* and the acknowledgments); upon their return to Providence, the videotapes are circulated among K'iche's who made donations.[44] Contributing to the *fiesta,* then, is another way of maintaining an "absent presence" and a connection with the home community and of showing one's transmigrant success (or at least one's nonfailure) to the home community. It is, moreover, the only time during which transmigrants *allá lejos* are formally acknowledged at the community level. Of course, returning home for the *fiesta* is an even stronger statement of success, indicating that one has time and money to spare and is not afraid of border crossing.[45] Some transmigrant Indians, moreover, now participate in the (previously Ladino-dominated) *pueblo convites* in addition to the Indian *zarabandas.* Thus, transnationalism does not erase the ethnic divide of the home community (so clearly symbolized in the *fiesta*), but it does change class positions.

Changes in Family and Gender Relations

The impact of transnationalism on K'iche' family relations can be highly paradoxical and wrought with problems. On the one hand, the transmigrant project is dependent on the family bonds of cooperation that have ideally formed part of traditional K'iche' identity. Because transmigration is often perceived as a project of the extended family, relations of exchange and reciprocity between those who leave and those who stay are ideally built into the family strategy. Among some older couples, women are left to administer local domestic concerns (such as hiring *mozos,* ensuring *milpa* maintenance, organizing the purchase of new property, and raising children) while their husbands send money for safekeeping or for *gastos.* Among younger couples, the wife will often stay with her in-laws, providing domestic labor until the day her husband returns to build a home or, alternatively, takes her with him to Providence. In the case of couples who leave together (or women who leave in search of their delinquent husbands), either maternal or paternal grandparents are usually given the responsibility of raising grandchildren in exchange for remittances and the company and domestic help provided by their grandchildren. Remaining children, for their part, are often expected to take on some of the roles of their absent parents, completing chores and helping with *milpa* labor. Often, these children remain the only family for widowed grandmothers whose own children have migrated, providing an important psychological reassurance and ensuring the continuation of progeny at home. As Doña Jacinta states:

> My grandchildren keep me happy, they help me and are my companions. If they were not here I would have nobody to keep me company. When my daughter left I became very sad, but since she has small children over there, they are more important than those who are here, so she had to stay over there.

Finally, parents who agree to sponsor their older children's *viaje* (that is, raise the funds or mortgage their land), and perhaps take care of administering savings, do so with the expectation that their children will fulfill the family obligation of sending money for *gastos*. Other relations of exchange might also take place between more distant family members—for example, nephews and cousins may agree to help tend the *milpa* or build new additions to a home with the agreement that they will eventually be sponsored to *viajar* by the transmigrant. Given the much longer history of seasonal and other migrations, such arrangements, which are meant both to facilitate the balance between maintaining the *milpa* and ensuring cash income, as well as to secure a certain degree of familial cohesion and continuity, are not new to the K'iche'.

On the other hand, the distance, uncertainty, lengthy separations, and the expectations related to remittances can lead to increased mistrust, fragmentation, and a disintegration of family bonds of respect and trust that were already devastated by *la violencia*. A whole range of resentments, fears, and criticisms are expressed toward family members at home and abroad on both ends of the transnational circuit. In Xinxuc, remaining family members are constantly preoccupied with the amount and pace of remittances, often comparing their own situation to other transmigrant families who seem to *superar* more rapidly. As Don Mingo, an elderly K'iche' man, says,

> I see that my children have not accomplished much (*no han hecho nada*), they have only been able to pay back their *deudas* and send our weekly *gastos*. They do not have anything. Who knows how other people make money, what they do to make their *centavos*. After only a few months over there, one or two years, they begin to build a big house or they can buy land. I don't know how they do it, I say that they probably steal or something because after only a little time one can see that there is a lot of money there.

This kind of competition, the fear that transmigrant kin will either *fracasar* (fail)—or appear to have *fracasado*—and the lavish displays of some returning transmigrants often lead dependent family members to put tremendous pressure on their relatives for more money and to question the manners in which they are spending both time and money in Providence. This in turn can cause anger and resentment among family members in Providence, particularly when their relatives at home do not appear to understand the amount of work and suffering that goes into sustaining a family on both sides of the border, or the cost of living in the United States. As one transmigrant woman in Providence says:

> Ah! Some people at home think that here one just comes to pick up money, that it is laying on the ground and one can sweep it up with a broom! It makes me mad, it is not true. Here one suffers to earn money! Here the person who does not work for just one day loses money. In Guatemala you do not lose anything if you do not work for a day. Here, with just one missed day, you earn less. Because you have to count the money you spend on rent, electricity, gas, the cable and the telephone, the food, the clothes. Here we suffer! But they don't think about this.

Another says:

> The problem is that here one can buy a car, to have a car, and one feels stronger, one feels better, but what we earn in a week is not much. So we pay car insurance, and we send money home, and if we want to have a drink or eat in a restaurant, there go $20, and if one invites friends, because here the loneliness necessitates friendships, and there goes the money. And so instead of sending money, there is no more money. And then if you have an accident, you must pay a fine, and so if you make what most of us make here, then with all these *gastos* there is hardly enough for the rent or for the family back there. And it is for that reason that the families start to fight, to divide completely.

Moreover, many Providence K'iche's do not trust their family members to spend remittances wisely. A few young transmigrants, for example, have been highly frustrated with their parents' poor investment choices at home. One, who states that his parents always *fracasan* and misspend his dollars (e.g., by buying animals that die), started to give clear instructions for remittance spending, incurring his parents' wrath. Another, whose father has at times spent remittances by lending money to other community members

who do not repay, angrily states "¡No gano dinero aca para otra persona!"
(I do not earn money over here for somebody else!). Other transmigrants,
moreover, fearful that their young wives will misspend their money, remit
only to their parents and ask them to allocate the wife's portion. Familial
mistrust over remittances, thus, occurs on both ends of the transnational
circuit.

A slow remittance pace can be extremely disquieting for those left
behind, particularly for wives who are forced to head their households on
their own. Often not even having taken part in their husband's decision
to migrate, these women are left with the very difficult situation of raising
children and managing the home and *milpa* on their own. Doña Ramona,
for example, is sad, desperate, and angry over her situation and the fact
that Virgilio's remittance money is too low to cover the couple's many obligations. Virgilio, who has no legal papers in Providence, has had a very
difficult time finding a steady job and enough weekly hours; in addition, he
was unable to work for six full months after being diagnosed with cancer
and undergoing chemotherapy. Ramona has been left to handle the huge
debt incurred by her husband back home, constantly fearing that she, her
mother, and her two daughters will be expelled from their home by the
moneylenders, who regularly come knocking. At the same time, she has a
difficult time making monthly remittances meet the many household needs
such as baby formula and medicine for her sick toddler, her daughter's
schooling, monthly *gastos,* and managing her *milpa* land. In the first year
of Virgilio's absence, Ramona had to travel alone to the *milpa,* located in
an *aldea* outside of the *pueblo,* to work on its cultivation, incurring much
criticism from other community members.

Indeed, not only do such wives need to reorganize their lives in order
to take on activities traditionally occupied by their husbands or to take on
new ones to supplement their remittances when necessary, but they also
must guard against the scorn and judgments made by the broader community for behaving too independently, fearing as well that their husbands
may hear negative rumors concerning their behavior and therefore stop
sending money. Ana, for example, begged me not to show her husband in
Providence a picture of her weaving *guipiles* as part of a PLANTAS crafts
project; as I found out, he had forbidden her to work outside the home and
she feared his anger if he were to find out. Ramona, on the few occasions
that she has wished to travel beyond the usual confines of daily life (once
for a religious pilgrimage, another time to visit a sibling in another department), made sure that she called Virgilio first to tell him, "before he hears
something bad over there." On the second occasion, Virgilio, who could
barely pay his rent money, did not accept her collect call, thus aggravating
Ramona's frustration.

By far the biggest fear for most women is that their husbands will find a new wife in Providence and terminate remittances, a possible scenario grounded not only in reality but also in the constant *chismes* (gossip) and rumors circulating between Xinxuc and Providence. A woman in Providence explains:

> There are some men who only think of finding another woman here, and the ones back home do not matter, or their children. These are men who have become totally lost and their women back home are in need. There are many men who do this, we see and we hear that women back home suffer because they have no money and their children are left alone.

For Ramona, like others, this fear even predated her husband's departure:

> When Virgilio said that he wanted to leave, I told him fine, well go, I was angry, I know that they go over there to find another woman. . . . And now he owes all this money and there is nothing I can do. I would like to get mad at him (*maltratarle*), but he is not even here for that!

The extreme uncertainty caused by a husband's absence (the constant concern over whether he is drinking or sick, why he is not calling and sends less money than others, whether he has lost his job or has a new woman) combined with women's feeling of abandonment (to raise children, tend the *milpa,* and fend off critics and moneylenders entirely on their own) can lead to a profound anxiety. Many women like Ramona, moreover, are unable to share these problems with others: Too afraid to tell her own family members that her home has been mortgaged for Virgilio's debt and fearful of the scorn from other women in the community, Ramona feels entirely isolated, cries often, and has chronic insomnia. This level of despair is shared by women in other situations, for example wives of transmigrants who are left behind to live with abusive in-laws. For all these reasons, it is not uncommon to hear of women who fall ill with *tristeza* (sadness) or *tiricia* due to their husband's departure. *Tiricia* is a traditional illness category among Mayans and other indigenous groups, caused by a rupture in emotional harmony due to the departure of a loved one or a sense of intense displacement and uprootedness following migration.[46] It is described as follows by Barrios:

> An illness occasioned by separation from a loved person or place, which causes extreme *tristeza*. Its symptoms are: yellowish skin,

inactivity, perhaps intestinal problems, a lack of appetite and fever. Its treatment is to return to the place or person with which one *se halle* (that one loves or is accustomed to) so that the symptoms stop; or, give the person consolation by telling them they will soon reunite with the loved person or place. The situation may be softened also by providing certain comforts to the person with *tiricia,* and by spoiling them. (1987: 67; my translation)

I heard of several cases of *tristeza* and *tiricia* caused by a husband's departure to the United States, a few that, it was said, had resulted in alcoholism and/or death. I met one young woman, for example, who had become completely despondent and exhibited numerous psychosomatic symptoms since her husband left for Providence. The husband was eventually forced to return to Xinxuc, though he soon decided to bring his cured wife back to the United States with him.

Again, however, this mistrust concerning spousal loyalty runs both ways. Men in Providence often fear that their wife at home will, in their absence, take on a new man and spend their hard-earned money on the new relationship. As evidenced by the following quote from a K'iche' woman in Providence, all of these fears reinforce each other, are further aggravated by the murky communication and rampant transnational rumor mill, and can lead to drastic transnational fights and separations:

Take the case of Juan downstairs, he is a humble man, he is
not abusive, he is responsible and sends money to his wife and
everything. Well there has been gossip that he has another woman
here. You know why they say this? Because he lives in an apartment
with two men, but they have a sister there. So in Guatemala they
don't think about how he lives there because he cannot afford his
own place, they think he is there because of the girl. How mean-
spirited! (*¡Que malpensados!*). That boy lives from work to home, he
comes home only to sleep, he goes to work, he is even thin, there
is no one to cook for him, he burns his fingers when he cooks!
And over there his wife is enjoying his money with another man,
because they say she has another one, and she sent word to him, by
telephone she told him she does not love him anymore, because over
there they are saying that he has another woman. It's a lie!
    And he has sent a lot of money, but now he doesn't anymore,
because of what she says. Can you imagine that? To spend years
here, working, earning that money, sending it to your wife, and why
does he send it? Because he has trust, because he wants her to be
his partner that he will always have, with children also. And then

your wife says you have another woman. And she tells him not to come home, to just stay here. It hurts when they say things like this! If it is true, it is one thing. But this man has no woman. You know what he does when he hears these things? He starts drinking, and he throws himself into the depths of alcohol. Why? Because his wife discourages him (*lo desanima*). . . . The women over there, whose husbands come here so that they can come out ahead (*para sacarlas adelante*), so that their children can come out ahead . . . but there is no more trust! If one's husband comes here one thinks: He is a lost husband. But it's not true! There are many men who come here to work, to sacrifice themselves for their families. But it is the gossip, the rumors, the *envidia* and the hatreds that we have, and there is nothing to be done.

Transmigration has also provoked numerous changes in parent-child relations. The absence of parents is often highly problematic for caretakers in Xinxuc, particularly as children grow older, causing a great degree of frustration and resentment. As many in Xinxuc say, this absence leads not only to children's growing lack of respect toward familial authority (toward the parent or grandparent at home, and toward the absent parent) but also to a lack of knowledge, skills, and desire necessary to learn and practice *milpa* maintenance and domestic chores, both of which, as part of *la experiencia,* are critical not only to survival but to the continuation of local Indian identity. Discussing how children are left *sin ninguna orientación* (without any guidance), one woman says:

My husband said that in order to avoid *la migra* over there he would move further away (*mas lejos*). I said, "Why go *mas lejos*? You will die over there. Come home to see your children so that they will respect you. They no longer respect me, they no longer carry the *leña* when I ask them to."

This woman's husband eventually returned for a visit but spent much of the time drinking heavily; her greatest fears remained not only the potential loss of remittances but the additional fact that her sons, without a solid male authority figure, were learning a bad example, no longer performed their duties, and would leave her also. Doña Jacinta—who, like many grandmothers, takes care of several grandchildren for her various transmigrant children—also complains that her two teenage daughters in Xinxuc are being brought up without their mother. As a result, she says, they are not learning how to do *oficios* (domestic duties) such as cooking and cleaning, do not obey her, will not learn how to be good wives, and will choose bad husbands:

> It think that if their parents were over there without children, it would be fine, but since they have children it is better that they return to show them how to do the work that we do here. But it is unfortunate for my grandchildren because they have them split up, some here and some there. Now I worry that these ones here are thinking of marrying, or something, and if the man is good it is one thing but otherwise. . . . You know today all the young women are having children without fathers, and that worries me. My granddaughters will suffer if they do not find good husbands. But their parents who are over there do not pay attention, they should come and see their children here. I've told them many times, but they do not come, they answer that they will come back in a few years and will see us then.

The concern with the loss of local values, work knowledge, and *experiencia* is also expressed with regard to K'iche' children growing up in the United States, who "no longer know how to cultivate the land." Summarizing the frustration felt by those who have grandchildren on both sides of the border, Doña Natalia explains:

> I think it is bad that they went over there, they forget how to cultivate the land, the children lose their customs, their language, they do not speak *dialecto*. They have left their land, and it is a pity because these children will not know how to live here. Over there, they only play, they do not learn to plant or to cut the *leña*. If they go there, they do not respect their parents anymore, because there it is different. Here, at eight or nine years, we learn to carry the *leña*, and one must accustom one's body to do that. There, they are sitting, they do not learn to carry *leña* with a *mecapal*, and then later they do not want to sow the *milpa*.
>   It's better if they stay here so that they do not forget how to cultivate the *milpa*. This year for example nobody will help me sow the *milpa*. The children are growing but the father is not there. The grandchildren do not want to help because they know that their parents will send money, so they do not want to work. The grandmother says work, it is for your good, to have the maize, but they do not respect one. Elena, for example, she does not want to sow the *milpa* or study, she just wants to go over there.

Parents of transmigrants, like wives, fear as well that in the absence of the family their children in Providence will abandon themselves to vice and moral or sexual laxity and will *portarse mal* (behave badly). While parents fear that their sons may become involved in suspect activities (drinking, crime) or become *perdido* (morally lost), both parents and male kin in Providence often discourage young women from making the *viaje,* arguing not only that the border crossing will compromise their chastity but also that K'iche' women in Providence become promiscuous:

> I do not want my daughters to go over there: My sons say that
> a cousin left, but she behaved very badly over there, she became
> arrogant (*creida*), she goes with men even if they are married, and
> these men start to mistreat their own wives because of this girl.

As we can see, transnationalism has, in many ways, disrupted the bonds of respect, obedience, and trust between couples and generations that have ideally governed K'iche' family relations. Such problems, however, are not necessarily new to the K'iche'. Indeed, González (1999) describes the types of family grievances among the K'iche' that have long been considered to transgress family norms and values and for which they have traditionally appealed to the informal, community justice system:

> Alcoholism, because it affects the man's responsibilities as a husband
> and father; disagreements and fights between husband and wife;
> the man's non-fulfillment in sustaining the household; the woman's
> non-fulfillment in her domestic obligations; the abandonment of
> the home; infidelity; arguments between parents and children,
> caused by a non-conformance in the distribution of inheritance;
> and disobedience on the part of children in not carrying out the
> agricultural work that their parents require. All of these are practices
> that disturb the family's harmony. (1999: 30; my translation)

Clearly, transnational migration has not only exacerbated the likelihood of such conflicts, but in addition the traditional mechanisms for resolving them, interference on the part of elders, is no longer possible given the distance between family members. And not only attitudes toward familial values of respect have been transformed, but the very relations to the land, *milpa,* and domestic work through which local K'iche' identity is both embodied and passed on to future generations have also been altered.

Although transnational migration has created a tremendous amount of mistrust and resentment among relatives at home, it should be pointed out that criticisms of those who leave are also highly ambivalent. Because people depend on remittances—or perhaps even plan to go to Providence eventually themselves—the frustration with absence and abandonment is often mixed with an acknowledgment that the migration provides people's livelihoods, as illustrated by these three quotes:

> Although one is always sad because one's children leave . . . well, if they return it is good, or if not, it is also good, those who send us money it is good.

> We don't know what to say about them because they make a lot of money there, but here they leave their children behind and everything.

> I am happy and I am sad that they are over there. For me, it doesn't seem good that they are not in their own country. It's better if they come home and plant their *milpa*, if they have land here. I think that maybe it is good that they went, but perhaps it is bad because they don't plant the corn on their land.

The "liminal" social position of transmigrants in Providence, thus, seems to be further reinforced by the ambivalence of those at home who, while often criticizing and blaming absent relatives for the disintegration of family and the values that comprise traditional identities, simultaneously count on them for the very survival and continuity of such identities in Xinxuc.

LOCAL IDIOMS IN TRANSNATIONALISM: INAUTHENTICITY, CHISMES, AND ENVIDIA

The transnational character of Xinxuc is in a process of evolution: people continue to leave and to return, and the transnational project has produced varying degrees of success and failure among individuals and families. At a broader community level, how do the K'iche' on either side of the border make sense of the vast social and economic changes, as well as the uncertainty, brought by transnational migration? What idioms do they use to make sense of the new competition, symbolic markers of difference and consumerism, and transformed values and expectations engendered by cross-border movement? Are these discourses continuous with older ways of coping with change and the threat caused by outside migration?

At a collective level, there exists a highly critical social discourse concerning transmigration, centered around the threat that this movement and its resulting displays of wealth and consumerism pose to local indig-

enous values of humility, hard work, and social conformity. Unlike the accusations and frustrations aimed at specific family members for particular
reasons (which cannot be publicly acknowledged), the social discourse has
a more diffused, unspecified target and is reflective of a more "imaginary"
and often highly creative discourse on transnationalism. The K'iche' in
Xinxuc (including transmigrant relatives and even returnees) often state
that those who leave take on *malas costumbres* (bad habits) such as drugs,
long hair and earrings, homosexuality, and crime. Others say that transmigrants become vulgar consumers who lose all sense of respect. Some say
that transmigrants leave their home only to work like dogs, get sick, and
die over there, while others on the contrary argue that transmigrants are
weak people who are lazy and are not able to work the land at home; the
proof, they say, is that they become fat. Some of the harshest criticisms are
reserved for those who return temporarily. The latter are often accused of
being *creido* (stuck up), proud, and disdainful, as well as of wasting their
money frivolously. An exaggerated version of this disapproval is given by
Gaspar, a young Mayanist who, while being a particularly severe critic of
transnationalism, nonetheless echoes the more veiled attitudes expressed
by others in Xinxuc:

> Those who are over there are like slaves, they are not part of
> anything. They just send money home to forget that they are slaves,
> and to forget their guilt, they only think about money, they stop
> thinking about their family, their land. They have lost their past, but
> they have no future. . . . The money that comes from there is just
> paper, just water (*puro papel, pura agua*), and those who come back
> are also paper people, they are not able to work here (*no aguantan
> trabajar aquí*), and the money they make, it's gone in a month. They
> go around showing their shoes, their clothes, inviting everyone to
> drink, and after a few months they have nothing left and they go
> back! We only make a little money here but with this we eat, we
> cultivate the land, and it lasts. Over there they make money, but they
> never rest!

Accusations of arrogance (*orgullo*) and a loss of respect, however, are
not expressed only by those at home but are extremely pronounced on
both sides of the border. Some K'iche's in Providence—particularly those
who maintain a stronger identification with the hometown, regardless of
their length of stay—tend to be quite critical of others whom they accuse of
denying their own background and *raza* (race). They often speak of other
transmigrants who become *creidos, orgullosos,* who "change" (*cambian*)
and act as though they are not "what they are" (*lo que son*) because they

do not want to be *de menor categoria* (of a lower category). The latter are contrasted to those who *siguen igual* (remain the same), as most assured me they had done. For example:

> The ones who really do harm are the youth, they think they are better (*se creen*), they have their cars and then they pretend they are not even Guatemalan.

> Some people become so arrogant here, they were already arrogant over there, but here they become even worse. Speaking of how they talk, how one carries oneself, and one's clothes: They dress better than one, they like good clothes, they don't let themselves look neglected, they don't allow people to tell them what to do (*ya no se dejen*).

The discourse on authenticity and change has long been part of Indian culture, since accusations of inauthenticity and ladinoization have often been made against Indians who have left the community and rural life. In part, then, the above statements might be read as the continuation of an ongoing historical dialogue within indigenous communities. In trans-nationalism, *cambiar* is not clearly associated with having left *campesino* life and one's land (since everyone in Providence has done this to some extent or another, and many in Xinxuc might expect to eventually), and it is not even necessarily attributed solely to improved social status (since class differences already existed before the migration); rather, it becomes an indirect notion of identity change associated with cultural attitudes and values. Moreover, as we have seen, K'iche's place a very negative value on displays of Otherness—such as conspicuous displays of wealth and behaving in ways that defy social norms of humility, conformity and respect. Becoming *orgulloso*, showing off, or losing touch with one's responsibilities at home clearly counter such traditional K'iche' values.

Herein lies one of the most profound contradictions of K'iche' trans-nationalism: While transnational success is based upon whether one is able to *superar* and therefore gain material wealth (a goal reinforced by the expectations and pressures put forth by family members at home as well as by American consumer society), the notion of standing out or displaying success is viewed with suspicion by the collectivity and can invite, from others in either the home or host community, *envidias* (envy), *chismes* (malicious gossip), and perhaps even *brujería* (witchcraft). Given the relatively large amounts of US dollars that some K'iche's are able to send home and the resulting threat of rapidly increased social inequalities, *envidia* has, indeed, been reappropriated as the most important explanatory model for the successes and failures of transnational migrants. *Envidia* seems to govern every aspect of transmigrants' lives. Those who succeed (in Providence, those who find good jobs or buy nice cars, and in Xinxuc, those who receive or return with substantial remittances) must be careful not to elicit *envidias*, which might lead to witchcraft and disaster. It is fairly common to hear, for example, of K'iche's who rebuff family or friends in Providence because they are *envidioso* that the latter had an easier border crossing or found a job quickly. At the same time, successful transmigrants might also be accused by others of having succeeded through having *envidiado* another person. Transmigrants who fail (*fracasan*), for their part, might suspect that somebody else had *envidias* for them. And those who behave in antisocial ways (e.g., Cipriano) are usually said to be highly *envidiosos* of other transmigrants (such as Inocente) who might *superar* further or faster than they do. Angelino, a thirty-five-year-old transmigrant, explains:

> There are many people, even from my own family, who were very happy when I used to drink, but when I stopped drinking, I bought a car, I bought some clothes, I had some nice things, and that bothered them. . . . And as I had my own place, my things in order, they didn't like it. And now it's worse because I have been able to get legal papers, and I have some cousins who have been here much longer than me. But I'll tell you, I didn't do this to get ahead of anyone, nor to say that I am better, no, I just came to this country, I wanted to get away from Guatemala, to see what is here. . . . But there is a lot of *envidia* because of this, but I do not want to get ahead of anyone.

Like other successful transmigrants, Angelino has been the subject of many *malas lenguas* (bad tongues) both in Providence and Xinxuc. In the postwar transnational context, social expressions of *envidia*—including malicious gossip about particular people (*chismes*), fantastic rumors (*rumores*) about unspecified persons, and *brujerías* (witchcraft)—have been refashioned as a primary means of social discourse within and between home and host communities. Given the ambivalence and ambiguity associated with the transnational project (which can be both beneficial and disastrous), these local idioms provide a more indirect form of expression and judgment than an overt, directed criticism, which is not socially sanctioned. Moreover, because of the distance created by transnationalism, communication between the two communities revolves largely around information conveyed orally by those who come and go or those can afford long telephone calls—that is, on the type of hearsay that defines rumors and gossip. Indeed, K'iche's in Providence often half-joke, "Over there they know what happens here before it even happens!" Or, as Estela says, "people's tongues are always fast, they run, they run, from there to here and back, they run to say everything!"

Both rumors and malicious gossip formed an important part of the "culture of terror" that preceded the migration and that, to some extent, continues to exist both in Xinxuc and Providence (where the conditions of fear and suspicion are compounded by the situation of illegality). During the war, rumors were used as a mechanism of control by the authorities, and the malicious gossip of the K'iche' was often transformed into deadly *denuncias* (denunciations) to the army. Still today in Guatemala—where the status and source of truth is always questionable—sensational rumors ripple every day throughout the country, resulting, for example, in the horrific "public lynchings" that have occurred in numerous highland villages. Some transnational rumors are clearly reminiscent of the fear produced by *la violencia*. For example, in discussing rumors concerning *denuncias* to the INS by community members, K'iche's often use the word *reportar*, which means to report or accuse (e.g., "Dicen que fue reportado." "They say he was reported."), rather than the word *deportar*, to deport. In another example, a K'iche' in Providence told me that "the *migra* here, it is like, as they said, the guerrillas over there, like touching an ant hole: If *la migra* is looking for one of us, we all run, run escaping, it is like the guerrilla." Such rumors also make it back to Xinxuc: A *campesino* there told me, for example, that he had heard that the INS had not yet arrived in Providence, though they were said to be close (thus likening them to the army or guerrillas).

Much of the gossip and rumors circulating between Xinxuc and Providence depict sad or sensational stories of wives abandoned by their husbands and living in dire poverty or dying of *tristeza*, or, at the other extreme, wives almost sadistically flaunting the fact that their husband's hard-earned money is going into the hands of a new lover. In Xinxuc, tales abound concerning husbands who take on new women in the United States; men who abandon themselves to lives of vice and crime; and Indian women who become lewd. These rumors, sometimes reflecting elements of people's real circumstances, sometimes not, are often widely embellished and exaggerated versions of simple events. Simply being seen speaking with the "wrong" person—just about anyone who is not from one's immediate family—can be enough to become a victim of the vicious transnational rumor mill. As one woman says:

> people often enlarge things, they do this because of *envidia*, or anger or hatred, who knows, but we see this a lot. . . . These are people who want to be enemies, they want to be more, they think they are better

than others.... This happened to me when my husband went back
to Guatemala, when he left here the people started talking about me,
that I had lovers, that I had a man here living with me. That never
happened, it was a lie. You know why people talk like this? I did not
have a car, I did not drive, I was a silly woman, I would go to work
walking and I suffered a lot when it snowed. I would fall and get up,
and fall again. So, because in this country there are many people
who know us, people we know from Guatemala, so when they see a
poor woman suffering, they offer you a ride and they do it with good
intentions, and with that cold, that exhaustion, or if one is sick one
says yes, when one trusts that person and knows they will not harm
one. Well, if another person saw you get into that car, they will think
the worst, they will think, that woman's husband left and now she
goes with any man. And these rumors go to Guatemala, this gossip,
and the family over there gossip among themselves, and it becomes
big, a huge rumor, and instead of blotting it out, instead of putting
water on it they put even more wood into the fire.

As Feldman points out, rumors reflect not only the sustained fear,
ambiguity, and collapse of established systems of reference (particularly
in a context of terror) but also counter-construct society by acting as "a
lens that identifies possible targets and accesses emerging social and personal needs, a calculus that organizes new relations between chance and
necessity" (1995: 234). Given the possibility that many K'iche's may find
themselves on either side of the transnational circuit at any time and given
the vital importance of maintaining social and familial connections, the
allegorical aspects of all these stories, and the threat that malicious gossip
might be told about oneself if one is not careful, serve to maintain social
links and reinforce some degree of social control and conformity between
communities. Underlying many rumors is the message that those who become *creidos* and make their dollars in dishonest ways will invite misfortune and *envidias*, or that those who abandon their familial responsibilities
will contribute to illness and catastrophe for themselves or others.
    Although malicious gossip can be extremely damaging to people, it is
the threat of such gossip, as well as the more diluted transnational rumors,
that serve to remind transmigrant K'iche's to *seguir igual*, to not forget or
abandon their family, land, and patrimony, and to remain *humilde* enough
not to disrupt the social balance that ideally enables indigenous communities to remain autonomous. Thus, not only do the tremendous *envidias*,
gossip, and rumors circulating in transnational space indicate the degree
of uncertainty, competition, and change produced by transnationalism, but
they are also traditional idioms used to effect a certain degree of social

and economic leveling and conformity, thereby ensuring that the gaze of the home community persists despite the spatial and temporal separations engendered by the migration to Providence.

Finally, it is important to point out that malicious gossip differs from rumor in that the harm intended is directed toward a particular person. In some cases such gossip—for example, that a son is not sending home money because he is not working or because he is drinking too much, or that a daughter-in-law is misbehaving in Providence—can result in chastising telephone calls or letters from home. However, it is widely believed among the K'iche' in both Xinxuc and Providence that both gossip and *envidia* may also result in *brujería*, or witchcraft. I heard of several transnational *brujerías* during my fieldwork. In one case, a K'iche' man whom I knew to be quite successful (having interviewed him and his family in his *pueblo* home, which was built with Providence money) later became hospitalized for psychiatric reasons back in Providence—the victim, I was told, of a witchcraft sent by his wife who had discovered he had another woman in Providence. In Chapter 6, moreover, we shall see how transnational *brujerías* are connected not only to success and *envidia* but also to resentments and fears lingering from the time of *la violencia*. Like *envidia*, then, *brujería* acts as a threat to those who may be neglecting their responsibilities, behaving in antisocial ways, or being too conspicuous, but it also serves as an explanatory category for many different types of misfortune, including the possible *fracaso* of transnational migration.

The notion that migration may lead to further class cleavages, ladinoization, and/or permanent abandonment has been well-known to K'iche's for centuries. Indeed, economic advancement through any means that push Indians into the nontraditional capitalist sector has long posed a threat to local indigenous identities. In this regard, Varese (1997) states:

> [F]rom the first years of the European invasion in the sixteenth
> century until the present, for the indigenous societies of America
> collective survival has constituted a recurring journey in the realm
> of ambiguity, a course between the difficult maintenance and
> reproduction of autonomous collective identities and existences, and
> the more illusory individual step to the nonindigenous sector that
> promises to compensate the abdication of one's ethnicity with the
> attraction of economic ascendance. (my translation)

This chapter has illustrated some of the material and organizational changes affecting the K'iche' in the wake of the transnational exodus, as well as the local idioms through which such transformations become part of an ongoing dialogue on identity between home and host communities. The difficult balance between striving to *superar* and maintaining a sense of local indigenous identity has become particularly challenging and paradoxical in the current period. On the one hand, transnationalism has produced increased tensions and divisions (in a community already fractured by the war), while, on the other, it has required a collective cooperation, for without the strong social networks existing between Xinxuc and Providence the entire project could not exist. The possibility of leaving one's culture and community behind, and the subsequent threat of *cambiar* (change), has increased in the context of globalization; at the same time, maintaining strong connections to home remains critical to most K'iche' transmigrants, given their unstable, liminal position. As we shall now see, superimposed onto these tensions—and onto the various local idioms through which they are interpreted—are newly revised ethnic discourses through which the K'iche' struggle to give meaning to or justify their decisions to stay, leave, or remain balancing in between.

CHAPTER 5

A DIALOGUE ON INDIANNESS
MAYA OR MOJADO?

Individual and collective identities are shaped not only by the everyday material life and social organization that govern people's existence but also by the more fluid "imaginaries" and symbols through which people give meaning to their past, present, and future lives. In this vein, geographer Catherine Nolin-Hanlon has noted that "[p]lace of origin shapes Mayan identity, yet with the shifting of place and time, identity does not fall apart. It is revitalized and re-shaped in a metamorphosis of meaning" (1995: 144). What are the new "imagined communities" of association and sentiment through which transnational K'iche's define Indianness and their membership in this group? How do the different forms of identification that comprise a sense of belonging—*natural, indígena, campesino,* Xinxucian, K'iche', Mayan, Guatemalan, *mojado,* illegal alien, factory worker—interact with self-conscious processes of ethnic identification across borders? How is Mayan ethnicity crosscut by the many other dimensions of identity—religion, gender, generation, political affiliation—that have been so affected by *la violencia*? By looking at dramatically different postwar contexts—one (Xinxuc) that encourages participation in the new construction of a Mayan "difference," and the other (Providence) that discourages any form of overt ethnic markings of Indianness—we can observe the various ways in which the K'iche' select different elements of their past culture to recompose the boundaries of identity and use these strategically within the context of transnationalism.

THE PAN-MAYA MOVEMENT:
NATIONAL DISCOURSE, LOCAL PRACTICE

The National Project

In the wake of the devastation produced by *la violencia* throughout the Indian highlands, the themes of ethnic and national identity, and their reconceptualization within the "democratizing" processes of the postwar period, have become paramount issues in Guatemala. Perhaps the most impressive accomplishment of the postwar period has been the tremendous work conducted by indigenous leaders, activists, intellectuals, and their allies to create a pan-Mayan ethnopolitical movement aimed toward reversing the historical oppression and silencing of Indian communities. The emergence of this movement defied not only the violence and oppression crystallized during the war, but also put into question the historically homogenizing concept of national identity that traditionally located indigenous identity within a hegemonic Ladino culture in which Indians were permitted to either assimilate or remain as subaltern Other. As such, pan-Mayanism has sought to highlight the manners in which ideologies of class, cultural difference, and national belonging have historically fused and produced a social order that has shaped the consciousness and constrained the options of Indians (Hale 1994). The movement has adopted self-conscious identity strategies and self-representations in order to enter civil society as a political force.

The development of the pan-Maya movement was situated not only within a national postwar period but also coincided with a growing continent-wide indigenous movement formed in the wake of the 1992 Columbus Quincentenniary celebrations, which brought together vastly different indigenous groups and sought to define a global discourse on indigenous identity, culture, and rights.[1] Within the past couple of decades, indigenous movements throughout South and Central America have increasingly worked within the frame of the ILO Convention 169 (1989) as well as the UN Working Group on Indigenous peoples (1990)[2] to advocate a list of rights surrounding issues of cultural practices, traditions, languages, land, legal systems, education, and political representation, and to argue for pluriethnic national models rather than separatism or state seizure.[3]

Neither monolithic nor static, the Maya movement contains a variety of streams and agendas that have worked together, conflicted, and overlapped at different moments. Indeed, the emerging and changing process of Mayan revitalization has been marked by contradiction and controversy. The "culturalist" current emphasizes racial discrimination as the basis for historic exploitation of Indians, thus stressing the importance of indigenous languages, native traditions, and cultural pride.[4] It includes various factions, ranging from those who desire total autonomy and oppose any cooperation with the Ladino state, to those who advocate bilingual, bicultural education for all Guatemalans. The "popular" current of Mayan revitalization, a grassroots movement embodied in localized Indian groups such as CERJ (Council of Ethnic Communities "Everyone United") and CONAVIGUA (National Coordinating Committee of Guatemalan Widows), addresses issues of land, poverty, class struggle, and social justice. This stream includes popular organizations fighting for human rights and postwar reconstruction and restitution projects such as linking families of the disappeared and exhuming clandestine graves. Its discourse is rooted in the materialist language of oppression and class conflict originating among leftists in the years preceding the violence. Discord between the two groups has ebbed and flowed. *Populares* have faulted culturalists for ignoring issues of class oppression, for collapsing cultural difference into biological essence, and for representing, basically, an elite perspective; culturalists, for their part, have criticized *populares* for their lack of a specific focus on cultural rights and for not directly challenging the hegemonic assumption of a natural hierarchy between Indians and Ladinos (Hale 1994).

In the early 1990s, the different streams of Mayanism developed a united front (COPMAGUA, the Coordination of Organizations of the Mayan Pueblo) in order to participate in the Peace Accords, calling for constitutional changes that would recognize and protect the languages, traditions, worldviews, and self-identification of indigenous people, as well as calling for steps toward land rights and measures to combat poverty. The common goal of taking advantage of the Peace Accords in order to effect changes in Guatemalan society created a constructive dialogue between the different currents of the Maya movement, whose perspectives became increasingly solidified.[5] Although the class/culture debate between culturalists and *populares* continues, these groups work together on concrete projects that integrate both cultural issues and material concerns. Mayan activists have sought to mobilize previously localized indigenous identities in order to negotiate self-determination at a national level. As such, they have (somewhat ironically) been profoundly influenced by the rhetoric and resources of the dominant culture—including the discourses of development and identity put forth by international and national organizations. Revitalization efforts focus primarily on cultural and educational projects, specifically the following: (1) language and literacy training in Mayan languages; (2) the revitalization of Mayan chronicles and sacred texts such as the *Popol Vuj* and the *Annals of the Kaqchiquels* and a focus on traditional Mayan time, calendars, numerics, astronomy, and ancient glyphs; (3) work with schools and teachers in promoting intercultural school programs and texts; (4) support for Maya leadership including *ancianos* (elders), *coma-dronas* (traditional midwives), and *aj q'ijab'* (shaman priests); and (5) "the dissemination of an internationally recognized discourse of indigenous rights, focusing on recognition and self-determination" (Warren 1998: 39). These projects have received funding from a wide array of sources, including the UN; European, American, and Canadian NGOs; the European Union; USAID; as well as the national government.

The Mayanist motto of "unity within diversity" reflects a model for participatory democracy that urges recognition of both the unifying and distinguishing characteristics of Guatemala's twenty-two Mayan language groups. Despite the wide variety of activities and streams of the movement, however, Mayanists generally assert that "there is a culturally specific indigenous way of knowing: a subject position no one else can occupy and political interests no one else has to defend" (Warren 1998: 37). This stance has elicited numerous criticisms, from both the right and left of the political spectrum, which have become part of the lively and contentious public debates surrounding culture and rights in Guatemala. Many Ladinos view the demand for indigenous rights as an attempt to "balkanize" the country and claim special privileges; others see it as a cynical attempt by a more privileged indigenous class to create ethnic polarization and attain power. Some critics of the movement have argued that pan-Mayanism essentializes and standardizes complex and heterogeneous indigenous identities, thus ignoring traditionally localized patterns of resistance that have long been a source of strength and cultural resilience; strong local identities, they argue, are what have prevented the state from "assaulting all Mayan communities at once" and have allowed communities to "push for economic advantage wherever openings or weaknesses exist, Mayanize useful western imports, and eject the assimilated from their communities" (Smith 1991: 31). Some have thus stated that the novelty of this new unified resistance could potentially result in the imposition of a rigid orthodoxy unable to represent the diverse local Mayan cultures and histories, or exclude those who do not "fit in" such as Protestant Indians or women who demand equal participation in male-dominated movements (Messer 1995: 65).

The positioning of anthropologists in these debates has been paradoxical. Like all "identity" struggles, the Maya movement has taken shape both through self-definition and by negotiating Others' gazes and representations of Indianness. This outside perspective has included the representations of anthropologists (which until the 1990s consisted primarily of the observations of non-Indians, and often non-Guatemalans). In a situation where genocidal violence has been followed by a political revitalization movement aimed at recapturing and asserting culture and ethnicity in the face of years (or centuries) of destruction, the "coherence" of anthropological knowledge and perspective can, indeed, help to fill in the memory gaps and holes left by the shards of violence and social fragmentation. These processes are susceptible to a dramatization (exaggeration) of certain cultural representations and essentializations in order to create a coherent mirror image that might compensate for profound disintegration and loss.

However, while the anthropological gaze gives a certain order to the idea of "culture" and can be reappropriated by ethnic and human rights leaders as a way of building a solid cultural movement and collective identity, this gaze, balanced uncomfortably between "us" and "them," is used partially and selectively. It can also be contested, as the somewhat tense and ambivalent relationship between Mayanists (including indigenous anthropologists) and foreign anthropologists attests (Nelson 1999a; Warren 1998; Fischer and Brown 1996).[6] While current cultural constructions of Indianness (by Mayanists, by anthropologists, and by development and human rights groups who utilize their discourse) increasingly influence indigenous community organization and forms of identification, they are part of a much broader arena of voices and perspectives, located both within and outside the boundaries of indigenous communities, contributing to emerging Indian identities in the postwar era.

Mayan activists have responded to some of the criticisms mentioned above by asserting that essentialization is necessary, tactical, and situational, a position necessary to subvert the authoritative representations of non-Maya (including Ladinos and foreign academics) and claim unique authority over their cultural difference (Warren 1998). Moreover, as Nelson (1999a) has demonstrated, Mayanists insist on local inclusion and participation, particularly since many local leaders are fully aware of such issues in their own communities. She argues that Mayan-controlled grassroots development projects are led by "Maya-hackers" who seek to transform the oppressive "orthopedic" of the Guatemalan nation-state precisely within the social spaces (language, education, law) wherein power is practiced.[7] As Warren also suggests, a simple "constructionist" perspective on the movement "avoids the serious engagement with the social practices, the everyday significance of the market, and the national and local politics to which this movement reacts as it struggles for the rights that have been denied much of the national population" (Warren 1998: 44). It also falls easily in with more conservative arguments that both caricature the movement and continue to see any form of indigenous mobilization as a national threat. Fischer (2001) expands on these views by noting that the "cultural logics" of the Maya movement tend to be continuous with, rather than distinct from, local identities and cognitive frames, and he argues that this convergence speaks to the authenticity of both national and local forms of Mayanness.

Some supporters of the movement also argue that Mayanism must be seen in terms of its historical continuity rather than as a radical change in ethnic mobilization rising out of the ashes of the war. Hale (1994) shows that both the culturalist and popular streams have grown out of a nation-state system rooted in the colonial era and predicated on a hegemonic cultural divide. From this perspective, the resources and discourse of the Maya movement are argued to be rooted in historic forms of power and subordination, as well as in long-term traditions of resistance and nego-tiation—even if they incorporate elements of modernity specific to the global era. And as Grandin argues, "[M]any of the questions regarding race, culture, gender and nationalism raised by today's pan-Maya move-ment ... have their origins in nineteenth century efforts by Ladinos to create a homogeneous national identity" (2000: 9). Rather than an entirely new project spawned from the ruins from a failed Ladino national proj-ect or from genocidal violence, he suggests that the movement's origins and development must be situated within a much broader history of state formation.

Perhaps the biggest difficulty encountered by the Maya movement at the local level is the very complexity and slipperiness of the ethnicity con-cept itself. As social scientists have often noted, ethnicity is something that is ascribed externally—usually by the nation-state, which uses hegemonic processes to place ethnic groups within a hierarchy of subject positions—and is also an affirmation of difference and belonging from within ethnic groups (Alonso 1994; Foster 1991). As such, ethnicity always exists in a historic dialogue with the broader social environment, and while it can be subject to collective validation by the ethnic group itself or even the Others against whom it is constructed, it can also incorporate the rage and indig-nation that results from exclusion and humiliation (Ibañez 2001). One of the problems with constructivist approaches toward identity—that is, those interested primarily in overtly political processes of ethnic transformation aimed at subverting older discourses in order to create new subject posi-tions—is that they often overemphasize the public articulations and con-structed character of identity while downplaying the everyday practices, sedimented meanings, and material conditions that influence the ways in which average people identify and recognize themselves but that might not fit in neatly with such projects.

Ibañez (2001) has proposed that a "historical-structural" approach, which emphasizes the notion of shared experience in identity, allows us to view identity as something that is never fixed or whole but rather situates people's practices and modes of life within collective narratives of the past, present, and future, which themselves are constantly revised within new contexts.[8] In this sense he incorporates the Marxist notion that everyday conditions of existence and practice determine consciousness, echoing Hall's argument that identity is always a matter of "becoming" as well as of "being" (Hall 1990: 225). This perspective is particularly useful for looking at local forms of identity construction in the Mayan case, since it allows us to observe at close range the manners in which people engage and incorporate (or not) the discourses on peace and ethnic revitalization, but it does not overdetermine such processes to the neglect of other equally salient local forms of cultural practice and consciousness rooted in the historical continuity of particular communities.

In order to understand processes of ethnic transformation in Guatemala today, it is thus crucial to look at the relationship between the mobilization of ethnicity at broader national and regional levels and the manner in which ethnic identity is practiced in communities still divided by the war and its aftermath. Because the Maya movement is recent, complex, and changing, it is difficult to assess its overall impact at this stage. Handy (2002) has argued that the drawbacks of the Maya movement are evident in its failure to garner substantive political support and in the fact that few of the measures outlined in the Accord on Indigenous Identity and Rights have been implemented. These failures are attributed, in part, to the movement's inability to adequately assess the current social realities and allegiances of indigenous groups at the community level. Indeed, like other political and ethnic movements, the pan-Maya movement has constituents and cannot claim to represent or include the identities of all indigenous people.

"Maya" Identity: Local Expressions

Field Notes, Xinxuc, November 1997

Today I visited Don Miguel, an *aj q'ij* who has had some experience in organizing small development projects and—as soon became obvious—trying to procure funds from international visitors. Upon my arrival, he promptly invited me to speak about "la cultura Maya" to a room full of Indian war widows who were gathered for a lesson on nutrition; this became quite an awkward anthropological moment as I tried unsuccessfully to persuade him that both he and the women know much more about their culture than this *gringa* possibly could. I proceeded to give a short faltering speech about the importance of remembering one's history and traditions especially now that the peace has been declared, adding that only they, and not I, could know what this history was. My talk was greeted by the women with the typical silence and weary gazes (reflecting so many years of hardship and violence) which might mask incomprehension, skepticism, antagonism, mistrust, fatigue, or most probably a mixture of all. Don Miguel's expression, on the other hand, clearly indicated that my hesitant talk was not what he had in mind. Later on in the day, he invited me to a ceremony in the mountains along with the widows and their children. During the *costumbre*, the only Spanish words (that is, not K'iche', which he knew I would not understand) spoken by him were those thanking God for my presence and praying for some financial aid from those countries such as ... Canada and the US!

Although the Peace Accords have attempted to forge a national "Mayan" solidarity, and although the movement has made some important inroads in some communities, others, like Xinxuc, have been quite slow to embrace such broader transformations. Unlike indigenous populations in some neighboring *municipios* that have a stronger NGO and/or UN presence, many of the Xinxuc K'iche', still traumatized by the army and PACs, have remained highly suspicious not only of the guerrillas but of organizations believed to have been affiliated with their cause, including human rights organizations or any form of social and political organization that does not fall into the established structures of the local *comites* or religious groups.

Here, the "imagined community" of Mayanism is, indeed, difficult to imagine: Xinxuc continues to be racked by internal divisions, and the majority of the K'iche' people remain illiterate, poor, and isolated from the national media and institutions within which Mayanist debates take place. Moreover, the local power structure, in which those in command are still Ladinos (or, in a few cases, K'iche' men who gained powerful positions during *la violencia*), has not changed. Most K'iche's in Xinxuc do not identify as "Maya" or speak about *la cultura Maya*. The shift from a long-term negative image of the colonized, dominated Indian Other and the extreme racism of *la violencia* to a sense of overt "Mayan pride" in languages and customs that have been denigrated for so long is (not surprisingly) not evident, either psychologically or socially.

Nonetheless, despite the apparent distance between the broader ethnopolitical movement and illiterate rural Xinxuc *campesinos*, projects and discourses based in the Mayan concept have trickled into this highland community in odd and uneven ways, primarily through the intermediary of a couple of local interest groups vying for financial support and local recognition: Ethnic revitalization, in Guatemala, has become a major initiative among international development donors. However, a less cynical reading of the Maya movement's seepage into local community life would argue that rather than simply providing a new vocabulary around which to solicit international aid, it provides a symbolic language which attempts to fill a space left by the destruction of the violence. As such, it encourages everyday forms of practice and identity that rework older forms of local culture, thereby empowering certain groups of Indians (who have little else to organize around) to contend with the new demands of postwar community life. Indeed, the practice of ethnicity in contemporary Xinxuc both escapes and is at some level shaped by the discourse on Mayanness and tradition in ways that seem at once primordial (it resurrects a common past rooted in tradition and culture), instrumental (it involves competing interpretations and interests that make sense within local boundaries), and "invented" (it creates and imposes a culture and history based in new concepts and struggles).

Although there is not a major ethnic revivalist movement in Xinxuc, it is (paradoxically) through the PLANTAS, a small European NGO established in this community in the early 1990s, that a burgeoning Mayanist organization has slowly developed in this community, though it has remained somewhat autonomous from regional or national forms of ethnic consolidation. As the only foreign NGO working in Xinxuc (and, indeed, the only NGO that has a substantial program in the community's hamlets), PLANTAS's main mandate has been to employ and train indigenous health promoters in the practice of traditional and herbal medicine in order to revitalize and validate older forms of health knowledge that utilize local plants and other resources in treating various local maladies.

Given the displacement of such traditional knowledge forms by modern medicine, new religions, and other sociocultural changes that have impinged on the oral transmission of local knowledge between generations, PLANTAS attempts to "reconstitute a collective memory in order to understand the alternative solutions that are already present, and systematize popular knowledge in order to return this knowledge to people themselves so that they may use it" (Bourgey 1997: 55; my translation). As such, PLANTAS health promoters also work closely with traditional healers (*curanderos*) and midwives (*comadronas*), as well as with certain *aj q'ijab'*, in the project to revitalize herbal remedies and traditional forms of categorizing, diagnosing, and treating illnesses. In a sense, PLANTAS has attempted to create a politically neutral space and discourse within fragmented Xinxuc by focusing on the relatively impartial notions of health and illness (rather than the more contentious issues of language, rights, or justice) and by framing its project within a collaborative rather than oppositional stance vis-à-vis the broader state system.[9] Nonetheless, the organization has also slowly moved toward a more "culturalist" position by promoting *costumbre* and encouraging both younger and older generations to practice *costumbrista* beliefs.

Wilson (1995) and Warren (1992) have described how ethnic revivalist movements in certain highland communities have been led by competing groups and actors of various religious and political persuasions who seek to reshape identities and meanings within local fields of power and history.[10] Both authors have shown how, ironically, it is the *catequistas* of Catholic Action, who for decades prior to the violence denounced with a class-based progressive political philosophy the pagan activities of *costumbristas*, that now seek to enact and revive elements of traditional culture (including the practice of *costumbre*) in order to create new local sociopolitical communities. Young Mayans, often the sons and daughters of earlier catechists, thus recreate and refashion local tradition through courses and *actos culturales* (cultural acts) that seek to integrate the knowledge of older traditionalists. In doing so, they selectively disregard or transform the meanings of previous practices or histories that are no longer considered appropriate or acceptable. The strategic focus on youth in such local movements is grounded in two fears: first, that younger people "who associate Mayan culture with agrarian poverty and marginalization will abandon their ethnicity altogether and use their education to disappear into Ladino society" (Warren 1992: 200), and second, that the growing evangelical churches will lure away Catholic youth, thus further atomizing Indian communities.

Many of the PLANTAS workers, likewise, come from families belonging to Catholic Action and having had no interest in (and indeed rejecting) traditional forms of knowledge or worship. A few leaders of the PLANTAS project, such as twenty-six-year-old Gaspar who is the local director, are children and grandchildren of catechists. For the younger K'iche', belonging to PLANTAS enables them, as one member describes, to "find my roots, find myself, my *pueblo*." It allows them as well to learn new skills and disseminate these in their hamlets, and to make contacts with organizations and persons from other communities working on health and development projects (some of whom also participate in broader national Mayanist projects).

Gaspar embodies the "new" Mayanism promoted by PLANTAS. During the week he organizes PLANTAS projects and workshops in Xinxuc (which include promoters from other municipalities), framing his classes on herbs and illness within a discourse that emphasizes the "forgotten" roots of indigenous culture and belief systems. He promotes the "new" traditionalism by staging elaborate public *costumbre* rituals on special days, and practices *costumbre* privately as well, though he and his wife remain active within the Catholic Church. He is studying to become an *aj q'ij* under the tutelage of a renowned elder shaman-priest in another department. On weekends Gaspar studies ethnomedicine at a German university in the capital in an advanced program that incorporates the hard sciences with "alternative medicine" (a degree being paid for through PLANTAS).

Through his work with the European and North American PLANTAS visitors who sporadically come to observe and study "ethnomedicine" in this remote town, Gaspar has acquired a taste for classical music and a collection of posters of Swiss Alp villas (which, when he was able to afford a home for his young family, he emulated by building on his mountain *milpa* a relatively lavish two-story home, not unlike those of transnational migrants whom he ironically criticizes). Gaspar sports a yin-yang necklace (a gift from a European visitor whose explanations of the dualities and cycles symbolized by the Chinese image resonated with Gaspar's study of Mayan cosmology) and a unique fashion aesthetic that favors leopard-print shirts, suspenders, and the traditional *moral*. Alongside his uncle Nicolas (who has spent two stints in Providence but now works as a PLANTAS leader as well) and his father, a poor and disabled *campesino,* Gaspar cultivates a small *milpa*. His young wife performs domestic chores and raises their four young children. Despite the "bricolage" of cultural identities (old and new, indigenous, Western and Eastern) that Gaspar creatively embodies, his discourse on Mayan culture and identity, which seeks to recapture a rather essentialized past, seems quite at odds with his cosmopolitan, if quirky, presentation.

Older K'iche's who work with or participate in PLANTAS projects often speak of their membership in terms of a continuity with the past, many recalling their grandparents who used to practice *costumbre* but were forced to "abandon their candles" to join Catholic Action. For them, the ethnic revitalization provides cultural capital that allows them to maintain a privileged status in the community (and, if remunerated by PLANTAS, a source of income). Their participation in the group also encourages and valorizes practices, skills, and knowledge (those of *aj q'ijab', comadronas,* and elders) that have long been devalued. One forty-five-year-old PLANTAS member, a hamlet *campesino* who converted from Catholicism to evangelicalism but has recently begun practicing *costumbre* with other PLANTAS promoters, explains:

> Before, with my parents and my grandparents, there was respect.
> My grandmother taught us many good things, she remembered a
> lot from before about plants, herbs, and she would light her candles,
> she would tell me we must venerate the land, that we must love the
> land because it gives us food. She taught us that the trees should

not be cut with machetes, because they are alive, and if we cut
them they cry, they bleed. . . . She also told us to respect the maize,
beans, that they also cry, because they are life, they are food. And
she told us to respect the people, the neighbors, greet them every
day, and not mistreat people, we must respect their land, the borders
of their land. . . . That we must thank God for the air, the sun, the
cardinal points, she was dedicated to these things, she lit candles. . . .
These days I have been thinking of this, because of my training, the
church, some sisters, and now the *Pop Vuh*, I see my own life, and I
start to think of the history, the customs of my grandparents which
were true because there it is in the *Pop Vuh*, their life is written
there, their religion, their beliefs. . . . I see that my blood continues
being the blood of my ancestors (*abuelos*), so how could I forget this,
I would be mocking my culture.

When Cristina (the European founder of PLANTAS) arrived, I
learned many things, about medicinal plants, conserving the land . . .
they awakened me (*me despertaron*), and we might have forgotten
all of this if PLANTAS had not arrived, and now my land is the way
it was before, I plant the way my ancestors did (without chemical
fertilizers). Now I have discovered that plants are spirits, they are
beings, there are sacred plants, sacred like the blood of Jesus. . . .
Now I thank God that Cristina and Gaspar and everyone we work
together, and even though Gaspar is younger than me he goes first
and I follow (laughs). . . . When I do my Mayan ceremony (*mi
ceremonia Maya*) I put my candles and do my asking, I give thanks
for the doctor Cristina, that God gave us this woman even though
we have such different skin . . . and I thank God that the diocese, the
bishop is concerned with the *campesinos*, the indigenous people, he
says that we must respect people's culture, so that is why these days
I dedicate myself to recuperating the culture, doing ceremonies. . . .
I notice that those who do their ceremonies, have a live faith, they
are more respectful, those who have their culture, their Mayan
culture. . . . I have been feeling peaceful (*tranquilo*), there is a hope,
it is a sacrifice to do all this work but I see it as a blessing.

Here we can see clearly the paradoxical effect of a "return" to older cultural beliefs through the introduction of a Western organization that has
provided this man with certain resources (for example, access to the *Popol
Vuh*) through which he rethinks connections to the ancestors and to his
grandparents. This refashioning is selective, however, as evidenced by his
acknowledgment that nowadays, indigenous youth (such as Gaspar) can

become *aj q'ijab* and leaders while older people follow—a structure at odds with the traditional "gerontocracy" of K'iche' *costumbre*.

Not all members of PLANTAS, however, have been totally swayed by the Mayanist discourse used by the group, maintaining rather an ambiguous and restrained perspective on some of its teachings. Virgilio, for example, a *catequista* who worked with PLANTAS before leaving to Providence, had mixed feelings about the group's emphasis on particular dimensions of Mayan culture such as the use of *lengua* (indigenous language), though he nonetheless acknowledges the worth of trying to recapture "true" feelings of Indianness:

> I worked with them, even though I don't really like medicinal plants, I prefer to buy a pill! And it's something strange because I, when we were speaking of culture and language . . . but with my wife I don't speak K'iche', so it is. . . . I used to have arguments with people who spoke of *lengua*. . . . But then on the other hand I think that sometimes it is worth it to be like, even though I don't speak, for example if I only spoke in Spanish, but my heart is Indian then, that is worth it. It would be worse to have a Ladino mind (*un pensamiento propiamente Ladino*) and speak only K'iche' but have a Ladino mind or feelings (*un sentimiento Ladino*), it would be much worse.

For Virgilio, who (as a catechist leader) places a high value on education (as does the Maya movement), learning to master Spanish, the language of power, is considered critical to the advancement of "his people": He believes that it is through learning to read and write in Spanish that one can gain the knowledge, power, and ability to negotiate within the Ladino power sphere. This theme was echoed repeatedly by many K'iche's in both Xinxuc and Providence: The historical manipulation of Indians by Ladinos—over issues ranging from unfair land titling to defending oneself during *la violencia*—has been largely abetted by Indians' inability to master the dominant language.

From this perspective, Spanish competence is seen as a more powerful tool for preserving indigenous identity (that is, for surviving) than the Mayanist focus on promoting indigenous language as a primary ethnic marker (for example, by alphabetizing and teaching indigenous languages). Moreover, the use of Spanish as a "common" medium of communication between K'iche's is more evident in Xinxuc than in other *pueblos* with more homogeneous, stable populations. This is because there has been some intermarriage between the different K'iche' ethnic groups (which use distinct dialects and modes of address) in Xinxuc, many people have spent lengthy periods of time on the coast or in urban areas, and increasing numbers of Indians have moved to the urban, "Ladino" *pueblo*. Virgilio sees Spanish language, rather than *lengua*, as a unifying tool for Indians; its mastery does not indicate for him a loss of indigenous identity, which runs deeper than language, rooted as it is in people's "hearts" and "minds."[11]

The historical heterogeneity, movement, and intermarriage acknowledged by Virgilio, which makes his discourse on PLANTAS ambivalent, are what Gaspar (Virgilio's nephew) argues to be precisely responsible for the "loss" of traditional culture that he seeks to revive. He contends that it is because of the different customs, dialects, and competition between groups (e.g., Max and *de corte* K'iche's, as Xinxuc K'iche's are often called, often compete over who is more clever and industrious), and because of both intermarriage and movements to Ladino areas, that many of the town's K'iche' have preferred to "dilute" their customs and language, for example by speaking Spanish. Gaspar also attributes to these ethnic divisions the facility with which the evangelical churches have been able to gain influence within the community. He promotes a K'iche' identity that seeks to bridge (or perhaps erase) internal difference, argues against longer-term migrations (e.g., to the capital, to the United States) by advocating community development on one's land, and proposes an "essential" Mayan identity that will enable Indians to achieve respect and dignity within the nation-state and vis-à-vis local Ladinos.

If Virgilio's assessment of PLANTAS's efforts to "revitalize" a common culture is ambivalent, the NGO's Mayanist tendencies are met with a fair bit of suspicion, skepticism, and/or incomprehension by some other groups in the community. This became apparent on the following occasion, where PLANTAS's "culturalism" appeared as an "invention of tradition" or as an outside discourse on identity imposed on people who did not appear to identify with the "essence" it sought to communicate:

Field Notes, Xinxuc, April 1997

This morning I attended the "Mayan New Year" ceremony organized by PLANTAS. The ceremony took place along the main road, in front of a hamlet church, and preceded a midday *bendición de semillas* (seed blessing) mass. A couple of elders sat chatting and smoking cigarettes as three K'iche's played *chirimias* (traditional flutes) and drums. Gaspar was dressed in the colorful costume from Chichicastenango, and sporadically performed a traditional dance (though not traditional to Xinxuc), hopping back and forth while holding onto a Christian-Maya *ídolo*. The women were all gathered in the back preparing food.

Slowly, two elders began to prepare the ceremonial space in front of the church. Gaspar explained to a gathering crowd that while in previous years *naturales* had been forced to perform their ceremonies in hidden places, they had decided on this day to perform a public ritual to show that they would not be intimidated or "laughed at." A large circle was drawn with sugar onto the ground, the four cardinal points indicated, and an outer circle of beautiful flower petals was ceremoniously prepared. In an extremely careful and lengthy process, dozens of colored candles, *pom* (incense), branches of various herbs, and numerous other materials were added to the circle resulting in a spectacular offering, much more striking than what I have seen in private *costumbres*. Loud *cuetes* (firecrackers) were released. The major expense of the ceremony, paid by PLANTAS and individual donations, comes at a time when most K'iche's are saving their *centavitos* for fertilizer and seed.

Gaspar and two elder *aj q'ijab'* affiliated with PLANTAS began to make speeches in K'iche' to the small crowd of forty to fifty people. They explained, as though teaching a class, the significance of the New Year in the Mayan calendar, to whom they were praying, the symbolism of all the offerings, and what was being asked for: "The herbs signify health, the limes cleanse and purge evil, the crackers and eggs symbolize the fruits of the earth which we pray for in the New Year. The cardinal points have many meanings, and connect us to the sun, earth and wind." Some people listened attentively, while others looked confused or skeptical; some chatted and bought sodas at the impromptu snack stand on the road. Gaspar then lit the *pom* and in an instant the beautiful montage became a mass of large flames. The two elders, swaying their incense holders, began invoking the *antepasados* (ancestors) and praying as the candles melted and the offering slowly became a mass of cinder under the hot sun.

Several MINUGUA vans drove by; one stopped and some Blue Berets, dressed in their military uniforms, jauntily came over to inquire about the fire. Rather than feeling intruded upon, Nicolas proudly shook their hands and launched into another lengthy explanation, directed at everyone assembled, concerning the purpose and meaning of the ritual. Then, he thanked us—Christine, Alain, Pierre (PLANTAS administrators), and myself—for coming to share this event even though we are not Guatemalan. Nicolas stated that "sometimes foreigners know more about our own customs and calendar than we ourselves know," as I felt numerous rather dubious eyes upon us. The four of us were then invited—along with the organizers, elders, and PLANTAS promoters—to a feast of *caldo*, *tamalitos*, tortillas, and coffee, while the women and children ate outside.

Despite the success of PLANTAS's work in hamlets promoting communal gardens and herbal remedies (a success rooted both in their thorough knowledge of the communities and the fact that they fill a tremendous need),[12] the organization's more recent attempts to promote *costumbre* have met with less success in the broader community. One of the elders who led the New Year ceremony explains the reluctance as follows:

> What we did the other day, that was when everyone had the same thought, everyone thought the same thing. Because that was a very special day for the Mayans a long time ago. . . . For example, the evangelicals, every few years they all get together in one place. And they all have different names, but on that day they all come together. And that is what we did on that day, we got together, *costumbristas* and Catholics, we all got together and we did a ceremony to give a general thanks, it was not just for one person.
>
> Some people here didn't agree with doing this ceremony, because they do not know, they are not used to ceremonies. Because before, the Ladinos told us that what we were doing was bad, but they were deceiving us (*nos engañaban*). And our people believed them, and thought that the ceremony ruins us (*es una perdición*). And that is why our people got used to not doing ceremonies. So now they are doubting us, they are saying *saber* (who knows), should we do ceremonies or not? But those who agree with us, they know. Before the Ladinos said ceremonies were *brujerías* (witchcraft). But it isn't, it is giving thanks, and *brujería* is something else. Of course there are some *sacerdotes* (shaman-priests) who do witchcraft too, but that is something else, it is not the same as the work of giving thanks, I don't know about witchcraft. So this is why our people cannot figure out what to do, because we have been deceived before. But perhaps slowly they will understand.

As this quote implies, the PLANTAS promoters are in competition with other groups in Xinxuc, in particular the large number of K'iche' evangelicals who converted during the violence and who look with antagonism upon PLANTAS's attempts to revive Mayan tradition. A young indigenous evangelical promoter, for example, adamantly expressed to me his opposition to PLANTAS's attempt to promote Mayan tradition (despite his collaboration in community health projects throughout the region with individuals and groups who are proponents of the movement). As he stated, those who promote *la cultura Maya* belong to exclusionist interest groups claiming to represent people they do not in fact represent. Moreover, he said, their beliefs in burning candles and ancestor worship are satanic, an antidevelopmental force that "does not help people to improve their lot." Another evangelical K'iche' development worker from a neighboring community told me that he believed the emphasis on indigenous identity and rights by MINUGUA, Mayan rights groups, and international NGOs were simply politically expedient ways of garnering international finances and support through an easy language that does not address the more complex, concrete problems faced by impoverished rural Indians. Evangelical opposition to PLANTAS, however, probably has as much to do with these developmentalist ideas (which in some respects resemble the critique leveled against culturalist Mayanists by the *populares*) as with wartime antagonisms between the Catholic Action catechists and evangelicals.

More ironically, it is the relationship of PLANTAS with certain *costumbristas*—many of whom, during the war, opposed the Catholic catechists and their outspoken progressive philosophy—that is perhaps most tense. While PLANTAS has recruited some elder *aj q'ijab'*, both to promote and give legitimacy to their "traditionalism" and to teach them about the "roots" of tradition, they are at odds with the dominant *aj q'ijab'* from Xinxuc's main traditionalist hamlet, including Don Miguel (referred to in this section's opening vignette) and his father. The resentment of Don Miguel and his father toward PLANTAS comes from the fact that, as authentic *costumbristas* who have never abandoned traditional practice, they now compete with the new young Catholic Mayanists for recognition from NGOs and international financiers interested in *la cultura Maya*. Don Miguel told me quite bitterly, for example, that neither he nor any of his hamlet's *costumbristas* were invited to participate in the Mayan New Year ceremony. For their part, the PLANTAS organizers tend to view Don Miguel's family with suspicion, stating that they are drunks who dishonestly manipulate others through *brujerías* and are not to be trusted.

Despite recent attempts by PLANTAS to revitalize and promote a Mayan culture, ethnic identity in Xinxuc thus remains, in the postwar era, up for grabs. Some view Mayanism positively as a form of cultural capital that, though brought to Xinxuc by foreigners and by the Catholic Church, nonetheless resounds with recollections of one's parents and grandparents—or perhaps with a more "imaginary" history comprised of wise ancestors—while also providing status (or even employment) within the community. Others view Mayanism as incongruous, suspicious, or opportunistic; however, they continue to tend their *milpas*, speak *lengua*, and engage in many of the social and economic activities that have been part of K'iche' culture for centuries, thereby structuring their lives in typically *natural* ways and, in some cases, practicing their own private *costumbres*.

Perhaps the biggest threat to Mayanism, however, is found not in the other religions or factions with which it competes locally, but rather in the large-scale transnational labor migration to the United States. Identities in Xinxuc compete not only over imagined pasts but also over imagined futures: For a large number of the K'iche', and particularly poorer youths, identity seems increasingly formed less around the place where they live than around *allá*, within the promise of Providence. In a place of such high unemployment and poverty, the promises of Mayanism—equality, respect, education, land, and justice at home—seem much more distant, in fact, than the dollars one can hope to make abroad. These, at least, can lead to the more immediate result of improving one's class status at home, perhaps even approximating that of Ladinos.

Ostensibly, PLANTAS members deplore transnationalism, arguing that it will spell the ruin of an already fragile cultural identity and that transmigrants become "cultureless" consumers. However, a number of PLANTAS promoters have family members in Providence, and some, like Nicolas, have spent years working in Providence factories. In addition, it is sometimes those youths who have been able to benefit from the remittances sent by their transmigrant relatives (for example, by receiving a higher education at home) that become interested in Mayanism. Cati, for example, Inocente and Estela's half-sister, is studying to become a Mayan priestess and works with PLANTAS. The ultimate irony, thus, seems to be that the "identity politics" of pan-Mayanism (while clearly rooted within evolving indigenous struggles) has been strongly influenced by globalization and transnationalism, benefiting from shared projects with indigenous groups in other nations as well as from funding and discourses imported from North America and Europe. At the same time, the movement competes—for constituents and for its local survival—with another dimension of transnationalism, the nuanced forms of identity created around undocumented labor migrations to *el Norte*, to which we shall now turn.

ETHNICITY IN PROVIDENCE:
SHAME AND SUBVERSION

My son, he is only four, but soon I will need him to learn
English well, I am very interested in him speaking English.
But when he speaks English well, he will have to learn
Spanish well too, because my Spanish is not very good, but
he will have to learn to speak and to write, in Spanish. And
when he knows those languages, when he is eight or ten say,

I will quickly teach him *dialecto* (K'iche'), and he has to learn my language. He has to learn because his grandmother is, yes, my blood, which he has, and so I do not want him to lose the traditions. I will have to tell him about our *fiesta* in Xinxuc, our saint, our traditions, we have so many, I will explain to him how my life was, I will explain how we ask a woman to marry in our language, in our customs, I will tell him everything. Because I need him to know what I have lived. Not the drama, not what they did to me, that they beat me and all, but . . . who knows how I will explain it. (Inocente, Providence)

The transformation of collective identities among displaced Mayans, both within and outside of Guatemala, has depended upon various factors relating to communities of origin and destination, including whether or not displaced Maya identify themselves as (and are identified by others as) official refugees, legal immigrants, undocumented *mojados* or *desplazados*. A number of studies concerning Mayan communities in the United States have shown how emerging ethnic identities among these groups come to integrate and overlap with new host country categorizations such as "migrant worker," "illegal alien," and "Hispanic" (Earle 1994; Burns 1993; Wellmeier 1998; Hagan 1994; Loucky and Moors 2000). Not only do Mayans become one among many minority and status groups, they also become subsumed into a new broader ethnic group (Latino or Hispanic).

While several of these authors have described the conflicts and competing interests that characterize the negotiation of Mayan identities in the host country, they tend nonetheless to analyze the retention and expression of Mayan "ethnicity" in terms of particular traits and customs such as dress, rituals, saints, and saint day celebrations (Wellmeier 1994, 1998; Burns 1993; Popkin 1999). In large part, they show that such "reproductions" of the culture of origin are almost always influenced by the new pan-Maya concept, which emphasizes particular traits, markers, and histories, and which enables individuals from different regions and municipalities to recreate a more unified identity. Though no longer existing *within* the Guatemalan nation-state, these identities continue to be defined *in relation* to the home nation; as such, they resemble what Clifford (1994) describes as "diasporas," whereby nostalgic representations of home merge past ethnic memories and future projects, thus forming a crucial component of collective identities in the host context.[13]

There are no such collective organizations or identities among the

K'iche' in Providence, as discussed in the previous chapter. Indeed, the articulation and practice of ethnic identity (which commonly relies on a sense of shared ancestry, history, place, and cultural traits, as well as common sociopolitical goals) is not an evident process for this community, divided and fragmented as it is by violence, dislocation, and invisibility. However, this does not mean that transnational K'iche's completely abandon all notions of home or indigenous culture. While the K'iche' in Providence clearly do not wish to enhance the visibility of Otherness, their identities become grounded in a flexible transnationalism that seeks to escape national projects of any sort. Indeed, a sense of collective transnational identity emerges in the new space of Providence, whereby certain hidden elements of Indian ethnicity and historical consciousness are reappropriated and transformed through discursive processes designed to incorporate both continuity and change.

If ethnic identity is based on contrasting oneself with a constructed Other (Barth 1969), the self-representations and narratives of K'iche' transmigrants reveal several Others against whom they constantly refashion shifting selves: The Other may be alternately represented as oneself in the past or the *indígena* in El Quiché; it may be other *indígenas* in the United States against whom one's transmigrant success or failure may be measured; the Other may be Ladinos in Guatemala, often portrayed as dominant and scornful *patrones*; or it may be Ladinos in the United States, whose social power has been dissolved as they work and live side-by-side with indigenous migrants. Finally, given the new multiethnic atmosphere of the United States, where class, race, and status shift radically from the Ladino/Indian divide of home, the Other also becomes other immigrants and minorities in the United States (Latino or other) with whom bonds of solidarity intertwine with strategies of differentiation and competition. And, of course, the Other may be the dominant *gringos* with whom most K'iche's interact primarily in institutional and work settings. This multiplicity of references across time and space creates different patterns and strategies of identity construction, both individual and collective.

Shame and Forgetting

> Here people don't want to talk about the past, because they have suffered too much and it was too hard, or because they were involved in *la violencia*. In either case, it is pain and hurt, here each person wants to calm himself, filling in his emptiness with each step he takes. (K'iche' man, Providence)

Many K'iche's appear to want to create a full and dramatic rupture with their past ethnic identity as *indígena*: practices such as speaking K'iche' in the presence of others, listening to traditional music, or displaying outward signs of Indianness through dress or behavior are often frowned upon by other K'iche's. Concealing the obvious habitus of Indianness becomes a primary collective concern in this setting, even though people's reasons may vary. The shame of being Indian in the United States implicitly refers to the temporal and spatial dimensions of home: The negative elements of identity that made, and continue to make, Indians suffer there (such as timidity, ignorance, manipulability, and poverty) must be abandoned in America. While shame is a response to the sufferings of the past (and a desire to forget the negative "gaze" of Ladinos), it is also constructed and imputed by certain K'iche's who "look down" on those who display signs of Indianness in Providence. For others, the shame of being Indian is more directly associated with the horrors of *la violencia* and with the negative role into which Indians were collectively forced (either as victims or perpetrators), a role that reinforced negative stereotypes of Indianness.[14] Moreover, as we have seen, the extreme psychological manipulation by the army and PACs in Xinxuc, combined with the general conformity of K'iche' culture, produced in some K'iche's a profound need to show allegiance to those in power, the Ladinos.

Though most transmigrants rarely discuss ethnic identity explicitly in relation to the violence, the internalized racism and fear resulting from the violence and the army's discourse and actions came through quite clearly, though in fragmented traces. The degree to which K'iche's from Xinxuc continue to fear both the association between Indian and subversive, and dangerous representations of Indians in general, was often revealed when I showed Providence K'iche's photographs of the guerrilla demobilization that had taken place near the village. Both the tremendous sorrow of the devastation, as well as the continuing fear of being seen as a subversive population, became evident, for example, in an emotional session with Petrona. Observing the photographs, she broke into tears, saying: "Oh, there is Doña Josefa, such a nice face, and her father was the same, so good, so humble, and they killed him just like that." Seconds later, stopping at a picture of a breast-feeding *guerrillera* wearing a *guipil* and handing in her rifle to the UN Blue Berets at the demobilization ceremony, she exclaimed: "How amazing! I do not like this picture, this woman who seems so humble and good, she is carrying a gun, she looks bad, how can she be a fighter, a *guerrillera,* with a baby in her arms, it is not possible!" On another occasion, Inocente, looking through the guerilla camp photos, said sadly:

I don't know what they were fighting for. It scares me to look at these pictures. . . . I'm afraid to go back there, especially with my children. It's that, the indigenous people, they are. . . . Do you think the UN knows that they are humble, ignorant, that the *guerrilleros* tricked them, that they don't even know how to write, to tell the time?

The tremendous fear of being seen collectively as "bad"—whether subversive or, in the context of Providence, criminal—is clearly evident in the often-repeated phrase told to me in Providence: "Solo por unos malos, sufrimos todos" (Because of a few bad ones, we all suffer).

Of course, given people's different levels and types of involvement in, or experience of, *la violencia*, it is difficult to generalize about the link between ethnicity and violence. To some extent, the desire to abandon one's Indianness can be seen as an internalization of racism and fear perpetuated by the army's discourse during the war. Those most concerned with creating a collective amnesia regarding home are some K'iche' ex–civil patrol *jefes* who, having utilized the army's discourse back home in order to justify the cruelty imparted on their own people, perpetuate the negative stereotypes of Indians in the host context. However, for most K'iche's, whose experience of the violence was more murky (that is, they may have been both victims and perpetrators, may have shifted alliances, and may have participated in the violence in indirect ways or by mere association), the need to distance oneself from the shame of past brutality is intertwined with a broader sense of remorse over what is seen to be the root cause of their involvement in the violence: the poverty, ignorance, conformity, and internal cleavages that drew indigenous people into manipulation by both external and local forces. Being illiterate, being unable to communicate or defend oneself, and being manipulated, all of which are seen as Indian traits from home, become profound sources of shame. The feeling of manipulation is not confined to the army's domination back home but extends to the influence of guerrillas and different religious groups as well, all of whom are depicted as negative influences who "tricked ignorant Indians" during *la violencia*.

Both the internalization of shame and its collective construction in Providence are also related to a broader sense of shame over one's origins and basic identity. This seems particularly true for poorer hamlet K'iche's who try to conceal their home identities. I encountered this sense of shame on a daily basis in Providence, and its deep-rootedness often resulted in behaviors that I found perplexing, as described here in my field notes:

Field Notes, Providence, August 1997
Today I dined with Antonio at X (a popular Guatemalan restaurant),
and I slowly noticed that he became extremely silent, nervous,
and uncomfortable when I referred to his home hamlet and some
innocuous news from there, which I thought might interest him. When
we left the restaurant an inebriated K'iche' man—stumbling toward us
with garbage in his hair—approached Antonio and began harassing
him by repeatedly asking if (or rather telling him that) he was from
Xinxuc. An equally drunk Ladino man for whom Antonio had bought
a beer came out and shooed the man away. Poor Antonio seemed
completely humiliated, and I felt that it was my fault for talking about
Xinxuc at all.

The sense of shame as well as sadness over home and its inhabitants
was made especially clear when I showed K'iche's pictures that I had taken
of the home setting, photographs that showed Xinxucians in their everyday
activities, unlike the typical Indian portraits for which people always get
areglados (cleaned up and formally dressed). In some cases, I had specifically asked people how they would want relatives in Providence to see them
in these informal pictures (which turned out to be, for example, working on
the *milpa*, fixing their homes, or planting a small herb garden). Dionisio's
nephew, browsing through my photos with a very gloomy look said: "¡Que
triste es!" (How sad it is!). When I asked him what was sad, he responded
rather incredulously: "Well look at the poverty, the dirt, the clothes, and
look at us here, our house, our car!" Antonio, looking at a picture of his
mother dressed in a rather tattered *traje* and head scarf (a picture that his
own father had loved, exclaiming how beautiful she was), repeated several
times with an extremely distressed expression, "Que pecado, que pecado"
(What a sin/shame). And many, upon seeing a picture of Nicolas, barefoot
and dirty as he leaned proudly against the house he was building with
Providence money—a photo he had purposefully asked me to take to show
in Providence—reacted by saying, "What a shame, look at him without
shoes, and he was even here for a while."

The internalized racism ensuing from the "hostile markings" (Nelson
1999a) of home was verbalized quite clearly in many of the interviews I
conducted in Providence, much more explicitly than in Xinxuc and in
response to a variety of questions on my part: "Our people are like that;
they don't want to liven up" (*No se quieren animar*). "They always just take
advantage" (*Siempre aprovechan*).[15] "They do not have the desire to excel,
to educate themselves" (*No les dan ganas de sobresalir*). "They are asleep"
(*Están dormidos*). "They are not trained, do not have their bearings" (*No
estan orientados*). "That is how we are, how we always are" (*Es asi que*

somos, siempre somos). Angelino, discussing the difficulties of organizing Indians either at home or in United States, says: "It's that we are ... I don't know, stupid, shy, lazy ... that is why we do not excel. Look at me, I do not know if I am stupid or lazy, but I have not accomplished anything here either."

This discourse on shame may be especially pronounced in the host context for a number of reasons. Those who have left Xinxuc may represent to some extent a select group of Xinxucians who have had particularly difficult experiences at home that they have sought to leave behind. The new context of relative wealth in Providence, in addition to the distance from home, where the ingrained dynamics of Ladino racism remain the stuff of everyday life, put into clear perspective and contrast the poverty and injustices suffered at home. It is not hard to see in these words the "hostile markings" of Ladino racism repeated by the K'iche'; it is no wonder, then, that consciously trying to put one's Indian identity behind becomes compelling in a setting such as Providence. Virgilio stated this explicitly one day as I showed him pictures of traditional embroideries made by Hmong refugees in Providence as part of a cultural project. He looked at them with a sort of hidden curiosity—carefully but without displaying too much interest—and simply said, when I asked him what he thought:

> We do not do anything like this because we want to forget our history, and our ancestors (*antepasados*), mostly because of Ladino culture. We want to forget that we are Indian, we do not want to return to what we were. . . . Most of us want to be like Ladinos because we have been so brainwashed about how inferior we were, how *inútil* (useless) we were, by the Ladinos from the *pueblo*.

Echoing my discussions with other K'iche's from the *pueblo*, he added, moreover, that it is mostly Indians from the *monte* (hamlets), that is, those who have suffered the most, who wish to put behind their Indianness:

> Here life is totally different. It's for this reason that many people want to forget everything, because here you come and operate a forklift and that is something that you would never do in Xinxuc. . . . A woman was saying to me, I don't eat *tortillas* anymore, I don't even speak Spanish. Those from the *campo* (hamlets) want to forget more than anything.

Such shame, combined with the marginality and isolation to which many are subjected in the United States, often becomes repeatedly rein-

forced through a chain reaction of events in Providence. Inocente, for example, due to his lack of knowledge and savoir faire upon arriving in the
United States, was swindled in the "asylum trap" by a man who demanded
large sums of money several times but never procured a temporary permit
for him. Too embarrassed to let anyone know that he had been cheated and
was still undocumented (which slots him as the lowest kind of *mojado,* particularly since he had been in Providence for years), Inocente anxiously hid
this fact from even his closer K'iche' friends. When it eventually became
clear to me that he had no documents at all and I offered to bring him to a
good immigration lawyer, he pleaded with me not to tell anyone, as he was
so chagrined that he had been taken advantage of and that people would
say he was a "stupid *indio.*" His feeling of humiliation had thus prevented
him from seeking help, which only reinforced the feelings of shame as well
as marginality.

Some K'iche's in Providence turn this shame onto their own people,
identifying in a sense with the oppressor or colonizer (i.e., Ladinos) by
ridiculing recently arrived *indios* or other Indians who behave in the docile
or conformist ways that mark them as *inditos* (little Indians). In this way
they express disdain for those who embody the submissiveness or inability
to communicate self-ascribed to *nuestra raza* (our race). The use of the
derogatory *indito* does not indicate, necessarily, a categorical rejection of
Indian identity; rather, it is used selectively and contextually to ridicule
those who are behaving, in their eyes, like the poor, manipulable Indians
of home.

This inverted racism, which expresses the degree to which shame is
interiorized rather than a racist position per se, becomes so profound for
some that it reaches what seems to be a sense of rage. In one particularly
violent episode, for example, Mariano—a K'iche' youth whose father died
in the violence, who had arrived in Providence at the age of fourteen, and
who often makes fun of other *inditos*—became enraged at his neighbor
for a seemingly innocent misunderstanding that had no relevance to the
content of his verbal attack and was certainly disproportionate to its ve-
hemence. Swearing at her in English and punching the wall next to her
head, he threatening to beat her, shouting that her new fiancé was a dirty,
ugly *pobre Indio* (poor Indian) and that she was a whore. He added, "When
I came to this country, I was a *pendejo* (a jerk, an idiot), I let people put
me down and scream at me . . . but now I do not let anyone do this, and
I no longer dress as an *indio!*" From what my informants told me, intense
expressions of both shame and rage explicitly related to being Indian came
out with most force either when people were very drunk (considered by
most K'iche's a state during which emotions not otherwise permitted can

be expressed) or during violent disputes. Because of my status as outsider and female I did not witness many such situations, though I did hear about them from closer informants.

The conscious verbalization of collective shame became particularly evident in my discussions of the use of K'iche' language (*dialecto,* or *lengua*) in Providence. Often, when I tried to show off some of my minimal K'iche' phrases with people whose relatives I had known back home, the immediate, almost visceral reaction (aside from surprise) was typically to make me stop: "Oouii, no, those words sound ugly to me!" Estela said the first time I tried, even though she told me, at a much later point, that she speaks K'iche' with her brother.[16] Ceasing to speak *lengua* becomes a primary indication in the host community that one is no longer the Indian "from home." Dionisio, for example, says, "When I first arrived here, Lazaro told me not to speak *lengua,* to forget about that because now we are in America." Virgilio, reflecting on this issue, states: "I think that people here need to speak in English . . . or that they feel badly when one speaks in *lengua.* Although some do speak it." While many K'iche's do speak *lengua* with people *de confianza* (trusted people), most give in to the collective pressure to conceal the traditional language. Nicolas, for example, remembers that in Providence "we sometimes spoke *dialecto,* with family or neighbors from here. But not with those ashamed of their language, right, because the person who is ashamed, well, he has his reason, and then we speak in Spanish." He adds, nonetheless, that "sometimes we liked to speak *lengua* there because nobody understands, not to make fun of anyone, but just because there are things that must stay hidden, so it is better to speak *lengua* (laughs)." Teresa, Virgilio's sister who longs for home, explicitly makes the connection between poverty, shame, and the desire to forget both language and origin:

> There are many people who speak *dialecto* but say they can't, many who come from the hamlets, and they say they are from the capital. . . . I say it is because of shame, they know that the indigenous language is shameful. . . . It is sad because it is part of where one was born, for me it should not be forgotten, I tell the children we must not forget. I think they say this because they think another person will belittle them (*le van a hacer de menos*), because that is what they do, at work, they look down on you, they think that if they say they are from the capital, they feel superior.

Indeed, as broached in the previous chapter, the K'iche' also sometimes speak about the notion of forgetting Indianness in terms of arrogance and pride, or acting as though one is not "what one is." Virgilio explains how this "arrogance" is, in fact, the flip side of shame and forgetting: It is based in the "shame" of being Indian in Providence and in the "arrogance" with which one represents oneself to the ever-present gaze of the home community:

> Most of us who have come here, we do not want to know, we do not want to return to being the same as before. . . . We have a bad habit, I don't know, we always like to say things that aren't true, to give ourselves importance. . . . For example, I am from Xinxuc but I say I am from the capital, or from the mountain but I say I'm from the *pueblo*. . . . So when people leave here, they say, "I was working in a big factory operating machines," and they will never say I came to do a work that many see as inferior. . . . So, to be here is different, it is much more, it is being much more important than being in or going back to Guatemala. . . . Some will even say, we are escaping from all that, the animals, the countryside.

Finally, the internalized shame of K'iche's is also maintained in part through the collective "gaze" of Ladinos in Providence, some of whom come from the eastern region of Guatemala and others who come from the same highland *pueblos* as Indians (including Xinxuc). This is illustrated in the following vignette:

Field Notes, Providence, September 1998

Yesterday, a newly formed organization Guatemalan Americans of Rhode Island, comprised primarily of Ladinos but including a few Indians, for the first time put on a *fiesta* for the Día de la Independencia (Independence Day). In true Guatemalan fashion, there was a beauty contest during which *reinas* (beauty queens) from the four representative departments, including El Quiché, competed—all were Ladina girls who dressed in *traje*, as well as fancy evening wear. Miss Quiché performed a dance of the corn (in *traje*) with a very bored look, and when asked to say a few words about home stated rather nervously that "we from El Quiché are very proud of our ancestors . . . the Aztecs!" Another *reina* lip-synched a perky Selena song, another danced to salsa music, and the fourth—the winner—performed an African dance number.

Soon, a middle-aged Ladina woman in Quiché costume, with long black braids taped onto her shortly cropped hair, did a corn dance around some tortilla stoneware. Behind her, a Ladino man, also dressed in *típico* clothing (though not from El Quiché) and with a *mecapal*[17] around his forehead, followed her at slow, heavy, downtrodden pace, eyes to the ground. At one point he stopped short, pulled a bottle of what was meant to be *cuxa* from his waist, took a sip and pretended to stumble to the ground. Most of the audience roared with laughter. Directly in front of me, a table full of indigenous youth, dressed in fancy eveningwear, stared ahead blankly.[18]

This type of racism extends to other Latino groups as well. I sometimes encountered patronizing and disdainful attitudes when I accompanied K'iche's to various places, particularly in social settings where there were many Dominicans and Puerto Ricans. The Latino community, as evidenced in most gatherings, whether religious or social, is structured around a clear hierarchy where smaller, darker *Guates*, particularly Indian *campesinos,* are seen to be at the "bottom of the heap."[19] I spent a particularly painful evening, for example, in a Latino discotheque: While the Dominican and Latin American salsa-dancing crowd "showed their stuff" on the dance floor, most of the Mayans (primarily male) stood in a silent row at the side of the floor, looking shy and mute. When I danced a merengue with a friend (a fashionable boy whose size and physical traits are distinctly K'iche'), he was greeted by the taller, whiter, better-dancing Latinos with looks that clearly mixed pity, amusement, and scorn. However, I also observed racism against Guatemalans in general (Ladinos and Indians);[20] indeed, as we shall see, the transformation of the Indian/Ladino divide in Providence within a multicultural setting creates a situation where all *Guates,* including Ladinos, are now perceived to some extent as subaltern *indios* (a comparison made explicitly by a K'iche' man).

The relation between ethnicity, violence, and racism in Providence is thus based in a number of factors: the internalized notion that Ladinos were smarter and more astute both before and during the war; the idea that Indians were ill-prepared, ignorant, divided, and therefore weak and manipulated during the violence; the continuing fear that Indians are considered "bad" (subversive, criminal); and, in part, the continuation of a negative "gaze" by some K'iche's, and by Latinos and Ladinos (although, as we shall see below, the latter is balanced as well by a more positive gaze). While the paranoid Indian ex-*jefes* desire to both "forget" (or consciously put behind) the past for reasons having to do more with fear of revenge and the need to justify their past actions, they are able to play on the internalized racism and shame already ingrained both before and during the war to manipulate others into creating this "community of forgetting." While most of the K'iche' do appear to want to abandon the more obvious ethnic markers and behaviors, the loss or retention of Indianness is contextual, multilayered, and shifting. Moreover, the ethnization process varies depending on cross-cutting factors such as generation, gender, religion, ethnic subgroup, and degree of attachment to home.

Cross-Sections: Generation, Gender, and Religion

Perceptions of the transnational "project" tend to vary across generations and genders, leading to different identity strategies. K'iche' youth in Providence are more likely to lose contact with the home community or at least to abandon the idea of returning permanently, which parallels what Bastos and Campus (1995) found with respect to indigenous migration to Guatemala City. The K'iche' youth are also more likely to clearly view de-ethnization as a rejection of poverty, embracing instead a future-oriented perspective in which *superar* (excelling) is crucial. For most, indeed, the *campesino* lifestyle of self-subsistence and *milpa* work is not an aspiration; though they continue to send remittances home as a part of their transnational "duty," younger K'iche's tend to lose interest in the idea of returning, other than for *una vuelta* (a visit).

The desire to forget the outer trappings of Indian identity is especially evident in the style of many K'iche' youths in Providence. Young girls who wore *traje* and dutifully attended to their domestic chores while in Xinxuc, and young boys who worked the land in dirty clothes, became acclimated to the Latino inner-city style of Providence: Mayan boys with gold jewelry, baggy pants, and trendy haircuts can often be seen cruising through the streets of the K'iche' neighborhoods, displaying their wheels and coolly inspecting the goings-on in the street. Indigenous girls can sometimes be seen wearing short skirts, dark lipstick, and heels, hair fashionably bunched up in Latina styles. These changes, though sometimes astonishingly rapid, are usually associated with length of time in the United States. It is not very difficult to distinguish the open, confident style of the K'iche' who have been in Providence for several years from the more reserved, quiet stance of recently arrived migrants. Larger or smaller changes in appearance among K'iche' youths do not necessarily indicate a total acculturation to Latino or American values; while some do begin to frequent discotheques, date non-Indians, or change their eating, clothing, and speech styles, most of the K'iche's I knew did so only to a small extent, preferring not to make *escandalos* (scandals) and thereby invite negative gossip or *envidias*.

Older K'iche's, usually male heads of families and women, tend to maintain a stronger identification with the hometown, both by supporting family and projects back home and by clearly stating that their goal is to return *ya mero* (soon). These transmigrants, who often maintain children, siblings, spouses, and/or parents in Xinxuc, tend to be quite critical of others (often youth, but also other adults) that they accuse of denying their *raza*. Dionisio, for example, criticizes the "arrogance" of youth and shows how he tries to "bring them back":

> The ones who really do harm are the youth, they think they are better (*se creen*), they have their cars and then they pretend they are not even Guatemalan. . . . I know one who is with us at work, and he said, "I am from the Oriente [eastern Ladino region of Guatemala]," but such bad luck he had that I knew his family, where he was born, everything. "And how can you say that you are from there, I know your parents and they are from X hamlet," I said. And I told him the truth, and he got mad at me because I told him the facts of where he was born and all.

Teresa concurs, speaking of a younger Mayan girl whom she describes here:

> There is a girl that I know here, she was already arrogant at home, but here when she goes to work she dresses up, she paints her face and does her hair, and on weekends she wears very short dresses, she walks around from one side to the other, she does her hair, she is *creida* (full of herself) I'm telling you, and even in her speech, though she hardly speaks at all.

(Here, she seems to attribute to this woman both the negative qualities of "arrogance" and the "typically" Indian "shame" of not speaking up.)

Some young Mayans considered to be *creidos* (that is, who obviously reject their "public" Indianness) discuss the sadness and shame regarding the poverty back home and the terrible suffering of their youth primarily in terms of their personal and familial stories. Angelino, Fidel, and Antonio, for example, have been tremendously scarred by the mistreatment and exploitation they received as children back home, forced to trail along with their fathers to the coast, carry massive amounts of *leña* (firewood) on their backs, walk barefoot, and so on. All three speak with resentment about the suffering of their childhood, and in particular about their own fathers' inability to protect them from such poverty. The psychological suffering of poverty and exploitation, for them, is seen as an essential attribute of Indianness; in many ways, the abandonment of Indianness is expressed not only in terms of a rejection of an unjust society but as part of a generational resentment and anger toward one's own kin. Fidel, for example, discussing his family with a mixture of resentment and sadness, says of his father:

Many of us could not go to school, where could we find the money, and we had to work, and my parents were incompetent, they could not maintain or educate us. . . . My father would go to the coast, go to work somewhere, sometimes he would take me, but mostly he would come see us and leave again.

Angelino, whose community in Providence consists primarily of the Latino Alcoholics Anonymous branch, which he says allows him to "stay far away from people and from vices," states:

My father always drank, especially at the *fiesta*. During the *fiesta*, he used to fall a lot because he drank, and he would find himself strewn next to a door, in the street. The people around there, the Ladinos would take hold of him, they would throw water on him, they would set the dogs on him. We had to wait there and watch this. There in Xinxuc there is a lot of scorn for our race (*hay mucho desprecio para la raza*). For this reason I left to the capital when I was ten. I have many resentments against Xinxuc.

Antonio, who has tried desperately to escape the "backwardness" of home, explains why he would prefer not to marry an Indian woman:

You know why, it is because I do not want to return back to the same (*no quiero volver en lo mismo*). I have to change, change the style of life, and if I stay with *mi gente* (my people), maybe they will not understand me, they won't understand.

As this quote shows, Antonio's desire to escape is rooted in a miserable and oppressive past, typical of many K'iche's, which he recounts in the following excerpt with an insistent bitterness. Here, the shame, suffering, and fear of being Indian are located in a painful past tainted by the inability to take advantage of the opportunities and patronage presented by others and by the danger of being seen as an Indian "troublemaker" like his brother. He is determined to avoid both in Providence:

There were eight of us but some of us died as children, I didn't know them. There is my oldest brother, Tomás then María, who died, another sister Rosa, then another María, whose husband died two years ago in a car accident, he was drunk. Then my brother Vicente who killed himself—he had many problems, he drank a lot, and he killed himself. He left his wife and two children. Tomás, he was married, he did his military service, but his problem was that he drank too much, he would come home late at night and beat his wife, and his children had nothing to eat, so his wife went back to her father.

My father could not maintain us, he could not maintain us all, he didn't make much money. Tomás went to work on a *finca* with Don Chepe [Ladino], who had many *fincas* and he even has a son studying at Boston University. Well back then he stopped giving Tomás work because he was drinking. But this man was good, he helped people, he let people plant their maize there, they can have their animals but they have to work on the coast. . . . Well, Tomás, we don't know much about him now, we think he is dead. He disappeared in 1982, but I've heard that he lives in Mexico, but sometimes you cannot believe people, so we're not sure if he is dead. . . . Well, he might have escaped because when he worked on the *finca* he had to travel a lot, he only was home every three months, so the military commissioners of Xinxuc said he was like a subversive, like a guerrilla, because he wasn't around much. He had been in the army, but still the commissioners and the *jefes* they started to slander him, and they said that because he did not join the patrols he was a guerrilla, and they took him, they put him away, they beat him and all that. And even though he explained everything, that he had even done his service, they almost killed him anyway, but they finally let him go because he had his papers. . . . So I think maybe he got scared, and he escaped. . . .

Well, eventually we had to leave the *finca*, and I went to work on the coast when I was ten. Oh! But it was so sad, so hard (*cuesta mucho*)! At that time I realized that those plantations are terrible, I said to myself I am not going to follow my father because he can't. . . . I must find another way to work. You go to the plantations and you wake up so early, it hurts a lot, you get wet, and you have to pick so much coffee or they do not pay you, it rains, there are snakes, animals, the mosquitoes eat you. . . . And there is so much smoke in the rooms because of the firewood, you get sick a lot, everyone is on top of one another, the smoke, the sickness, there is no toilet. . . . And dad didn't even seem to notice! Because all he wants is to work and make some little money for the family. . . . Then I went to work on a cardamom plantation, it was better, and I was able to go to school until sixth grade, and the owner helped me. . . . But only for a few years, because I wanted to help my father, I didn't want him to work too much. . . . So maybe if he had made more of an effort to give me some more education, but I saw that the situation was bad. . . .

And from that time I grew apart from my father, I began to work alone, I worked in a supermarket, and as a bus attendant, and then I became smarter (*mas vivo*) in the city. . . . I decided alone, I do not want to work with dad, because it was too hard for me. . . . So from my youth I hardly was in Xinxuc, mostly I've been in the city, because like I say I like to make my life myself, not follow my father, because he does not do anything/has no trade (*no se dedica a nada*)! So I looked for work myself, I looked for a way to distance myself and find things that were better, to have something in this world, something for me, something for me.

In my discussions with young men such as Antonio, Fidel, and Angelino, their own explanations for the distance they seek to create from their "people" are quite different from the shame/arrogance discourse of those who judge them. Mostly, they say, they do not feel part of the community because from an early age they traveled to the coast or to the capital, learning to "pass" and losing their ties to home; they tell me that their lack of K'iche' language is real and that they did not even speak it at home. All three expressed sadness and alienation because they are not totally accepted either by Ladinos or Indians, and because they are constantly criticized for being *creidos*: They simply want to get away from the many problems and pains associated with their past suffering. Sometimes they express the view that not only ignorance but also the divisions and *envidias* of K'iche's contribute to shame and suffering in Providence. Angelino, for example, who makes a point of maintaining a distance from other K'iche's in Providence, states that he stays away from *mi gente* (my people) on account of the *malas lenguas* (bad tongues), *envidias*, and witchcrafts circulating in the community, which he sees as the product of a damaged and cruel culture and which have caused him much harm in the past.

Ethnic transformation in Providence is also crosscut by religious differences, which have been both divisive and fluid at home, where many people have over time changed religions or practiced a syncretism of several religions. Despite the more general sense of ethnic rupture discussed above, a handful of K'iche' families in Providence, led by Virgilio (who was the leading Catholic Action catechist in Xinxuc), have organized an informal rosary group, gathering once a week (Saturday evenings) to pray and socialize with people *de confianza*, sing songs from home (accompanied by guitars and an accordion), speak *lengua*, eat *comida típica* (traditional foods), and sometimes even wear *traje*. Virgilio explains his leadership of the group in terms of his dissatisfaction with the charismatic church (which has the largest Catholic Latino congregation in the city, gives masses in Spanish, and is attended by Latinos of multiple national origins, classes, and races).[21] He states that charismatic preaching is "irrelevant" and "superficial" as it avoids addressing issues of poverty and injustice, omits any discussion of home, and does not, unlike Catholic Action in Guatemala, create a sense of solidarity and community (though he does concede that the Latino charismatics are engaged in issues concerning the legal situation of Hispanic immigrants). Virgilio states:

> What some people lose here is religion, or some on the other hand become even more converted (*muy convertido*). But here religion is softer, here they don't speak of poverty, of sacrificing oneself to serve others in a meaningful way, here it is just loving God, it is very soft, and people think it is better like this, because they do not want to think of poverty, no. . . . I was saying to someone, here everyone works, not like over there, so here we do not have to fight for our land, because we are not from here, people just want to be in their homes and that's all. Over there we talk more about land, poverty, it is harder. Here the people do not need to ask help for schools, for potable water, for health, everything is different here. . . .
>
> One day, the day of the holy family, I was hoping they [the charismatic priests] would talk, talk about the family that we have left behind, the suffering, right, both of those who stay there, and those who recently arrive, and those who live here too, how to love their family . . . but they spoke of Joseph and Mary, they didn't speak of real life. . . . When I speak I talk about daily life, because God is not superficial, those who only think of what is above, they do not have their feet on the ground. That is why in the prayer group I speak about life here and life back home.

The rosary group uses the *directiva* structure of Catholic Action communities at home, and different members are responsible for various tasks. The group has raised small amounts of money that have been sent to Xinxuc (to family members) for projects such as renovating a hamlet church. For special religious occasions, rosary group members attempt to reproduce some of the traditions of the home community. Around Christmastime, for example, they recreate the *posadas* of the hamlets, which traditionally take place the week before Christmas. In Xinxuc, hamlet Indians collectively reenact the holy family's journey in search of a shelter, walking through the mountains, stopping at various homes for refreshments and prayers, and ending with a nativity scene. Due to the heavy work schedule in Providence, rosary members perform the *posadas* each Saturday of December. Given the spatial layout of Providence neighborhoods, as well as the cold and snow, they create a caravan of packed cars that stop at a chosen member's house on each Saturday. Attesting to the seriousness of preparations and the significance of the event, Estela, who was in charge of purchasing the plastic doll used to represent the baby Jesus, became wildly anxious in November, unable to find a suitable doll in Providence. Insisting that it had to come from Guatemala, she made a special order at one of the Guatemalan-run *panaderías* that ship items from home, and, indeed, within two weeks the plastic Jesus doll had arrived.

Although one of the rosary group's main purposes is to maintain some continuity with home, some of its members explain this connection less in terms of a continuity of ethnic identity per se than as a way of maintaining the moral and community standards of home by preventing "bad behavior" (e.g., drinking or womanizing on Saturday nights), thus ensuring that negative rumors do not reach their families at home (the group has, for this purpose, sent videos of prayer sessions to Xinxuc). As one member explains:

> It is on the basis of religion that we get together, it is religious and friendly, and also so that we do not lose our customs that we have there in Guatemala. Because there are many people, most of the men, who leave their wives back home, well they forget them when they come here.

This small group, however, is not typical of the wider community in Providence, and its activities are looked down upon by other K'iche's who scorn the group's members for behaving as *indios*. One female member told me that on a couple of occasions she had put on a *traje* that her mother had sent from home—once at Christmas (when they took a video of the event to send home), and once on a fall outing to the park (the purpose, again, was to send the pictures home). When I asked her how people in Providence had reacted to the latter occasion, she said:

> Well the Americans more than anything like to see those costumes, they know that they are *trajes típicos*. But the people who know us, they make fun of us. Because they are ignorant, they should not do that because they know very well that these are the clothes that we use over there, and that if we don't use them here it's because it is not practical. . . . So they make fun, they say, "Aai, look at those *indios*, they think they are in Guatemala," they say, "here we are in America," that is what they tell us.

Even the K'iche' who belong to the prayer group make a clear distinction between "Indian" behavior and language allowed within the group but not in other contexts. While speaking K'iche', singing typical songs, dressing one's daughter in *traje*, or carrying one's baby in a *perraje*[22] might be acceptable there, it is not in public. Moreover, whether or not one feels comfortable behaving in "Indian" ways might depend on which members of the group are present. Indeed, as Virgilio explains, the evolution and composition of the group itself has been contentious from the beginning, and its members have been at odds about how much of a connection with the home culture they wish to maintain:

> When we first organized, we were speaking of having a party where there would be a dance and musical groups, like American or Puerto Rican or English, and I said let's put some marimba and they said we don't want to. When we started out it was for birthdays and parties, but then we said we should pray too. But when the group continued without the motive of parties, and became religious, only some of us stayed on, we are the ones who are the organizers.
>
> And once in a while those who were not the organizers would come too, but they started to say what are you doing, we are here in America! . . . They did not want to pray the way we did, in the style of home, to play the guitar or sing the songs from home, no. . . . They are ingrates for sure, and then they started to say, for example to Inocente, right to his face they told him that they did not like this, that we should not do this because we are here and not in Guatemala, you are not in X [hamlet] anymore they said.

Ironically, those most critical of the rosary group (for behaving too much like Indians) are a group of Max K'iche's who were *costumbristas* back home. When I ask Virgilio if he thinks the Max are trying to deny their Indianness through such criticisms, he answers:

> Well no, there are many who claim to be Indian, pure Max, but in their own way. . . . For example, well they will say that between here and Quiché we are different and we do things differently, and not even a Ladino will take anything away from us. "Here we are proud to be in the US and we are going to live in our way, and better yet if we speak another language like English," they say, for example. . . . And some of them even have candles of different colors in their homes, I have heard this but I haven't seen it, I have heard that they are doing *costumbres*. So that is part of them too, and they are also

bad, they have *envidias*, they criticize. . . . They are the ones who were criticizing the group that we formed.

Thus, members of the prayer group—which is based on the catechist model that in previous years had put down *costumbristas* for being pagan and backwards—are now being ridiculed by *costumbristas* for their "Indian" practices in Providence. The *orgullo* Virgilio attributes to the Max and their attempts to belittle the prayer group are thus described not in terms of a "denial" of Indianness or desire to behave like a Ladino, but rather as a continuation of the historical competitions and cleavages between Max and non-Max K'iche's, which, as we have seen, were also exploited during the war. We can see here how the complex historical mixture of religious and ethnic factions have not been forgotten in Providence, where notions of *indio,* and of "Indian," are constructed, redefined, and proscribed in numerous ways.

Finally, many K'iche's in Providence join evangelical *cultos,* including K'iche's who were evangelicals at home as well as a number of *costumbristas* who have also converted in Providence. Many Catholics, for their part, have joined the charismatic church. Both of these congregations tend to emphasize a common Latino ethnicity rather than national or ethnic difference, and, as Virgilio described, they do not address the social and political issues articulated by progressive catechists. Most *costumbristas,* nonetheless, continue to send money to their families in Xinxuc for *ceremonías* (thus paying *una multa,* or a "fine," which goes toward both the *aj q'ij* and the materials necessary for the *costumbre*). Family members ask that the *aj q'ij* pray for ancestral protection from *la migra* and illness or accident, and for help (*ayuda*) to ensure work and ward off *envidias.*

Back home, as well, transmigrant family members, and wives in particular, visit *aj q'ijab'* to ask them to divine whether various rumors concerning their spouses are true and to pray that their husband stay safe, keep his job, remain faithful, and send money. I became friendly with a young Mayan priestess (trained through the pan-Maya movement) in Joyabaj who had developed a successful business divining the plight of transmigrant husbands and performing ceremonies for K'iche' women (who preferred, in the new era of female *aj q'ijab',* to visit her). She also housed them, at a fee, in her home, since many had to make daylong trips into the *pueblo* from their hamlets and sometimes required several ceremonies. In addition, some K'iche's in both Providence and Xinxuc also visit (or send money for) *ajitz*—shamans who specialize in bringing harm—to ask that illness or accident be sent upon their enemy or the person toward whom they have *envidias.* Indeed, both transnational *costumbre* and witchcraft have become lucrative endeavors for those at home who can perform such ceremonies.

As we have seen, ethnic shame and forgetting are, on the surface, primary characteristics of the K'iche' community in Providence and are linked to a distinct lack of ethnic organizing or solidarity. The K'iche' address ethnicity and identity rather indirectly through the notions of shame and arrogance, both in their discussions with me and in their behavior and speech with each other. It is important, however, to make a distinction between shame and forgetting. While shame is usually a more unconscious, internalized process related to years, or centuries, of racism, suffering, and violence, choosing to consciously "forget" certain elements of Indianness is considered a necessary step in survival. Forgetting, or putting the past behind, is spoken of directly as being a conscious choice that people can make—even if it is an uneven, fragmentary choice, as described in the next chapter. However, this desire to forget competes with an important opposing need: to maintain one's roots and links with home, for practical purposes, since one never knows when one will be sent back, as well as for psychological reasons, since coping with the tremendous marginality and uncertainty of transmigration also requires positive identity constructs, both subjective and collective.

Subverting the Indian/Ladino Power Divide

Nelson argues that in Guatemala "[t]he way power demands authentic difference from its others . . . seems to be a disavowal of the tenuousness of its own identification—as non-Indian, as male, as modern, as legitimate, and so on" (1999a: 134). In Providence, this tenuousness becomes apparent as the dissolution of Ladino power and the Ladino Other creates a situation where the categorical identities of both Indians and Ladinos—the imputed contrast that makes both racism and submission to it possible—dissipate. In Providence, living and working with other ethnic groups, including other Latino groups such as Dominicans and Puerto Ricans, as well as Haitians and Africans, allows the K'iche' to open the Indian/Ladino lock to new perceptions of ethnicity and nationality, and, indeed, to situate themselves on an equal footing with Ladinos. Despite the negative "gaze" of Latinos and Ladinos described above, the new context also allows for positive identifications of Indianness since, within a much more diverse ethnic context, Indians and Ladinos—whether *mojados* or legalized—are situated on an equal footing. As Inocente explains:

> Thanks to God, Patricia, I have to tell you that since I came to this country, I suffered a lot when I came, then after two to three years

here, when I had my job, I started to know the city, and I found people around, Ladino people, I look at them as though nothing, and it is not that I am trying to be so strong or proud or anything, because I don't have anything. But you know when I see Ladinos, I see them as nothing. Thanks to some Dominicans at work, I was telling one of them about how the Ladinos treat us at home, and he said, "How can it be, they should be the ones feeling badly when they call you *indio*, because you are *indio*, and you should be proud of it!" He said, "They should be the ones feeling badly, to be in a country that is indigenous, because they are the ones who were brought over to Guatemala, and you, you who are really from there are the real Chapines, the Ladinos are the ones who were brought over! So you should not feel offended when they say this."

And so I know now that when a Dominican or a Colombian see us here, for them there is no difference between a Ladino and an Indian. You know what they call us? A Guatemalan. That is what they say: A Guatemalan. There is no difference. But then crossing the border into my country, then we know who is Ladino and who is Indian. [sighs.]

Indeed, the discourse on ethnicity shifts quite radically away from notions of shame and forgetting when K'iche's compare themselves more specifically to Providence Ladinos. Virtually all K'iche's (representing the many religions, generations, ethnic subgroups, and degrees of "home" attachment) echo Inocente's recognition of the change in power structure and the consequences of the new "equal playing field" on their own identity as constructed vis-à-vis Ladinos:

The Ladinos think they are kings, but here our people, we are all equal here in this country, there is more respect here, because there is law here, but not over there, we are less. (Josefa)

I say the relation [between Indians and Ladinos] is better here. . . . I think about this, and here the indigenous people have their apartment like the Ladinos, with a carpet, a bed, everything the same. And they wear the same clothes. (Angelino)

Over there Ladinos feel arrogant, but here we all have the same work, we're in the same boat, here we can see the señoras Ladinas in the Laundromat, and it's the same for everyone. Ladinos have to talk to us here, everyone needs help, so out of necessity one has to speak with someone, whether they are Indian or Ladino. (Teresa)

Here they [Ladinos] behave more or less with us because they know that in this country we are worth the same. Ladinos and *naturales*, we are of equal worth. But in Guatemala there is a difference because they think they are better, they are arrogant, they can explain themselves better, and they treat us badly. Here they control themselves, because they know we are worth the same, here natural and Ladino does not exist. . . .*La raza* (race), here *la raza* does not exist. (Estela)

In this respect, a common refrain by K'iche' migrants of different genera-tions is, "I am not afraid of anything!"[23] In context, "anything" often refers to Ladinos and to the notion that they might see or treat one as *indito*. This attitude is especially present among younger male Indians who take on a rather macho stance of defense against being treated as an *indio*. Angelino, for example, told me numerous stories regarding injustices and insults at work directed toward either himself or other Indians and against which he has defended himself ("No me deje." "I didn't let them abuse me"). As he says, "I will defend my people, if that person is not doing anything, is a humble person." Fidel, a muscular, tough young Indian, told me that he has often gotten into fistfights with Ladinos in Providence.[24] As he says,

There is one thing, when I am with a Ladino . . . for example when they are angry they call us *indios*, but with me they never have. Because I do not like it for a Ladino to say this, and I've already punched someone because of this. . . . If I have a friend and they call him by his [Indian name], I tell them they can't do this, and then they say "sorry" (*no tengas pena*).

Both young men vehemently state that their response to such racism—whether on the part of Ladinos or other Latinos—has been to point out that the attackers in fact are the inferior, stupid ones, since even with an education and/or legal papers they are still relegated to working in the same menial jobs as Indian *mojados*. Ironically, both Angelino and Fidel (who defend "their people") are, as we have seen, considered by other K'iche's as being "arrogant" and trying to be "what they are not," and they state them-selves that they have distanced themselves from the K'iche' community.

The discourse on equality shifts even more radically when K'iche's compare themselves to Ladinos more specifically in terms of their plight as transmigrants or *mojados*. K'iche's in Providence discuss with pride the superior abilities of Indians to learn English, find jobs, be smart enough

to survive creatively in such demanding circumstances, and to put up with
the harshness and instability of being marginal, exploited, and invisible:

> Here we *naturales* learn fast, we learn to speak and understand. But
> the Ladino here is a *pendejo* (fool, jerk), he doesn't learn anything!
> (Estela)

> In this country, coming from Guatemala, whether one is indigenous
> or Ladino, whether one has studied, it is worth nothing. Even better,
> here in this country *naturales* progress more than Ladinos because
> Ladinos who come here are . . . it's that here in this country it is
> different, at least the language here, so sometimes even though
> Ladinos have studied, it is hard for them, they can't get used to the
> language, or even to the work. If a *natural* is *listo*, here he progresses
> faster than a Ladino. Because I'll tell you something, *naturales* have
> suffered too much in their country, and here they find a place, work,
> well it is easy. But over there, one has to fight, struggle, be strong, to
> work in the mud, under the rain, in the hot sun, on the coast. . . . So
> here we find a place where the work is easier, they come here well
> they feel better, and what's more we concentrate more on the work,
> we give more importance than the Ladinos. (Antonio)

> Ladinos do work but they have an aspect . . . they do not have much
> success because they almost cannot put up with the work. It's hard
> work, and it is very heavy. (Fidel)

> You can't see the difference like over there, there is no difference
> like over there. . . . Because here we are doing well and also, because
> sometimes the Indian has better work than the Ladino, sometimes
> they help them, right, and also because they have the same clothes,
> they are in the same place, whereas over there they live in different
> places, so they feel more important than us: Ladinos with Ladinos,
> Indians with Indians. . . . Here, perhaps they don't really mix, but
> for example at work they can't tell us *vos andate por allá!* (you
> [diminutive] do this or that!) anymore. (Virgilio)

Even Xinxuc's Ladino ex-PAC *jefe*—who is responsible for the deaths
of hundreds of Indians at home and now lives in Providence—seems to
concur with the sentiment that K'iche's advance faster in the United States.
Discussing the fact that many Indian men in Providence are rapidly able
to purchase a car (an essential sign of status), he made this symbolically

poignant statement, with a somewhat bitter laugh: "Back home, we run them over; here, they are running us over!"

As these quotes show, America is not only seen as the great equalizer, but furthermore as a place where the Ladino/Indian power relation can be subverted. In the "equal playing field" of transnational migration, Indians see themselves not as equal to Ladinos but, in fact, as superior transmigrants. That Indians continue, to a large extent, to construct identities in relation to Ladinos in the new context (rather than vis-à-vis other ethnic groups or the dominant culture) is hardly surprising. First, because of the structure of the transmigrant community, Indians are in more contact with Ladinos than with other groups. Second, given that Indian identity at home has for centuries been constructed as a colonized Other, the relation to the colonizing Other—in particular to the *pueblo* Ladinos, whose domination has been experienced in the past as more obvious, direct, and violent than a broader state hegemony—is not likely to simply be dismantled upon migration, especially since many people are in limbo or coming and going between home and host contexts. Freed from the oppressive local structures of home, K'iche's can now reinvent and indeed subvert that power dynamic, both through more equal class relations and also through a self-conscious collective narrative on identity that places them above Ladinos.

The Essentialized *Mojado*

This indigenous discourse of resistance vis-à-vis Ladinos takes shape within the new space of Providence, but it is also framed within a positive ethnic memory that links past and present, and that creates continuity between life back home and in the United States. For example, one critical aspect of transmigrant identity is having the competence to balance several references and skills—whether this relates to economic opportunities, languages, places, or cultural styles. For K'iche's, the ability to adopt multiple identities and to leave options open is already vital back in El Quiché, where the instability caused by poor weather and crops, an insecure economic environment, poor health, and social strife lead most K'iche's to learn to be flexible and, above all, *listo* (literally to be ready, or on one's toes) for whatever opportunities present themselves. Many K'iche's in both home and host communities have thus learned to balance numerous jobs and survival strategies, having worked back home as *campesinos*, as merchants, on development projects, and so on, and in Providence in fish packing, restaurants, agriculture, and factory work. In the uncertain, liminal atmosphere of undocumented transnationalism, the ability to hustle, learn new skills, and keep options open—in other words, to be *listo*—becomes a crucial attribute that differentiates them from Ladinos.

Another way the K'iche' construct themselves as better able to endure the exigencies of transnationalism is through their abilities to use their subaltern identity to play a game of power with authorities. As discussed in Chapter 2, indigenous notions of resistance in Guatemala have often led Mayan Indians to find ways of positioning themselves advantageously within a social hierarchy that they cannot (or may not wish to) radically change. In this respect, finding clever ways to negotiate with those in power, and utilizing intelligence and wit (*ser vivo*, to be alive, or smart) in doing so, are important components of K'iche' survival and identity. This indigenous view of relation to authority is represented in the multitude of Mayan folktales, which, passed down through the generations, center around tales of weak but clever animals who outsmart strong but stupid ones, as well as indigenous "tricksters" who defeat Ladinos through ingenious *trampas*, or tricks (Peñalosa 1996: 9).[25] Playing this psychological game of wits with the oppressor—by calling people's bluff and tripping them on their own weaknesses—was already sharpened during the violence; Virgilio, for example, told me on numerous occasions that his ability to stay alive during *la violencia* (against all odds) was a consequence of his clever word games with the PACs.[26]

This game of wits becomes particularly important for undocumented immigrants, who throughout the transmigrant circuit must habitually contend with authorities such as *la migra*, the police, and bosses; their stories of success in getting out of jams often use this language of being *listo* and *vivo*, even if they do not always succeed. Ironically, one of the ways transnational K'iche' manage in the game is by playing the "dumb *indio*," in order to appease others, "give them what they want," and catch them in their own *trampas*. I witnessed this game on many occasions in Providence, where K'iche's played the mute or overly courteous Indian role with both ex-PACs as well as the American police. Of course, this "trickster" mentality, which involves among other things perfecting one's bluffing skills, is one that tends to be used by illicit border-crossers (*mojados*) in general (Olmos 2001). It is both a coping mechanism used by those who have little to lose but always something to gain and an adaptive response to a stressful and unstable situation in which one actually has little control over one's life. For transnational K'iche's, however, it is this essentialized indigenous trait—cleverness—that becomes integrated into the *mojado* identity and that indeed operates as a powerful counterpoint to internalized shame and fearfulness. Unlike the *porisal* described by Montejo (1999), however, the trickster identity is not viewed in Providence as a ladinoized trait, but rather as a clearly indigenous, subaltern one that enables Indians to outdo Ladinos in the transnational field.

Finally, K'iche's in Providence more specifically place their claims to being better transmigrants within a collective Indian history of previous migrations to the coastal plantations or to the capital. As we have seen, while older K'iche's have usually had a history of cyclical migration to the coastal plantations in Guatemala, many younger K'iche's had migrated to the capital around the time of the violence. Many women I spoke with, moreover, had at some point worked as domestics outside of Xinxuc. Already preceding the move to Providence, these different histories of migration had led to variable levels of ethnic retention or rejection. Indeed, Bastos and Camus (1995) have shown that within Guatemala both coastal and urban migrants exhibit various patterns of identity transformation, with some Maya rejecting Indianness outright, others hiding the external markers of Indian identity when outside their community but maintaining it in the home context, and others accentuating and relocalizing the trappings of Indian ethnicity in the "outside" context. For most, who maintain some degree of attachment to home, the ability to shift identities in different contexts comprises the essence of a hybrid indigeneity. "Chameleon strategies"—the capacity to separate and balance different spatial and laboral contexts, juggle cultural references, and hide some elements of identity in some contexts and reproduce them in others—are thus essential components of this migrant Indian identity.

As discussed in the previous chapter, the memory of these internal migrations enables the K'iche's, to some extent, to organize themselves strategically within transnationalism. Here, I argue in addition that this memory comprises a key theme around which transnational identity becomes asserted, enabling K'iche's to construct a continuity with the past through localized historical understandings. Indeed, as Max Weber pointed out in his seminal essay on ethnicity, ethnic groups integrate people who "entertain a subjective belief in their common descent because of similarities of physical type or of customs or both, or because of memories of colonization *and migration*" (Weber 1997; my emphasis). In *la costa del Norte*, K'iche's draw on previous experiences of movement within Guatemala to make sense out of their current displacement and forge new transnational identities. Though the anguish and abuse of their mobile history form part of the painful memories from which they seek to escape, transmigrant K'iche's nonetheless use the lessons of a past filled with distress and dislocation in order to cope with their vulnerability and preserve a sense of control. In this respect, knowing how to *aguantar* (endure) suffering and frustration, when to *aprovechar* (take advantage of) life's opportunities, and, importantly, being able to cope with the distance from one's land and family, all become important indigenous traits that differentiate them positively from their Ladino counterparts. Whether the K'iche' in Providence do, in reality, achieve more material success than Ladinos is beyond the scope of this research. However, the space of transnationalism clearly has permitted them, to some extent at least, to escape the oppressive structures of home and simultaneously reappropriate historical elements of Indianness in order to transform them into a source of relative collective strength.

THE MANY FACES OF K'ICHE' ETHNICITY

Constructions of Indianness among the Providence K'iche' thus have little to do with either the folkloric representations of traditional ethnographies (speaking *lengua*, wearing *traje*, practicing *costumbre*, etc.) or with the discourse on Mayanism in Guatemala, which has reappropriated some of these essentialized cultural traits to create a political project. Here, I have approached the issue of identity as a way of life, a historically grounded sense of survival and adaptability, a set of very complex, changing, and intersecting worldviews, which rather than disappearing through displacement become consciously reinterpreted to meet the demands of the present. Transnational Indians subvert representations imposed on them and reappropriate space in order to create something different; in doing so, they generate their own essentializations, based in a long history of migration and multiplicity, and particularly useful for the transnational project. For these transnational actors, "hybrid identities" have less to do with the juxtapositions of tradition and modernity engendered by fluid borders than with historically grounded coping mechanisms devised to struggle against profound violence and dislocation. Their own brand of ethnic identity integrates the realities of displacement and globalization within a reconstructed discourse concerning what it means to be and to act like Indians.

It is interesting to add to this discussion how the Mayanist project is perceived by the Providence K'iche', who are removed from both the cultural and larger human rights projects of home. While many of the K'iche' in Providence left Guatemala before these movements gained momentum, some have heard glimpses and rumors concerning the postwar developments at home. Some, like Antonio, openly mock and reject the Maya movement; when I showed him pictures of the Mayan New Year ceremony led by Gaspar and attended by his own father (an *aj q'ij* who works with PLANTAS), he cynically called it a *mafia*, and then said they are free to do what they like. Others make little connection between the new Mayanism, which they relate to those "ancient Maya" of long ago, and the practices of Indians today. Dionisio, for example, says:

The problem is that when I grew up my parents converted to Catholicism, but they were of *costumbre*, but not in this way [points to the picture]. What they would do is find a man dedicated to doing that, a bit like a *catequista*, and then bring candles, incense, flowers, but they only listen but they don't participate, and when the prayers are over they go home. Now the traditional *costumbre*, that is totally Maya, what they are doing there with the four cardinal points, that is something else, that is more like a mass where many people go, it is more like the Catholics, and the *costumbristas* are getting involved in it too now, because now everyone does his own thing. . . . What we saw in the photo, that is from long ago, from the Rey Quiché, and now it is not only for one person but for the public. They used to do this before in the time of Tecún Umán,[27] but because of all the divisions it was impossible to keep people together, so everyone, what they remembered, what they adapted, what they saw, what they heard from their parents was passed down, and each one did what he wanted what he felt like, what he could still remember.

As this quote shows and as this chapter illustrates, the concept of Indian identity is extremely confusing in the postwar context, particularly for those who find themselves removed from the boundaries of Xinxuc—a home context where, despite continuing factionalism, the references of land, family, and custom, combined with the discourse on Indian rights, create a sense of a collective identity grounded in space and time. For the K'iche' in Providence, this identity becomes "up for grabs" and replete with contradictions. The same person might display a tremendous ethnic shame (surrounding the negative attributes ascribed to and felt by Indians) and simultaneously integrate the collective discourse on the superiority of transmigrant Indians vis-à-vis Ladinos.

The difficult balancing act between distancing oneself from this shame (by discarding certain elements of Indianness) and maintaining one's roots and being true to oneself (by "not changing," or not becoming too arrogant to be Indian) became particularly clear to me during a long interview with Estela and Magdalena, two women with whom I spent much time and who formed part of the rosary group. Throughout the interview, Magdalena (whose parents are traditional *costumbristas*) smirked, giggled, rolled her eyes, and dismissed most of my questions concerning some of the more obvious reminders of Indianness from home. When I asked her if she could describe how her father used to do *costumbre* at home, she said abruptly, "I don't remember, I didn't pay attention to him"; when I asked her if she speaks in K'iche' she replied, "I can but never do," and when I asked why not, she quite adamantly said, "No!" (i.e., "I don't like it, it is awful, it does not deserve an explanation"); when I asked if she ever misses the *temascal* (traditional steam bath), she laughed and said "that oven?"; and, the *co-fradías* were "a diversion for the drunks," she told me with a smirk. Estela also on many occasions made derogatory comments about things Indian (I overheard her once, for example, joking about an *indito* with another K'iche'). However, when I turned the conversation more directly to a discussion about cultural remembering and forgetting in the context of Mayanism, their responses changed; indeed, they connected it immediately to the self-conscious process of remembering and forgetting in Providence:

[P: Do your brothers still practice *costumbre* at home?]

M: No, that is something the old people practiced before. . . .

[P: And today?]

E: Those people do it but they are little old people (*viejitos*) who still believe in the times from many years ago. But today, with the years that go by, people are becoming smarter, they are awakening more (*van despertando mas*). . . . If they go to church it is better because then they learn to be directed (*orientado*) about spiritual things, and God. But those little old ones who do those things are those who really live in the past. They are stuck there (*fijen ellos allí*), acting the way their grandparents or parents taught them to. There are many who still believe in the old beliefs, but there are many who do not. . . . We believed in that before, and now anyone can do their thing, and we say okay, everyone can adore God in his way. . . .

[P: What do you think of the ceremony that I showed you in the pictures, where Gaspar is doing a Mayan New Year offering with candles in front of the church?]

E: Well what must have happened is that they did it in the way it was done many, many years ago, but that is not something of *aj q'ijab'*, that is a religious culture from many years ago. They do that so that the cultures from many years ago, of the Mayans and stuff, I don't know how it's called, so that it doesn't get lost. In other words there are things that are no longer done because of the times we live in. But then if they do it is so that it does not get lost. Like us here, for example: If we want we can learn English, and if we want we can forget our language. . . .

M: [emphatically] But that can't be lost! That cannot be forgotten because one brings it with one!

E: Yes, but if one wants to say, "I'm not going to speak anymore, I'm going to learn something else," then with time one forgets!

So what they are doing is that they do not want to forget. . . .
I have a cassette here that is a *cántico* (canticle) in K'iche', and
there it explains how one must not forget, forget the culture, of
the Mayans. . . .

[P: Where did you get that cassette?]

M: My mother gave it to me. . . .

E: So it's there that one realizes that, one mustn't forget what one is!
We have many people who just don't want that, who go back to
Guatemala arrogant, stuck up, and they don't want to remember
that they can speak in *dialecto*. . . . Many people do that! They
don't want speak over there, let alone here. But we are, . . . we
stay the same, because we continue to talk here. . . .

[P: But Magdalena, you told me you don't like to speak in
lengua. . . .]

M: [defensively] I like to, I like to. . . .

Given the large and growing numbers of Guatemalan Indians migrating to the United States to work as labor migrants in places such as
Providence, it is clear that the notion of indigenous identity needs to be
rethought, not merely in terms of colonial relations or identity politics
or vis-à-vis host communities, but in a broader context characterized by
global movement and transnational dialogue. In transnationalism, where
the boundaries of state become elastic, neither ladinoization, assimilation
to some generic Latino identity, nor ethnic crystallization are adequate
explanations for ethnic transformation, which is multilayered and shifting.
Moreover, as Bastos and Camus (1995) have already argued with respect to
indigenous migration at home, what might often appear as the "ladinoization" of Indian migrants is often a superficial change for pragmatic purposes, remaining only an external expression of identity: It does not entail
the assumption of a Ladino identity or the appropriation of Otherness. As
I have illustrated here, in both Xinxuc and in Providence debates about the
"invention" or loss of culture seem superfluous since, as Kay Warren says, it
is "the continued practice of embracing and rejecting all sorts of intersecting ideas and identities" (1998: 12) that broadly characterizes culture and
survival among Guatemalan Indians. Or, as Virgilio says:

For me there is not one way of being indigenous, there are so many
ways to be indigenous: One can have an Indian heart and not
speak *lengua*, one may or may not listen to marimba, one can be
Catholic or evangelical or *costumbrista*, there are so may ways, it is
very difficult to say only one . . . and it is normal I think because
it is like saying that an American is, is someone who eats a lot of

hamburgers! [Laughs.] . . . If [Mayanists back home] do it with all their heart and that is how they feel, if one feels it and wants to do it, it is good . . . that is what is important. . . . All things that are invented or are done for the good, so that people feel good, then it is important, that is what I always say.

Chapter 6

Memory and Guilt

The previous chapters have examined how various types of memory, including the reorganization of older social practices and ethnic representations, have been reworked *aquí* and *allá* in order to create various types of symbolic capital through which transnational K'iche's reconstitute identities in the aftermath of war and rupture. However, the agency and resilience of transnational K'iche's, that is, their ability to draw upon various cultural frames in order to maintain some sense of coherence, must not be overstated. Indeed, personal and collective suffering continue to dominate the lives of many of the K'iche' both at home and abroad, effected by poverty, mistreatment, racism, sickness, political violence, fear, psychological abuse, death, dislocation, cultural rupture, illegality, marginality, and uncertainty.

I now shift the lens to a more subjective dimension of identity, in particular the memory processes through which the K'iche' revisit (or choose not to revisit) the tremendous violence of the past and make sense out of the chaotic events that propelled the migration. In Xinxuc, such personal and collective memories are ambivalently situated within the context of national projects to recuperate historical memory that have formed part of the postwar reconciliation effort. For the Providence K'iche' (who are removed from such projects), memory processes are complex: While *la violencia* is (negatively) conflated with Xinxuc, "home" can also come to represent, symbolically at least, a place of the past and future that stands as a counterpoint to the drudgery and alienation experienced in Providence. At the same time, however, memories of home often elicit painful emotions—the guilt of having left, the fear of being forgotten—which then become connected to *la violencia* in various ways.

This chapter thus highlights two questions that have been put in motion in the previous pages: How do the different social spaces of Xinxuc and Providence influence the memory processes that enable people to cope with past horror and go on with life? And how is the synchronous temporality of transnationalism—where "here" and "there" no longer correspond to "before" and "after"—reconstituted in such transnational memory processes? This final discussion, which draws upon current understandings of the connections between culture, trauma, and social suffering (Kleinman et al. 1997; Das et al. 2000, 2001), seeks to offer a constructive critique of some of the institutional and psychological models used on a broad scale to promote healing and justice among "postconflict" and displaced populations.

The concept of memory has long fascinated scholars from all disciplines.[1] Anthropologists have evoked the notion of embodied memory, which serves to transmit tradition and history through ceremony, everyday ritual, and bodily practices (Connerton 1989). This type of social memory forms the basis of Bourdieu's concept of habitus, or "history turned into nature" (Bourdieu 1977: 78), whereby embodied memory (and forgetting) play a vital role in forming and articulating the signs, practices, and images that become taken for granted and habit-forming in the present. I have described some of these notions in past chapters as they relate to concrete and symbolic forms of identity reorganization among the transnational K'iche'. In examining postwar memories of violence and dislocation here, I shall focus more particularly on narrative memory, that is, the ways in which people revisit, transform, and seek to give meaning to past experience through language.[2] Critical to this approach is the idea that processes of remembering and forgetting are always framed vis-à-vis present political and social spaces and audiences, as well as visions of the future. As Antze and Lambek state, "[M]emories are never simply records of the past, but are interpretive reconstructions that bear the imprint of local narrative conventions, cultural assumptions, discursive formations and practices, and social contexts of recall and commemoration" (1996: vii).

The process of remembering is an intersubjective one, shaped by a constant interplay between individual and collective forms of giving meaning to past experiences. It is therefore defined by membership in a community and requires a shared sense of values, expectations, and "speech genres" (Morris 1997: 33). It also requires a sense of emplotment, whereby sequence and causality are ordered within an explanatory logic that enables the person to communicate meaning to others and shape experience for himself or herself (Feldman 1991: 14; Ricoeur 1984; Good 1994). Within such culturally situated meanings, shared moral notions of good, evil, hero, victim, justice, and the like come to be created in the present. The process of remembering may also, conversely, shatter repetitive or conclusive images of the past, thereby creating fragments of memory and reinscribing new imaginary possibilities into the present (Ricoeur 1984: 219). The presence of silences, uncertainties, and metaphors in people's representations can thus illuminate the many areas of ambiguity and longing in people's subjective worlds (DelVecchio Good, Munakata, and Kobayashi 1993).[3]

Clearly, the experience of prolonged terror and persecution can grossly interrupt the possibility of constructing meaningful narratives of the past and present. The narratives of those who have witnessed an "unmaking of the world" (Scarry 1985) are thus often couched in denial, suppression, rationalization, and guilt (Suarez-Orozco 1990). Both mental health and sociopolitical projects oriented toward healing the wounds of those who have suffered political violence—projects ranging from individual therapeutic models to collective testimonial projects and truth commissions—seek to create a social space within which people's past suffering can be renarrated, transformed, and communicated in ways that both validate and give meaning to past suffering. In war-torn countries where silence, denial, and the suppression of memory were not only concrete strategies utilized by authorities to instill fear and confusion but also became critical survival mechanisms during periods of paralyzing terror, learning to narrate a new social memory that counters the cruel distortions of "official stories" can lead to an important recognition and validation of past injustice (Martín-Baró 1996; Summerfield 1998; Bracken 1998; Lira 1997).

Recent transcultural literature on trauma and memory, however, cautions against a universal application of Western trauma models that posit memories as discrete entities which, if repressed or blocked, may be retrieved within the self and processed through different types of intervention (Bracken and Petty 1998). In this respect, the very notion of memory—its placement within a particular cosmological and epistemological order, and its relation to cultural notions of time, space, and causality—must be understood within specific worldviews (Bracken 1998). Indeed, among non-Western persons, notions of self, community, time, history, death, suffering, culpability, and fate are often embedded in ontologies that differ radically from the chronotopic conventions (that is, how experience is constituted by and embedded within particular spatiotemporal dimensions) implicit in Western models.

Kay Warren states that "memory and its various embodiments—recalling, forgetting, denying, repressing, erasing, revitalizing, replacing, veiling, rejecting, reenacting—have always been preoccupations in Mayan communities" (1992: 193). Other authors have shown how Indian communities in Guatemala have often "Mayanized" outside time and experience by using local cyclical memory—encompassing local beliefs, practices, and relationships to the ancestors and ecology—to make sense of changing social processes (Tedlock 1982; Bourgey 1997; Earle 1986; Burgos-Debray 1983). In other words, as Arias (1997) argues, it is by placing the outside within local worldviews and perceptions of time and causality, and by bringing their own particular knowledge to bear on the framing of issues, that Indian communities have been able to preserve continuity and maintain their autonomy and identity through time. By continuously adding new circumstances to older repertoires rather than simply replacing them, "the burdens of time do not so much change as accumulate" (Tedlock 1982: 176).

How do the postwar K'iche', whose "shared moral worlds" and cultural models have been so shattered by violence and dislocation, reemplot the past within the different spaces of transnationalism? In the following sections, I illustrate how people's memories of the past in Xinxuc integrate local conflicts and moral frames that do not always fit with the "counter-discourse" on justice and accountability of official memory projects. In Providence, on the other hand, there exists a public "moral community of forgetting," that is, a tacit collective impetus to suppress and deny the past, as well as a lack of institutional categories or spaces within which memories can be formally or purposefully narrated (such as human rights courts, testimonial projects, political asylum hearings, or psychiatric evaluations).[4] Nonetheless, traces of past violence constantly resurface, inextricably intermingled with painful memories of home that elicit guilt, accusation, sadness, and the ever-present need to both understand and justify one's own and others' actions of the past and present.

REMEMBERING LA VIOLENCIA IN XINXUC

Institutional Memory Projects

Numerous human rights, historical memory, and mental health projects have been established in postwar Guatemala. Their mandate, broadly speaking, has been to respond to the profound social and psychological damage produced by la violencia, which led to a vicious cycle of collective fear and silencing and denial. The process of peace and reconciliation in Guatemala called for the difficult task of coming to terms with a blood-spilled past, including documenting wartime abuses by all actors and setting up institutional mechanisms for justice and healing. One of the main accomplishments of the Peace Accords in this regard was the establishment of an independent Truth Commission (formally known as the Comisión para el Esclarecimiento Histórico, Commission for Historical Clarification or CEH). This project resulted, in 1999, in the publication of a lengthy report entitled "Guatemala: Memory of Silence," which contradicted years of official denial concerning the massacres, tortures, disappearances, and executions that resulted in the deaths of over two hundred thousand civilians during the thirty-six-year war.[5] Through the use of detailed statistical and historical data, the CEH report "officialized" information that although previously known—relegated to human rights reports and academic publications—had rarely reached the mainstream media either nationally or internationally. It documented many of the social realities of the war previously silenced by the mechanisms of state terror and repression: that the large majority of the violence was attributable to the army and sustained through the support of its military allies;[6] that the "excesses" committed were not the result of local disputes or overeager military subordinates but of explicit counterinsurgency strategies to divide and terrorize the population; and that the scorched-earth policies and massacres of the early 1980s constituted an act of genocide against the Indian population (CEH 1999).[7]

The CEH project followed (and complemented) an earlier report put forth by RHEMI (Interdiocesan Project of Recuperation of Historic Memory), entitled "Guatemala: Nunca Más" and directed by Bishop Juan Gerardi, who had worked near Xinxuc during the worst period of the violence. Underlying both the CEH and RHEMI projects was the idea that a just future can only be realized by recounting the truth in all its horror and coming to terms with its causes. The RHEMI project sought to cope with the difficult ambiguities and moral chaos of past violence by working within individual communities (with victims and perpetrators) and by promoting local notions of justice and healing. Two days before the report's publication in 1998, Bishop Gerardi was brutally assassinated, and the subsequent attempts to cover up the political nature of the murder were bitter reminders of the aura of violence and terror remaining from the civil war.[8] As his death sadly showed, memory is a dangerous political tool in Guatemala; this brutal killing was also a symbolic one, an attempt to obliterate the possibility of revisiting past truths.

The concepts of "truth" and "memory" continue to be critical—and lethal—sociopolitical issues in Guatemala. Their presumed tangibility underlies the foundations of both the Peace Accords and the multitude of human rights organizations working in the country. In terms of understanding the sociological roots and consequences of violence, and of denouncing those responsible for its orchestration and their international allies, the political significance of memory projects such as the CEH and RHEMI cannot be disputed. Indeed, both projects contextualized the violence within both the authoritarian and racist state model and the highly unequal economic structure spawned by colonization and reinforced by a weak state, Cold War alliances, and a hegemonic military apparatus. These projects enabled thousands of victims of the civil war to voice their stories of suffering by providing testimonials; for individuals who contributed to them, the feeling of vindication and clarity that such official documents bestow on a long-manipulated and distorted social reality was significant.[9]

However, as Gerardi's assassination pointed to, the reception of such collective memory projects within an ongoing political climate of fear and impunity was problematic. Although both reports showed clearly that a majority of the destruction was a direct result of government policy, the official CEH stopped short of identifying individuals responsible for the massacres—a decision widely criticized by human rights advocates but compelled by the army, who otherwise threatened not to cooperate with the project during the peace negotiations.[10] The Guatemalan government's official response to the CEH project, moreover, was far from conciliatory: It rejected the majority of recommendations suggested by the CEH, claiming that most had already been met. These factors, in addition to the 1996 Law of National Reconciliation, which extinguished political liability for crimes committed during the war, contributed to a tangible aura of impunity throughout the country in the years following the signing of the peace. Although the Truth Commission's accusations of genocide did, in the end, open up "the possibility of indictments against individual officers, since the amnesty did not cover crimes against humanity" (Goldman 1999), in many highland areas people remain too terrorized to implement accusations in the courts. Indeed, a significant number of cases that have been brought to court for wartime human rights violations have been marred by judicial "complications," often being extended for years or culminating in acquittals, short sentences, or refusals to condemn higher-ranking authors of human rights abuses.

A related area, the exhumation of the multitude of mass graves strewn throughout the countryside, has received much support at the international level. But again, although close to two hundred mass graves and clandestine cemeteries have been unearthed to date by teams of forensic anthropologists and human rights workers, the UN has conceded that prosecutors have used forensic evidence against suspected killers in only a minority of cases where criminal complaints have been filed by survivors. The UN blames these omissions on the consistent climate of fear and intimidation, and has documented dozens of cases of threats against those filing charges as well as human rights workers involved in the excavations (Weissert 2000). The continued impunity enjoyed by most perpetrators of past violence, the government's response to the Truth Commission, and the 1999 defeat of a national referendum that proposed to implement many of the recommendations of the CEH and Peace Accords, all point to the profoundly political and conflictive nature of postwar projects that seek to build peace through the recapturing of a collective "social memory" of violence. They also put into question the universal viability of internationally imposed reconciliation efforts in a context of continuing divisiveness.

Both the RHEMI and CEH reports go to great lengths to describe and denounce pernicious wartime strategies that have resulted in present social fragmentation—a fragmentation that, ironically, makes the project of "recuperating" a common memory problematic throughout the highlands. In particular, the reports point to the army's use of forced complicity (which compelled people to witness or execute acts of brutality against their own) and the criminalization of victims (which turned anyone who acknowledged or questioned the army's brutality into "legitimate" targets of repression), both of which "deeply affected values and behavioral patterns, as violence became a normal method of confronting conflictive situations and promoted contempt for the lives of others" (CEH 1999). In addition, as the CEH points out, guerrilla tactics of temporary occupation and "retreat" (which often left sympathetic Indian communities vulnerable to brutal army attacks) created a profound sense of abandonment and deception, sometimes leading entire communities to turn themselves over completely to the army.

These divisions, changing alliances, and complicities of the past, as well as the heterogeneous nature of *la violencia* (which was experienced in different ways from one community to the next) have had a profound impact on local reconstructions and remembrances of the war in the present. In many communities, the line between forced and willing complicity, between actual participation in violence and necessary allegiance with killers, and between who was "right" and who was "wrong" remains extremely confusing and fuzzy. In places such as Xinxuc, where, despite minimal guerrilla activity, merely being Indian and Catholic, being related to a "suspect" person, or living in a "suspect" hamlet could all spell a death sentence, people were forced to make sudden, radical shifts (in religion, living quarters, political allegiance, and morality) during the war and then internalize a logic to either justify their own actions or simply survive. Moreover, the broader terror often became intimately intertwined with preexisting local power dynamics, land feuds, and interpersonal or familial *envidias* (Hale 1997; Stoll 1999). What sort of collective narrative or common "moral community" could encompass the profound personal and communal cleavages created by such chaos?

Herein lies one of the biggest paradoxes and obstacles faced by institutional memory projects in Guatemala and in other postconflict regions (aside from the ongoing repression and lack of accountability within which they often seek to be heard): While pointing out and examining the tremendous divisions and distortions produced by terror, which destroy collective mechanisms for speaking out and making sense in the present, they simultaneously propose the idea of a "collective" memory. However, the underlying idea that either social memory or cultural interpretations of violence can be framed or narrated coherently at all remains highly problematic, since the very success of this type of state terror is to dramatically divide communities and to destroy the cultural models through which people have previously sought meaning. In this context, the recollection of murky and often shameful events cannot be neatly subsumed into the larger narrative and logic of a national collective memory project. Moreover, for the many Mayans who internalized (partially or fully) the categorical and authoritative logic of the army—that the violence was necessary in order to protect the community from "evil" guerrillas—projects such as the Truth Commission are not only baffling but also threatening: either because they question and oppose the authority of the army (and are therefore dangerous) or because they reopen extremely painful and frightening memories without really being able to offer a resolution to one's past suffering or sins, or those of one's neighbors.

Beyond the Boundaries of Institutional Memory

Given this present context, it is perhaps not surprising that, despite the collection of a large number of testimonies, the majority of Mayans did not come forward to participate in these projects. As the CEH itself states, "[A] large number of people continue to remain silent about their past and present suffering, while the internalization of traumas prevents the healing of their wounds." The report's authors attribute this reticence to fear, since the perpetrators of violence continue to live in the highlands. In communities such as Xinxuc, however, where most people lived through brutal violence but did not participate in either the CEH or the RHEMI projects, reasons for withholding testimonials went beyond the fear of their persecutors. For many, the CEH seemed to represent one more foreign body that had parachuted in, urging them to join a cause that could help them. Based on past experiences, many believed that *los Derechos Humanos* ("the Human Rights," a personification of the abstract concept of human rights),[11] like previous outsiders soliciting their participation (whether the army or the guerrillas), must not be trusted.[12]

Unlike some other southern Quiché communities (such as Santa Cruz del Quiché, Joyabaj, and San Andrés Sajcabajá, for example), which had a much larger group of both national and international NGOs encouraging relationships between such institutional groups and community members, most of Xinxuc's population had little trust in outside groups. Others simply did not believe in the usefulness of revisiting the past: Such memory projects could not bring back their loved ones, could not bring to "justice" those responsible, and could bring back only the memory of profound suffering and pain.[13] The only justice, many implied, was a divine or cosmic one, just as the only true knowledge of what had happened lay with God: "Solo Dios sabe lo que pasó." In explaining why they did not contribute to the memory projects, several Xinxuc widows stated that everyone (Indians and Ladinos) already know why their husbands had been targeted: because they were poor, Catholic, and Indian. Retelling their stories would only reinforce this painful fact and would indeed make the wartime polarities even clearer to all those who continue to hate, or fear, Indians.

Moreover, the idea of digging up the "truth" is not seen as catharsis or justice but rather as potentially leading to further conflict and, many say, a resumption of violence. Indeed, the ongoing climate of violence and fear reflected in high levels of delinquency, public lynchings, and human rights violations, as well as continuing inequality, provides a highly precarious context for institutional memory projects. One K'iche' woman stated:

> We don't know if there will be peace, because now we see how the
> prices are increasing, for sugar, soap, salt, everything. And that
> is when the violence will start again. Why do I say this? Because
> there are people who can buy these things and there are those who
> cannot and they start to rob things, and to claim things, and to fight
> with others, and they will kill you. We hear about this happening
> in the capital. They say there will be peace, with the army, with the
> guerrillas, but who knows, it is not happening. We hope to God that
> it happens, but who knows. Because the Ladino people do not like
> us.

As Zur (1998) has shown, given the devastation of the past and the instability of the present, local reconstructions of meaning among K'iche' Mayans remain highly ambiguous. They often rely upon a multitude of layers of discourse, resulting in open-ended, shifting explanations and stories, rather than upon a coherent narrative of the past. Alternative interpretations of past violence shift between a variety of presently available discourses, depending on the present context, place, and audience; differing concepts of culpability and justice are balanced between various public and private reconstructions of the past. Some of these discourses have been part of the Mayan cultural fabric for centuries and are drawn from traditional categories of causation based in the concepts of fate (*suerte*), *envidia*, *brujería*, and ancestral punishment (*castigo*), thus privileging notions of the supernatural, the return of ancestral spirits, and the cyclical nature of time. Others frame the reconstruction of memory within a religious or sociological language stemming from the years preceding or concurrent with the civil war (e.g., the language of liberation theology, which seeks to remember the "martyrs" of the violence, or political explanations pointing to Ladino domination and racism). Yet others employ discourses imported from the outside and widely propagated during the period of national reconciliation (the discourse of "human rights" and "indigenous rights"), discourses that respond to the devastation of the war by invoking a national ethnic resurgence and its placement within civil society. While alternatively utilizing several of these frames and discourses in reconstructing memories, people may also balance internalized "official stories" of the violence as propagated by the army (e.g., "the guerrillas were bad people against whom we had to defend ourselves") while simultaneously conjuring contradictory personal memories (e.g., "we know that it was not the guerrillas committing violence, as we never saw them").

Since any one person may utilize several or all of these discourses in describing and explaining past violence, it is difficult, from a more rigid Western perspective that values logical consistency, to comprehend how the radically different assumptions of each can be balanced within a coherent worldview or moral frame: The splitting, ambivalences, and contradictions of such narratives seem profound. Explanations of past violence embedded in notions of fate, witchcraft, or ancestral punishment entail self-blame (e.g., "the ancestors were punishing us for past misdeeds") or the suspicion of *envidia* (e.g., "someone harmed us because they envied what we had"); in these cases the underlying explanation for suffering might be paraphrased as, "we were punished for being a sinner or antisocial." The apparent political neutrality and passivity of such cosmological explanations seem irreconcilable with the free-will rationality and active stance implicit in social justice and restitution models (of "new" Catholic and human rights groups), where "good" and "evil," "victim" and "perpetrator" stand in binary opposition rather than as part and parcel of a common reality of personhood or community, as in the traditional ontology. Here, rather than self-blame or fate, the active construction of victimhood prevails. Depending on which explanation is privileged, models of justice and action will differ significantly. For instance, a belief in witchcraft or *envidia* as an explanation for one's suffering might entail supernatural retribution characterized by caution, secrecy, and patience. In contrast, a belief in the human rights model suggests taking a public stand and speaking out against a perpetrator. How are these conflicting explanations and responses balanced?

The ability to syncretize various influences—ontologies, languages, and practices—has characterized Mayan survival strategies through centuries of struggle and repression. The "tolerance for alternative explanations" (Zur 1998), which may appear as a profound ambiguity or ambivalence (a lack of logical unity), represents a historical form of resistance against the oppressive encroachment of outside influences. Indigenous syncretism can be described as a culturally embedded tendency to draw on and combine internal and external (or traditional and modern) discourses, worldviews, and practices for the sake of survival. This blending of cultural models is, and has long been for Mayans, a successful way of keeping options open and hence surviving within unequal power dynamics.

As a mechanism for coping with past violence, the generation of syncretistic explanatory models and narratives seems to be an adaptive way to "re-member" the chaos of the past, since no single explanation could possibly explain the level of brutality committed by one's own kin and neighbors, and, perhaps, by oneself. Annis states that many Indians "have not mythified themselves or heroized their resistance" but feel instead that whole communities "fell victim to temporary madness" (Annis 1988: 173). In order to cope with this intolerable past and the unbearable guilt and suffering of having been forced to witness or participate in brutalities external to their moral worlds, a variety of memory strategies are utilized, fluctuating between continuity and disjuncture with the past, between different explanatory models for the violence, and between various representations of self. Mayan reconstructions of past violence thus rarely revolve around one coherent logic or metanarrative; instead, they weave together various threads of meaning that stem from fragments of both past and present cultural models and references.

While some of the K'iche' are able to balance several different explanatory frames to achieve some sense of meaning, others have suffered a total loss of faith in any system of meaning, feeling deceived by God, the ancestors, the army, the guerrillas, and their own family members. Such individuals, unable to integrate past memories into the present, are often "isolated within their own physical and emotional conditions, deprived of any vehicle through which their experience can be made meaningful, and therefore, sufferable" (Zur 1998: 248). For them, silence may often be the most valuable coping mechanism. However, such silence does not necessarily represent a traumatic reaction, a form of repressed memory or dissociation. It might be read, instead, as a self-conscious acknowledgment, a communal agreement, that past brutality was indeed too horrific to comprehend or "make sense out of" (Zur 1998: 166).[14] Moreover, like syncretism, silence and secretiveness are historically rooted forms of communal resistance, elements of the profound pride and inviolability characterizing Mayan discourses on identity and the past. Elusiveness vis-à-vis outsiders is used to maintain a distance from and to ward off intruders who might seek to appropriate such secrets into their own discourse and hence acquire power—a dangerous power extending beyond economic and political forms—over the community (Burgos-Debray 1983). The silences resulting from the traumatic violence of the civil war may, therefore, represent a powerful form of coping with past suffering and resisting any form of further manipulation by outsiders.

"Truth" and "Memory" in Theory and in Practice

Thus, while collective memory projects serve important political, social, and psychological purposes, they are not able to encompass the "social memory" of a population or the many heterogeneous truths and memories dwelling in the hearts and minds of a large majority. The "justice" of the Truth Commission, based on the notion that responsibility must be assigned to the broader geopolitical and national interests within which the war took place, does not always integrate local experiences and interpretations of the violence. As Wilson points out, the clarity necessitated by such institutional models tends to decontextualize the complexity of such past experiences, thus "[stripping] events of the subjectivities of victims who may have practiced resistance, neutralism, collaboration, or a tactical mixture of all available strategies" (1997a: 834; 1997b). Despite a methodology that clearly avoided an ethnocentric framework and included a wide range of verbatim testimonies within its broad historical documentation, the perceived "victim" identity required by the CEH did not necessarily ring true to the self-perceptions of many of the Xinxuc K'iche' as both guilty participants as well as pawns in the violence, and it could not encompass the messiness of such memories or the understandable desire to forget or deny their shame and guilt.

This argument does not seek to undermine important efforts to recuperate and validate the voices and memories of thousands of victims silenced through years of terror and fear. I seek, rather, to contextualize notions of "truth" and "memory," concepts that often remain unproblematized in the dominant media and among the organizations developed to foster them. In this respect, it is useful here to briefly refer back to the academic debates surrounding David Stoll's criticisms of Rigoberta Menchú's testimonial *I, Rigoberta Menchú: An Indian Woman in Guatemala* (Burgos-Debray 1983), since these concerned problems of representation and "social memory" in Guatemala and, more specifically, within a K'iche' community.[15] In *Rigoberta Menchú and the Story of All Poor Guatemalans* (1999), Stoll argued that rather than representing a wider or collective "truth" encompassing the experience of Guatemalan Indians, Menchú's testimonial narrative was an ideological construction—framed within the rationalizing discourse of

the EGP—which essentialized and victimized Mayan Indians by using ex-
aggerations, omissions, fabrications, and misrepresentations, thus obscuring the important local complexities and contradictions of the war. Among
other things, Stoll provided explicit historical data showing that Rigoberta's
depiction of a unified, harmonious indigenous identity and social "awakening" prior to the army's counterinsurgency veiled the many preexisting
ethnic, religious, and territorial antagonisms among the K'iche' people;
that her portrayal of popular indigenous support for the EGP in the face
of unprovoked Ladino and army brutality distorted a complicated local
history and was not generalizable; and that her own self-description as a
poor, illiterate *costumbrista* contradicted her relatively well-off, educated
catequista upbringing.

Stoll's questioning of Menchú's testimonial was vociferously contested
by numerous scholars on several fronts (see Arias 2001). Many argued that
his reading of Rigoberta's narrative failed to place it within the personal,
political, and cultural context within which it was recounted, pointing out
that she had to frame the story in a particular way in order to garner
international attention and support. Others stated that Rigoberta's narrative was an attempt to define herself, both as an Indian woman and as a
political subject, in the midst of profound collective trauma, destruction,
and instability (Le Bot and Rousseau 2000). Several scholars responded to
Stoll's criticism of Rigoberta's claim to represent her "people" by evoking
the particular narrative style of Mayan oral culture, where individual and
collective voices, voices of the past and the present, tend to be blended
within the same narrative to recount and resituate histories of suffering
(Lovell and Lutz 2001). Through an overly positivist and personalized reading of Rigoberta's testimony, many argued, Stoll obscured the larger "truth"
and belittled the critical importance of Menchú's testimonial in seeking to
break out of the silence and paralyzing terror to which Mayans had been
subjected.[16]

Stoll addressed a number of these issues in his book, arguing nonetheless that even if "the truth is unknowable, because the milieu is too
ambiguous and fraught with repression to have confidence in any particular version" (1999: 63), "it is a mistake to assume that epistemic validity
matters only in the western tradition" (189). An account such as his, which
"encompasses a wider range of versions" and "deals with contradictions"
(65), he states, is more reliable. Ironically, however, while pointing to the
political repercussions of Rigoberta's framing of the story, Stoll concealed
the dangerous consequences of his own "truthful" representation. The most
harmful aspect of Stoll's book, indeed, was his choice to target such an important figure of the Mayan resistance and publish his exposé on the eve of

the Truth Commission—thus playing into the military's justifications that Indian "subversives" were to blame for the carnage and that indigenous accounts were not reliable.

However, Stoll's arguments do point to some important issues relating to postwar collective memory projects, namely the tremendous complexity of situating personal, local narratives (each with their own motivations and plots) within a broader social memory seeking historical justice; and, conversely, the problem of constructing a collective story (also emplotted for an audience) from individual ones, particularly in a context of continuing fear and divisiveness. Stoll argues that Rigoberta's claim to represent a "collective memory" through her testimony "dodges an important question: What parts of her testimony might not be so collective, reflecting a perspective at odds with many of her people?" (1999: 190). Although the CEH and RHEMI projects integrated many testimonies and provided a balanced and comprehensive view of *la violencia*, a similar question might be posed relative to these projects. In a sense, they proposed a new language and new categories through which the destructive and chaotic experiences of the war might be articulated and transformed in a meaningful way.

But what of the thousands of Mayan voices that do not fit into this new language and "collective memory"? How useful are such projects for those whose recollections of the war revolve around highly localized personal, land, and power disputes, whose explanatory logic lies in traditional idioms of *envidia* and ancestral punishment, or for whom the line between coercion, survival, and willful action remains a blur of guilt, denial, and trauma? Most importantly, could it even be damaging to assert or impose a collective "truth" or "memory" that represents all Indians as victims of army brutality without paying attention to the more perplexing and intricate historical factors and cultural relations that led to varying responses and degrees of local violence in different communities—factors that continue to persist in many *municipios* of the highlands today? As I suggest above, any broader effort to understand, reconcile, and attempt to prevent what happened in Guatemala must reveal the full extent of atrocities committed but must also take into account the many nebulous voices that fall outside of institutional projects and that continue to guide people to think and act in a highly unstable present.

The memories of *la violencia* among the Xinxuc K'iche' tend to be situated "betwixt and between" several explanations: an often internalized official army/PAC discourse, which claims that those missing or dead (or those associated with them) were "subversives" and therefore guilty; a counter-memory reinforced by the UN and the Catholic Church (both of which, in the eyes of most Guatemalans, are far from politically neutral), which argues, conversely, that the army (and those who carried out its evil deeds) are primarily to blame; and local explanations, which tend to point to personal betrayals and *envidias*. In Xinxuc, these contradictory moral frames lead people to depict an ambiguous scenario where all community members, including the *conocidos* (acquaintances) who carried out violence as well as their dead victims and surviving relatives, are both guilty *and* guiltless, to varying degrees.

As Zur notes, the guilt of many of the K'iche' is a "complicated, ambiguous" one, rooted not only in past situations and actions that took place in a moral vacuum of chaos and helplessness but also in a present that is continually subject to "interpretive understanding by victims burdened by the question of their own role in [the violence]" (1998: 184). Such intolerable memories are "perhaps memorable in some form but not necessarily accessible or speakable" and, in the end, "can neither be remembered nor truly forgotten" (188). Moreover, in a context where the justice system remains marred in corruption and impunity (no matter how the past is recounted), the urge toward silence and forgetting, in the public sphere at least, is further reinforced, contested only by the few individuals with the resources, energy, and will to do battle in the legal and political realms.[17]

If silence can be seen, in part, as a culturally ingrained mechanism for coping with *la violencia,* the verbal silence forced upon many Indians must also be analyzed with respect to the many embodied idioms of distress that have been observed throughout the highland population in the postwar period. As the CEH, RHEMI, and several authors (Green 1999; Zur 1998; Lykes et al. 1993; Garrard-Burnet 2000) have pointed out, the continuing feelings of sadness, anxiety, and helplessness resulting from terror are expressed in a slew of psychosomatic symptoms among the indigenous population, including headaches, stomachaches, chest pains, gastric problems, and sleep disturbances, as well as traditional categories of illness such as *tristeza* and *susto*.[18]

A significant proportion of PLANTAS's clients are, indeed, people (often women) from Xinxuc and surrounding towns who suffer from psychosomatic illnesses and who are able to find some degree of comfort through the herbal and other traditional prescriptions offered by PLANTAS practitioners. PLANTAS serves, in a sense, as a neutral space within which past and present injustices or deeds can be indirectly (or sometimes directly) expressed through long-standing cultural idioms and without the threat that some perceive in more politicized approaches to recognizing the past. The embodied impacts of terror, moreover, are usually gendered (Green 1999; Zur 1998); while K'iche' women often seem to internalize or somatize sadness and helplessness, men express the rage and frustration resulting

from their vulnerability, guilt, or shame through increased alcohol consumption and domestic violence. It has been found that the excessive use
of alcohol has gone up substantially following the war, among both victims
and perpetrators of violence, and it is also related to an increased incidence
of child and wife abuse among male victims of the violence (Garrard-
Burnet 2000).

If most of the K'iche' in Xinxuc have not voiced their memories within
the more public and political sphere of collective memory projects, private
memories of *la violencia* (as told to me at least) are usually recounted in
narrative form within the context of the broader life changes, dislocations,
and separations that wreaked havoc on—and continue to dramatically impact—people's everyday lives (unlike the more discrete events referred to
in institutional memory projects). With respect to K'iche' war widows,
Zur (1998: 183) notes that "it was not only *la violencia* which changed the
women's lives; it was only the beginning of the dramatic change, particularly in widow's [*sic*] lives following the loss of male kin and the shattering of world views. Because of this disjuncture, the period of *la violencia*
maintains biographical relevance to the present."

The context of everyday life, its physical boundaries and activities,
and, in particular, changes such as the loss of loved ones due to death or
dislocation are daily reminders of this terrible period, even if this is rarely
overtly expressed. In transnational communities like Xinxuc, the absence
of relatives who have left to Providence, in particular, often becomes part
of this sad and painful past, though it is paradoxically associated as well
with escape and economic advancement. When asked to recount the period surrounding the exodus to Providence or to discuss the impact of
the migration more broadly, some of the K'iche' tended to shift between
relatively coherent, linear story lines describing the general dislocations of
la violencia and how the migration has influenced their lives in positive
and negative ways, and sudden "flashbacks"—sometimes highly emotional
and often rapid, hushed, and confusing details of the events surrounding
the deaths or disappearances of loved ones. Doña Jacinta recounts:

> Before, the place where we lived was very tranquil, we were happy,
> we had animals and harvests. When the war began, I suffered so
> much because they killed so many people. Before they killed my
> husband, we had planted a great harvest of maize and beans, and I
> was not preoccupied because I had everything I needed at my reach.
> When my husband was here we had firewood, *gastos*, money, but the
> day the war came all my children went to the capital, my oldest son
> left, my children became divided and went to different places. They

told my oldest son that they would kill him, as they had killed his
father, and so he went to the capital. I stayed alone with my youngest
daughter. I was very sad because it was not because of a deed of
God that we were divided but because of these people who
were killing us here. The people who did this were known to us
(*conocidos*).

My son went to the US for three years and so he was able to
have the house where they now live. Before our house was very
small, made with reeds. Now it is big because he went to the US to
earn money. Because he went he could earn money, buy his house,
but at first I suffered so much. When I stayed alone I had to work
on the *milpa*, bring my own firewood, harvest alone because I did
not have my husband. My children went to the US because in the
hamlet they were killing a lot of people, they wanted to kill us, so
they left there. . . . And now I am sad, but I am also happy, because
my children are living in peace over there, with their families, they
are happy, they do not have problems like before.

Jacinta's private "reframing" of the past in terms of the more positive aspects
brought by her children's migration seems, in some ways, to enable her to
resituate herself and her children within a longer story wherein, if they
fell victim to a terrible and unjust brutality, they were also able to resist,
through their own agency, becoming subsumed or engulfed by it. Rather
than conclusive, however, this narrative reframing continues to incorporate
as well the unfathomable violence from which it cannot escape, and that
becomes revealed a few seconds later in this uncanny juxtaposition:

I give thanks to God that I have many grandchildren, I even have
great-grandchildren over there. My children over there have work,
they have the possibility of earning their living there, and here
they don't. You know before in a tomb near here they buried five
catechists. The secretary, they cut off his fingers, and others their
ears and lips. And some their eyes. Some they left hanging in trees,
others they burned, and others lying there like dogs.

If Jacinta's struggle to create a meaningful story in the present while
incorporating the incoherent horror of *la violencia* is difficult, the attempt
to emplot and narrate the past is even more problematic for those who,
having encouraged their kin to migrate for reasons related both to the
violence and economic duty, incorporate feelings of guilt into their present
stories. Guilt sometimes seems to weigh heavily, for example, on parents
who, having helped their children to leave by paying for their *viaje*, have

lost the ability to "keep an eye on" and guide them in Providence. One widow says:

> people were saying that over there one can make a lot of money. For this reason I sent my children, and now I do not know if I did the right thing or not, because I sent them for *pura obligación*, they did not want to go. I sent them, I took care of it, I went to borrow money for their passage. The desire I had when they left was that they would help pay the *gastos* because I had grown tired of maintaining them, and I wanted them to earn their livings themselves. Maybe, I think that perhaps I sent them into some sort of slavery, because they were still very young.
>
> And so, they have not accomplished anything (*no han hecho nada de aprovecho*). Because they were very small when their father died. I think about my son, I made him suffer because I sent him by force (*a pura fuerza*) to work over there, so that he would send money for his siblings. But he did fulfill his duty that I had decided for him, he paid his debt and helped me, he found a job and sent money for his siblings and me. . . . Now I am more worried about the other two because they have not been able to repay their debt. So I think I am to blame (*fui la culpable*) because I forced them to leave, and now I realize that I am to blame because I asked for the loan and now they have the debt and they have to pay it. . . .
>
> But I struggled for them before, I did not abandon them but rather I fought to take care of them and now they can decide whether or not to send me my *centavitos* or not. Because I fought for you and didn't give you away to anyone else, if I had been another person I would have given you away, but I did not, I struggled with you to not abandon you.

Alongside this tremendous guilt, any rumors of "bad behavior" on the part of their absent children (e.g., drinking, unemployment, or decreased remittances) or any misfortune such as illness become, in part, a reflection of their parents' past decision to send them away. As such, guilt is at times transformed into expressions of resentment and anger toward kin, who are feared to be abandoning or losing respect for their family and values, as described in previous chapters. Thus, in addition to the multiplicity of "collective frames" within which K'iche' memories of *la violencia* are situated, conflicting and complex elements of sadness, desperation, guilt, and accusation surrounding the subsequent transnational separations provide a further element of ambiguity—incorporating again both guilt and guiltlessness—in people's reconstructions of the past.

MEMORY AND FORGETTING IN PROVIDENCE: A FRAGILE VACILLATION

The Moral Community of Forgetting

Providence offers a completely different spatial, social, and political context within which the K'iche' frame and reterritorialize their memories of the violence. Removed from both the broader political projects and local boundaries of the home community, the social impetus, physical cues, and temporal markers that remind one of the past—or remind one to reflect on *la violencia*—do not exist here. Moreover, as we have already seen in the prior chapter, there exists a self-conscious "community of forgetting" in Providence, where both the past suffering and poverty associated with Indianness and any discussion of the war itself are proscribed at the collective level. When asked about *la violencia,* most K'iche's immediately state that they do not wish to (like to, try to, want to) remember or talk about this period. This shared agreement to "forget" the past exists for several reasons. The "political ethos of the culture of terror" (Jenkins 1991) seems, at one level, to have remained frozen in time, more deeply ingrained than at home: Many of the K'iche' in Providence have not witnessed the recent peace process at home and the human rights discourse surrounding it. In addition, a number of ex–civil patrol *jefes,* as well as ex-guerrillas, now live in Providence. Thus, lingering fears and divisions in the host context partially explain the unwillingness to speak about the violence:

> We do not talk about any of this because among us there may be one of those. One of those people, you know, and they might say why are you remembering all this . . . because one never knows about people. . . . It could be that, well as we never saw who were the *guerrilleros,* perhaps, of all those who are in the US, maybe there are some who were with the guerrillas, and it is ugly to talk about that.

Perhaps more significantly, however, the tacit agreement to put the past behind exists because Providence is seen to offer a new slate to all: Here, both victims and perpetrators have a chance to escape both past sins and accusations, whether fabricated (i.e., false accusations of subversion by PACs) or real (i.e., abuses by civil patrollers). The new "moral community," then, is one of nonjudgment: By not voicing judgment over others, one hopes not to be judged oneself. Nonetheless, despite initial assertions that *la violencia* is not something to be remembered or discussed, many of the Providence K'iche' immediately follow their statements with evidence that, in fact, it is clearly remembered in the private realm.

Between us we do not talk about that, because it is ugly, sad, it is horrible, it makes you feel afraid. . . . But I think that everyone, I think they remember that . . . I imagine that each family must remember this in their hearts, and they must talk about it between themselves, but we do not get together to talk about it because it is ugly.

As in Xinxuc, the painful details of the war are inescapable, often pouring forth in a sort of built-up cadence, for example:

Those things are not to be remembered (*eso no se recuerda*), no, I don't really remember all that. . . . Nobody speaks about that, of those things like the killings and everything, no. . . . It is not because they are afraid, it is simply that they don't want to remember because, there were people who . . . for example the family X, they are one of those that . . . their father was taken away. They were coming from the coast and umm, some men came and they say they just took him, they simply said get up, he got up, they took him to the bus . . . his son just watched, he alone watched them take his father, and oooi, quickly like that . . . he lost him from sight, they never knew more about his father . . . they never found out. And many people, I know many people that they killed in the hamlet . . . they were the presidents, secretaries of the Voice of God, an organization they had, just like our little rosary group . . . they killed them, they tortured them, along the roads, we would pass to go grind the corn or to fetch water and everything, and I know all the places where they killed them, they left them there strewn, hanging, others say they cut off their fingers, they took out their eyes, they did everything to them. Many people that were *conocidos*.

Some deny remembering the violence but then recount gruesome details through startling emotions that appear to reflect the horrific absurdity of both the war and of its silencing:

I hardly remember about all that, that is all far away. They killed a brother of my mother. . . . And my aunt became a widow, with two children. He went with the *guerrilleros*, probably they advised him (*le aconsejaron*) and he went with them, and then when he tried to get out he couldn't and they killed him [laughs, giggles] . . . and my father was a *patrullero* (civil patroller). . . . What I remember is that the *guerrilleros* wanted to enter Xinxuc. So they [the PACs] put signs up, posters, papers, saying they were going to come, and that

everyone should be ready so that they could not enter [laughs]. . . .
They said they were going to invade Xinxuc, the *guerrilleros*, but
they never entered [laughs]!

Internalized Rhetoric, Personal Countermemories, and the Ambiguous Space in Between

However, if in Providence there is no "public space of memory"
within which to make sense out of the violence, and if there are no formal
"counterdiscourses" to subvert the army/PAC ideology, the new space of
Providence does, within its more private memory spaces, paradoxically
seem to allow for a more open and nuanced reflection on the ambiguous
and confusing events and allegiances of the past. Indeed, perhaps *because*
there is no institutionally imposed exegesis of the war that directly counters
years of silencing and army ideology (and that, in a still divided and fearful
Xinxuc, leads many people to simply avoid collective explanations for the
past altogether), people in Providence tend to struggle to make sense of
their own dubious, confusing, and painful experiences during *la violencia*.
Their narratives reflect a profound internalization of past "official" rhetoric; however, they simultaneously integrate personal "counternarratives"
that question, contradict, explain, and destabilize these "fixed" stories and
explanations of the past.

At one level, the army/PAC discourse is clearly evident in the narratives of both victims and perpetrators. For example, the PACs' assertions
that there was not much violence in Xinxuc, unlike in other villages with
widespread Indian support for the EGP (a rationale that back home served
to reward the K'iche' people for their submission and to threaten further
violence if they did not comply), is apparent in statements that deny or at
least downplay the extent of horror in Xinxuc:

> Well in Xinxuc, I do not think it was that bad. But if we talk about
> the towns around us, all those hamlets around there, haaaii, there
> it was painful, because when we would go to X, we would see all
> those dead people on the road there. The dogs were opening their
> stomachs and eating them, I saw a lot of that, people without
> heads. . . . In Xinxuc there were some but not many. In the
> mountains they say there were many, many, but not in Xinxuc.

In Providence, moreover, the most brutal civil patrol *jefes* are described
very ambivalently (in particular those who are still alive, and especially
those who live in Providence), even if their violent deeds are well known

to the narrator. The contradictory role of patrol *jefes* as both respectful, fair, friendly, and protective, and as violent perpetrators of random atrocities is one that enabled them to maintain the "epistemic murk" of the violence. In its immediate aftermath, moreover, their justification of atrocities as "ordered from above," or as a necessary strategy to eliminate the enemy, was further reinforced through the official army discourse. In Providence (where many K'iche's arrived in the late 1980s or early 1990s, when the PACs still maintained a strong hold on Xinxuc), the K'iche' often describe such *jefes* by stating that perhaps they were only doing their jobs, perhaps they were only "bad" (*malos*) in an evil context (and are reformed in the new space of Providence), perhaps they are both good and evil. Indeed, Xinxuc's Ladino ex-PAC *jefe*—who, as described earlier, was known to be one of the most brutal PAC leaders in the country and is responsible for hundreds of deaths—now lives a humble life in Providence, working as a landscape gardener. He is addressed by many with the same affectionate name he used in Guatemala (something that would resemble "Uncle Johnny") and is often asked to be godfather to the children of Ladinos and (some) K'iche's—though he did insinuate obliquely to me in an interview that he is uneasy about enemy reprisals even in Providence, which he gave as a reason for no longer drinking in bars.

The moral confusion among some of the K'iche' concerning the culpability of perpetrators is pronounced. One woman, after a long, confusing description of the deaths of her husband, her father, and her brother-in-law, along with her own imprisonment in a Quiché jail, describes the return to her hamlet where she encountered a *jefe* who had taken part in ordering these deaths:

> There are people like X, he, for me, with us, that man saved my
> mother's life. Yes! Because that man also, well I don't know in truth,
> they say that one part of him behaved badly with other people,
> and another part behaved well. Because there are some that are
> good and others no. So that man said to my mother please, leave
> here today because it looks like they are going to burn the houses,
> go to the *pueblo*, and so my mother fled, everyone to the *pueblo*,
> and like he said in two days they burnt all our houses. When my
> mother returned there are dead people hanging, she said they were
> very burnt, dead. . . . These are stories that we can never . . . when I
> remember more than anything I feel sad in my whole body, I always
> had a stomachache when I was there, aii my God, I didn't eat, I was
> very sick and my mother too, we were so frightened, and all my
> family got separated.

After I described to one K'iche' woman in Providence the accusation (by a group of Indians from a *municipio* close to Xinxuc) and current trial of the town's military commissioner for countless atrocities, she responded, even after acknowledging his role in the carnage:

> Wow. I didn't know that poor man was in jail, and because of that, because of the guerrilla. But how can they only blame one person? It is good that they got him but how can he pay for the faults of many other people? What's more, they didn't do all that because they wanted to, but because the soldiers ordered them. They had to kill.

In a community where civil patrollers ranged from vicious murderers to those who simply complied to survive (with various levels of complicity in between), and where victims became perpetrators, the line of accountability has become terribly blurred. For this reason, all patrollers (which may include oneself, one's husband or son) must be, to some extent, exculpated in Providence:

> The patrollers . . . it's that they didn't know, how could they know when it is really the soldiers? The patrollers when they killed innocent people, it was not their fault, only simply that the soldiers told them: This is a suspicious person and he has to die. On this night you must come and kill him. They would send them. That happened a lot.

As we can see in the quote preceding the last one, moreover, the ultimate blame for *la violencia*—in concordance with the army's rhetoric—is often placed on *la guerrilla*. In the following passage, we can detect how the very astute logic utilized by the army and PACs not only demonized the guerrillas but also described their actions in terms that made sense to many of the K'iche', thereby ensuring their compliance. One K'iche' ex-patroller says:

> Well those people [the guerrillas] said that we had rights, and that we deserved to live, but what they did was the opposite, they did bad things, and then the authorities came. Because the government built the road, and it was a good road, we could now go to the capital without ending up in the mud, or going by foot, we didn't have to be late anymore. . . . They built good bridges, a health center, new municipalities, but those people came and ended it all because they were against the government, but that money to build didn't only come from the government but from our own community. That is what we understood later, what we heard when we formed the

patrols: that these people were trying to harm the government, but they were really harming us. Because we had to have a tax before in the community, we could not do a business or sell chickens without that tax. Well that money slowly it grew and it was sent to the state, and that is why we could build a school, a road, have water and energy. . . . But then when they destroyed these things we couldn't move around anymore, we couldn't take the bus, and so instead of doing good they did bad.

However, it is important to point out that, if the above quotes reflect an internalization of the "fallacious reality" through which the PAC *jefes* asserted their power, they also describe a reality directly experienced and remembered by the K'iche', a certain degree of "truth" that for them cannot be denied: The PACs *did* "save" some lives while destroying others; the "justice" of accusing one *jefe* in lieu of all *is* dubious; most patrollers *were* forced to participate at the risk of losing their own lives; and, the guerrillas *did* destroy the local infrastructures that many K'iche's had perceived as enabling progress. These acknowledgments do not preclude the other "truth" that, as everyone knows, the murderers were the army and patrol *jefes,* and not the invisible, abstract, and unseen *guerrilleros*—assertions that are often vehemently stressed by most Providence K'iche's, including many of those quoted above.

Indeed, if these memories of and explanations for *la violencia* are, at one level, steeped in the institutional discourse of pre-peace Guatemala, the narratives of Providence K'iche's, who find themselves removed from both past and present structures of violence and peace at home, also seem more open to uncertainty, contradiction, and questioning than those in Xinxuc. The bewildering reality of local violence, for example, is described as follows:

We never knew any guerrillas, we don't know who they are. They told us they were like Germans, like monsters! We heard about them, the soldiers said the guerrillas, the guerrillas . . . but we did know who the soldiers were because we saw them . . . and there were people from Xinxuc who killed innocent people. And they are afraid now that there will be revenge. Those are people who . . . who knows, who knows what they . . . well for example X, and Y, they did things like that. They tortured and burned the mother of Z, yes they robbed them and everything, they did too much harm. But it was not the *guerrilleros* who did that. He was involved in, [hushed and fast] he was a patroller, no he was with the guerrilla. . . . And he, how do you say, how to say . . . he went with both sides, so they didn't kill him. He participated with the guerrillas, and also with the soldiers. So for this, he knew very well, he knew where our homes were, he was a known, trusted person there (*una persona de confianza*), but what a lie it was, it was because of him that they burned our home and everything, they took Z's mother, they tied up her husband and burned him, and they raped her, in front of her children. And one of those people is here now.

Moreover, a number of the Providence K'iche' engaged in lengthy political discussions with me concerning their disagreement with past guerrilla strategies and goals—explanations that went beyond the army's justifications and that reflected, rather, a K'iche' worldview in profound disagreement with the revolutionaries. One man states, for example:

Well, I don't understand all of this of the guerrillas because it is very complicated, and I don't want to, because it is madness, imagine that there are guerrillas in the mountains, suffering under the rain, just so that the soldiers come and kill them! It's just stupid. What they should have done is, each in his own way (*cada quien por su lado*) should look for work and gain his life and be happy, and if one complies with the government, the government protects one, they protect. Well perhaps they don't always give you what you want, but what they wanted was to appropriate everything . . . and that is not easy! The government, sometimes we visit them, we need help, and maybe they take a while but they do give. . . . But the guerrillas did not have patience, they wanted things too quickly, and that is impossible!

Another questions:

I would like to know what the guerrillas were fighting for. . . . [P: They said they were fighting against poverty and the government was not helping the poor.] But really, the poverty is not the fault of the government. It is not the fault of one person. Because there are many people in this world, and each person has his destiny. How can God, who leads us in this world, with so many people, so many heads, how can he give a home to everyone? He can't, and he has to leave some people poor, and some people rich.

These explanations of the guerrilla's shortcomings integrate various levels of discourse: the notion of destiny, which may connote a religious explanation or the K'iche' belief in *suerte* (fate); a model of "limited good," which forms part of the *envidia* economy; and the social conservatism and caution engrained in K'iche' culture, which rejected (and still rejects) the guerrillas' "impatience," destruction, and disrespect for the existing authority structure. Although these statements might be read as a sort of retrospective justification for having sided with the "winners" (the army/PACs), they also reveal much more complex, culturally informed past and present understandings of the war. In addition, some Providence narratives show how *la violencia* was characterized by various changes in allegiances and ideologies—and led some of the K'iche', for example, to initially consider the EGP's message, then disagree with its tactics, and then be forced to join the other side (which some did adamantly, fearing reprisal from the EGP). In striving to "make sense" of this messy past, Dionisio (a catechist community organizer turned hamlet *jefe*), for example, described to me the radical shifts in moral frames and logic that he had to make in order to "survive" in the midst of excruciating events, coercions, and choices. The following excerpt reveals as well the association many K'iche's currently make between *Los Derechos Humanos* and the guerrillas, as noted earlier:

> The Human Rights, they are the rights of the land, of indigenous people. But they take over the *fincas*, the haciendas, because they feel that they belong to them. That is what happened the other day. When I was in the *patrulla*, the ones who talked about rights were the guerrillas. For me it is the right to defend your life, to make a living, to have a tranquil life: It is not to take what does not belong to you. . . . For me the right is to send your children to school, to speak, to write. And they did not give us those rights. And I spoke about those rights. For example, that those who were going to the coast were being paid too little. We have rights, we have to work and to defend ourselves, and I spoke about this before. But they [the guerrillas] asked us to go with them. The Human Rights said that Ladinos come from somewhere else, that us *naturales* are from here, we have the right. They said, you buy the worst coffee, you could harvest the best coffee here for yourselves! You can't even harvest cilantro, they said. And I said, and why don't you plant cilantro then? I didn't go with them.
>
> In the hamlets, I used to motivate people, I taught them how to plant different things, I tried to show them and help them, I told them not to let other people's animals graze on their land, because the Ladinos let their animals loose on our lands, their animals eat our *milpa*, and we cannot grow avocados, apples, bananas, *guisquiles*, only the Ladinos could have these things, not the poor, *natural* people. And so when I said this is not fair, the Ladino says, he is a

guerrillero, he wants to do things his own way. The Ladino speaks of communism and guerrillas, but that is not it, it was just to defend our property, our lands.

[Later] When I became the patrol *jefe*, it was to unite people, Catholics, evangelicals, *costumbristas*, all had to come. Because it was said that if the person does not come, he is against the patrols, so he had to come. That is what was said. And for me I saw a unity of all the people, the family, maybe it was forced but . . . there was a lot of togetherness (*convivencia*), a lot of union, and everyone realized that it is good to be united, because it was only then that we were able to get the water project in the hamlet, so it was through the patrol meetings really, we always talked about that, the road, the school, the bridges, the water. . . . So I brought a bit of union there, so to speak.

This narrative reveals the narrator's present struggle to alternatively situate himself within and be critical of both "sides," and to define himself as both a victim and as a political subject who made choices based on his own understandings of the world. As we can see, while he had believed in rights and progress, he also viewed the guerrilla's strategies as no different from the oppressive Ladinos' (since in his view both involved abuses of power and forceful acquisition). Forced to submit to the army, he then became a *jefe*, even though this meant siding with the Ladino patrols. In the present, he still tries to make sense of such chaos, in part by justifying his *jefe* position by claiming that it brought unity (and water) to his hamlet. In addition, he illustrates how the profound rejection of the EGP's idea of "rights" (which many of the K'iche' saw as simply appropriating what belongs to someone else) has led to a broader rejection of *los Derechos Humanos* in the present, which partially explains Xinxucians mistrust of the Truth Commission. Indeed, all of these tremendously complex "memory processes," which involve various levels of denial, guilt, rationalization, forgetting, and remembering, and which integrate the multiple allegiances of the past, are not only narrated in the present with much difficulty but also seem almost impossible to place within a single collective memory frame.

Thus, in Providence, despite the conscious (and collectively sanctioned) desire to put such a horrible and complicated past behind, many of the contradictions and multiple perspectives of this past come clearly to the surface. Notwithstanding the new "moral world" of "nonjudgment" and forgetting, the uncertainties, contradictions, fears, and ambivalences of the past become superimposed onto a present narrative frame, as illustrated in the following passage by Antonio, whose brother was "disappeared" by the civil patrols:

Here in this country and in this city, I know many people who, when
I was younger, did a lot of harm to my brother. And I have seen
those people but . . . they try to forget it. But I cannot forget it but
. . . I have seen that man here, the man that took my brother, and did
calumnias against him, and brought him to the military zone, where
they nearly killed him. I know that man, he is here. Sometimes
those people [patrol *jefes*] talk to me, and I speak to him, but those
are things of the past, no? Like that, perhaps they were just doing
their work, right? So I don't offend them, I don't tell them they are
bad, maybe the justice system was ordering him . . . but no, he was
wrong, no, it was his mistake. Because my brother was not bad, he
was a worker. . . .

For me, the past is past. It doesn't matter to me how, perhaps it
was an order from someone in the army . . . but I never forget that
when I see those people, I know that person, he is bad, but me when
I see him I . . . I know what he has done, and, but, if he is repentant
of what he did, then . . . for me there is no vengeance, I only ask
God that things go well and that he won't bother me. But I don't
want revenge, those are things of the past . . . I know those people,
but they had orders. It's like if I work for an organization and they
give an order, do it, or we will kill you. Well, to save myself, I do it,
so maybe that is what happened, I am nobody to criticize or judge
him, and he already did it, he did it but he is repentant. Well, I am
not sure if he is repentant but . . . either way, he already did it! And I
am nobody to judge him.

These are things of the past that are, they are forgotten, one
remembers them because sometimes it makes one sad because
they did harm and said things, and it is not true, it is not fair what
they did. So sometimes it makes one angry, no. . . . Sometimes I am
angry, but I have forgotten all that. That doesn't matter to me right,
it is a past. And my brother does not exist anymore, maybe he died,
I don't know. . . . But to put myself into problems it is not worth it,
it is all lost already, and perhaps it would put me in problems with
the law, better to leave this behind, these things of the past. . . . Aah,
it is not worth it because, in any way, if you are going to fight over
something that is lost, it will never be returned anyhow, even if you
punish people . . . it's useless (*por gusto*), it's better to forget and let's
continue anew, and hope that there is no more of this.

Finally, the "ambiguous guilt" of the K'iche' often becomes translated,
in Providence, into a tremendous fear that one's "escape" from home might
be seen as evidence of past bad behavior at home. Because one may be per-

ceived to have left in order to flee the PACs or, conversely, to have escaped reprisal due to one's PAC activities, many K'iche's take concerted efforts to explain that they left out of *pura necesidad* and nothing else. When asked whether some people may be afraid of returning to Xinxuc now that a Truth Commission was underway, one woman quickly answers:

> As God knows we never put our hands in the game, all that of killing people or harming them. God sees that. The ones who are afraid are those who did things. Those who are afraid are those who did things. But the one who is not afraid it is because he has not done anything. But me, I do not return [to Guatemala] because I do not have the capacity to further my children's good (*sacar a mis hijos adelante*). Because if it were for me, I would return, alone, I wouldn't be here, I would be there, enjoying the life in Guatemala. . . . I am here because of my children. But I am not afraid of anyone.

Indeed, in a community as divided as Xinxuc, perhaps the only way to cope with the past without reviving tremendous pain, prolonging the conflict, and falling prey to an unbearable guilt is (as many of the K'iche' believe) to let the final judge be God, whose gaze, situated beyond institutional, ideological, and religious divisions, is seen to reflect the only possible "truth":

> The word peace must mean to forget, for example we must forget all these past things, all that happen, all these killings that I've been telling you about. I know many people who want to do harm, or some who want to claim something, but for what, what will they gain, what would I gain if I do that and my husband doesn't exist anymore, he is not here, and there will never be anything we can do! If he were in jail maybe I could do something, but it has been nearly fifteen years and it is the time to say there, there, he is dead and there is nothing to be done. . . . And we can only think that God knows what happened!

Alternative Memories of "Home": Nostalgia and Guilt

There are several other elements of the memory process in Providence that resist the collective impetus to forget both home and the suffering associated with it. Indeed, because the K'iche' in Providence are, in a sense, both refugees from violence and undocumented labor migrants, various dimensions of memory work operate to connect (and disconnect) them from home and from the past. As we have seen in the last chapters, immigrants often revise memories in order to reinvent identities and situate themselves in an ambiguous present. In order to resist the rapid, alienating change imposed by displacement and the pressures of industrial work and marginality, migrants often create memories of the past that are unchanging, incorruptible, and harmonious (Feldman Bianco 1992). And, in order to justify difficult lives in the present, they often imagine futures full of hope and promise. In this sense, "home" can become, in the migrant sensibility, "something to be regained, created, discovered or mourned"; it is "not where we are in time or space, but where we dream of being" (Thelen 1989). Moreover, despite the "simultaneity" of transnational migration, even a couple of years abroad can create a specifically "nonsynchronous memory," since the "community one remembers or returns to is not only a different space. It is also a different social time, with a different pace or pattern" (Karrer 1994: 130).

For migrants in a host country, this temporal displacement of the "homeland" can lead to a particularly nostalgic sensibility, often evident in narratives, whereby the home community becomes an idealization of both past memories and future projects. This nostalgia can be inscribed in migrant narratives at two levels: (1) as a form of yearning for, or mourning, something lost, and (2) as a practical, active nostalgia that connotes transformative action with a connective purpose. This first form of nostalgia dwells in representations of the past and connotes false contact with a fantasized past; in a present experienced as a hollow absence, such nostalgia serves to permeate the present void by infusing it, overwhelmingly, with separate temporalities (past and future) conceptualized as the place of "home." The second nostalgia functions rather as a powerful force for social reconnection and for attempting to project and control the future (Battaglia 1995: 78). It opens individuals to creative reconfiguration and self-problematization, which can function as a positive vehicle for present and future knowledge and experience.[19] According to Battaglia, the first form of nostalgia may mask, but may also become transformed into, a substantive one where a more dynamic relation between past and future can be engaged and become an empowering force in the present.

With respect to transmigrants in particular, Rouse (1989) has shown that displaced people often use nostalgia as a coping mechanism to make the ambiguities, insecurities, and constant changes of life in the host country more bearable. He states that nostalgia creates an idealization not only of the world from which one came or where one wishes to return, but also an idealization of one's own identity: In the difficult space of transnationalism, nostalgia permits the individual to see his true and desired identity as realizable only "at home." Although he does not seem as optimistic as Battaglia about the transformative, empowering potential of nostalgia for transmigrants—and in fact suggests that the ability to envision one's real identity only in another place is somewhat tragic—he at least sees migrant nostalgia as a coping mechanism rather than a total or deluded evasion of the present.

Nostalgia for "home" is closely linked to the possibility and dreams of return. The notion of utopia thus also plays a large part in the experience of displacement and in the tension between "roots and routes." As Gilroy (1993) argues, the utopic sensibility is linked to a "politics of fulfillment" whereby the migrant hopes that a future society will be able to realize the social and political promise that the present neglects. In fact, the "migrant dreaming," with its promise of utopia, begins not in the host country but rather at home (Berger and Mohr 1975), where the host country may take on utopic proportions (in this case, the "American Dream" as projected through the media, pop culture, as well as the discourses of visiting return migrants). Premigratory mythical representations of the host country will justify and give impulsion to migration. While in the host country, these utopian desires may be turned back to the home community, which is remembered nostalgically and projected through memory into an ideal future return. In a sense, there is an involution of the spatiotemporal cycle of transmigration. The "myth of return," thus, may become a powerful discourse in which the home community is envisioned as a place where the migrant hopes to return to live a better life, to achieve a more secure position, to meet a spouse, or to help bring about other changes. The final return is thus mythic in the sense that "it gives meaning to what might otherwise be meaningless. . . . It is the stuff of longing and prayers. But it is also mythic in the sense that, as imagined, it never happens. There is no final return" (Berger and Mohr 1975: 216).

Whether or not such "idealized" memories of home become integrated into the complex narratives of the Providence K'iche' depends on how they position themselves with respect to the home community. The project of return, while often construed and narrated as the primary motivator for their difficult existence in the host country, is an ambiguous one in reality. As we have seen, some K'iche's plan to return home within a specific period of time (or when they have made a specific amount of money); many postpone their return indefinitely as they become accustomed to the host community, extend their work to pay off debts, or acquire new responsibilities such as spouses or children. Or, if they have not succeeded in the host country, some cannot fathom returning to Xinxuc, fearful that they will be poorly received and will disappoint family members. Others may return home only to find their utopian dreams shattered as they encounter an unfamiliarity with local circumstances, economic stagnation, and an unfriendly, or at best cool, welcome to their identities, which have been transformed abroad.

K'iche's who recount nostalgic memories of home are usually those who are not able to return in the present but who maintain a strong emotional connection with their families and land and cannot envision remaining in the United States forever. These are usually women, undocumented K'iche's, and poorer *campesinos* for whom it would be particularly difficult (or expensive) to cross the border a second time. For them, while *la violencia* is (negatively) conflated with Xinxuc, "home" can also come to represent a meaningful, though often imaginary, place of the past and future that stands as a counterpoint to the drudgery and marginality of Providence. In order to fill in the "liminal" and often lonely time of transnationalism, they narrate nostalgic visions of a Xinxuc that is peaceful and *alegre* (happy, convivial).[20] This intact, prewar haven to which one hopes to return contrasts markedly with both the alienation of urban Providence and the terror produced by *la violencia*. One woman explains:

> I remember the holy week, the day of saints in October, Christmas and New Year's, and our *fiesta*. I remember all this because over there it is more *alegre* (joyful), everyone remembers, but here, all of these *fiestas*, nothing, there is nothing *alegre*. . . . Sometimes during the day, when the children are playing and I am all alone, with nobody to speak to, I start to think, I tell myself if I were over there I would be doing this, I would be by the river, I like being by the river and fetching the water, and washing the clothes, I don't know, I prefer that, being in the mountains walking, seeing the animals. . . . I like living like that better. That is what I think when I am alone and with no one to talk to. Here life is very boring for me. If I were there, with the children we would go to the mountains, they would run, they would play. But no, here one only goes out to the street, and you have to be careful with the cars and this and that, and I don't like it . . . I don't like it.

Another K'iche' remembers:

> In the countryside one has to go look for firewood, we had to go fetch water at the well, and so many things. And then one has to work outside for eight hours, and when one has time to rest one has to go fetch more firewood because otherwise it might get wet if it rains and the fire won't start and then you cannot cook. So for me the *campo* is very grueling (*costoso*) . . . but it is *alegre*, also. It is *alegre* because there no one bothers you, not like in the *pueblo* where one cannot even have little animals, because they go into the street and get lost or are stolen, you cannot have little pigs or hens.

But in the *monte* it is *alegre*, you can have all the little animals you want. There it is really *alegre*, and I like it. I say that the day I leave if God wills I will be able to build a house in the *monte*, and if there is water and electricity, for me it is a good life there. I like to have everything. It would not be strange because I know that living in the *monte* is very *alegre*, one can plant fruits, vegetables, all sorts of things.

And a third states:

I would rather be in the *pueblo*, it is more *alegre*. . . . Here it is more comfortable and everything but it is better there in Guatemala, where there is no problem with papers, with anything, it is free.

All three of the above narrators have remained in Providence for years, primarily, they say, for the sake of their children. Such nostalgia is, however, not restricted to those with children: It also appears in the narratives of young men who fantasize about returning to settle with an indigenous wife (even if they frequent discotheques and non-K'iche' women), and in those of *campesinos* who sometimes recount their lives on the *milpa,* with their animals and family, in a highly idealized way. Most people, however, also acknowledge that the "good life" (one that includes proper health care, nutrition, and safety) is more accessible in the United States and that poverty and unemployment at home made life very difficult, though they usually mention this when justifying why they have not returned. Indeed, people's narratives often alternate between different visions of home, depending on the present frame or argument they are making: the violence, oppression, and suffering of home and the benefits of the host society (which justify their continued presence in Providence) are juxtaposed with recollections and projections of a lovely, harmonious countryside where they can (or could) breathe the air and feel free. Within the highly liminal and unstable present, such shifts, rather than pointing to a hollow or paralyzing nostalgia, seem to enable people to cope with the multiple possibilities and options that define their "in-between" lives, while also providing an imaginary space within which sadness and loss—of family bonds, of cultural practices, of prewar community and *alegría* (happiness)—can temporarily be "territorialized."

Just as in Xinxuc, where memories of *la violencia* are also associated with the rupture caused by transnational migration, memories of home among the Providence K'iche' often elicit painful emotions associated with absence. As Sayad states, the "double absence" of transnational migrants— who are at once partially absent from home and partially absent from

the host context where they are never complete—can lead to a deeply felt
"sentiment de faute" (sentiment of culpability), which might become an
"obsession du retour au passé" (an obsession with returning to the past)
(1999: 207). Among the Providence K'iche', the tremendous feelings of
guilt over having left wives, children, and parents, and the fear of being
forgotten by these, come through in many indirect ways, and sometimes
become interrelated with memories of *la violencia*. This feeling of guilt
is represented, for example, in the narrative of a son who—despite his
mother's assertion in Xinxuc that she had sent him away to avoid the army
draft and violence—feels both guilty and resentful for having left home:

> [P: Do you speak much with your mother?]
> Well that is the problem that I have. I am not a very good son to
> her I think. Because I am bad, and that is the sadness that I have,
> because sometimes I ask myself, I wonder why. Why did I decide to
> make this decision to leave? Because like I say, if I make a decision,
> it has to take a lot of time, it has to be well thought out. So, it is
> difficult for me to say but I made a decision very quickly, I was
> in error, it is a rancor that one regrets. . . . Well I will tell you. The
> whole time I have been here [seven years], I have not spoken with
> my mother on the telephone. So you see that is it, I am not good. It's
> because when I arrived in this country, I was a bit like the chick that
> gets lost, that is distanced from his mother, and I felt badly because I
> came here and it was not easy. Now I am happy because I am what I
> am, but I also feel absent because . . . because I never had the love of
> my mother.

This guilt and its rationalization is also present in the thoughts of a mother,
who describes the child she has left behind:

> I have not returned home, because I have to think of my children,
> and I want what is good for them, I do not want them to suffer
> as I suffered. But I am sad because my son is over there, and I
> am not with him. I have not been at his side, and the love that he
> needed from me when he was a baby, he did not have it. From his
> grandmother yes, he had her affection and love. But he understands
> this now! He writes to me now that he is older, and says now I know
> why I have all that I need, it is because of you, because if you were
> not in that far away country, he says, I would not have everything I
> have. He always has what he needs, enough to eat, clothes, but when
> we were little we had no way to eat, we couldn't! He knows that each
> check I receive will go towards him. If it weren't for my mother, he

says, I wouldn't be alive. . . . He understands that I could not bring him with me because I could not bring a baby with me on the trip. I write to him a lot now that he can read, I ask him to forgive me, I tell him to behave well, I tell him that I had to do this, and he says I know *mamita*, I know you have suffered a lot for us, and when I am fourteen I will work to help you, to help pay for you.

Finally, the guilt of not being with loved ones in times of difficulty (illness, death, drought, etc.), the fear that one will eventually forget them altogether, and the fear that one, in turn, will be forgotten (or, in particular, that one's wife will find another man and have children)—all anxieties rarely expressed or narrated directly—nonetheless form part of the tremendous loneliness of Providence and of the "imagined" memories or future visions of home. One man, for example, who has not seen his wife and children for ten years, told me of a recurring dream that incorporates these worries:

Last night, for example, I dreamed that my mother [at home] was sick, she was sleeping with some little girls. I came into the house through the other door. A woman was grinding *pepita de aguacate* (avocado seeds), making medicine for her mother. And you, what family do you come from, I asked her. She said, don't you know me? I said I do not. I felt badly. A little boy came. And who is he? I don't know you. The little boy came to give me a hug, congratulations, I said, but who are you. . . . And then I woke up.

Some authors argue that, particularly among victims of trauma and displacement, the "necessary oscillations of memory between disclosure and avoidance" become critical coping mechanisms, since on the one hand, "[l]iving permanently with disclosure can be unbearable" and, on the other, "[t]otal avoidance . . . leads to meaninglessness" (Rousseau et al. 2001: 161; see Ricoeur 1976). The ambivalent narratives recounted above seem to illustrate this need to simultaneously appropriate and distance oneself from a past and a home that, on the one hand, resurrect memories and feelings of horror, sadness, guilt, and shame and, on the other, allow one to project a positive "place" of return or fulfillment. It is by vacillating between these two poles, indeed, that transnational K'iche's are able to produce "meaningful" narratives at all, rather than falling into either the vacuum of total forgetfulness or the unbearable suffering of total remembrance.

THE STORY OF DIONISIO

As we have seen, the moral communities and spatiotemporal contexts of Xinxuc and Providence shape the ways in which the K'iche' in either place are able to narrate the past. In most of the narratives discussed above, memories often appear fragmented and shifting, at once restricted and opened up by the "current context of their retrieval"—that is, both the larger sociopolitical context and the immediate situation (the retelling of one's past to an anthropologist who was perceived in various ways by different respondents). In this final section, I illustrate what can happen to this memory process in the absence of the usual marks and boundaries that confine self-conscious narratives of the past. Here, I depict the nuanced and fluid nature of memory as constructed by one K'iche' man, Dionisio. Although the events surrounding his story are unique and his story is not generalizable, this narrative contains many elements echoed, in a more veiled manner, in the other K'iche' narratives. Dionisio's story is situated within an unusual episode, whereby isolation and medication have blurred the boundaries of real and unreal: The crystallization of memories and events is framed within a dramatic context of crisis. His narrative in effect synthesizes (and Dionisio himself embodies) many of the broader themes discussed throughout this book. However, it seems that it is only in this "transitional" space of profound crisis, a "turning point" of sorts, that the suffering, resilience, and many contradictions of the past and present can come together and be expressed with such poignancy.

Don Dionisio's story finds no place in the present nation-building project of Guatemala nor, indeed, in any legitimized space of public solidarity. His present, moreover, is situated in an ambivalent, unstable transnational space, and his future lies in the hands of the US Immigration Service, an American plastic surgeon, and, as he often states, God. Like many Xinxuc K'iche's, he grew up in a hamlet, and his family subsisted by planting corn and coffee in their small *milpa* and migrating yearly to work on the coastal coffee plantations. He never went to school and did not learn to speak Spanish until he was a young adult; his speech is still often interspersed with K'iche' words. In the early 1980s, Dionisio was working as a health promoter in Xinxuc, counseling people on nutrition and agriculture. Like many Indian lay Catholics, he was also a catechist with Catholic Action. When the violence started, Dionisio was targeted by the army as a probable guerrilla. Hearing that the army was coming to get him in his home, he fled into the mountains for three days, and when he returned he burned all of his health promotion literature, as well as anything that identified him as Catholic.[21] To further obliterate his past identity, he became the head civil patroller in his hamlet, stating that he did so in order both to stay alive and to continue organizing the community. Soon, Dionisio was forced to become an *oreja* (ear), a spy for the army, to eavesdrop and report on religious and other meetings. He was ultimately appointed to be the military commissioner for his hamlet, thus becoming a further accomplice to the violence. He describes his forced indoctrination from progressive community organizer to PAC *jefe*:

> I was military commissioner in 1982 and 1983. When they organized the patrol, that is what they made me. Because you see, as the time went on, we saw that if one behaved badly—um, sorry, I mean behaved well—they give him a position. It is because I had been in the army much earlier, and my name was on a list, and they told me to present myself. Well I got scared, because I did not know, they told me to come at a certain time and place. I presented myself to the *comandante*, he was the *comisionado* of the *pueblo*, and they said now you will be one of us. They told me to organize people, organize them to do their military service. Because it is there in the constitution of the republic to be patriotic and do our service, but a lot of people defended themselves against that, and even I used to do that before, I would run away, I wanted to harm the *comisionado*, I wanted to hurt him. But it is because I did not understand my responsibility as a Guatemalan, to the constitution of the republic. There it says everything, to be patriotic is to do your service.

The tremendous fear caused by his forced "conversion" to the civil patrols led him to drop Catholicism altogether: As he says, he withdrew from the church because there was no life there, it only brought death. However, he resisted the pressures exerted by the evangelical churches to join their religion. Although many in Xinxuc converted, Dionisio refused this final form of indoctrination.

Dionisio decided to leave his family in 1989 to undertake the difficult trip *al Norte*, hoping to make some cash in the United States to send back home (and to move away from horrible memories). Dionisio, whose temporary work permit has run out, lives in constant fear of being deported. He spent seven years working in a Providence textile factory, sending money home regularly, until the day his hand got caught in some machinery and was nearly torn off. The factory owners, in order to avoid a legal suit and the disastrous possibility of being exposed for their hiring of undocumented workers (and their failure to abide by minimal safety standards), decided to provide Dionisio with the best medical care possible. With only two remaining fingers on his right hand and impaired mobility in his arm, he has undergone a series of painful reconstructive operations and numerous skin grafts, and he has remained unable to work or to return home.

Following his factory accident, Dionisio was taken to the hospital for immediate surgery. He subsequently recounted to me at length the tremendous pain and struggle of his first three days in hospital, during which he was strongly medicated. He told me about the unwanted visits he received in his hospital room, which caused him much greater torment than his quasi-amputation. Though I had previously heard a distorted version of this story from his daughter back home, I had not addressed it with Dionisio due to the delicate nature of its contents. His narrative sprung forth unsolicited during one of our many visits, and I was taken aback by its candor as well as its vivid and numerous details.

Dionisio's openness with me, less common among many other Mayans who were more guarded, was grounded in several factors. First, I knew both him and his extended family in El Quiché well, and I had brought them, in my travels back and forth, gifts and news from each other. I also helped Dionisio to communicate with various institutions and persons related to his recovery, which included social workers, physiotherapists, and a psychiatrist. I represented, in a sense, a neutral interpreter and friend who, while knowledgeable of the two contexts between which his life was balanced, did not seek to manipulate him, as he felt so many others around him were trying to do. Given his inability to work and the empty time that he sought to fill, we spent many hours discussing the state of his present life and his future options. Memories of Dionisio's past, his family, and the violence saturated these discussions, although usually in oblique and diffuse ways. In the following story, which he recounted on one of these occasions, we can see Dionisio's past and present, conscious and subconscious converge in a three-day period of intense agony and revised memory.

Dionisio's hospital visitors shift from being real people to spirits, voices, children, animals, people in the United States, people at home. The main "visitor," the one giving orders to all the others, is, in real life, Cipriano, a K'iche' ex–civil patrol leader renowned for his brutal killings back home during the war. Cipriano, who has been able to obtain US citizenship, converted to an evangelical sect following his migration (although he and others in his family are also rumored to practice *brujería*). As we saw earlier, he has strived to maintain his power in Providence through various forms of intimidation and threat. He returns regularly to Guatemala, transforming his home into a loud evangelical *culto* for days at a time, slaughtering cows and inviting the *pueblo* to join him by shrieking through loudspeakers that sinners must be saved and that he has met God.[22] His overt use of religion to pressure others to forget the past (that is, their sins as well as his own) manipulates the "salvation-oriented" message of evangelicalism to exploit the shame and fear of other K'iche's and their desire to put the past behind. His ability to return home regularly also permits him to acquire knowledge of what is transpiring there and to use this information back in the United States, creating uncertainties and fears among those who cannot return. This man is powerful—both hated and feared by many in this community—and Dionisio knows him well despite his efforts to avoid him. Dionisio recounts:

> When I went to the hospital it brought back many things from my life. In the dream, I was like dreaming, but it was not a sleeping dream but a wakeful one. . . . They brought me taped cassettes, I heard, which were from my family over there. They were saying that the wife had gone off with another man. And then she got sick. And when she got sick, those who brought the cassette had taped her voice over there. I could hear her noise, and my children being raped, and she was crying, saying that why did this happen, that before she was a good Catholic. . . . And she lamented also that I had loved her very much, but that the one who is doing this now, the one who is with her does not love them like that. . . . And that is what is what she lamented in her suffering, which was on the cassette that they brought me.
>
> [P: Who brought you the cassette?] Well you see, I did not totally see those people, but I put the blame on a person who visited me, who was an evangelical, full of prayers, huh? And those orations that he did, well that same person was talking to me in the dream. . . . I didn't see him, but he started to speak to me with his own voice, and I know that voice. They [the spirits] arrived, and unfortunately my room was the last one near the exit, like a final passage, so to speak. They came in through the air vent, some of them hid behind the wall and others in the ceiling. . . . Soon, they started to say so many prayers, they were calling me, they were telling me to leave the hospital because the medicine they were giving me was no good, it was only a partial medicine. . . .
>
> What they brought for me was a message from God, and God will cure me if I go with them. . . . And after that they offered me food, all sorts of food that we eat: They started with *atol* (corn drink), coffee, *mosh* (oatmeal), chocolate, meat, beans, *tortillas*, and other things. . . . And then the one on top became transparent, like an alert eye, transparent like a glass window. . . . And I saw that they started to look for me, I heard them tell me not to move, not to speak, they were looking for where I had my mouth, so that they could put the food into me, they tried to enter into my mouth. They

could not find it, and they said turn around because you are hidden, inverted, and they wanted to see my mouth so they could put the food into me. And the ones who were behind the wall were praying, singing. . . .

Then I heard, the law came, law from here, the police came, and then they [the spirits] started to run . . . but those above me became calm, they whispered between themselves, slowly, so that no one could hear them. Unfortunately they were calling me with a voice that was very familiar to me, from my family so to speak. This person, I know her, she is almost very close to me, they had her voice which was calling me, saying come here, where are you, this is not reality, that we are reality, yes, that here is the God that will heal you. And they even offered me a woman, they said here is the most loving, beautiful woman, the woman you hoped for. . . .

And they said that while I was sending money to my family in Guatemala, someone else was eating up this money, that my wife was giving this money to another man, and me not knowing this because I never ask anyone what is going on with my family. But they knew, but I did not ask. They said that is what happens, because I do not speak, I do not speak with people. . . . All night they played those cassettes, of my wife and children crying, of the word of God, and of hymns. . . . And I said to myself, I do not need these people, and I made myself strong. They kept calling and I didn't speak to them, I ignored them, I wouldn't speak. I could hear the voice near the door, but when I tried to see it, to look for it, it would hide, disappear, it wouldn't let me see it, but I wouldn't speak to it either. . . .

There were four men who came to sleep by my side that night. It started to rain, and the one sleeping at my side said, "This brother is going to get soaked, we will not let the water fall on this brother. We will cover him with some plastic." . . . I was very preoccupied, and I asked the nurses to not open the door, to keep it locked. But they [the spirits] left me cassettes through the bottom of the door, money, religious pamphlets. I heard them say, leave these and he will soon realize. . . . And the person whose voice was calling me, who is of my family, she said, you, come back. Here we are waiting for you and you can see my son here is dying for you, because of you he is dying of the cold. But I know that in him there is salvation. This son will be your path, through his suffering, he will be your salvation, so that you can be with God, his suffering is your guide, I hear her say. . . . In the morning, the nurses cleaned me, changed me, and then I felt a bit better, I thought: I won, and I thanked God that the new day had come.[23]

This first part of Dionisio's narrative sets forth the flow, the backdrop, and many of the themes characterizing his broader story. In this passage, he introduces several events and imaginings through which he weaves together a past and present filled not only with terror and suffering but also elements of struggle, agency, and resilience. From the beginning, he broaches, through various forms of imagery, the elements of fear, guilt, and confusion that characterize both his present and past lives. He alludes several times, for example, to his inability to see clearly what is happening, only to hear. Indeed, even when the spirits speak to him in a familiar voice, he is unable to cast a clear eye on them, to confront them directly. This overreliance on hearsay and lack of visual clarity reflects several aspects of Dionisio's life. It describes the time of violence, which many of the K'iche' people characterize as a hazy, murky period when what one heard (or was told) did not correspond to what one saw (or did not see). Hearsay, in the absence of "visual" truth, was enough to mark one for death, and the power of language shamelessly contradicted what was happening in reality (for example, the army's discourse of peace and development in the context of terror). However, people's attitude toward hearsay during the war was ambiguous: While it was not to be trusted, careful listening was also crucial since a verbal tip from a friend could also mean the difference between life and death.

At the same time, this theme reflects Dionisio's current dependence on, and aversion to, transnational rumors and hearsay, as well as his tremendous feeling of impotence stemming from the inability to verify such rumors. As described earlier, rumors form a major part of the K'iche' transnational experience, engendering a constant state of distrust, anxiety, and ambiguity (both at home and abroad) regarding the situation "over there." The distance from home, bridged only by telephone calls, letters, cassettes, and individuals who travel back and forth, creates a troubled sense of "not really knowing" what is actually happening at the other end, particularly with respect to one's absent kin or spouse. Thus, while hearsay becomes the most viable way of maintaining links with home and therefore retaining at least the illusion of a stable base in the world, one can never fully trust the messenger (whether it comes in the form of cassettes or spirits). The confusion of voices, whereby both familiar and dangerous voices are both seductive and threatening, thus reflects the disorientation and apprehension that Dionisio has felt at different periods regarding who is a friend, who is suspicious foe, and the dim line in between.

The constant allusion, throughout this narrative, to hiding and silence parallels the inability to see clearly and the mistrust of words. As mentioned, Dionisio has had to make himself "invisible" several times during his life. When he hides from the spirits who are trying to find him to administer the "medicine," he might remember hiding from the Guatemalan army (his experience in the mountains), from the evangelicals trying to convert him, or from dangerous fellow immigrants such as Cipriano. The "alert eye" that is "transparent" might represent the fear of *envidias,* of being watched by envious and dangerous eyes without knowing who they are.[24] He might be hiding as well from the North American authorities such as the police or immigration officers—as illustrated by the police siren, which forces the spirits to hide, as well as the plastic rain shelter, which evokes the cross-border journey of *mojados* who make the difficult trip from Guatemala to the United States.

More nefariously, the pervasive imagery of invisibility and hiding may also be related to Dionisio's guilt over having been an *oreja,* or traitor, back home. Like the evil spirits of his "dream," he had made himself invisible in order to spy on and harm others; as such, he was not only a victim of the "epistemic murk" (Taussig 1987) of the violence, but also a participant in its performance. The value of silence, like his reliance on hearsay, has been an ambivalent one. Although Dionisio heroizes his ability to remain silent, to refrain from speaking to the spirits (and others who have tried to coerce him)—silence, in this sense, being an admirable form of resistance—he also acknowledges that his silence is disempowering, as it prevents him from communicating with others and finding out what is really happening.

The tremendous guilt and fear relating to Dionisio's marital situation is one experienced by many K'iche's who have left their families in Guatemala, particularly for such an extended period of time. Because it is considered unnatural and undesirable for a married woman to be left alone and unprotected, Dionisio is wracked with guilt and pain for having left his wife and children behind to fend for themselves. At the same time, he suffers great fear and pain in imagining that his hard-earned dollars may be reaching another man's pockets and that his sacrifices in *el Norte* (which now include losing a hand) are being abused—a fear that is compounded not only by vicious rumors but also the hard reality of long-term displacement.

During his first days in the hospital, it seems clear that Dionisio felt that he was going to die, that he was in the "last passage." In part, then, his struggle with the spirits constitutes a "final judgment" whereby he is being assessed in terms of all of his previous betrayals and loyalties, moral weaknesses and heroisms. Dionisio's confusing and ambivalent relation to the three worldviews that have shaped his life (the "new" progressive Catholicism, traditional Mayan beliefs, and conservative evangelicalism), as well as their political and cultural meanings and repercussions, are thus central to his story. The battle between religious loyalties shapes both the recall and narration of his memories, and frames as well his search for meaning, identity, judgment, and salvation. He has been both seduced and threatened by all three religions, and his delirious struggle in the hospital seems to encapsulate the profound spiritual disorientation he has suffered through the violence, his uprootedness, and now his nearly fatal accident. He continues:

> And then I heard a bunch of children under the bed, and they were blowing, they started talking about papers again, that they were bringing papers, newspapers, anything, but from Guatemala, those papers were on fire, and they were blowing so that the paper would burn, and I could feel the heat. And that man started to speak again, and he was telling them to bring more papers, so we could feel more relief. . . . But then after a while I heard them say goodbye, they said, "All right, well we'll see you, if you don't want anything then so be it, go ahead, go and see your catechist, go see your priest, go find your incense, your candle, and burn it, see if it helps you, only don't complain later on." . . . And that voice I know well, she said, you know that I was Catholic, and what did it bring me, nothing, only separation. Being Catholic is not worth it, so that is why now I have found God, now I am my true self, at peace. . . . And that cassette stayed in my mind, and I thought, it is time to leave the hospital, to go back to my land. . . .
>
> [P: Do you think this was just a dream?] No, I have no doubt that they came, not alive, but as spirits, maybe they did a prayer, and sent visits back home, and asked God to do this, so that . . . well you see before I was very active in Catholicism, not like now, so this happened. . . . Oh, I even had music, I have some music from over there that is native, and at that moment they were telling me that music I listen to, I must leave that behind, forget all that . . . that I must pray to God. They say that they speak directly with God, God tells them what will happen tomorrow, and those people can also tell you what will happen. . . . But those people cannot convert me to their religion, they cannot. I still feel Catholic, so to speak, though I don't practice like a Catholic. That religion helped me before because . . . when I think of how it helped me, what it gave me, it was good. But because of the situation, because of the moment and everything, I had to leave it . . . but not leave God altogether. I know that the church is not responsible, is not guilty, nor the Bible. We used to speak of the Bible, of exploitation, of humiliation, and that Jesus himself told us that he came to save the slaves, he did not come for those who live well, but for the slaves. And he made things better,

and I cannot forget that. I don't forget that, it's always in my head, I always have that, until now.

The voices that come to Dionisio are, on the one hand, perceived by him as evangelical "spirits" that have come to pressure him to convert once again, as they had in Guatemala in times of danger and chaos. The tremendous seduction of evangelicalism has been a difficult battle for Dionisio to fight: The spirits woo him not only with traditional food, a loving woman, warmth, and safety (symbolizing all the elements he lacks in his current life), but also with survival and salvation. They try to appease his guilty conscience for having left his children behind to sickness and poverty by claiming that their "suffering" will be his "salvation." They purport to provide a direct link to God, which the tragic experience with Catholicism in Guatemala was unable to offer him, and they claim to know the future, a compelling lure for someone whose future is so uncertain.

The spirits represent the concrete safety and survival he had sought during the violence—when evangelicals were rumored to have been given protective "identity cards" by the army (significantly, Dionisio's visitor also has "legal" papers in the United States, making him doubly powerful). More broadly, however, they are attractive because they speak out, they are not timid, they are open both in their proselytizing and in their power to state clearly and safely where they stand, in opposition to the hiding and silences that have so tormented Mayans such as Dionisio. Despite their powerful appeal, Don Dionisio sees these spirits as malevolent and diabolical ones that prey on the sick and weak. For him, giving in to evangelicalism represents a total subjugation to all the evil forces that have molded his life. In this sense the voices are metaphorical representations of the broader political and moral evil of men such as his visitor. Though his one heroic tendency throughout the story is his ability to fight the alluring spirits, to remain true to himself by battling them courageously, he also acknowledges that he has fallen prey to them in the past—one of several weaknesses upon which he might be currently judged.

However, these spirits are also very real to Dionisio. In an alternative explanation for the "visits," he states that the spirits have been sent to him through witchcraft, dispatched by Cipriano to confuse and harm him. As he told me, "Los brujos llegaron invisible" (the witches arrived invisible). The supernatural transformation of humans, in particular *brujos* (witches), into spirits or the physical form of their animal counterparts (*naguals*) is basic to both ancient and contemporary Mayan mythology and cosmovision. In this case, the evil sent to him has come transformed and disguised not only as killer insects, children, and clouds but also as evangelical spirits. Since the notion of being invaded by supernatural beings is essential to both traditionalist and evangelical belief systems (in particular Pentecostals, who have a strong presence in Xinxuc) and since his enemy practices both, this blending of spirits and their multiple disguises make sense to him. In an interesting transnational "twist" to his witchcraft, Cipriano was able, Dionisio explains, to send the spirits back home to gather information on his wife and children.

Dionisio believes that Cipriano is trying to harm him through witchcraft because of Dionisio's own stubborn resistance to him, both back home and in Providence. Though Dionisio has mentioned on another occasion that Cipriano has had *envidias* toward him in the past (enough to warrant this type of supernatural revenge),[25] he implies in his narrative that the main motivation for the witchcraft is Cipriano's anger toward Dionisio for refusing to convert, refusing to be coerced, and, most importantly, refusing to forget the past. The seduction of putting the past behind is symbolized at various points in Dionisio's narrative through the imagery of papers being burned.[26] As he says, the heat from the fire, kindled by Cipriano's spirits, is meant to provide relief from his many tormenting memories. In America, according to the evangelical Cipriano, solace and absolution from the pain and guilt of past violence must be found by forgetting all cultural and religious ties to the past and embracing the new God.[27] In addition, the symbolism of fire in traditional Mayan rituals also represents cleansing and renewal, necessary to envision and enact the future. The spirits thus seem to be playing on this traditional imagery, just as the army had manipulated such beliefs during the war to attract Indians to their side.

While this denial of the past is seductive in terms of both psychological reassurance and physical safety, Dionisio has continuously refused it. He has been reprimanded by Cipriano (and other K'iche's) in Providence not only for refusing to convert, but for speaking K'iche' in public, listening to traditional music, and maintaining other elements of his past identity. Because of the collective nature of guilt in this community, Dionisio's unwillingness to cooperate is a tremendous threat to those, like Cipriano, who wish to put the past behind. The burning of papers also evokes the memory of all the documents he himself burned back home in an effort to destroy his previous identity as a Catholic and community organizer. Not once, but twice, has Dionisio had to purge his past identity. Like everything else in his life, thus, the struggle between remembering and forgetting has been a profoundly ambivalent one.

Finally, it is clear that while Dionisio has felt disappointed with Catholicism in the past (and, by extension, with the optimistic promises and social projects of the "new" Catholicism), he also suffers much guilt and pain over having left this religion. Some of the voices in his dream (in particular, female ones) lament the fact that Catholicism brought nothing but separation and death. In addition to the literal death for which catechists back home were targeted, Dionisio feels disappointed and sad about the wartime fragmentation and divisiveness (of the community and of the family), which he sometimes attributes to the prewar belligerence of the more progressive elements of his community (the outspoken catechists) who invited the army's wrath. At the same time, he was deeply involved with the new Catholic movement, having placed much of his faith in the impetus to organize and improve the community. For him, the Catholicism of the poor was a just religion, and just as he will not forget Jesus' message, he will not forget the social values that came with it.

On many other occasions, Dionisio spoke to me about his previous work, giving me detailed accounts of the agricultural and educational projects he organized throughout his community and speaking nostalgically of the various plants and animals that were once part of his life. He also often mentioned separation: As this particular narrative shows, his guilt over having left the church is conflated with his guilt over having subsequently left his wife and children behind, and for having "escaped" to the United States. When I asked him why he thought the factory accident had happened to him, he indicated that it was most probably punishment—by the ancestors, by God, or perhaps by both—"because I abandoned God and I abandoned my family" (*porque deje a Dios y deje a mi familia*).[28]

Although Dionisio's story is more extraordinary and unguarded than most, it reflects many of the tensions and sufferings of other K'iche' people in Providence. In this sense it is paradigmatic, a magnified view of memory processes as they occur outside of a habitual setting. Dionisio's narrative of his hospital experience, told to me in retrospect, seems to superimpose a delirium caused by trauma and medication with a powerful cultural interpretation. Moreover, Dionisio at times refers to this episode as a dream, which is significant in that Mayan Indians tend to view dreams as powerful and compelling media for cultural interpretation, enabling people to communicate with the ancestors and perhaps to explain the inexplicable. Indeed, it seems that his detailed recall of this convoluted episode was possible only because it had such profound signification. I believe that Dionisio's very openness in recounting the story to me resulted, in part, from the remarkable context within which the episode took place: It is only by recounting this "altered state," when his body had been invaded by exterior forces (medicine, spirits), that he can speak so clearly and poignantly of his suffering and guilt.

Although the possible interpretations of Dionisio's visions are my own, he has offered his own explanations for some of the themes, both during the telling of this narrative and subsequently. The very pronounced element of inner struggle throughout his story—a moral battle between good and evil, strength and weakness, past and present, and between different religions and political stances—seems to merge all of Dionisio's past tribulations into the ultimate one, the fight against death (and against an unfavorable judgment). The trials of his past and present come together in a cacophony of voices that appear to ask: Is Dionisio a hero or a sinner? Dionisio has no doubt that he was close to dying and that this was a spirit invasion, a witchcraft performed by his visitor and facilitated by his weakened physical state. However, he also offers alternate explanations: perhaps it was partly the medication; perhaps it was a message from God, testing him to find out if he can really live without God. Or, he says several times, perhaps it was truly the Devil trying to win him over.

Dionisio's story represents a synthesis of several of the themes explored in this chapter. His narrative points to the arbitrariness of the line between good and evil in reconstructing memories of chaotic violence, a line crucial to institutionalized notions of justice, rights, and other models of restitution. In communities like Xinxuc, people who considered themselves "good" did, thought, witnessed, or were allied in various direct and indirect ways with "evil" deeds. For them, everyone in the community is guilty by association, and everyone knows it. Unable to live with the idea of being evil, everyone must (and can, to some extent, in the United States) also be absolved. However, the desire for absolution, framed within a community that ostensibly seeks to forget the past, is combined with individual traces of guilt, victimhood, and accusation, thereby creating ambiguous personal narratives and memories.

Dionisio's narrative, moreover, shows how subjective memories incorporate personal histories in which traces of social violence intermingle with other elements of the past and present that are not directly related to the violence. The subjective weight of memory enters into both individual and intersubjective (or collective) memory processes, as illustrated by the dimension of accusation, blame, and guilt in his story. His son-in-law back home explains his accident in *el Norte* as punishment for bad deeds committed during the violence; his daughter blames his distressful hospital visits on *envidia,* caused by his visitor's anger over Dionisio's success as a transmigrant (implicitly, she blames her own father for inviting such *envidia* by having left home); Dionisio's visitor simultaneously blames him for having been a Catholic "subversive" and for refusing to cooperate with him in erasing the past. As the narrative shows, these various explanations for his misfortune are incorporated into Dionisio's own ambivalent interpretations.

In other contexts, however, he explains the links between past and present in more rational terms, arguing that the violence and the disasters it brought to his life were the outcome of both guerrilla belligerence and army brutality. These seemingly dissonant explanations, rather than representing a negative "splitting" of memory and identity or a form of dissociation, are balanced and alternately accessed by Dionisio, who recognizes that the pain and suffering of his life are rooted both in an externally imposed war and in his own actions. In the absence of either a unified "moral community," institutional ideology, or other collective options for absolving guilt in the present (Young 1995), this ability to balance various worldviews and explanations in the recollection of memories becomes a crucial coping mechanism.

MULTIPLE IDENTITIES

By examining the movements of people, money, commodities, and symbols between a small K'iche' Maya community in rural Guatemala and the US urban landscape, this book has illustrated some of the new global twists and contradictions created by recent patterns of globalization and transnational movement. Emerging K'iche' identities—situated between *milpa* and US assembly line, between postwar ethnopolitical movements at home and anti-immigrant policies abroad, between Guatemalan peacetime projects to "recapture" memories of the recent civil war and the desire to forget the brutal suffering of the past—are embedded within a whirlwind of global social change.

In Xinxuc, we have seen how the postwar K'iche' negotiate the "identity politics" of the Maya movement through local contestations and appropriations of Mayanism. In Providence, on the other hand, the K'iche' have fashioned a discourse on migration that enables them to construct a sense of spatial and historical continuity despite their dislocation. I argue that the political subjectivity of variously situated K'iche's, who use multiple strategies to reshape their identities in response to transnational liminality, is no less "resistant" than the overt Mayanist discourses and strategies that are constructed vis-à-vis the Guatemalan state and international organizations. The "hybrid" identity strategies of transnational K'iche' labor migrants, indeed, are based within a historical consciousness and sense of agency that has long enabled them to respond to precarious and changing social conditions.

For a few of the K'iche', the choice between Mayanism and transnational migration is mutually exclusive: Some Mayanists view transnationalism as a total affront to indigenous values and culture, and some transmigrants mock or are skeptical about the Mayan revival. Most K'iche's, however, cautiously view these different identity strategies as two options—both emanating in the wake of a profoundly destructive violence—that may (or may not) allow them to achieve the indigenous ideal of simultaneously maintaining autonomy and advancing economically. Whether the "globalizing" tendencies of transnationalism described here—increased social inequalities, heightened consumer culture, and so forth—eventually work against or with "localizing" ones (e.g., the Mayanist project or simply the desire to remain on one's land) remains to be seen. In the end, this book has provided a detailed snapshot of a group of indigenous people in a small Guatemalan town who move to an American inner city in which they find themselves marginalized within a complex society that is in fact a compendium of such communities. And yet, within this microcosm, as within the microcosm of this narrative, we see the dreams and the horrors, the promises and the failures, the voices and the silences, of whole worlds.

EPILOGUE

In August 2001, Inocente and Magdalena called me in Montreal, excitedly asking me to meet them at the Niagara Falls border the following month. They had decided to join a bus caravan organized by their church, which was to drive from Providence to the Canadian border and back, along the way advocating a pro-immigrant message that would rally people to support an amnesty for undocumented immigrants. The news was exciting indeed, given how terrified both had been to discuss any matter relating to immigration just a couple of years earlier. The time was right, they explained, and President Bush seemed to be warming up to the idea. A few weeks later, the terrorist attacks on the World Trade Center took place, the world changed momentously, and the trip was cancelled. In the months that followed, life was to become increasingly difficult for all immigrants in the country, including the K'iche' people in Providence. As the economy took a dip, undocumented immigrants were the first to lose jobs, and it became harder to find new ones. Virgilio, however, explained to me over the phone that for those like himself who could still find work in the jewelry factories, things weren't too bad: In this time of national mourning, the demand for pins, belt buckles, and other adornments in the shape of the US flag had superceded the usual demand for class rings and other custom jewelry.

Despite this short-lived break, increasingly tough immigration laws and border security concerns have made life extremely precarious for the K'iche' and millions of immigrants like them since 9/11. The USA Patriot Act widely expanded the list of "crimes" for which noncitizens could be deported, and it also permitted indefinite incarceration prior to deportation. Over the past years, tens of thousands of immigrants have come to populate federal, state, and private prisons, many accused only of immigration offenses. The average amount of time served by immigration offenders has soared, leading the federal government to increasingly contract private prisons and county jails. By 2003, a few of my K'iche' friends had been imprisoned, and some deported. Most of the latter were men whose wives and children in Providence chose to remain in the United States rather than return home. Having lost their primary source of income and with an increasingly vitriolic anti-immigrant sentiment palpable throughout the country, these migrant families have not had an easy life. For those returning to Guatemala, things are perhaps even harder. Although MINUGUA's ten-year peace mission in Guatemala ended in 2004, there has been an alarming increase in social violence throughout the country, with drug- and gang-related violence in particular on the rise in the countryside. Jobs are still hard to come by in Xinxuc.

Transnationalism certainly takes different routes, as unpredictable as life itself. In 2001, Estela, who had fought so much hardship with spirit and strength, died of cancer at the age of thirty-four. Though Doña Isidra was initially denied a travel visa to the United States to say goodbye to her dying daughter, Estela's American social worker managed to persuade a state politician with connections to make an exception. On my last visit with Estela, I saw her elderly mother standing in front of the New England house in her *guipil* and *corte,* looking forlorn and devastated against the Providence evening sky. Just a year earlier, Estela, who had been able to mourn her abusive past, had married and had a baby. Members of Estela and Inocente's church raised money so that her body could be flown to Xinxuc and receive a proper burial. It was said that the entire community of Ladinos and K'iche's came to pay their respects. Inocente, for his part, adopted Estela's children and has been able to save enough money to buy a house in Providence. Dionisio finally returned to Xinxuc, though his *pueblo* house remains empty: Ana, his wife, still prefers to live in the hamlet. Virgilio remains in Providence, still hoping to receive legal papers, and still hoping to see his family.

GLOSSARY

aj q'ij—shaman-priest practicing *costumbre* who can be an initiated calendar diviner, dream interpreter, and curer (plural *aj q'ijab'*)

aldea—rural hamlet

azadón—hoe

brujería—witchcraft

cabecera—municipal town center or *pueblo*

campesino—peasant

cantina—bar; saloon

castigo—ancestral punishment

cofradía—religious brotherhoods in indigenous villages that incorporate Christian saint worship

comerciante—merchant

conocido—acquaintance

contratista—labor contractor

compadrazgo—fictive kinship relationship of being a godparent or sponsoring a child at baptism

corte—traditional skirt worn by Mayan women

costumbre—indigenous code of conduct and belief practiced ritually through ceremonies venerating the ancestors, the natural elements, and the land

costumbrista—follower and/or practicioner of *costumbre*

coyote—human smuggler

CUC—Comité de Unidad Campesina—peasant organization founded in El Quiché in the 1970s that eventually joined the EGP in the armed struggle

cuxa—local firewater

deuda—debt

DC—Democracia Cristiana—left-leaning political party allied with the Catholic Action

EGP—Ejercito Guerrillero de los Pobres

envidia—the intense desire to possess what is owned by another *finca*—plantation

fracasar—to fail

gastos—daily household expenses

guipil—traditional woven blouse worn by Mayan women

hacienda—plantation

jefe—leader of the PAC (civil defense patrol)

jornalero—day laborer

leña—firewood

marimba—musical instrument similar to a xylophone used in most traditional Guatemalan music

mecapal—band made of leather used by indigenous men and women around their forehead to carry heavy loads

milpa—cornfield

(la) Migra—INS (Immigration and Naturalization Service)

mojado—illicit border crosser

mozo—hired hand

municipio—municipality, town

nagual—animal spirit that many Mayan Indians believe children to be born with

PACs (Patrullas de Autodefensia Civil)—Civil Defense Patrols

patrón—boss; employer

principal—elder

reina—beauty queen

suerte—fate; luck

susto—traditional illness category explained as a sudden fright caused by an external event and the resulting loss of a vital substance or soul that ensues

traje—traditional Mayan female costume composed of *guipil* and *corte*

tristeza—traditional illness category indicating the embodiment of suffering

URNG—Unidad Revolucionaria Nacional Guatemalteca—Marxist guerrilla movement uniting the different organizations involved in the armed struggle, including the EGP

APPENDIX

THREE TRANSNATIONAL K'ICHE' FAMILIES

DOÑA NATALIA'S FAMILY

Doña Natalia is a fifty-seven-year-old K'iche' widow who lives in a hamlet close to Xinxuc's *pueblo*. Four of her ten children have died: One, along with her husband, was killed by Xinxuc's civil patrollers during *la violencia,* and three died of childhood illnesses. Three of her remaining children—Virgilio, Gonzalo, and Teresa—live in Providence. Two of her daughters (Tomasa and Marta) have stayed with Doña Natalia in Xinxuc, and her son Nicolas has migrated to Providence on two occasions but now lives in the hamlet with his family. Doña Natalia was married to a landless *campesino,* living for a long time on a hamlet *finca* owned by a wealthy Ladino. In exchange for their small *milpa,* she and her family spent five months a year working on his southern coffee plantation. Eventually the *finca* owner pushed them off the land. They sold their animals to buy land in a hamlet close to the *pueblo.* With the help of her three sons (who were working in small businesses on the coast) and income from her daughters (who went to work as domestics in the capital), she and her husband saved some money and bought more land.

La violencia was a devastating time for Doña Natalia's family. In 1980, Virgilio had become the town's leading indigenous *catequista* and was appointed president of the parish. Soon, he was accused by some locals of collaborating with the guerrillas. He fled to the coast but was eventually forced to return, as the PACs had signaled their discontent to him by killing his father and brother. In the meantime his brother Gonzalo had been recruited to the army.

The first family member to go to Providence was Teresa, who left in 1988 to join her husband Santiago, a small pig *comerciante.* After a year working in Providence, Santiago came back to fetch Teresa and their baby;

they have had four more children in Providence. Shortly thereafter, Gonzalo and his wife Petrona followed suit; they had two children in Providence. Soon, Virgilio, who had acquired a massive debt after having started a co-operative in Xinxuc (whose members, he states, never paid back the credit they loaned), decided to leave as well, leaving behind his wife Ramona and their two daughters. Marta's husband, a *jornalero,* also left to Providence, telling her that he would return in three years; within two, however, he was run over by a car and died (it was rumored that he had been staggering drunk in a city street after hearing of his father's death back home). Her mother-in-law, now blaming Marta for her son's death, made life impossible for her, so Marta moved out. With some of her husband's remittance money, she bought some land, built a house, and remarried. Though she had wished to go to Providence, her brothers forbade her to leave her children behind with their mother. Tomasa, who has never wished to make the *viaje* to Providence, has thirteen children. Her oldest son is Gaspar, a young Mayanist who works for PLANTAS. Nicolas, for his part, upon returning from his second stint working in the Providence factories, joined Gaspar and now holds a leading position in the organization; he has six children in Xinxuc.

DOÑA ISIDRA'S FAMILY

Doña Isidra, a sixty-year-old widow, has a pretty, broad face that hides many years of suffering and poverty. Isidra had four children with her first husband (the father of Inocente and Estela), a landless pig *comerciante* whose business failed, like so many, due to accrued debts and environmental factors (his animals kept dying), and whose drinking problem resulted in an early death. Soon thereafter, the family found itself expelled from its land by Isidra's own in-laws. This forced her, for the next years, to move from home to home and live on rented land that she could not afford. Eventually, she rented a small plot from a Ladino family in return for working on their land. With the help of her children, who performed chores for the landowner, she was soon able to cultivate a small *milpa* and construct a home (that is, a dirt-floor hut with laminate roof) in the hamlet. Within a couple of years, however, her oldest son died following an incident of heavy drinking, leaving the family once again in dire straits.

Isidra's second son, Inocente, found himself responsible for his family at age fourteen. He vaguely remembers a childhood spent cleaning the landlord's stables, carrying firewood and pine, being beaten by his older brother, and going hungry. After his brother died, Inocente worked for a short while as a health promoter in his hamlet. Eventually, he found a job in the capital working in a butcher store, improved his Spanish, and within a few months was able to send home money for the family's daily *gastos* and *milpa* maintenance. Estela went to work at age eleven as a domestic for a wealthy family in the capital and was able to send home money regularly. Micaela, Isidra's other daughter, stayed with her mother to help with chores.

Around the time of *la violencia* Isidra found herself once again kicked off the land. Inocente returned to his family, selling the furniture and clothes he had been able to buy in the capital. Back in Xinxuc, there were no jobs to be found, and Inocente was forced to join the civil patrols. At this time, Isidra decided to marry Don Santos, a widowed K'iche' pig *comerciante* and *costumbrista* for whom she had worked as a servant washing clothes and making tortillas while his wife was alive. Like many others, Don Santos moved his new family from the hamlet to the *pueblo* during the war. They soon had a daughter, Cati, but within a year and a half of their marriage, Don Santos got ill and died. Don Santos's children from his previous marriage—in particular the two eldest, Cipriano and Martina—had encouraged the marriage, hoping that Isidra's servant status and humility would make her easily manipulated. Inocente and Estela opposed the marriage. Santos's children became tremendously fearful that their father's land would be inherited by Isidra's children, rather than by them. When he died, however, Santos left Isidra and her children landless once again and unable to pay the rent of their *pueblo* home. The issue of Santos's inheritance nonetheless created an intense animosity on the part of his children toward Isidra's family.

During Isidra's brief second marriage, *la violencia* was in full swing, and her son-in-law Cipriano became one of the most feared and ruthless of the K'iche' civil patrol members, often bringing along Martina's husband Miguel on terrorizing patrol duties and massacres. Knowing that Cipriano was capable of killing and denouncing anyone who got in his way, Isidra's children both feared and acquiesced to him. Cipriano used this power to control Isidra's family, for example by both threatening them and allowing them to take *posada* (shelter) for a while in their home during the worst of *la violencia*. Eventually, the violence calmed down. Isidra returned to a destroyed and burnt-down hamlet, trying once again to rebuild a *milpa* on rented land. Pained to know that his mother was now working the land entirely on her own, Inocente again decided to return home, this time investing some of the capital earned in the capital in a pig-selling business.

In 1984, Cipriano and Miguel decided to go to Providence, having heard that there was work and money there and also fearing revenge on the part of their victims' families. They were among the first of the Xinxuc K'iche' to *viajar,* and they have brought their wives and all their children to Providence. Two years after their departure, Inocente, engaged to be married but without land or inheritance, decided to make a try for *el Norte* as well. He left his mother moneyless, sad and worried that she would be unable to pay off his travel debt and the weekly dues required by the civil patrollers in his absence. Estela soon followed Inocente to Providence in search of her estranged husband, and left her baby boy with Doña Isidra. After five years in Providence, learning that their mother was sick, both Inocente and Estela returned to Xinxuc for a six-month visit. Inocente also had other matters to take care of: His sister Isabel's husband was jobless, drunk, violently abusive, and spending their remittance money frivolously. (Eventually, Inocente would try to resolve this problem by sponsoring his brother-in-law to come to Providence "so that he would not kill her, and so that he could *salir adelante* (get ahead)." The plan backfired, however, since the brother-in-law ended up fathering a child with another woman in Providence.) During his visit, Inocente also took the opportunity to build, on his own, a new *casita* on the *pueblo* lot he had bought with Providence dollars; he planned to return, eventually, for further extensions. During this visit he also met Magdalena. Once back in Providence, he asked her to come join him and then paid for and arranged her trip across the border. They have two children and live with Estela and her second child.

DOÑA JACINTA'S FAMILY

Before *la violencia,* Doña Jacinta led a comfortable life by Xinxuc standards. Her husband was a successful pig *comerciante* who had been able to buy a fair bit of land. When *la violencia* started, her husband was one of the first *catequistas* killed by the civil patrols and army, as were the husbands of Jacinta's two daughters, Petrona and Jacinta. Doña Jacinta's oldest daughter also died during this time and is rumored to have died of *cólera* (anger) after her husband left her and their five children for another woman in a nearby *municipio.*

Six of Doña Jacinta's eight living children—including her two widowed daughters—now live in Providence. One of her sons has returned from there after five years to build a hamlet home for his family next to Doña Jacinta's, though he works in the capital and is often gone for long stretches of time. Jacinta's youngest son was the first to leave to Providence, around 1987. Following his departure, his wife fell prey to the "vice" of alcohol in Xinxuc, having heard rumors that her husband was spending money on another woman. Eventually, he came to fetch his wife and children and brought them back to Providence. Both Petrona and Jacinta (Doña Jacinta's widowed daughters) have remarried and live with their husbands and children in Providence. Both, also, have left children from their previous marriages with their mother, who has raised her grandchildren on the *milpa* with the remittances she receives from her various children. Doña Jacinta's daughter Ana has never been to Providence, though her husband, Dionisio, has lived there for nine years. She looks after the empty home Dionisio bought in the *pueblo* with Providence dollars, but she prefers to stay on their *milpa*, located in a distant hamlet without electricity. Due to a serious industrial accident sustained in Providence, his lengthy rehabilitation, and incapacity to work, Dionisio's return to Xinxuc remains pending, and his remittances have dwindled.

Notes

PREFACE

1. The K'iche' form the largest of the twenty-two Mayan language groups in Guatemala.

2. The name of Xinxuc is a pseudonym, used here because of this book's delicate subject matter and to protect the anonymity of participants. Given the small size of the home community, the context of past and ongoing violence and tensions, and the extremely sensitive nature of working with undocumented persons in the United States, I assured respondents during my fieldwork that I would not reveal the name of the particular home town, and would conceal individual identities, in the final manuscript.

3. This research was based on my participation in a broader project directed by Dr. Cécile Rousseau concerning psychosocial risk and protective factors in the adaptation of adolescent children of refugees.

4. Following regional peace efforts outlined by the Esquipulas II agreements, Marxist guerrillas of the FMLN (Farabundo Martí National Liberation Front) had signed peace accords with the Salvadoran government in 1992, and those of URNG (Guatemalan National Revolutionary Unity) were in the process of negotiating the conditions for ending the war with the Guatemalan army.

5. Adding to the political volatility of the Zapatista uprising, camp refugees in Chiapas had been held in suspicion, by both the Guatemalan and Mexican governments, of being a front for the guerrilla movement in Guatemala; they were also suspected by some authorities to be in cahoots with the Zapatistas.

6. On October 5, 1995, twenty-six Guatemalan soldiers opened fire on approximately two hundred unarmed returnees in Aurora 8 de Octubre, Xamán, a hamlet in the Chisec *municipio* of Alta Verapaz. Eleven villagers were killed and more than thirty were wounded. At the time of the massacre, the community had been preparing to celebrate its first anniversary in Xamán. It was not until 2004, following years of official investigation

      thwarted by threats to victims and their lawyers, that a lieutenant and thirteen soldiers were each sentenced to forty years in prison for the killings.

7. The savage murder of Myrna Mack (a Guatemalan anthropologist working closely with internal and returning refugees) in 1990 by soldiers clearly demonstrates the politically sensitive nature of this topic and the insidious extent to which the military would go to suppress information relating to these matters.

8. See, for example, the courageous work put forth by Falla (1994), Carmack (1988), Manz (1988) and Stoll (1993), and the biographical testimonials of Victor Montejo (1987) and Rigoberta Menchú (Burgos-Debray 1983) among others around this time.

9. Burns 1993; Earle 1994; Wellmeier 1994; Jonas 1995; Hagan 1994.

10. See George Lovell's remarkable collection of essays in *A Beauty that Hurts: Life and Death in Guatemala* (1995).

11. See for example Appadurai 1990, 1991, 1996; Kearney 1995; Gupta and Ferguson 1997; Hannerz 1990; Harvey 1989; Marcus 1995; Ong 1999; Rouse 1991.

12. The increased export of capital from richer to poorer countries was argued to be resulting in rapid cycles of booms and depressions in the latter, provoking uneven development and thereby triggering emigration (Hamilton and Chinchilla 1991). Growing evidence has shown, moreover, that international economic pacts such as the North American Free Trade Agreement (NAFTA) have pushed poor farmers in some peripheral regions off their land by flooding such areas with cheap agricultural products, leading to a devaluation of local currency and hence a boom in cross-border migrations (Audley et al. 2003). The many protests throughout Central America against NAFTA's successor, CAFTA (the Central American Free Trade Agreement), have been rooted in fears that the latter will have a similar impact in these countries.

13. More specifically, the process of deindustrialization in rich countries such as the United States, whereby core industrial sector jobs were increasingly being moved to manufacturing industries abroad, was, in conjunction with a shortage of native workers willing to take remaining jobs in the secondary sector of the economy (usually physically hazardous jobs with limited benefits or opportunities for advancement), leading to the increased recruitment and often the spontaneous flow of unskilled labor willing to take these jobs. As Guarnizo put it, "transnationalism from below" (the increased movement of people across borders in search of better wages and work conditions) was a reaction to "transnationalism from above" (the movement of capital across borders by corporations and states in search of cheaper labor). Guarnizo 1997. See also Massey et al. 1994; Georges 1990; Glick Schiller et al. 1992; and Basch et al. 1994.

14. Clearly, not all transnational social actors who retain ties in more than one place are motivated strictly by economic vulnerability. The position and identities of transnational businessmen, professionals and travelers—not

usually considered migrants—cannot be compared to those of unskilled (and often undocumented) workers, and to those who come from communities where transnationalism has become a normative coping strategy, as discussed further.

15. See Glick Schiller et al. 1992; Basch et al. 1994; Rouse 1990; Levitt 2001; Lamphere 1992; Mahler 1998.

16. In the United States, the growth of such communities is especially evident in the large waves of Hispanics arriving over the past twenty years, a demographic shift that has led to increasingly polarized immigration debates throughout the country. Since the 1970s, and particularly over the past twenty years, migrations from Mexico, Central America, the Caribbean, and Latin America have mushroomed. It was estimated that in 2002 approximately 13.3 percent of Americans (roughly 37.4 million) were Hispanic (US Census Bureau 2003). A majority of the country's approximately 10.3 million undocumented immigrants in 2003 were Hispanic, with the top three countries of origin for this population Mexico, El Salvador, and Guatemala. Over the past twenty years, Hispanic immigrants have increasingly included persons from poor and marginal regions, many of whom (though clearly not all) maintain significant ties with their home communities. (Previous waves of immigrants from Latin and Central America tended to be smaller and emerged most often from middle-class, educated sectors.) Mexican migration to the United States, on the other hand, already had a long history preceding this period, due to Mexico's proximity and historic border relations with the United States, and programs such as the *bracero* or guest farm-worker program implemented between the 1940s and 1960s. Certain waves of Caribbean immigrants (Basch et al. 1994; Levitt 2001) have also had long and significant migration histories to the United States.

17. Levitt and Glick Schiller 2004. See also Rouse 1989, 1991; Georges 1990; Glick Schiller et al. 1992; Basch et al.1994; Massey et al. 1994; Kearney 1995; and Levitt 2001. While some scholars assert that patterns of movement in which migrants maintain enduring contacts and interests in both home and host communities are hardly new (Foner 2003; Portes 2003), most agree that the scale and intensity of such patterns have greatly increased over the past few decades. As Glick Schiller (2003) points out, moreover, earlier "transnational" migratory patterns, such as those of the late nineteenth and early twentieth centuries, have long been obscured by the assimilationist model adopted by dominant migration studies.

18. The point of departure for these discussions is the idea that national and ethnic identities have been naturalized historically through the logic of nation-building, and that it is through power-laden processes of spatialization and temporalization that nation-states have been able to solidify and hierarchize group identities and place national subjects within a temporal frame marked by a national narrative of progress and linearity (Anderson 1993; Gellner 1983; Foster 1991; Malkki 1992; Alonso 1994; Hobsbawm

1990). Others have pointed to the social sciences' (and anthropology's) own epistemological assumptions, which have served to reinforce the nation's classifications (Handler 1988). Malkki (1992), for example, argued that the "sedentary metaphysics" of anthropology has situated people morally in national soils and geographically rooted identities; within this framework, the "natural" order is perceived in terms of stability and social coherence, whereas movement and mobility are regarded as fringe phenomena. Fabian (1983) argued, moreover, that anthropology has also historically reinforced the sense of a linear national time line by assigning evolutionary value to categories of "traditional/modern," "peasant/industrial," "rural/urban," and the like and by typologizing various forms of organization and identity along the scale of progress. Many postcolonial writers have noted that national narratives and identities have never been either totalizing or linear and that "countermodernities" have always existed in tension with the homogenizing, "progress-oriented" logic of nationalism (Bhabha 1995). Nonetheless, the notion of "methodological nationalism"—the assumption that the nation-state is not only a given, bounded category but is also a natural unit of analysis—is important to recognize when studying contemporary migration since it has "fundamentally shaped" the notions of immigrant acculturation and incorporation (Glick Schiller 2003).

19. Of course, the traditional concepts of assimilation and acculturation, which assumed a linear direction of cultural conversion toward the receiving country culture, have long been revised by many social scientists (Del Baso 1984; Portes and Rumbaut 1996). Some researchers have framed acculturation as a bidirectional adjustment or multilinear phenomenon whereby individuals adopt differing degrees and alternatives of acculturation in different settings, thus entailing varying degrees of assimilation to the "majority" culture and of retention to the "minority" culture. However, many researchers continue to perceive changes in migrant identities from the perspective of the host country, often perpetuating an assumed dichotomy between "traditional" (premigratory) and "modern" (Western, egalitarian) values and identities, and often viewing both home and host "cultures" as somewhat homogeneous entities (see Portes and Rumbaut's [1996] notion of "segmented assimilation" for a critique of this model).

20. See Ong 1999; Nonini and Ong 1997; Clifford 1994; Basch et al. 1994; Kearney 1998. Some of the more recent literature has looked at how specific models of citizenship (on either side of the border) influence not only the nature of dislocation and relocation for particular groups, but also the very fabric and sustainability of transnational activities (Ong 1999; Sassen 1999; Nell 2004). These critiques are especially useful in the post-9/11 era of tightened border security.

21. As Portes et al. have pointed out, transnationalism has been discussed through a range of conceptual premises, and the field seems to lack "both a well-defined theoretical framework and analytical rigor," using "disparate units of analysis" and mixing "diverse levels of abstraction" (1999: 218).

22. See Levitt et al. 2003; Portes et al. 1999; Portes 2003; Castles 2003; Levitt and Glick Schiller 2004. For overviews of the literature on transnational migration, see the special issues of *Ethnic and Racial Studies* 1999 and of *International Migration Review* 2003; Glick Schiller 2003; and Levitt and Glick Schiller 2004.

23. Poerregaard suggests that in places where it is widely practiced, transnational migration should be seen as a "state of being which any subject . . . may pass through during his or her lifetime" (1997: 40). See also Kearney 1998; DeGenova 2002; Chavez 1998. The liminal position refers specifically to the idea that transmigrants find it difficult to become incorporated either at home or abroad. As many K'iche' people told me, being *ni de aquí, ni de allá* ("neither from here nor from there") is the flip side of *con un pié aquí y otro allá* ("with one foot here and one foot there").

24. Chavez describes undocumented liminality as follows: "These people never accumulate enough links of incorporation—secure employment, family formation, the establishment of credit, capital accumulation, competency in English, and so forth—to allow them to become settlers and feel part of the new society. They remain 'liminals,' outsiders during their stay in the US, often returning to their country of origin after a relatively brief time. . . . [E]ven individuals who have accumulated a great number of such links may find full incorporation into the new society blocked because of their undocumented status and the larger society's view of them as 'illegal aliens'" (1998: 5). See also DeGenova 2002.

25. See Georges 1990. Tough transnational passages, for example, often come to be seen as "rites of passage" for young men, a new way of constructing manhood, even as women have increasingly joined transnational migratory flows.

26. Such authors argue that these concepts should not be extended to all displaced people who keep in touch with home, or all contemporary forms of "hybrid" identity construction, and that the study of transnational migration should focus primarily on individuals who engage in specific, routine, and regular cross-border activities (Castles 2003; Portes et al. 1999; Portes 2003). From this perspective, "temporary labor migrants who work abroad for a few years, send back remittances, communicate with their family at home, and visit them occasionally are not necessarily transmigrants," and "similarly, permanent migrants who leave their country of origin forever and simply retain loose contact with their homeland are not transmigrants because their life focus is on the country of settlement" (Castles 2003: 435).

27. Glick Schiller identifies at least five sets of transnational actors: "(1) circulating migrants within a transnational network who travel between their new land and homeland, (2) transmigrants who maintain multiple connections across borders and who may or may not travel, (3) immigrants and their descendants who may maintain only one or two types of transnational connections, such as family and friendship, (4) immigrants and their descendants who do not maintain their transnational connections

but participate in networks with people who do maintain such ties, and (5) circulating migrants, transmigrants, and immigrants and their descendants who utilize various forms of media, including the internet, to obtain information about the homeland and utilize this information in their day-to-day interactions and decision making" (2003: 119).

28. The "firm and lasting" peace was signed between the Guatemalan army and guerrilla forces of the URNG (Guatemalan National Revolutionary Unity) on December 29, 1996, marking the official end to the thirty-six-year civil war (see Chapter 2).

29. Indian *campesinos* or peasants in Guatemala have long referred to themselves as *indígena* or *natural,* an ethnic category that differentiates them from non-Indians, or Ladinos; as discussed in Chapter 2, the concept of being "Mayan" is a fairly new one, particularly in the countryside. Throughout this book, however, I use the concept of Indian, *indígena,* and Mayan fairly interchangeably, though I use the latter primarily to discuss current-day indigenous persons and, often, those who identify with the pan-Maya movement.

30. Traditional woven blouse and skirt worn by most indigenous women; together these are called *traje.* The municipality-specific *traje típico* has served, since colonial times, to identify locality (municipality), thereby both marking local identity and facilitating the colonizers's domination. Somewhat ironically, *traje típico* is now one of the "cultural markers" emphasized by the Maya movement. While in some highland villages men also continue to wear *traje,* most indigenous men, in particular younger generations, have abandoned this practice.

31. Most rural indigenous women make soft *tortillas* daily by removing corn from cobs harvested on their *milpa,* soaking the corn with lime and water, grinding the mixture on a *molino* (grinding stone), flattening and shaping the tortillas with their hands, and cooking them on a wood stove.

32. *Costumbre* (literally "custom") generally connotes an indigenous code of conduct emphasizing ties to the ancestors, a close spiritual relation to one's land, and respect between generations and within the family (Warren 1978; Tedlock 1982; Earle 1986). As discussed further on, it is practiced ritually by *costumbristas* (traditionalists) through ceremonies venerating the ancestors, the natural elements, and the land, and has been emphasized by some in the Maya movement as an essential element of indigenous identity.

33. Throughout this book, the term "bilingual" refers to Indians who speak both *lengua* (one of the twenty-two Mayan languages) and Spanish, and "monolingual" refers to those who speak only their indigenous language. Currently, most monolingual Indians are older or female and tend to live in hamlets; Indian youth (who have had some formal education) and men (who tend to travel more widely for economic reasons) tend to be bilingual. Some of the K'iche' described in this ethnography no longer speak their *lengua* at all, though they still identify—in some contexts at least—as Indian.

34. The term "Ladino" refers generally to non-Indians. It has undergone historical changes in meaning, pointing to the somewhat fluid nature of both ethnic categories. In colonial times, Ladinos referred to Indians who had lost their ties to their communities and hence their cultural distinctiveness and language. By independence, Ladinos were people of mixed Spanish and Indian descent; however, because racial descent was difficult to label, the term actually referred to anyone who was not considered culturally Indian and continued to include Indians who "passed." And, by the early twentieth century, the Ladino in Guatemala came to refer primarily to a non-Indian elite in the highlands, as well as permanent workers in the cities and lowland plantations (Smith 1990b; Colby and van den Berghe 1969).

35. As a number of scholars have pointed out, hybridity in this sense has been part of (and perhaps constitutive of) local sociocultural processes for most colonized people since the inception of nation-states, since the latter have long used hybrid strategies to manipulate structural hierarchies and widen access to resources at the center and the margins (Chaterjee 1993; Warren 1998; Bhabha 1990, 1994). Chanady (1994) has argued that such hybridity has been an essential cultural element among indigenous groups in South and Central America.

36. This can be attributed in part to the fact that the social science and psychological literature has often replicated conventional distinctions made between "refugees" and "immigrants," where the former are perceived as vulnerable, persecuted populations in need of particular forms of institutional assistance (Malkki 1995; Zarowsky 2004), while the latter are assumed to be either active agents seeking economic opportunity or exploited victims of economic oppression. Most literature on Guatemalan immigrants does, of course, take into account—to a greater or lesser extent—the violence that led people to leave (see Hagan 1994; Hamilton and Chinchilla 2001; Loucky and Moors 2000; Popkin 1999; Montejo 1999; Jenkins 1991; Mahler 1998; Fink 2003; Nolin Hanlon 2000; Burns 1993; Wellmeier 1998). Some of these authors have focused quite specifically on how the violence and responses to it have affected specific processes of accommodation in the host context (e.g., Fink 2003, who looks at how labor union organization in the United States is informed by hometown political experiences, and Jenkins (1991), who examines mental health processes in the host environment). Few if any studies, however, have examined how such violence comes to shape actual transnational processes.

37. While the dynamics of *la violencia* in Xinxuc are critical to an understanding of its postwar migrations (and are elaborated upon in Chapters 3 and 6), the brunt of research and analysis focuses on the question of transnational indigenous mobility. An in-depth historiographywould clearly compromise the anonymity promised to my interlocutors, whose vulnerable positions created by undocumented status in the United States and ongoing wartime fears I have sought to protect. For some excellent writings

focused specifically on reconstructing the political dynamics surrounding *la violencia*, see for example Kobrak 1997; EAFG 1997; Remijnse 2002; McAllister 2000; Stoll 1999; Wilkinson 2002; Grandin 2004; Sanford 2003; González 2000; CEH 1999; and ODHAG 1998b.

CHAPTER 1. ENTERING THE FIELD

1. This term is used in Guatemala (as in other Central American countries) to refer to the most brutal period of the thirty-six-year civil war, roughly between 1978 and 1983. The neutrality of the term is but one of many ways in which Guatemalans have learned to modify their language to conceal any sort of political allegiance and to express the chaotic nature of the war.
2. The very high proportion of transport accidents, both in rural areas and larger cities, is in part due to the corruption inherent in this unregulated business. Buses are often packed to over twice the legal limits, and the police often accept *mordidas* (bribes) to turn a blind eye to this practice. Moreover, since the privatization of bus services in the early 1990s, drivers and their *ayudantes* (assistants) are sometimes known to fix prices and negotiate bus routes, leading to unregulated fares as well as violent rivalries (for example, the *cantina* dispute in Joyabaj which led to the public lynching was between bus owners from the capital and Joyabaj).
3. *Cancha* and *canchita* are slang terms often used to designate fair-skinned *gringas*.
4. *Mojado* quite literally means "wet back" and refers to illicit border-crossers; though used derogatorily, is also a term of self-identification used by many undocumented migrants.
5. The structure of municipalities in rural highland Guatemala revolves around the *cabecera*, the center of political, economic, and social life (often described as the *pueblo* or "urban center"), and its *aldeas, cacerios,* and *cantónes* (hamlets), described as the "rural area," *el campo* ("the countryside"), or *el monte* ("the mountain"). While some *cabeceras* are populated primarily by Indians, others (such as those of Joyabaj and Xinxuc) are Ladino-dominated.
6. This musical style was popularized in the 1990s by Mexican musicians such as Los Tigres del Norte and Juan Gabriel, and picked up by a host of more current musical groups whose lyrics often speak of the difficulties of being a transnational *mojado*, including themes such as broken love stories, loss of language and culture, difficult border crossings, drug trafficking, and racism.
7. As Nelson points out, such macabre humor is entrenched in Guatemalan culture, serving as a tool to recode, deflect, and structure the tremendous anxieties of living with the legacy of a profound and irrational violence (1999a: 173).

8. Many transmigrants who return to Guatemala worry that they are targeted by criminals due to their perceived wealth.

9. This is a pseudonym for the organization.

10. The continuing association between the notion of "human rights" and the URNG guerrillas throughout this region is discussed in further chapters.

11. Slang used to refer to the American Immigration and Naturalization Service (INS).

12. As illustrated in Chapter 4, fears, rumors, and what appears as paranoia in Guatemala are rarely irrational and tend to be rooted in a broader social reality. In the case of this particular rumor, what appeared initially as a generalized phobia about my presence came closer to reality a few months later. In Providence, I was asked by an American police detective trying to break a local car-theft ring run by Guatemalans to jot down license plate numbers from Rhode Island when I returned to the village (I did not).

13. *Cuxa* is a locally distilled moonshine or firewater produced, in its pure form, from sugarcane, though often "cut" with a variety of chemical substances such as fertilizers.

14. See Appendix for descriptions of three of the extended families I worked with extensively.

15. Interviews in K'iche' were translated into Spanish by Juanita during the transcription, and I have sought to faithfully preserve the style and meaning of these narratives in the English-language exerpts included here.

16. See, for example *El Senor Presidente* by Miguel Angel Asturias (1991).

17. As a friend from the capital asked me, laughing: "Do you know of any other country where people not only send sympathy cards for the relatives of the kidnapped, but also thank you notes for those sympathy cards?"

18. The target of this rumor, its content, and the time at which it came about are interesting: Throughout the period surrounding the signing of the peace, ubiquitous Pepsi banners, vans, and other forms of advertisement proudly proclaimed that the company was a sponsor of the peace. One interpretation of the rumor suggests that the peace—which has brought in vast amounts development, human rights and other foreign workers, as well as the apparent promise of better times to come by foreign corporate interests such as Pepsi—is connected in people's minds with a fear of "foreign bodies" that can, if consumed, lead to (physical or social) illness, death, and destruction.

19. The civil defense patrols were paramilitary groups instituted during the war, through which the Guatemalan army forced male villagers to participate in surveilling their communities (often through extremely brutal means), purportedly to guard against the guerrilla "threat." As discussed in Chapters 2 and 3, PAC leaders in some communities (including Xinxuc) were notoriously ruthless and used their position to exert considerable control over the community.

20. During my fieldwork two important historical memory projects were in process. On one occasion, an aging widow from another municipality who

heard about these projects (and happened to be visiting one of my "transnational" interlocutors) suddenly recounted to me in gruesome detail and at length the massacres and disappearances her family were subject to during the violence, asking me to make sure I wrote down the entire story. Clearly she had thought that as a *gringa* soliciting stories I must be a human rights worker.

21. Roberta Menchú is a renowned K'iche' Mayan political figure who won the 1992 Nobel Peace Prize.

22. This joke, which was made repeatedly during my fieldwork, seemed to rely on both the supernatural belief among some of the K'iche' people that humans can change shape and form, as well as the ambivalence with which Western medicine and pills (which can be either powerful or evil) are perceived.

23. I found myself quite regularly at the police station, negotiating various types of traffic tickets with frustrated state policemen and detectives (see chapter 4).

24. The *guisach* is a person, without formal title, acting as intermediary for rural Indians in legal matters due to the lack of official lawyers in the countryside; he can be either Ladino or an influential Indian from the community.

25. Stoll explains: "*Guisachs* are often the only recourse for a *campesino* in legal straits. . . . But inevitably, their performance reflects the available opportunities for redress, which are few, and exploitation, which are many, and they tend to become an extension of power" (1993: 69).

26. Procuring a driver's license is one of the first things undocumented migrants attempt, as it is a way of obtaining an identification card. For Mayan *campesinos* who have never driven, this process entails borrowing a car, being taught how to drive, and taking the driver's test—all part of the "networks" described in Chapter 4. Since this fieldwork, of course, it has become much more difficult for undocumented immigrants to obtain driver's licenses in many states, which have either denied licenses without proof of citizenship or provided special identification cards for noncitizens.

27. One of the few ways to obtain legal papers for most Mayans at the time of this study was to marry an American. Such arrangements could be beneficial to both parties, as the immigrant (usually male) would usually provide economic support to the household while the "legalized" partner (usually a Dominican or Puerto Rican woman) would provide legal status.

28. Given the extreme divisions existing in this community, as well as the use of witchcraft to harm others (and the purported use of photographs in sending curses), I was careful to distribute photos only to close family members.

29. As we shall see in Chapter 4, these videos are brought back by particular transnational migrants who are able to attend the *fiesta* and who distribute the video to community members in Providence.

30. Guatemaltecos Unidos is composed of middle-class, legalized Ladinos

organized years earlier to protest discriminatory immigration laws (see Chapter 4).

31. I had heard about this broadcast, aired a few years earlier, from a contact in Joyabaj, who told me that the representations of El Quiché as a wretched, poverty-stricken place, and of Guatemalan immigrants as criminals with false documents, had created a fury among members of the community.

32. One notable exception was the aforementioned broadcaster, who told me in disgusted tones about this influx of people "breaking the law" and violating the "work ethic." Of El Quiché, he said: "It was as though I had been transplanted several centuries backward. . . . I've also heard the Mayan Indians have been in the middle of some conflict." When I asked if I could see the broadcast, he told me (perhaps sensing my unease with his statements) that it had been "accidentally erased."

33. This is the local term used to describe the staff of the United Nations Human Rights Mission, whose departmental headquarters were situated in Santa Cruz del Quiché.

34. See Chapter 3 for a discussion of *envidia*.

CHAPTER 2. MAYAN IDENTITIES THROUGH HISTORY

1. In this model, members of the community combined forces to promote the common good and spread the burden and risk of hardship; the "corporate" aspect denotes the idea that members' identification with the group was not limited to rights and obligations but that the group in fact became an extension of the individual and his/her permanent social identity (Farriss 1984: 138).

2. See Stavenhagen 1975; Guzmán Böckler and Herbert 1970; Adams 1970. Martinez Peláez (1973) and Friedlander (1975) argued that Indian culture was a colonial artifact, which, while perhaps having had existed "for real" in precapitalist times, in the modern world only served (like religion) to conceal class oppression and contribute to further subordination.

3. The closed corporate community has been criticized by social scientists (including Wolf himself) for its assumption of generalizability, its lack of theoretical space for understanding broader economic processes of capitalist exploitation, and its overemphasis on the "closed" nature of communities. As Watanabe argues, however, it is not Wolf's theory but rather its simplified interpretation by subsequent anthropologists that has made it problematic: Naive reifications have "reduced Mayan communities to little more than intricate but fragile mosaics of "shared poverty," political insularity, and cultural inscrutability that then shatter irrevocably under the impact of global modernity" (Watanabe 1990: 201). The second approach has been criticized for portraying Guatemalan Indians as simply passive victims of an unjust social order, and thus leaving little room for

human agency or social struggle. A big problem with both approaches has been the tendency to either generalize findings from one community to an entire region and period or, conversely, to assume that general trends occur at the same pace and in the same manner in all communities. As Warren argues, these perspectives also ignore "overwhelming evidence that individuals and communities continually rework identities" in the face of numerous historical and economic pressures, and are not merely passive victims of historical circumstance and social insularity (1998: 71).

4. "Passing" is usually described in the literature as the process of individual detachment from Indian communities, one that removes people from the locus of tradition and custom that forms, maintains, and validates indigenous identity. Nash argues that it is different from acculturation, which implies that cultural traits from the dominant tradition will change an entire community (Nash 1989). Stoll distinguishes three types of ladinoizing processes: (1) individuals moving away from the community; (2) communities adopting Ladino practices but preserving a sense of indigenous identity; and (3) the gradual community-wide erosion of indigenous custom and tradition (Stoll 1993: 209).

5. Guatemalan Marxists argued that both exploited Indians and poor Ladinos formed part of the same social class; here the binary opposition was between marginalized groups and the Ladino-dominated state rather than between ethnic groups per se, though the conflation of class and ethnicity was clearly acknowledged. As we shall see further on, the URNG's discourse on Indian culture has undergone changes since the 1970s, as a result of shifting strategic imperatives during the war and in the period of peace.

6. In eastern Guatemala, slavery, mining and indigo plantations, land expropriation, and miscegenation nearly destroyed Indian culture and resulted in a largely Ladino population (Smith 1988; Smith 1990b; Lovell 1988). Smith ascribes the relative neglect of the highlands to the preconquest nature of its K'iche' communities, which had achieved stronger state-level integration than their neighbors and were thus more able to resist colonial labor drafts and more difficult to control (Smith 1993). Due to this resistance, and because the remote area of the northwestern highlands was perceived as economically unattractive by the colonists (Lovell 1988: 31), Spanish involvement in this area throughout the colonial period remained relatively negligible.

7. By the 1700s, given a depleted Indian work force, colonists gradually focused more on the acquisition of land through the *composición de tierras*, a royal order designed to supplement the royal treasury through the sale of land to Spaniards (Lovell 1988: 30).

8. *Ejidos* are ancestral areas of communal land.

9. *Hacienda* refers to large Ladino-run farms and plantations, including for example cattle ranches as well as agricultural properties such as coffee and sugar plantations.

10. Moreover, as both Farris (1984) and Smith (1993) point out, in many areas the closed corporate community developed not out of a response to encroaching *haciendas*—since there were few of them at the time and still ample space for Maya to move around—but rather as a response to state taxation and authority.

11. According to Smith (1993), Indians were therefore able to retain greater political autonomy, even as they were later absorbed into larger economic systems. She argues that it is precisely this political relationship with the outside that enabled indigenous community organization and culture to endure after elements of the closed corporate community (such as the *cargo* system discussed further) had, four centuries after the conquest, long vanished. The corporate nature of the colonial Indian community is problematized as well by scholars who argue that *parcialidades*, or preconquest "endogamous kindreds holding rights to corporate property" (Smith 1993), coexisted with *municipios* well into the nineteenth and twentieth century; in this sense, highland communities were comprised of distinct and heterogeneous social, cultural, and economic entities rather than forming a single corporate body (Lovell 1988, 1995). As evidence of long-lasting resistance to forced resettlement, *parcialidades* continue to exist as corporate units today and have in fact withstood centuries of state manipulation much better than municipal institutions such as the *cargo* (Smith 1993: 82; Lovell 1985).

12. Trouillot (1991) argued that the colonists' expectations regarding the "primitive" had already been instilled before their arrival in the Americas. Beginning with the expulsion of the Moors (before the discovery of the New World), the construction of "Others" as primitive, barbaric, dangerous, or docile enabled Europeans, in part, to construct their own identity as enlightened, civilized, rational, and Christian.

13. Exotic characterizations of native South Americans can be traced back to the early explorers and missionaries including Columbus, Pizarro, and Bartolomé de las Casas, among others (Todorov 1984).

14. Although the Liberal reforms theoretically favored natives by promoting legal equality and access to more land, most Indians had neither the resources nor the education to exploit them.

15. Some historians view this period as unlike any other in Guatemalan history, as it used national resources for the benefit of the majority indigenous communities (Burns 1986). McCreery (1990), for example, argues that Carrera's conservative policies permitted rural communities to emphasize subsistence rather than exports, hence reinforcing local culture. Others, on the other hand, argue that the main beneficiaries of the revolt were not Indians but the aristocratic, conservative élite from the capital, many clergymen who had been exiled during the Liberal period. Smith (1993), moreover, questions the degree of both protection and isolation of Indian communities during this period. Indeed, she states that the creation of new indigenous-run markets, combined with increased local economic spe-

cialization and commerce, undermined the closed corporate community and led to an economic differentiation within and between communities that paved the way for increased class distinctions exploited by subsequent plantation system (Smith 1993: 85–97).

16. By 1905, Guatemala controlled 14 percent of the world trade in coffee, which comprised 85 percent of Guatemalan export revenues (Perera 1993: 8).

17. The latifundia system in Guatemala comprised large tracts of land owned by a wealthy few, operated exclusively for export production, and relied largely on a cheap forced labor and foreign investment. Smith (1993) states that this system was not necessarily the product of colonialism but persisted rather due to the fact that only large producers had the political and economic power to afford forced labor. She argues that the latifundia system was ultimately inefficient compared, for example, to Costa Rica, where coffee production has historically taken place on small holdings.

18. Carmack (1990), for example, points to the case of Momostenango, where severely dispossessed Indians waged a violent reprisal against perceived state encroachment during the first Liberal period. By the end of the 1800s, however, Ladinos had created a highly paternalisitic system of status inequality within the community, in part through tight state control and the co-optation of some local natives.

19. Through the *cofradía* and *fiesta* systems, Indians have traditionally spent a large part of their yearly wages during the weeklong *fiesta* on the purchase of alcohol, candles, incense, firecrackers, food, and other *fiesta*-related goods. As we shall see in Chapter 4, the *fiesta* continues to be an opportunity for heavy spending and consumption, even in communities where the *cofradías* have vanished or are watered down.

20. By the end of the nineteenth century, although *jornaleros* constituted two-thirds of employed persons in the Indian highlands, Swetnam concludes that "nonagricultural occupations must have provided alternative employment to a significant number of laborers" (1989: 101). This conclusion takes into account the possibility that some nonagricultural jobs were held by the Ladino minority.

21. Despite Ubico's historical reputation as a ruthless dictator who exploited Indian labor, McCreery (1994) has shown that his centralized rule in effect weakened the power of provincial Ladinos in many places, which partially explains the strong support he received from many Indians who, though they "reaped no great benefit from these changes . . . may well have perceived Ubico's edicts as bringing minimal relief from the most immediate and tangible sources of oppression" (Hale 1997: 819).

22. LaFarge and Byers (1931), for example, were concerned with the relationship between indigenous culture in Jacaltenango and the Classic Mayan civilization. Bunzel's study of Chichicastenango (1952) provided a detailed ethnography of economic life, family life, local government, *fiestas*, beliefs,

and rituals in that *municipio*. Oakes (1951) described the customs and ceremonies—including the intricacies of maintaining the *caja real* and interpreting the Mayan calendar—in Todos Santos. Wagley (1941; 1949) described *cargo* systems, traditional religion, clan lineage, native agriculture, and elements of social life such as fear, envy, and rumors, as well as the growing inequality of landholding in Chichicastenango.

23. As we shall see in the next chapters, K'iche's from Chichicastenango (Maxeños) have a reputation among some other K'iche' groups as well for being both industrious and arrogant.

24. Both of these municipalities, indeed, currently have thriving tourist markets, which points perhaps to their particular inclination toward "penny capitalism" and clearly sets them apart from towns like Xinxuc.

25. The *indigenismo* of this period resembled the "Enlightenment Liberal" ideology of the first Liberal period (1830s), which emphasized Indians' redeemability through assimilation, more than the neoliberal ideology of the plantation period, which perceived Indians as "probably essentially and certainly in the short run unalterably inferior" (McCreery 1994: 175). As Hale argues, the ultimate failure of power holders in Guatemala to effectively create "even a plausible assimilationist (i.e. 'Enlightenment Liberal') discourse of national identity, much less one based on the principle of ethnic or racial equality" (1997: 819), might be explained by the constant tensions between these two perspectives (Indian as inferior but redeemable vs. Indian as inferior and exploitable).

26. Grandin (2000) has described in detail, for example, the formation of "anti-communist" committees organized by élite K'iche's in Quetzaltenango during this period, which pitched, often in violent ways, indigenous municipal authorities against poor Indian *campesinos*.

27. Montejo (1993) points out that the effects of this intercommunity violence are still present today in many indigenous villages that are reluctant to support the notion of land reform.

28. Schlesinger and Kinzer (1982) document in fascinating detail the role of the United States (including the CIA, journalists, UFCo lobbyists and publishers, ambassadors, and senators) in the coup against Arbenz (labeled "Operation Success"). Arbenz, along with Arevalo (who was clearly anticommunist) and anyone else promoting land reform, was branded as a communist by American intelligence. Handy, however, cautions that US concerns over communist influence during this period should not be seen as a mere smokescreen for economic imperialism or a conspiracy inspired by UFCo; he argues that the fear of communist elements was not totally unfounded, given the Ccold War context (Handy 1994: 117).

29. Although the coastal plantations still required both permanent and seasonal labor, the mechanization of agricultural production increasingly necessitated permanent laborers, who were given access to small plots in return for their labor.

30. Although the governments of Arevalo and Arbenz had relaxed much of the anticlericalism set forth by the Barrios's Liberal government, it was not until 1956 that foreign clergy were formally permitted to enter the country.

31. The rabid anticommunism of the Spanish Church is explained, in part at least, by Spain's recent civil war (1936–1939), which was considered "a crusade or almost a holy war against communism"; in the case of other missionaries, the church's conservative and defensive stance must be understood in light of the Cold War and the fear of Soviet expansionism (Diocesis del Quiché 1994: 32, my translation).

32. Liberation theology was defined by the Second Vatican Council and the 1968 Latin American Bishops' Conference held in Medellín. Throughout Latin and Central America in the 1960s and 1970s, the establishment of base ecclesial communities at the local level "contributed to a delegitimation of established structures and leaders, and laid a foundation for new kinds of leaders and solidarities. In so doing, they . . . created tension within the church itself, at the national and international levels, and within local polities" (Eckstein 1989: 30).

33. As Annis (1987) argues, the already dwindling *cargo* system throughout much of the highlands facilitated the conversion to orthodox Catholicism. In many *municipios*, civil-religious hierarchies continued to lose their privileged position as the perpetuators of Indian identity, and in some communities these systems became relegated to *fiesta* organization of a much more limited (less traditional) type.

34. Despite the rabid anticommunism of the army and government during the Arevalo-Arbenz period (a rhetoric that made its way to conservative factions in rural areas), Marxist ideology had not yet been transformed into an active resistance movement at that time in Guatemala.

35. The writings of Guzmán Böckler and Herbert (1970), while radically romanticizing Indian culture, similarly explained Indian culture as a mere product of the labor demands produced by capitalist markets.

36. *Foco* theory, implemented in Cuba by Che Guevara and Fidel Castro and exported to revolutionary organizations throughout Latin America, rested on the idea that "a few committed militants could become catalysts for revolution, without the long, painstaking task of first organizing the local population" (Stoll 1993: 66–67).

37. Waldemar Smith's (1977) study of San Pedro Sacatepequez, for example, shows that some community members distinguished themselves from *naturales,* or traditional Mayan corn farmers, but preferred to see themselves as *civilizados* rather than Ladinos, thus indicating a more complex class-ethnic transformation than ladinoization. Colby and van den Berghe's influential ethnography (1969) showed that local relations between Indians and Ladinos in the Ixil area of El Quiché were highly instrumental and functionally specific, circumscribed by struggles for wealth and power on the part of both groups. As they illustrated, there was a certain amount of commuting between cultural systems, whereby temporary "passing" al-

lowed Indians to behave as Ladinos in certain contexts, as needed. In their account, ethnic boundaries were maintained through relations with Ladinos that involved cooperation, conflict, *and* subordination; the "closed" and "corporate" nature of the Indian community was conserved to some degree due to a selective incorporation of new values, and cultural difference was maintained through shared hierarchical institutions and networks. In describing the relations between catechists and traditionalists in San Andrés Semetabaj, Warren (1978) similarly defined the existence of two competing cultural alternatives—separation and subordination—between which Indian ethnic identity was constantly vacillating and being negotiated. She described a complex process whereby traditionalists (who espoused separation and the maintenance of an indigenous moral order) and CA catechists (who promoted universal religion as a way of overcoming subordination within the biethnic hierarchy) self-consciously reformulated cultural identity, conceptions of the moral order, and alternatives to subordination, thus creating a shifting dialogue on identity during a period of rapid social change rather than positing indigenous culture as either static or in need of outside agents of change.

38. This organization, based in El Quiché, started out as a peasant league and eventually moved toward the armed struggle, as we shall see in the following chapter.

39. Though several authors have argued that the army's most persistent and brutal attacks were targeted toward areas of strong Indian political and economic organization, several postwar ethnographies have shown that the beginnings (as well as the subsequent years) of *la violencia* varied throughout regions and municipalities. Stoll (1993) and Le Bot (1992) have shown the army's targeting strategy following the guerrillas' routes down from the northern Quiché and Huehuetenango south to Chimaltenango. Although Stoll argues that the guerrillas' strategy of provoking the army in particular communities eventually came to play (at least) as important a role as the preexisting level of political and economic development in bringing about the army's brutal reprisals, Schirmer notes that this was "an army that was already poised to operationalize [a] logic of brutality" (2003: 71).

40. Revolutionary calls for the "kingdom of God on earth" and promises of a future religious golden age gave the rural movement a millenarian, utopian mantle (Wilson 1991, 1995; Le Bot 1992).

41. This massacre killed thirty-seven people, leaving Maximo Cajal y Lopez, then Spanish ambassador to Guatemala, as the only survivor.

42. The EGP operated in the capital and in the departments of Sacatepequez, Chimaltenango, El Quiché, Huehuetenango, and the Verapaces. The ORPA operated in San Marcos, Quetzaltenango, Solola, and Chimaltenango The FAR, or Rebel Armed Forces, operated primarily in El Petén, and the PGT, or Guatemalan Labor Party, operated in Guatemala City and the southern Coast. In 1982, the four groups joined to form the Guatemalan National Revolutionary Unity (URNG).

43. The different factions of the guerrilla movement did not hold a unified viewpoint concerning Indian culture; the ORPA, for example, stressed a national model that would liberate Indian oppression, while the EGP's discourse was a more orthodox Marxist one of class struggle. Such viewpoints changed over time as the war progressed and strategies shifted. While the ORPA tried to avoid exposing civilians to army attacks, the EGP's strategy of prolonged popular struggle sought to involve the population in military strategy, a method that they later conceded enabled the army to justify its massacres.

44. At the height of the violence (1981–1982), it is estimated that the URNG counted 250,000 supporters and 6,000 armed combatants; by 1983, fewer than 2,500 guerrillas remained (Le Bot 1992: 195).

45. According to Stoll, in a number of communities the guerrillas' radical message was neither evident nor accepted unanimously by Indians, since the "broader enemies" they spoke of ("plantation owners for whom they [were] no longer forced to work, an army that ha[d] yet to arrive, and a capitalist system that allow[ed] them to improve their lot in small, incremental ways") were not necessarily perceived as enemies but as necessary, if dominant, sources of livelihood or survival, and perhaps even as benefactors (1999: 96).

46. Through this sinister tactic for dividing indigenous resistance, the army's foot soldiers were forcefully recruited from Indian villages and then stationed in areas outside of their ethnic group. Schirmer (1998) has described some of the brutal tactics through which the army instilled aggression into soldiers, training them to hate, torture, and kill other indigenous people.

47. This is exemplified by an army colonel in Cobán who stated: "We liken ourselves to the mountain spirits because like them, we dominate the land, we command over all who are in our territory" (Wilson 1995: 242), and by the use of the term "Kaibil" for the most brutal counterinsurgency units, named after a Mayan ruler who had resisted the Spanish conquest. For a particularly horrific example of how the mass rape of Mayan women was used to terrorize communities, see González 2000.

48. Montejo's testimonial writings (1987), which include his own and others' firsthand experience of terror and torture, constitutes one of the most chilling accounts of this period.

49. Wearne and Calvert point out the Orwellian nature of the military rhetoric used for civic projects such as *Frijoles y Fusiles* (Beans and Rifles), *Techo, Trabajo y Tortilla* (Roof, Work, and Food), and *Paz y Tranquilidad* (Peace and Harmony), where, for example, "food for work" means forced labor, "search and rescue" means hunt and capture, "secure and protect" means neutralize and imprison (1989: 21).

50. Model villages and development poles essentially consisted of regularly laid out wood and tin huts, where displaced indigenous groups were subjected to military control and strict limitations on mobility. Model villages have

been described as re-education camps designed for ideological indoctrination into "antisubversive" models for the nation (Manz 1988; Wilson 1995), though Stoll claims that some Indians experienced them as something of a relief from war-torn areas (Stoll 1993: 158). Following the war, a number of displaced people returned home or went elsewhere, while others remained living in the model villages, having become used to the environment and community. Other strategies of civilian control used by the army included Inter-Institutional Coordinating Councils, which placed all "development projects" in the hands of the military, thus merging together the notions of counterinsurgency and development throughout the countryside (Jonas 1988: 37). In addition, the army's S-5 and G-5 units, in charge of "civic action" programs and the civilian population, worked in tandem with the S-2 and G-2, who were in charge of kidnappings and murders, to instill fear and violence in Indian villages.

51. Civilian responses to the PACs varied, and while in some communities members were seriously co-opted, acting as perpetrators of interethnic and intercommunity violence (Handy 1992), others participated unwillingly as a survival strategy. Thus, on the one hand, Perera offered the following image of PACs: "There is no more humiliating spectacle in the highlands than the sight of schoolboys and gray-haired elders reduced to a common degradation as they shuffle along a country road, cowed and glassy-eyed, carrying wooden rifles—or old M-1's—and a Guatemalan flag" (1993: 92); on the other hand, there have also been chilling accounts of brutal violence by PAC members against civilians, as we shall see in Chapter 3.

52. As Zur notes, suspects' kin were also targeted because "until *la violencia* shattered family solidarity, people were identified by their household or extended family rather than as individuals with their own allegiances. The fear generated by having a dead or disappeared relative among one's kin is driven by the residuals of this traditional way of identifying and placing others. It was a time of multiple betrayals and these betrayals have scarred the community more than the deaths themselves" (1998: 98).

53. Since the 1976 earthquake, Protestant clergy—most coming from the United States—had become increasingly involved in Indian communities, loaning money, helping to obtain material goods, and intervening in local politics (Manz 1988). In addition to state violence, growing marginalization, landlessness, and the increased likelihood of obtaining foreign aid from Protestant groups are all seen to have contributed to the high conversion rates to evangelical sects (Wilson 1995; Stoll 1993).

54. As Le Bot notes, an element of utopianism and millenarianism is also present in the new evangelical sects, replacing the utopianism of previous catechists and revolutionaries (Le Bot 1992).

55. In the highlands, it was often rumored that evangelicals had "identity cards," or papers that allowed the army to recognize them as nonsubversive.

56. Smith, for example, argues that while many Indians in Huehuetenango and

El Quiché joined the guerrilla movement, those in Totonicapán, who had long been challenging Ladino economic and political monopolies through peaceful means (and were therefore able to drive out most Ladino traders and politicians), were able to maintain a more neutral stance, a factor she attributes to their strong sense of local, rather than class-based, identity (Smith 1990c, 1991; Carmack 1988). Watanabe (1992) similarly argues that Chimaltenango successfully resisted the upheaval, partly due to local aspects such as the absence of nearby *haciendas* (which eliminated the presence of an immediate enemy), partly due to the wealth that this *municipio* had been developing through local coffee cash-cropping, and partly due to a very strong sense of place, morality, mutual obligations, and everyday cultural forms that circumscribed the community and its ethnic distinctiveness. He argues that Chimbal's cohesiveness served the community well during the war, as its members did not denounce each other to the army out of self-aggrandizement, revenge, or fear. These ethnographies contest the widespread assumption that the main dynamic of the war was that of a generalized Indian economic oppression and a popular or unified uprising against its representatives (the army, Ladinos), and they demonstrate that different communities had very different agendas than the revolutionary leadership (Smith 1990c).

57.   Efforts to remember the violence, long silenced by the official discourse and brutal actions of the military, have been documented not only within a public political domain by Mayan and human rights advocates (see Chapter 6) but also by anthropologists (Wilson 1995; Warren 1998; Stoll 1999; Zur 1998; Green 1999; Hale 1997; Remijnse 2002; Wilkinson 2002).

58.   The institution of civilian government, the "democratic opening," and the discourse of pacification at this time, however, were more a cosmetic shift in "public relations strategies intended for foreign consumption" (Perera 1993: 48) on the part of the government than an effort to restore peace. The return to civilian law was orchestrated in the early 1980s by the army, which sought to appease international criticism, attract foreign aid, and establish some stability and legitimacy, and in doing so claim credit for restoring civilian rule (Jonas 1988; Manz 1988). Given the naturalization of military control, the army no longer needed its dictatorship to maintain power in the countryside (Manz 1988: 21). Trudeau points out more generally that "democratization" processes throughout Latin America, while optimistically pointing to the possibility of restoring democracy through empowering popular movements and civil society, may also mask or preserve oppressive power structures while appealing to international legitimacy and funding (Trudeau 1993: 236).

59.   The 1993 "auto-coup" attempted by then-president Serrano added to the loss of confidence felt by most Guatemalans regarding government credibility and democracy.

60.   By 1995, MINUGUA had established eight regional offices and five subregional offices across the country, and included 339 staff members (includ-

ing UN volunteers, administrative and logistical functionaries, military officers, and police observers, as well as local hires). Most of MINUGUA's funding has come from Norway and the United States.

61. In addition, they have worked closely with other UN agencies, in particular UNDP (United Nations Development Program) and UNHCR, the latter working toward the reintegration of returning refugees.

62. It has been argued that the institution's difficulties, initially at least, extended from its insistence on a narrow definition of the verification mandate and on a lack of UN organizational experience and culture for dealing with rights issues that lie outside of the civil and political realm—including cultural and economic rights, which have been at the core of the Peace Accords (Baranyi 1995). MINUGUA has also been alternately accused of overstepping its boundaries through its political declarations and public actions, of being partial to the guerrillas, and of being ineffective or not doing enough (see McCleary 1997; ICCHRLA 1995). It has also been accused of excessively bureaucratizing the process of postconflict social movement and change in Guatemala, thereby weakening the sustainability of local programs. For an overview of MINUGUA's strengths and limitations, see Baranyi 1999.

63. The following agreements in particular were drawn: (1) The Comprehensive Accord on Human Rights, (2) The Accord for the Resettlement of Populations Uprooted by the Armed Conflict, (3) The Accord on the Establishment of a Commission to Clarify Human Rights Violations and Acts of Violence that have Caused the Guatemalan people to Suffer, (4) The Accord on the Rights and Identity of Indigenous peoples, (5) The Accord on Socioeconomic Aspects and the Agrarian Situation, (6) The Accord on Strengthening Civil Society and the Role of the Army in a Democratic Society, (7) The Accord on Constitutional Reform and Electoral Regime, and (8) The Accord on the Integration of the URNG to Legality.

64. Through their inclusion of other issues such corruption, tax reform, the decentralization of institutions and budgets, and local participation, the Peace Accords have also functioned as a guide for the multitude of bilateral and multilateral international organizations—UNDP, the World Bank, the International Monetary Fund (IMF), the European Union, and the Inter-American Development Bank (IDB)—whose funding for reconstruction projects was linked to compliance with the mission's recommendations. Throughout its tenure, MINUGUA has reported on the progress of the accords through a series of reports identifying advances and limitations in their implementation.

65. Guatemala City is reported by the Human Rights International (2000) as the third most violent city in Latin America.

66. Most cases that have captivated international attention have involved mob attacks against foreigners, such as the March 1994 brutal assault on American environmentalist June Weinstock, which left her in a long-lasting coma, and the April 2000 attack against a Japanese tour bus in Todos

Santos, in which a tourist and the tour bus driver were stoned to death. In both cases the victims were believed by villagers to be baby snatchers, a widespread rumor connected to the fear of organ trafficking and of strangers. As with most rumors in Guatemala, the foundations for this one rest in some element of truth, in this case the corruption surrounding the international adoption system in Guatemala and some of its local legal representatives.

67. Some authorities, however, have attempted to categorize these lynchings as "a centuries-old tradition in Guatemala's mostly Indian rural areas . . . to rid themselves of rivals," despite the fact that such occurrences rarely, if ever, occurred before the war (Weissert 2000).

68. As in many other poor countries, structural adjustment policies (SAPs) endorsed by international financial institutions and donor governments have stipulated "cuts in government subsidies and spending on education and health, the liberalization of trade and financial markets, the privatization of public enterprises, and general deregulation to attract foreign investment and promote export production" (North and Simmons 1999: 14). These policies, which privileged the private sector at the expense of popular classes, have had a deleterious impact on poor Guatemalans who have increasingly seen their wages held down, inflation and interest rates soar, and purchasing power decrease. This has led, say North and Simmons, to a "doubtful compatibility between SAPS, the peace agreements, and the creation of conditions for long-term peace and democratization" (1999: 14).

69. It remains tied with Brazil in this respect.

70. Many of these refugees, moreover, were already fairly politicized back home, having had contact with or belonging to either the guerrilla movement or other leftist groups.

71. These actors include the UNHCR and specially created government organizations—COMAR, the Mexican Commission for Aid to Refugees, and CEAR (Comisión Especial para la Atención de Repatriados, the Guatemalan organization designed to assist returning refugees)—as well as numerous NGOs.

72. Credits promised by the government for the purchase of land did not come through for many returnees, and often the lands that were allocated were insufficient and lacked the most basic infrastructure. Contestations over land and other resources resulted in numerous antagonisms between returnee and nonreturnee populations in some areas (Stoll 1997). Some of the major issues related to land problems include that (1) families had grown in exile, and original plots were too small to sustain them; (2) refugees were encouraged to buy land through credit, but many were told that the land they request is too expensive; (3) land titles and documentation were lost or are considered invalid by the government; and (4) original lands were claimed by other indigenous people or the army (Manz 1988), often leading to hostilities between *antiguos* who fled the violence and *nuevos* resettled by the army (Ferris 1993: 210; Stoll 1997).

73. In addition, because the experience in Mexico had created many new expectations (e.g., the availability of potable water, schools, clinics, etc.), as well as new organizational forms and power relations (e.g., a dissolution of traditional authority relations), the return to difficult conditions—both material and political—in Guatemala sometimes contributed to internal dissention between different groups of return refugees (men and women, adults and adolescents, representatives of different organizations, etc.), as well as to psychosocial problems, within several returnee communities (Rousseau et al. 2001; Crosby 1999).

74. According to Dunkerly (1988: 496) at least one hundred thousand *campesinos* fled to the plantation area after 1982. A smaller number of refugees (totaling 7,700) fled to neighboring countries, the majority to Belize, followed by Honduras, Nicaragua, and Costa Rica (Nolin Hanlon 1995). By the mid-1990s, the majority of those in Honduras returned to Guatemala, while most in Belize remained in that country (Castillo 1999).

75. While some were originally part of the official camps and chose to leave or form new communities, others tried to integrate themselves directly into rural Mexican farms and plantations or to seek refuge in urban centers from Tapachula to Mexico City (Ferris 1993; Earle 1994; Casillas and Castillo 1994).

76. The agricultural practices and indigenous groups living in these regions, along with the closeness to home, offered some degree of familiarity and respite for these exiles.

77. Like the CCPPs, ARDIGUA sought to create an "imagined community" of exiled Mayan refugees by "infusing an ethnic and class consciousness with a claim to Guatemalan nationality"; unlike them, however, it substituted a "shared refugee identity with one that focused on the population's shared experience as self-settled, non-documented refugees" (Wolfensohn 2001: 28). For ARDIGUA, spatial dispersal and illegality became the primary identifying features of the *disperso* population.

78. Their demographic impact, nonetheless, has been substantial. Gellert (1999) shows that both internal migrants and returning refugees in the northern Petén and Alta Verapaz regions have led to an overall population growth of 251 percent in the area, with some *municipios* increasing up to tenfold since the beginning of the 1980s.

79. Bastos and Camus (1994; 1995) have documented the extremely precarious conditions of these indigenous urban migrants, as well as the multiplicity of family strategies, connections to the home community, and ethnic retention and change among this population.

80. Indeed, it is only by examining how such internal cleavages and interests have developed that it becomes possible to engage some of the broader contradictions of local indigenous identity, for example, why many Indians have historically supported repressive governments or how local identities have persisted and transformed despite such encroachment.

81. Despite the sedentary and "territorializing" tendencies of traditional an-

thropology, there has been a rich ethnographic history of movement and migration ranging from early diffusionist approaches to studies of rural-urban migrations in Africa and Latin America in the 1950s and 1960s (Glick Schiller 2003).

82. As Fabri notes, however, this certainly does not mean that all indigenous *desplazados* in the capital by any means have such a positive outlook on their displacement, as many live in conditions of tremendous poverty, fear, and racism. Moreover, she notes, Mayans migrating to the capital during and after the violence often label themselves as "economic migrants" to "camouflage, for both their own psychological benefit and their reception by the public, the political underpinnings of their migration" (2000: 60).

CHAPTER 3. THE K'ICHE' OF XINXUC

1. This is an estimate based on averaging numbers provided by the national census in 1994, which reported Xinxuc's population to be around six thousand, and a development plan organized by the municipality and NGOs, which placed Xinxuc's population at around eight thousand, a testament to the large fluctuations between data sources in Guatemala. As Gellert has stated, Guatemala is a "country without information"; most data available for social and policy analysis are based on "projections or estimates generated by various national and international organizations on the basis of scattered and incomplete statistics" (1999: 116). Clearly, some of the statistics presented in this chapter have changed since the time of my fieldwork.

2. Binge drinking that is, drinking oneself into a stupor for days at a time, is not uncommon among Indian men, and hearing news about someone dying or being hospitalized for alcohol-related illness is a regular occurrence.

3. Allegedly designed to promote community participation, the *comites* were actually developed to centralize and control community projects their donors and recipients. They are limited to public infrastructure projects—building schools, roads, and water systems—and often continue to be run by influential Ladinos.

4. Charismatics "prefer a degree of independence from the hierarchically structured Catholic Church that dictates norms for engaging in spiritual reflection" (Popkin 1999: 271). Like Protestants, charismatics "address each other as 'brother' and 'sister,' invoke the Holy Spirit, speak in tongues, heal by faith and prophesy" (Zur 1998: 44; Stoll 1993). In Guatemala, tensions have arisen between charismatics, who consider themselves part of the mainline Catholic Church, and Catholic Action members, who perceive the conservative political posture of charismatics on par with evangelicals.

5. *Aj q'ijab'*, or "day keepers," are "active practitioners of the indigenous religion who are initiated calendar diviners, dream interpreters, and curers. . . . [They] are empowered to make prayers to the gods and the ancestors on behalf of lay people" (Tedlock 1982: 47).

6. It is common to see Indian *campesinos* dowsing their *milpas*, unprotected, with these highly toxic fertilizers.

7. The planting of corn is associated with the sexual act (Wilson 1995: 111), and for women to be seen conducting this activity can be a sign of "serious aberration in the family" (Zur 1998: 61).

8. A couple of *aldeas* comprised of merchant families, however, have been spared this negative image.

9. The notion of duality stems from *costumbrista* beliefs and rituals emphasizing the harmony of nature (symbolized by the four cardinal points), the cyclical nature of time (represented in the 260-day calendar of the Cholq'ij, which is interpreted by *aj q'ijab'*), and the need to keep the ancestral spirits pleased. Through this dialectic view of humans, nature, and the supernatural, dualities (male/female, human/spirit, earth/sky, hot/cold, good/evil) are seen to complement rather than clash with one another, and nothing exists without its opposite. Earle (1986), Tedlock (1982), and Bourgey (1997) have described this region's *costumbrista* beliefs and practices in detail.

10. Bourgey (1997), for example, has described how notions of balance and harmony through which the K'iche' view the healthy human body and mind are reflected in sociocultural values and structures, and, conversely, how biological illness is seen to be rooted in social disharmony.

11. Indeed, local *aj q'ijab'* continue to be consulted by traditionalists and Catholics alike in times of difficulty and illness or for special requests for protection from the ancestors; and, as we shall see in the following chapter, the new generation of *costumbristas* spawned from the Mayanist revival attempt to work with older traditionalists.

12. Although the "image of limited good" has been criticized and is not considered "an adequate general psychological model of peasant behavior" (Dow 1981), there is no doubt that *envidia* has long formed part of Mesoamerican culture, as documented by numerous anthropologists.

13. As Fischer states: "If variant behavior is motivated and interpreted in relation to a normative model, then that model is still symbolically and practically valid, regardless of the frequency of non-normative instantiations. This is not to deny the primacy of practice as the subject of anthropology, but practice should encompass more than materially observable behavior, namely the culturally conditioned cognitive frameworks that give rise to concrete activity" (2001: 144).

14. Indigenous coastal migrations continue to fuel the export economy that remains the mainstay of the Guatemalan nation. The current number of *jornaleros* is estimated to be approximately one half million (Flores Alvarado 1995).

15. Plantation *contratistas* are required to fill quotas for *jornales* (days of work) rather than specific numbers of workers; the latter are paid for the weight of produce picked per *jornal*.

16. In some cases, *jornaleros* are "positively reinforced" for high productivity through gifts of radios and other consumer goods.

17. Translated from the French: "Les gens du Quiché partagent cette inclination au voyage et à l'entreprise hasardeuse avec tous les autochtones de cette région du monde pour qui le sentiment d'ancrage sur un territoir ancestral semble n'avoir jamais exclu le désir de voler de sommet en sommet, ni l'habitude du commerce et de la multiplication des alliances. Cette habilité à tirer parti de la mosaïque écologique dont le dessin se modifie au rythme de l'activité volcanique et de l'intempérance des climats tropicaux, cette compréhension familière de la diversité géographique sont les atomes lourds d'une expérience humaine vivace, exprimée dans une constellation culturelle particulièrement dynamique. . . . Il est donc impropre de s'en tenir à la notion d'une autochtonie qui restreint sa portée à l'experience de la communauté localisée, territorialisée dans la finitude de frontières imperméables." (Lartigue 1991: 280–81).

18. These tensions became particularly strong following the loss of control by the K'iche' people over Chichicastenango after the Guatemalan independence.

19. As Earle (1982) notes, such differentiation also occurred among the local Ladino population.

20. Though not originally espousing armed confrontation, the CUC would become more militant after 1978, when the army made clear its intention to destroy all popular movements, and it effectively joined the Guerrilla Army of the Poor (EGP) by 1980.

21. According to the Guatemalan military's intelligence, approximately 360,000 people—including regular fighters, local irregular fighters, and sympathizers—supported EGP alone (Schirmer 1998). The different EGP fronts were named Che Guevara (Huehuetenango), Augusto Cesar Sandino, and Ho Chi Minh (Northern and Southern Quiché).

22. As Earle states, "[T]he evil men included guerrillas, military, civil patrol leaders, ex-*comisionados*, and violence opportunists who profited by the arrival of de facto martial law, using it as an excuse to settle long-standing scores." (2001: 302). Even at the time of the peace, many K'iche' still referred to both the army and guerrillas as *esos hombres* ("those men").

23. As many scholars have pointed out, it is crucial to take into account the deep psychological impact of militarization and years of psychological indoctrination on people's reconstructions of *la violencia*, in particular their need to justify their collaboration with the army in retrospect and to downplay (or deny) supporting the guerrilla movement (Kobrak 1997; Hale 1997). The profound difficulties K'iche' people continue to have in giving shape and meaning to this period are explored in depth in Chapter 6. Nonetheless, contacts within the EGP itself asserted to me that the guerrillas in fact strategically avoided Xinxuc, particularly after 1981, due to the town's rapidly acquired reputation as being under total army and PAC control. Of the nearly three thousand guerrillas demobilized after 1996, only one was listed as originating from Xinxuc.

24. As Schirmer has shown, corruption often played a large role in giving PACs power, and "get-rich-quick stories of corruption by several PAC leaders abound" (1998: 95). See González (2000) for a description of this pattern in San Bartolomé, Jocotenango.

25. For example, when some *campesino* PAC members, fed up with the corruption of the patrols, explained to the *jefes* that they wanted to quit, they were accused of being guerrilla collaborators, were issued death threats, and were eventually forced to leave the community altogether.

26. The department of El Quiché, with its predominantly Indian population, had the most extensive PAC network in the highlands (Zur 1998: 96).

27. Because this area is far from the Mexican border, fleeing across the border was not an option.

28. *Compadre* designates a fictive kinship relation that bounds people through godparenting.

29. In 1986, a new hamlet was founded by refugees and was eventually split in two due to problems between evangelicals and other groups.

30. It is well-known that most people sent to Santa Cruz del Quiché under suspicion of guerrilla activity or knowledge for such "declarations" were usually brutally tortured, if not killed, by the army and police.

31. This metaphor is often used by the K'iche' to express their treatment at the hands of Ladinos, both on the coast and at home, attesting to the long-term, severe humiliation experienced by this population.

32. Most of these organizations had unofficial links throughout the war with the URNG, which integrated armed struggle and popular movements into its revolutionary agenda; indeed, the EGP is often said to have grown out of the CUC, while other organizations such as CONAVIGUA were created in response to the devastation produced by army and paramilitary massacres that produced thousands of widows and orphans.

33. *Saber*, roughly signifying "who knows?" is often used in Guatemala to answer even the most unthreatening, mundane questions. As Zur notes, when used in reference to *la violencia*, *saber* reflects not only a statement of neutrality (i.e., a safe answer) but also a "deeply discouraged view of things, expressed as an abdication of responsibility. . . . *Saber* is also the least presumptuous answer; for the K'iche', presuming to know such answers is like playing God" (1998: 246).

34. After two appeals and the eventual involvement of Amnesty International, the accused was finally judged guilty in 1999 and sentenced to 220 years in prison, though he could only serve a maximum of 30 years under Guatemalan law.

35. Because of the notoriously corrupt and ineffective Guatemalan justice system, continuing fear and intimidation in highland communities, the lack of clarity surrounding the Law of National Reconciliation (passed in December 1996) whereby judges could grant amnesty for certain crimes committed in the context of counterinsurgency, and the general lack of trust in

the official legal system, relatively few indigenous victims have ventured to approach the courts regarding wartime human rights violations, despite the multitude of forensic evidence showing up throughout the highlands as mass graves were exhumed.

CHAPTER 4. LA COSTA DEL NORTE

1. As an example of this massive local inflation, land in the *pueblo* rose from approximately Q500 to Q1,000 per *cuerda* (0.045 of an hectare) to between Q20,000 and Q50,000 per *cuerda* at the end of the 1990s. The value of hamlet land has also soared (ranging from one hundred to five hundred times its early 1980s value) as a result of both the tremendous local purchasing power of the dollar and the increased desirability of land in certain privileged areas.

2. Due to the sudden large flows of Latin and Central Americans coming through the border in the 1990s, the Mexican government, with support from the United States, drastically stepped up deportation measures. While only 1,308 Central Americans were expelled from Mexico in 1987, this number had soared to 120,000 annually since 1990—amounting to a weekly deportation rate equal to the yearly rate for 1987 (Chinchilla and Hamilton 1999; Popkin 1999).

3. The border has become a conflict zone, where INS border patrollers, US anti-immigrant vigilante groups, and pro-immigrant organizations (often church-run) seek to implement their respective agendas. The latter have tried to lessen the hardship and death rate by supplying water stations and welcome posts.

4. These include not only Mexican slang and expressions, but also particular Spanish words that are used differently in the two countries. For example, *coyotes* warn Guatemalans not to use the word *chumpa* for sweater-jacket, but rather the Mexican *chamarra* (which in Guatemala means blanket), and to avoid referring to money as *pisto* or to children as *patójos*.

5. This was the approximate fare during the late 1990s. The prices charged by coyotes rose in following decade, particular after September 11, 2001, when border security became tighter and crossings more difficult.

6. Currently, for migrants who wish to leave immediately, interest is as high as 20 percent.

7. According to a bank manager from Joyabaj, the banks turn a blind eye to this practice, since transmigrants are more likely to be able to repay these loans if they migrate than if they remain on their land.

8. In the first instance, thus, *suerte* refers more to the notion of fate, while in the second it connotes luck; as seen in the previous chapter, *suerte* can signify either.

9. Although they charge less than the courier services, even small letters and packages can cost several dollars to send in either direction.

10. It is not uncommon to visit a family and find that someone has *viajado* in the previous days without having let others know.

11. The last category does not exist since the migration is not conceived as a political exile by Xinxucians.

12. According to the International Insitute, a local institution providing legal and social counseling to immigrants, Guatemalans are estimated to form approximately 25 percent of the Hispanic population in Providence.

13. The *panaderías* sell not only a variety of Guatemalan breads and typical foods, but also a number of consumption articles that are difficult to find in the United States—including the crafts and textiles usually sold to tourists in Guatemala. The *panaderías* also serve as an important social space for Guatemalans, who often run into *conocidos* and friends and catch up with news and gossip.

14. The sudden arrival of K'iche's in Providence has been less problematic than in some other areas of the United States where cultural clashes between Mayans and relatively homogeneous American populations have produced much tension and sometimes violence. This may be explained because (1) this region has a long history of welcoming immigrants, (2) its very economy is largely dependent on their labor, and (3) Guatemalans have arrived roughly at the same time as a number of other immigrant groups.

15. Illiterate K'iche's dictate formal and brief letters; in the home community, the "service" of writing or reading letters is sometimes provided by the courier office at a fee, while in Providence K'iche's usually find a family member to write or read letters for them. These letters are always in Spanish since, until recently, indigenous languages have not been taught in written form. For all these reasons, letters tend to be very brief and include only critical information (usually concerning issues of health and financial need).

16. War widows usually remain unable to remarry officially: Because they lack the documentation confirming their husbands' death (unavailable for *desaparecidos* of the violence) or are still too terrified to request such a document back home, they cannot enter into a second official marriage, even if they have children with their current partners. This obstruction creates a number of pragmatic difficulties for couples and their children in both Xinxuc and Providence, in addition to the clear psychological torment of not having been able to fully grieve their husbands' deaths.

17. These problems have also been reported in other Central American and Mexican immigrant communities.

18. The notion of abiding by the law, when one by definition embodies criminality in the host context (by being categorized as an "illegal alien"), illustrates the contradiction and logical inconsistency governing the lives of many undocumented immigrants.

19. Although the INS and police serve entirely different functions and collaborate primarily in the apprehension and deportation of serious criminals, most K'iche's are terrified of being stopped by the police and deported.

20. There are cases of "green card marriages" among K'iche's (as among many immigrant groups). These, however, have become much more difficult since the passage of the Marriage Fraud Act (1986), "which established large fines for people engaging in such marriages and required spouses to prove the validity of their marriage for two years before a permanent green card could be issued" (Mahler 1998: 167). These arrangements can be a source of much stress, however, as utilitarian and amorous motivations are not always clear to both parties and since government authorities, in order to prevent "marriage fraud," keep track of the marriage for several years before granting legal status.

21. This backlash was epitomized by Proposition 189 in California, which sought to bar public services to undocumented workers (and restrict those provided for legal immigrants).

22. In 1997, "Guatemalan deportation numbers ranked third of all national groups and exceeded 2,300 deportations," representing a 36 percent rise since 1995 (Popkin 1999: 274). Under the IIRIRA laws, undocumented immigrants who had been ordered to be deported before April 1, 1997, could solicit a "cancellation of removal" if they could prove that they had lived at least seven years in the United States, under "good conduct," and that leaving would cause suffering and damage to one's family. If the process of deportation was initiated after that date, however, the immigrant would need to prove ten years of residence and show that deportation would cause "extreme and unusual" hardship—a poorly defined requirement that most Guatemalans could not document.

23. Approval rates for Guatemalan asylum applicants have been consistently low, ranging around 1 to 2 percent. In some cases, bogus *notarios* do not even bother to fill in the applications but continue to request money from unsuspecting clients.

24. In 1998, there were 105,209 pending Guatemalan asylum cases in the United States.

25. Unfortunately, a number of these people could, if properly advised, have applied in 1998 for a suspension of deportation or cancellation of removal under the Nicaraguan Adjustment and Central American Relief Act (NACARA) and perhaps eventually even regularized their status. Although some K'iche's were able to obtain legal status under NACARA, many missed this opportunity either because of fear or because they did not fit into the legislation's deadlines.

26. The IRCA stipulation against the hiring of "illegal aliens" has been difficult to implement given the abundance of counterfeit documents and the supply of cheap labor. In Providence, the INS focused its "crackdown" on apprehending undocumented criminals and conducting a few unexpected factory raids.

27. As mentioned earlier, this situation changed in Providence as in the rest of the country after 2002, when federal legislation made it more difficult for institutions to accommodate undocumented immigrants. Nonetheless,

government and private institutions continue to provide services and jobs to this population.

28. Numerous think tanks and research groups representing both sides have emerged over the past few years, attempting to influence government policy.

29. The Coalición de Inmigrantes Guatemaltecos en los EEUU (Coalition of Guatemalan Immigrants in the US) and the Congreso Nacional de Organizaciones Guatemaltecos (National Congress of Guatemalan Organizations), for example, seek to unify disparate Guatemalan communities on a national basis and to negotiate more political clout for immigrant communities back in Guatemala (e.g., the right to vote at home).

30. In 1997, when the United States began to threaten the deportation of large numbers of Guatemalans, the home government took notice of the potentially devastating economic and social impacts on transnational communities supported largely by remittances. At this point, the government joined other Central American presidents in diplomatic campaigns seeking the protection and legalization of undocumented Central American migrants, claiming that this population had fled persecution in their countries—and therefore contradicting their own country's wartime assertions that refugees were subversives with unsubstantiated claims to asylum in the United States (Popkin 1999; Mahler 1998).

31. In most cases, these are not Ladinos from El Quiché but those coming from other departments or the small group of well-educated, middle-class Guatemalans who had been living in Providence since the 1960s or 1970s, well before the massive exodus of the 1980s.

32. An example of this cultural appropriation is provided in Chapter 5.

33. Although my failure was certainly due in part to my odd status in the community, Virgilio also attempted on two occasions to gather other K'iche' people to discuss the new immigration laws, and not a single person came to the meetings.

34. The media that might enable K'iche' people to become part of a more organized community often have little relevance to their world and are inaccessible. For example, the GARI newspaper usually includes features such as a literary article about Miguel Angel Asturias or an interview with a cordon-bleu chef in Providence. Unfortunately, important articles such as those warning Guatemalans not to place their trust in bogus *notarios* are lost on those who need them the most—illiterate *campesinos*.

35. This phenomenon is not unique to Guatemala; the economies of Mexico and El Salvador (and more recently those of countries such as Ecuador, which have seen a large increase in transnational migration) have also become dependent upon massive remittances coming from immigrants in the United States.

36. These include two homes that were undergoing major renovations. A 1995 survey counted 550 total households in the *pueblo*. My survey did not

take into account the time of construction, but it is likely that many of the homes built from remittances have been constructed since that survey.

37. These numbers are likely to underestimate the Providence-bound population, as our methodology was necessarily cautious. Given the tremendous sensitivity of the subject and people's fears concerning the immigration situation, my assistants (one Indian and one Ladino, both of whom had grown up in the *pueblo*, and one of whom had lived in Providence) walked through the *pueblo* with me and provided the required information about each household to the best of their knowledge. This method seemed much more productive than seeking to interview people in their homes, since they often either refused to answer or gave contradictory answers. Although the 1994 national census had included two questions regarding emigration to another country, so few people had answered the questions that the census bureau never tabulated the results.

38. Because there was too much fear in these hamlets to conduct a reliable house-to-house survey, I asked a community leader in each to count the number of households with members who had gone, stayed in Providence, and returned to either the hamlet or elsewhere in the *municipio*.

39. These three hamlets were selected for their known transmigrant population; because of the "chain reaction" of transmigration, some hamlets have seen a much larger exodus toward Providence than others—though these patterns, of course, are constantly changing.

40. Cipriano's son married a white American woman and brought her to Xinxuc. Several of the K'iche' told me that he "paraded" her around the town in his new car. He returned to Xinxuc the following year and conceived a baby with a K'iche' girl from the *pueblo*, to whom he now sends remittances.

41. Given the difficulties and costs of border crossing, they usually stay on for several months and return to Providence when they are low on money.

42. This differentiates them from other Mayan communities in the United States. Popkin (1999), Burns (1993), Wellmeier (1998), and others have described the reproduction and enactment of the *fiesta* concept in different US contexts, which sometimes incorporate Indians from various *municipios*.

43. This practice began around 1993.

44. All of this is very far removed, of course, from the traditional *fiesta* system, when the main contributors were elders (*principales*) who had made their way up the civil-religious hierarchy. However, it has been a long time since this system existed in Xinxuc, and its demise happened long before transnationalism.

45. Indeed, transmigrants who have truly *superado* are those who have legal papers in the United States and can afford to fly home and back.

46. The term *tiricia* is also used in the Andes to describe a similar illness category, and it is thought to have etymological roots in colonial Castillian.

CHAPTER 5. A DIALOGUE ON INDIANNESS

1. This broad transnational movement was labeled he Coalition of Five Hundred Years of Indigenous, Black, and Popular Resistance.

2. The first of these is the final product of deliberations started in 1957 with ILO Convention 107 Concerning the Protection and Integration of Indigenous and Other Tribal and Semi-Tribal Populations in Independent Countries; the second is the latest declaration of a draft product that took root in 1982. Both declarations have evolved with the increasing participation of indigenous groups in their drafting.

3. Sometimes they even bypass the state and negotiate demands (such as land rights) directly with international organizations such as the UN, the World Bank, and the International Monetary Fund.

4. This current is represented by intellectuals such as Narciso Cojtí (a Kakchiquel linguist) and Demetrio Cojtí Cuxil (a professor at the university of San Carlos), and at the organizational level by the Council of Maya Organizations (COMG).

5. Rigoberta Menchú, for example, whose vision has clearly been based in a more *popular* perspective, uses a strong culturalist discourse as well (Burgos Debray 1983), while many Mayan intellectuals do address issues of land and human rights.

6. In addition, as we shall see in Chapter 6, the contention surrounding the history of Rigoberta Menchú's narrative on Indian identity, first published by French anthropologist Elizabeth Burgos-Debray and then criticized by American anthropologist David Stoll, points clearly to competing representations of Indianness by foreign anthropologists who have their own diverging political and theoretical perspectives and agendas.

7. "Like computer hackers, who do not control the systems they work in but intimately understand their technologies and codes, the Maya are appropriating so-called modern technology and knowledges while refusing to be appropriated into the ladino nation" (Nelson 1999a: 249). She argues that while Maya-hackers do not challenge state and Ladino power directly, they are primarily concerned with sharing information and creating networks in numerous ways, thus "reprogramming from the bottom up" (257).

8. Like individual identity, then, ethnic identities involve multiple identifications that are transformed through specific social and material articulations. At the same time, such identities cannot exist unless the group is trying to fix (to capture or repair) a position within the broader social realm (Nelson 1999a).

9. For example, at a national level PLANTAS collaborates with regional and national public health efforts by integrating alternative medicine within the existing formal health system (e.g., through trainings and educational projects).

10. Wilson describes the case of Q'eqchi' Mayans in Alta Verapaz, and Warren discusses the Kaqchikel Maya in San Andrés.

11. Moreover, Virgilio seems to allude here to some K'iche' ex-civil patrollers who, while speaking primarily *lengua* and perhaps practicing *costumbre* (two identity dimensions emphasized by Mayanists) nonetheless turned viciously against other Indians during the time of *la violencia*.

12. Since morbidity and poverty rates are very high, many cannot afford basic health care.

13. A number of authors have shown how the crystallization of ethnic identity become most important when it seems threatened, as in situations following war and migration. In such contexts, "conspicuous forms of boundary maintenance" often become particularly salient for a group: the sentiments of belonging and continuity become psychologically reassuring mechanisms that ensure a source of self-respect and personal or collective authenticity (Eriksen 1993; Smith 1991; Pellizzi 1988; Diskin 1989; Camino and Krulfeld 1994; Daniel 1996; Malkki 1995; Warren 1992, 1998; Goldin 1999).

14. Already during the war, concealing ethnic markers by fleeing to the capital and abandoning native clothes and tongue sometimes became an important survival strategy (Lovell 1988: 47).

15. *Aprovechar* (to take advantage of), in this sense, is used negatively, as in making unfair use of something or capitalizing on things by being lazy, rather than in the positive sense of taking advantage of a good opportunity.

16. This type of reaction never occurred in Xinxuc, where most people I knew seemed pleasantly surprised by my attempt at speaking K'iche' and usually corrected me or tried to teach me new words.

17. A *mecapal* is a harness worn by Indian men around their forehead to carry heavy loads of firewood or produce.

18. Alcoholism is a top cause of morbidity and mortality in much of the highlands, symptomatic of the extreme poverty and hardship in which many Mayans live.

19. Because the sense of Latino unity, however, is an important essential element of political identity for this ethnic group, there is also a clear ambivalence in the community regarding how social, cultural, racial, and class differences are constructed and recognized.

20. I was told by Latinos around the neighborhood, for example: "I don't want my daughter to marry one" (Dominican man), "they are beneath us" (Puerto Rican policeman), or "I wouldn't rent my house to a Guatemalan family" (my non-Hispanic landlord). On one occasion, a Dominican night club owner told me: "They are like sleeping shrimp, you know they just let themselves be swept away by the current because they are asleep. . . . Guatemalans arrive here, put one foot forward but then do not know what to do, so they stay illegal and have low-paying, unstable jobs. They never quite make it here because they are always thinking of home. They do not learn English, they do not get their papers in order even if they have the opportunity to. We are different, we are Latin American, we know what to do to survive!"

21. As mentioned previously, the style of the charismatics is closer to evangelical religions. In Providence as in other places, the charismatics worship by holding hands and clapping, and the language of salvation is emphasized.

22. A *perraje* is the typical cloth used by indigenous women to carry babies on their backs.

23. This refrain is clearly contradicted by tremendous fear among the K'iche' of the authorities, of being deported, and of each other.

24. Fidel is reputed by other K'iche' to steal cars and make false documents, though it was impossible for me to verify this.

25. As Peñalosa states, it has also been suggested that "the popularity of these kinds of tales derives from the inability of the Maya directly to confront their Spanish-speaking oppressors."

26. For example, when accused of being a *guerrillero* by local PACs, he responded that the only way they could know this information would be if they, too, were subversives. He claims that this logic is what kept him alive.

27. Tecún Umán was the revered Mayan prince who resisted Pedro de Alvarado at the time of conquest and whose refusal to submit to religious or cultural conversion resulted in his death at the hands of the Spaniards.

CHAPTER 6. MEMORY AND GUILT

1. These disciplinary perspectives range from philosophical conceptions emphasizing memory as the primary basis for self-recognition and consciousness through time, to psychoanalytic models exploring the role of the subconscious and early childhood experience in individual memory processes, all the way to social scientists examining the role of historical memory in creating and contesting national identities (see Boyarin 1994).

2. Narrativity is seen in many disciplines (psychoanalysis, literary criticism, medical anthropology) as a fundamental means through which human beings create meaning, both individually and collectively. The dialectical relationship between experience and narrative is such that "as humans, we draw on our experience to shape narratives about our lives, but equally, our identity and character are shaped by our narratives" (Antze and Lambek 1996: xviii).

3. Here it is interesting to think of Salman Rushdie's notion of memory as a broken mirror, the shards of which are represented in narratives through partial, fragmented memories; rather than being destructive, however, this fragmentation can give memories greater resonance by making trivial things seem like symbols and providing luminous qualities to the mundane (1991: 11).

4. Most K'iche' do not have access to psychiatric or psychological care in Providence, and most of their health care revolves around prenatal care and emergency hospitalization.

5. Of these deaths, 42,275 occurred during *la violencia*, and 83 percent of victims were indigenous.

6. The compilation of the report was aided by the declassification during the 1990s of many security documents that were held by the US government and that indicated the extent of American involvement in and awareness of the violence.

7. The notion of genocide has consistently been rejected by both the army and some intellectuals who argue that the counterinsurgency was targeted toward subversives (guerrillas) and their supporters, who themselves are equally responsible for the violence (an argument clearly refuted by CEH statistics, which show the guerrillas responsible for only 3 percent of human rights violations during the war). The CEH justifies the use of the term "genocide" by evoking the definition provided by the Convention on the Prevention and Punishment of the Crime of Genocide as adopted by the UN General Assembly on December 9, 1948. As the CEH states, "[T]he army, inspired by the National Security Doctrine, defined a concept of internal enemy that went beyond guerrilla sympathizers, combatants or militants to include civilians from specific ethnic groups" (CEH 1999, item 110). As such, killings, massacres, and disappearances were systematically directed against groups of the Mayan population, most often the noncombatant civilian population.

8. It was not until 2001, after a lengthy and highly problematic process in which several judges and witnesses were threatened with death (some seeking political asylum abroad), that three military officers were finally convicted of Gerardi's assassination.

9. Approximately 8,000 testimonials were gathered by the CEH, and another 6,494 by RHEMI. As Helen Mack—whose sister Myrna Mack, an anthropologist, was killed by the army in 1990 for her research on refugees—said after the official reading of the report, "[W]e the victims feel vindicated. No one can now tell us we're following lies or ghosts any more." In addition, an entire volume of the four-volume RHEMI report was dedicated to listing and identifying those who were reported by witnesses as killed, disappeared, and tortured during the violence—a chilling index that, judging from the listing given for Xinxuc, is not complete.

10. Following the report's publication, the CEH reasserted that one of its main recommendations was that the Guatemalan government move ahead with judicial trials against war criminals.

11. Many people in this area, particularly from the outlying hamlets, perceive *los Derechos Humanos*—broadly categorized as the UN Human Rights Mission (MINUGUA), the CEH, and any other organization utilizing the language of rights—as an extension of the guerrillas. There are several reasons for this: First, the guerrillas themselves had used the language of rights (the right to land, education, and health) to rally people in villages to support their cause. Second, during the period of armed struggle, the URNG also participated in popular human rights organizations as part of their social

strategy. And third, the army, in implementing its counterinsurgency and fear tactics, had used a discourse which demonized those who spoke of *derechos humanos*. This negative discourse on human rights continues to reach every level of society; in September 1998, President Arzú told a group of graduating military cadets that human rights activists are "nearly traitors to the fatherland" (Goldman 1999).

12. In the case of the RHEMI project, which trained local leaders to gather testimonies, lingering mistrust within the community itself impeded participation.

13. The Guatemalan justice system is notoriously corrupt and ineffectual in general. The situation is particularly difficult for poor Mayan peasants with poor Spanish-language skills and little social clout. Though there have been particular attempts to bring war criminals to justice through legal cases, in many regions people remain too fearful or skeptical to press charges.

14. As Zur states, "[S]ilence and forgetting are present absences or negative spaces shaping what is remembered. . . . Knowing what not to know is a major coping response to terror" (1998: 164).

15. The life story narrated by Menchú to anthropologist Elizabeth Burgos-Debray at the height of *la violencia* focused international attention on army brutality in Guatemala and eventually led Menchú to receive the 1992 Nobel Peace Prize.

16. As Nelson (1999b) states: "One doesn't have to be a post-modernist to know that the binary of true or not true may not always be clear cut, and may actually impoverish our understanding of complex realities. There are truths in the story a woman tells about searching for a disappeared child that are not contained in the aggregates reported by Amnesty International, which are also true. It is probably true that Ms. Menchú's family was involved in internecine struggles over land, but it is no less true . . . that Guatemala has one of the most unequal land distributions in the hemisphere. Does the obsessive personalizing of the coverage simply obscure the larger question of why there was not enough land to live on? . . . Reducing such truths to an individual issue especially as Ms. Menchú makes it clear she is trying to tell a larger story is obscurantist and de-historicizing."

17. In 1997, for example, in one of the few judicial trials of its kind, thirty-six K'iche' Mayans, represented by a Catholic human rights organization, testified against a Ladino ex-military commissioner for countless brutalities committed within their hamlet during the violence. The defendant was absolved due to inconsistencies and contradictions in the witnesses' testimonies, despite the provision of ample forensic evidence. The racist environment of the courtroom, wherein the defendant and his supporters smirked openly at the poor Spanish-language skills of the Mayans and one of the three judges slept, made clear the point that narratives of remembrance, like all discourse, are framed, privileged, and given credence (or not) within particular hierarchies of powers. This particular case was retried twice in 1999. It was not until the second appeal, and after Amnesty

International (AI) became involved and publicized the case internationally, that the defendant was eventually found guilty and given an appropriate sentence. Without the strong support of authoritative human rights groups such as AI and others, it is unlikely that this case would have reached the appeals court a second time.

18. *Tristeza* refers to the embodiment of suffering and sadness; *susto* is a folk illness produced by a sudden fright or fear. These illness categories can be manifested through symptoms such as listnessness, despondency, nevousness, insomnia, nightmares, diarrhea, shaking, and others.

19. Strathern similarly differentiates between a synthetic nostalgia, which posits a clear break between the "traditional" past and the "modern" present, and substantive nostalgia, which is a relational view of past and present, tradition and modernity (1995: 113).

20. As pointed out to me by anthropologist Alain Breton, *alegre* also connotes togetherness, being with a group of people like oneself, and therefore the opposite of loneliness.

21. As González has pointed out, in heavily militarized communities at this time one had two choices: to become a patrol member trained to persecute one's own people, or to flee into the mountains. Those who hid in the mountains were "thought of as enemies, people without land, rootless, savage people who wandered through the night in places where the animals live, strange people who didn't have homes, who didn't eat hot tortillas, animal-like people who could be persecuted and hunted" (2000: 326).

22. Cipriano often tries to schedule his visits during the period surrounding the *fiesta*. González has brilliantly described the use of loudspeakers and aggressive noise and music by powerful men—that is, ex-PAC *jefes*—during the *fiesta* in San Bartolo, Jocotenango. This over-the-top loudness "expresses their need for a noisy clamour to deafen their consciences. They need the noise to cover the silence of the dead and of those living who still remember the way in which the deaths occurred. They—the real leaders of the village—need to demonstrate to themselves and to the neighbouring villages that San Bartolo is no longer a place where everyone knows—but keeps quiet about—what happened. They need to impose their noise on the silence that reproaches them for the crimes they committed and for their continued abuse of power. They are showing the neighbouring villages and the country as a whole that they—and not the silence of the dead—are in control of San Bartolo" (2000:334).

23. Though this narrative has been edited I have tried to maintain the sequence and thematic content of its lengthier version.

24. As Gilligan points out, the Latin word for envy literally means to "see/against" (1996: 68).

25. In one instance (in Xinxuc) because Dionisio was asked to be godfather to a child that the visitor felt he had claim to, in another (also back home) because the visitor's wife had sought refuge in Dionisio's house following a bad beating by her husband.

26. I've included only one such passage, though there are several.

27. As Zur notes, "Evangelicals tend to deny "real" events and emphasize the hoped-for better after-life. Their sects are attractive to people who wish to escape (psychologically) from the intolerable events surrounding them" (1998: 250, footnote 180).

28. The concept of *castigo*, or ancestral punishment, is, like *envidia*, a powerful explanatory model for illness, accidents, violence, and other forms of suffering among the K'iche'. As Zur states, "[T]he ancestors are said to punish people who maintain anti-social attitudes . . . by seizing their spirits, causing them illness or even death" (1998: 232).

BIBLIOGRAPHY

Adams, Richard N.
1970.   *Crucifixion by power: Essays on Guatemalan national social structure,
        1944–1966.* Austin: University of Texas Press.
1990.   Ethnic images and strategies in 1944. In *Guatemalan Indians and the
        state: 1540 to 1988*, ed. C. Smith, with the assistance of Marilyn N.
        Moors, 141–62. Austin: University of Texas Press.

Alonso, Ana Maria.
1994.   The politics of space, time and substance: State formation,
        nationalism and ethnicity. *Annual Review of Anthropology* 23:
        379–405.

Amnesty International.
1997.   *Annual report 1997.* www.amnesty.org.
1998.   *Annual report 1998.* www.amnesty.org.
1999.   *Annual report 1999.* www.amnesty.org.
2000a. *Annual report 2000.* www.amnesty.org.

Anderson, Benedict.
1993.   *Imagined communities: Reflections on the origin and spread of
        nationalism.* Revised Edition. London: Verso.

Annis, Sheldon.
1987.   *God and production in a Guatemalan town.* Austin: University of
        Texas Press.
1988.   Story from a peaceful town: San Antonio Aguas Calientes. In *Harvest
        of violence: The Maya Indians and the Guatemalan crisis*, ed. M.
        Carmack, 155–73. Norman: University of Oklahoma Press.

Antze, Paul, and Michael Lambek, eds.
1996.   *Tense past: Cultural essays in trauma and memory.* New York:
        Routledge.

Appadurai, Arjun.
1990.   Disjuncture and difference in the global cultural economy. In
        Global Culture: Nationalism, globalization, and modernity, ed. M.
        Featherstone. London: Sage.

1991.   Global ethnoscapes: Notes and queries for a transnational anthropology. In *Recapturing anthropology: Working in the present*, ed. Richard Fox. Santa Fe, NM: School of American Research Press.

1996.   *Modernity at large: Cultural dimensions of globalization*. Minneapolis: University of Minnesota Press.

Arias, Arturo.
1990.   Changing Indian identity: Guatemala's violent transition to modernity. In *Guatemalan Indians and the State: 1540 to 1988*, ed. C. Smith, with the assistance of Marilyn N. Moors, 230–57. Austin: University of Texas Press.

1997.   Comment: Consciousness, violence, and the politics of memory in Guatemala. *Current Anthropology* 38 (5): 824–26.

Arias, Arturo, ed.
2001.   *The Rigoberta Menchú controversy* . With a response by David Stoll. Minneapolis: University of Minnesota Press.

Asturias, Miguel Ángel.
1991.   *El señor presidente*. Guatemala: Editorial Piedra Santa.

Audley, John J., Demetrios G. Papademetriou, Sandra Polaski and Scott Vaughn.
2003.   *NAFTA's Promise and Reality: Lessons from Mexico for the Hemisphere*. Washington, D.C.: Carnegie Endowment for International Peace.

AVANCSO.
1992.   *¿Donde esta el futuro? Procesos de reintegración en comunidades de retornados*. Asociación para el Avance de las Ciencias Sociales en Guatemala. Cuadernos de Investigación No. 8.

Baranyi, Stephen.
1995.   The challenge in Guatemala: Verifying human rights, strengthening national institutions and enhancing an integrated approach to peace. London: Centre for the Study of Global Governance, London School of Economics.

1999.   Maximizing the benefits of UN involvement in the Guatemala peace process. In *Journeys of fear: Refugee return and national transformation in Guatemala*, ed. Liisa L. North and Alan B. Simmons, 74–94. Montreal: McGill-Queen's University Press.

Basch, Linda, Nina Glick Schiller, and Cristina Szanton Blanc, eds.
1994.   *Nations unbound: Transnational projects, postcolonial predicaments and deterritorialized nation-states*. Basel, Switzerland: Gordon and Breach.

Barrios, Lina.
1987   Análisis antropológico del grupo étnico Quiché. Unpublished report, Cooperación Guatemalteca Alemana Alimentos por Trabajo (COGAAT). Santa Cruz del Quiché, Guatemala.

Barth, Fredrik.
1969.   *Ethnic groups and boundaries: The social organization of cultural difference.* London: Allen and Unwin.

Bastos, Santiago, and Manuela Camus.
1994.   *Sombras de una batalla: Los desplazados por la violencia en la ciudad de Guatemala.* Publicación de la Facultad Latinoamericana de Ciencias Sociales, FLASCO, Programa Guatemala.
1995.   *Los Mayas de la Capital: Un estudio sobre identidad étnica y mundo urbano.* Publicación de la Facultad Latinoamericana de Ciences Sociales, FLASCO, Programa Guatemala.

Battaglia, Debbora.
1995.   On practical nostalgia: Self-prospecting among urban Trobrianders. In *Rhetorics of self-making,* ed. D. Battaglia. Berkeley and Los Angeles: University of California Press.

Beaucage, Pierre.
1994.   The opossum and the coyote: Ethnic identity and ethnohistory in the Sierra Norte de Puebla (Mexico). In *Latin American identity and constructions of difference,* ed. A. Chanady, 149–86. Minneapolis: University of Minnesota Press.

Berger, John, and Jean Mohr.
1975.   *A seventh man: Migrant workers in Europe.* New York: Viking Press.

Bhabha, Homi.
1990.   Introduction: Narrating the nation. In *Nation and narration,* ed. H. Bhabha. New York: Routledge.
1994.   *The location of culture.* New York: Routledge.
1995.   Freedom's basis in the indeterminate. In *The identity in question,* ed. John Raichman. New York: Routledge.

Bottinelli, Maria Cristina, Ignacio Maldonado, Estela Troya, Pablo Herrera, and Carlos Rodriguez.
1990.   *Psychological impacts of exile: Salvadoran and Guatemalan families in Mexico.* Hemispheric Migration Project, Center for Immigration Policy and Refugee Assistance, Georgetown University.

Bourgey, Anne.
1997.   *La Maladie dans les communautes Maya-Kiché (Guatemala): Essai d'harmonisation entre l'approche anthropo-medicale, sociale et culturelle de ces medecines et l'approche occidentale. Un exemple pratique: "el susto" et "la perdida del alma."* Ph.D. dissertation, University of North Paris, Bobigny School of Medicine.

Boyarin, Jonathan, ed.
1994.   *Remapping memory: The politics of time and space.* Minneapolis: University of Minnesota Press.

Bracken, Patrick J.
1998.   Hidden agendas: Deconstructing post-traumatic stress disorder. In *Rethinking the trauma of war*, ed P. J. Bracken and C. Petty. London: Free Association Books.

Bracken, Patrick J., and Celia Petty, eds.
1998.   *Rethinking the trauma of war.* London: Free Association Books.

Brettell, Caroline B.
2000.   Theorizing migration in anthropology: The social construction of networks, identities, communities, and globalscapes. In *Migration theory: Talking across disciplines*, ed. Caroline B. Brettell and James F. Hollifield. New York: Routledge.

Breton, Alain, and Jacques Arnaud, eds.
1991.   *Mayas: La passion des ancêtres, le désir de durer.* Paris: Autrement.

Brintnall, Douglas E.
1979.   *Revolt against the dead: The modernization of a Mayan community in the highlands of Guatemala.* New York: Gordon and Breach.

Buchner, Florian.
1997.   *Untersuchungen von Krankenversicherungsansatzen im Rahmen des GTZ-Projektes Landliches Basisgesundheitsprogramm Guatemala* (Investigation of basic health insurance within the GTZ-project Rural basic health program in Guatemala). Master's thesis. Department of Public Health, Ludwig Maximilians University, Münich, Germany.

Burgos-Debray, Elisabeth.
1983.   *I, Rigoberta Menchú: An Indian woman in Guatemala.* London: Verso.

Bunzel, Ruth.
1952.   *Chichicastenango: A Guatemalan village.* Publication of the American Ethnological Society 22. Locust Valley, NY: J. J. Augustin.

Burns, Allan F.
1993.   *Maya in exile: Guatemalans in Florida.* Philadelphia: Temple University Press.

Burns, Bradford E.
1986.   *Edward Muybridge in Guatemala, 1875: The photographer as social recorder.* Berkeley and Los Angeles: University of California Press.

Camino, Linda A., and Ruth M. Krulfeld, eds.
1994.   *Reconstructing lives, recapturing meaning: Refugee identity, gender, and cultural change.* Basel: Gordon and Breach.

Carmack, Robert M.
1981.   *The Quiché Mayas of Utatlan: The evolution of a highland Guatemala kingdom.* Norman: University of Oklahoma Press.

1990.   State and community in nineteenth-century Guatemala: The
        Momostenango case. In *Guatemalan Indians and the state: 1540 to
        1988*, ed. C. Smith, with the assistance of Marilyn N. Moors, 116–40.
        Austin: University of Texas Press.

Carmack, Robert M., ed.
1988.   *Harvest of violence: The Maya Indians and the Guatemalan crisis.*
        Norman: University of Oklahoma Press.

Casillas, R. Rodolfo.
1995.   *Central American migration to Mexico and the United States in the era
        of NAFTA.* Hemispheric Migration Project, Center for Inter-Cultural
        Education and Development, Georgetown University, Washington,
        D.C.

Casillas R., Rodolfo, and Manuel Angel Castillo.
1994.   *Los flujos migratorios internacionales en la frontera sur de Mexico.*
        Mexico: Secretaria del Trabajo y Prevision Social, Consejo Nacional
        de Poblacion.

Castillo, Manuel Angel.
1999.   Exodus and return with a changing migration system. In *Journeys
        of fear: Refugee return and national transformation in Guatemala*,
        ed. Liisa L. North and Alan B. Simmons, 130–54. Montreal: McGill-
        Queen's University Press.

Castillo, Manuel Angel, and Rodolfo Casillas R.
1988.   Características básicas de la migración guatemalteca al Sonconusco
        chiapaneco. *Estudios Demográficos y Urbanos* 3 (3): 537–62.

Castles, Stephen.
2003.   Transnational communities: A new form of social relations under
        conditions of globalization? In *Host Societies and the Reception of
        Immigrants*, ed. Jeffrey G. Reitz. Center for Comparative Immigration
        Studies, University of California, San Diego.

CEH (Comisión para el Esclarecimiento Histórico).
1999.   Guatemala: Memoria del silencio. Guatemala.

Chanady, Amaryll.
1994.   Introduction: Latin American imagined communities and the
        postmodern challenge. In *Latin American identity and constructions of
        difference*, ed. A. Chanady, ix–xlvi. Hispanic Issues v. 10. Minneapolis:
        University of Minnesota Press.

Chatterjee, Partha.
1993.   *The nation and its fragments: Colonial and postcolonial histories.*
        Princeton: Princeton University Press.

Chavez, Leo.
　1998.　*Shadowed lives: Undocumented immigrants in American society.* 2nd
　　　　ed. Fort Worth, TX: Harcourt Brace College Publishers.

Chinchilla, Norma Stoltz, and Nora Hamilton.
　1999.　Changing networks and alliances in a transnational context:
　　　　Salavdoran and Guatemalan immigrants in southern California.
　　　　Social Justice 26 (3): 4–26.

Clifford, James.
　1994.　Diasporas. *Cultural Anthropology* 9 (3): 302–38.

Colby, Benjamin N., and Pierre van den Berghe.
　1969.　*Ixil country: A plural society in Guatemala.* Berkeley: University of
　　　　California Press.

Connerton, Paul.
　1989.　*How societies remember.* Cambridge: Cambridge University Press.

Crosby, Alison.
　1999.　To whom shall the nation belong? The gender and ethnic dimension
　　　　of refugee return and the struggle for peace in Guatemala. In *Journeys
　　　　of fear: Refugee return and national transformation in Guatemala.*
　　　　ed. Liisa L. North and Alan B. Simmons, 176–95. Montreal: McGill-
　　　　Queen's University Press.

Davis, Shelton H.
　1988.　Introduction: Sowing the seeds of violence. In *Harvest of violence: The
　　　　Maya Indians and the Guatemalan crisis,* ed. R. M. Carmack, 3–38.
　　　　Norman: University of Oklahoma Press.

Daniel, Valentine E.
　1996.　*Charred lullabies: Chapters in an anthropography of violence.*
　　　　Princeton: Princeton University Press.

Das, Veena, Arthur Kleinman, Mamphela Ramphele, and Pamela Reynolds, eds.
　2000.　*Violence and subjectivity.* Berkeley: University of California Press.

Das, Veena, Arthur Kleinman, Margaret Lock, Mamphela Ramphele, and
　　　　Pamela Reynolds, eds.
　2001.　*Remaking a world: Violence, social suffering, and recovery.* Berkeley:
　　　　University of California Press.

DeGenova, Nicholas.
　2002.　Migrant "illegality" and deportability in everyday life. *Annual Review
　　　　of Anthropology* 31: 419–47.

Del Baso, M.
　1984.　L'assimilation et les études ethniques en Amerique du Nord. *Cahiers
　　　　de Recherche Sociologique (UQAM)* 2 (2): 49–73.

DelVecchio Good, Mary-Jo, Tseunetsugu Munakata, and Yasuki Kobayashi.
  1993.   Temps narratif et incertitude en médecine clinique. *Anthropologie et Sociétés* 17 (1–2): 79–98.

Diocesis Del Quiché.
  1994.   *El Quiché: El pueblo y su iglesia 1960–1980*. Santa Cruz del Quiché, Guatemala, Julio 1994.

Diskin, Martin.
  1989.   Revolution and ethnic identity: The Nicaraguan case. In *Conflict, migration, and the expression of ethnicity*, ed. N. L. Gonzalez and C. S. McCommon. Boulder, CO: Westview Press.

Dow, James.
  1981.   The image of limited production: Envy and the domestic mode of production in peasant society. *Human Organization* 40 (4): 360–63.

Dunkerley, James.
  1988.   *Power in the isthmus: A political history of modern Central America.* London: Verso.

EAFG. Equipo de Antropología Forense de Guatemala.
  1997.   *Las massacres en Rabinal: Estudio histórico antropológico de las Masacres de Plan de Sánchez, Chichupac y Río Negro.* Guatemala: Equipo de Antropología Forense de Guatemala.

Earle, Duncan.
  1982.   Changes in ethnic population proportions in the Quiché Basin: A case of reconquest. In *The historical demography of highland Guatemala*, ed. Robert M. Carmack, John Early and Christopher Lutz. Albany, NY: Institute for Mesoamerican Studies, State University of New York.

  1986.   The metaphor of the day in Quiché: Notes on the nature of everyday life. In *Symbol and meaning beyond the closed community: Essays in Mesoamerican ideas*, ed. Gary Gossen. Austin: University of Texas Press.

  1988.   Mayas aiding Mayas: Guatemalan refugees in Chiapas, Mexico. In *Harvest of violence: The Maya Indians and the Guatemalan crisis*, ed. R. M. Carmack, 256–73. Norman: University of Oklahoma Press.

  1990.   Appropriating the enemy: Maya religious organization and community survival. In *Class, politics, and popular religion in Mexico and Central America*, ed. Lynn Stephen and James W. Dow. Washington, DC: American Anthropological Association.

  1994.   Constructions of refugee ethnic identity: Guatemalan Mayas in Mexico and south Florida. In *Reconstructing lives, recapturing meaning: Refugee identity, gender, and culture change*, ed. L. A. Camino and R. M. Krulfeld. Basel: Gordon and Breach.

  2001.   Menchú tales and Maya social landscapes: The silencing of words and worlds. In *The Rigoberta Menchú controversy*, ed. Arturo Arias, with a response by David Stoll. Minneapolis: University of Minnesota Press.

Early, Jon D.
  1983.   A demographic survey of contemporary Guatemalan Maya. In *Heritage of conquest thirty years later,* ed. C. Kendall, J. Hawkins, and L. Bossen. Albuquerque: University of New Mexico Press.

Eckstein, Susan.
  1989.   Power and popular protest in Latin America. In *Power and popular protest: Latin American social movements,* ed. Susan Eckstein, 1–60. Berkeley and Los Angeles: University of California Press.

Eriksen, Thomas Hylland.
  1993.   *Ethnicity and nationalism: Anthropological perspectives.* Chicago: Pluto Press.

Fabian, Johannes.
  1983.   *Time and the Other: How Anthropology Makes Its Object.* New York: Columbia University Press.

Fabri, Antonella.
  2000.   Space and identity in testimonies of displacement: Maya migration to Guatemala City in the 1980s. In *The Maya diaspora: Guatemalan roots, new American lives,* ed. James Loucky and Marilyn M. Moors. Philadelphia: Temple University Press.

Falla, Ricardo.
  1980.   *Quiché rebelde.* Coleccion "Realidad Nuestra," v. 7. Editorial Universitaria de Guatemala.
  1994.   *Massacres in the jungle: Ixcan, Guatemala, 1975–1982.* Boulder, CO: Westview Press.
  1997.   Comment: Consciousness, violence, and the politics of memory in Guatemala. *Current Anthropology* 38 (5): 826–28.

Farriss, Nancy M.
  1984.   *Maya society under colonial rule: The collective enterprise of survival.* Princeton, NJ: Princeton University Press.

Feldman, Allen.
  1991.   *Formations of violence: The narrative of the body and political terror in Northern Ireland.* Chicago: University of Chicago Press.
  1995.   Ethnographic states of emergency. In *Fieldwork under fire: Contemporary studies of violence and survival,* ed. Carolyn Nordstrom and Antonius C. G. M. Robben, 224–52. Berkeley and Los Angeles: University of California Press.

Feldman-Bianco, Bela.
    1992.   Multiple layers of time and space: The construction of class, ethnicity, and nationalism among Portuguese immigrants. In *Towards a transnational perspective on migration: Race, class, ethnicity and nationalism reconsidered*, ed. Nina Glick Schiller et al., 145–74. Annals of the New York Academy of Sciences, vol. 645. New York: New York Academy of Sciences.

Ferris, Elizabeth G.
    1993.   *Beyond borders: Refugees, migrants and human rights in the post-cold war era.* Geneva: WCC Publications (World Council of Churches).

Field, Les W.
    1994.   Who are the Indians? Reconceptualizing indigenous identity, resistance and the role of social science in Latin America. *Latin American Research Review* 29 (3): 237–48.

Fink, Leon.
    2003.   *The Maya of Morganton: Work and community in the Nuevo New South.* Chapel Hill: University of North Carolina Press.

Fischer, Edward T.
    2001.   *Cultural logics and global economies: Maya identity in thought and practice.* Austin: University of Texas Press.

Fischer, Edward T., and R. McKenna Brown, eds.
    1996.   *Maya Cultural Activism in Guatemala.* Austin: University of Texas Press.

Flores Alvarado, Humberto.
    1995.   *Migración de jornaleros.* Materiales de Estudio y Trabajo 5. Guatemala: Fondo de Cultura Editorial, Ciudad de Guatemala.

Foner, Nancy.
    2003.   Introduction: Anthropology and contemporary immigration to the United States—where we have been and where we are going. In *American arrivals: Anthropology engages the new immigration*, ed. N. Foner. Santa Fe: School of American Research Press.

Foster, George M.
    1965.   Peasant society and the image of the limited good. *American Anthropologist* 67: 293–315.
    1972.   The anatomy of envy: A study in symbolic behavior. *Current Anthropology* 16 (1): 73–92.

Foster, Robert J.
   1991.   Making national cultures in the global ecumene. *Annual Review of Anthropology* 20: 2325–60.

Fox, Richard, and Orin Starn, eds.
   1997.   *Between resistance and revolution: Cultural politics and social protest.* New Brunswick, NJ: Rutgers University Press.

Friedlander, Jonathan.
   1975.   *Being Indian in Hueyapan: A study of forced identity in contemporary Mexico.* New York: St. Martin's.

Friedman, Jonathan.
   1990.   Being in the world: Globalization and localization. In *Global culture: Nationalism, globalization and modernity*, ed. M. Featherstone. London: Sage.

Galeano, Eduardo.
   1967.   *Guatemala: País ocupado.* Mexico: Editorial Nuestro Tiempo.

Garrard–Burnet, Virginia.
   2000.   Aftermath: Women and gender issues in postconflict Guatemala. Center for Development Information and Evaluation, Working Paper No. 311. U.S. Agency for International Development. Washington, DC.

Gellert, Gisela.
   1999.   Migration and the displaced in Guatemala City in the context of a flawed national transformation. In *Journeys of fear: Refugee return and national transformation in Guatemala*, ed. Liisa L. North and Alan B. Simmons, 112–29. Montreal: McGill-Queen's University Press.

Gellner, Ernest.
   1983.   *Nations and Nationalism.* Oxford: Basil Blackwell.

Georges, Eugenia.
   1990.   *The making of a transnational community: Migration, development, and cultural change in the Dominican Republic.* New York: Columbia University Press.

Gilligan, James.
   1996.   *Violence: Reflections on a national epidemic.* New York: Vintage Books.

Gilroy, Paul.
   1993.   *The black Atlantic: Modernity and double consciousness.* Boston: Harvard University Press.

Gleijesis, Piero.
  1991.   *Shattered hope: The Guatemalan revolution and the United States,*
          1944–1954. Princeton, NJ: Princeton University Press.

Glick Schiller, Nina.
  2003.   The centrality of ethnography in the study of transnational migration:
          Seeing the wetlands instead of the swamp. In *American arrivals:*
          Anthropology engages the new immigration, ed. Nancy Foner. Santa Fe:
          School of American Research Press.

Glick Schiller, Nina, Linda Basch, and Cristina Blanc-Szanton, eds.
  1992.   *Towards a transnational perspective on migration: Race, class, ethnicity*
          and nationalism reconsidered. Annals of the New York Academy of
          Sciences, vol. 645. New York: New York Academy of Sciences.

Goldin, Liliana, ed.
  1999.   *Identities on the move: Transnational processes in North America and*
          the Caribbean basin. Institute for Mesoamerican Studies. Albany, New
          York: University at Albany.

Goldman, Francisco.
  1992.   *The long night of white chickens.* New York: Atlantic Monthly Press.
  1999.   Murder comes for the bishop. *New Yorker,* March 15, 1999, 60–77.

González, Juan de Dios, ed.
  1999.   *El sistema jurídico K'iché: Una aproximación.* Guatemala: Universidad
          Rafael Landivar, IDIES.

Gonzalez, Matilde.
  2000.   The man who brought the danger to the village: Representations of
          the armed conflict in Guatemala from a local perspective. *Journal*
          of Southern African Studies. Special Issue: Popular Culture and
          Democracy (26) 2: 317–35.

Good, Byron.
  1994.   *Medicine, rationality, and experience: An anthropological perspective.*
          Cambridge: Cambridge University Press.

Good, Byron, and Mary-Jo DelVecchio Good.
  1993.   Au mode subjonctif: La construction narrative des crises d'épilepsie
          en Turquie. *Anthropologies et Sociétés* 17 (1–2): 21–42.

Gossen, Gary.
  1986.   Mesoamerican ideas as a foundation for regional synthesis. In *Symbol*
          and meaning beyond the closed community, ed. Gary Gossen. Albany:
          Institution for Mesoamerican Studies, State University of New York.

Grandin, Greg.
  2000.   *The blood of Guatemala: History of race and nation.* Durham, NC:
          Duke University Press.

2004.   *The last colonial massacre: Latin America in the cold war.* Chicago: University of Chicago Press.

Green, Linda.
1999.   *Fear as a way of life: Mayan widows in rural Guatemala.* New York: Columbia University Press.

Guarnizo, Luis Eduardo.
1997.   The emergence of a transnational social formation and the mirage of return migration among Dominican transmigrants. *Identities* 4 (2): 281–322.

Guidieri, Remo, and Pellizzi, Franscesco.
1988.   Introduction: Smoking mirrors—modern polity and ethnicity. In *Ethnicities and nations: Processes of interethnic relations in Latin America, Southeast Asia, and the Pacific,* ed. R. Guidieri, F. Pellizzi, and S. Tambiah. Austin: University of Texas Press.

Gupta, Akhil, and James Ferguson.
1992.   Beyond "culture": Space, identity, and the politics of difference. *Cultural Anthropology* 7 (1): 6–23.

Gupta, Akhil, and James Ferguson, eds.
1997.   *Anthropological locations: Boundaries and grounds of a field science.* Berkeley and Los Angeles: University of California Press.

Guzmán Böckler, Carlos, and Jean-Loup Herbert.
1970.   *Guatemala: Una interpretación histórico-social.* 1st ed. México: Siglo Veintiuno.

Hagan, Jacqueline Maria.
1994.   *Deciding to be legal: A Mayan community in Houston.* Philadelphia: Temple University Press.

Hale, Charles R.
1994.   Between Che Guevara and the Pachamama: Mestizos, Indians and identity politics in the anti quincentenary campaign. *Critique of Anthropology* 14 (1): 9–39.
1997.   Consciousness, violence, and the politics of memory in Guatemala. *Current Anthropology* 38 (5): 817–24.

Hall, Stuart.
1990.   Cultural identity and diaspora. In *Identity, community, culture, difference,* ed. J. Rutherford. London: Lawrence & Wishart.
1996.   Cultural studies and its theoretical legacies. In *Cultural studies,* ed. Lawrence Grossberg, Cary Nelson, and Paula A. Treichler, 277–85. New York: Routledge.

Hamilton, Nora, and Norma Stoltz Chinchilla.
  1991. Central American migration: A framework for analysis. *Latin American Research Review* 26 (1): 75–110.

Hamilton, Nora, and Norma Stoltz Chinchilla.
  2001. *Seeking community in a global city. Guatemalans and Salvadorans in Los Angeles.* Philadelphia: Temple University Press.

Handler, Richard.
  1988. *Nationalism and the politics of culture in Quebec.* Madison: University of Wisconsin Press.

Handy, Jim.
  1984. *Gift of the devil: A history of Guatemala.* Toronto, ON: Between the Lines.
  1990. The corporate community, campesino organizations, and agrarian reform: 1950–1954. In *Guatemalan Indians and the state: 1540 to 1988,* ed. C. Smith, with the assistance of Marilyn N. Moors, 163–82. Austin: University of Texas Press.
  1992. Guatemala: A tenacious despotism. *NACLA Report on the Americas.* 26 (3): 31–37.
  1994. *Revolution in the countryside: Rural conflict and agrarian reform in Guatemala, 1944–1954.* Chapel Hill: University of North Carolina Press.
  2002. Democratizing what?: Some reflections on nation, state, ethnicity, modernity, community and democracy in Guatemala. *Canadian Journal of Latin American and Caribbean Studies* 27 (53): 35–71.

Hanks, William F.
  1990. *Referential practice: Language and lived space among the Maya.* Chicago: University of Chicago Press.

Hannerz, Ulf.
  1990. Cosmopolitans and locals in world culture. In *Global culture: Nationalism, globalization and modernity,* ed. M. Featherstone. London: Sage.

Harbury, Jennifer.
  1994. *Bridge of courage: Life stories of the Guatemalan compañeros and compañeras.* Montreal: Vehicule Press.

Harvey, David.
  1989. *The condition of postmodernity.* London: Blackwell.

Hobsbawm, Eric.
  1990. *Nations and nationalism since 1780: Programme, myths, reality.* Cambridge: Cambridge University Press.

Hobsbawm, Eric, and Terence Ranger, eds.
  1983. *The invention of tradition.* New York: Columbia University Press.

House, Krista L., and W. George Lovell.
  1999.   Transmigrant labour and the impact of foreign remittances in rural
          Guatemala: The case of Nueva Unión Maya. Paper presented at the
          International Seminar on the Population of the Central American
          Isthmus at the End of the Millenium, Jacó, Costa Rica.

Human Rights Watch.
  1998.   *World Report 1998.* www.hrw.org.
  1999.   *World Report 1999.* www.hrw.org.
  2000.   *World Report 2000.* www.hrw.org.

Ibañez, Jorge L.
  2001.   The concept of identity. In *National identities and socio-political
          changes in Latin America,* ed. M. Durán-Cogan and A. Gómez-
          Moriana. New York: Routledge.

Interamerican Development Bank.
  2000.   *Poverty in Guatemala.* Washington, DC: Interamerican Development
          Bank.

ICCHRLA (Inter-Church Committee on Human Rights in Latin America).
  1995.   *Crisis of state—state of crisis: Human rights in Guatemala.* Special
          Report, June, 1995. Toronto, ON: ICCHRLA.

Immerman, Richard.
  1982.   *The CIA in Guatemala: The foreign policy of intervention.* Austin:
          University of Texas Press.

Jenkins, Janis H.
  1991.   The state construction of affect: Political ethos and mental health
          among Salvadoran refugees. *Culture, Medicine and Psychiatry* 15 (2).

Jonas, Suzanne.
  1988.   Contradictions of Guatemala's "political opening." *Latin American
          Perspectives* 15 (3): 26–46.
  1991.   *The battle for Guatemala: Rebels, death squads, and US power.*
          Boulder, CO: Westview Press.
  1995.   Transnational realities and anti-immigrant state policies: Issues raised
          by the experiences of Central American immigrants and refugees
          in a trinational region. *Estudios Internacionales,* Revista del IRIPAZ
          (Instituto de Relaciones Internacionales y de Investigacion para la
          Paz) 6 (11): 17–29.

Karrer, Wolfgang.
  1994.   Nostalgia, amnesia and grandmothers: The use of memory in Albert
          Murray, Sabine Ulibarri, Paula Gunn Allen, and Alice Walker. In
          *Memory, narrative, and identity: New essays in ethnic American
          literatures,* ed. Amritjit Singh, Joseph T. Skerret Jr., and Robert E.
          Hogan. Boston: Northeastern University Press.

Kearney, Michael.
1986.   From the invisible hand to visible feet: Anthropological studies of
        migration and development. *Annual Review of Anthropology* 15:
        331–61.
1995.   The local and the global: The anthropology of globalization and
        transnationalism. *Annual Review of Anthropology* 24: 547–65.
1996.   *Reconceptualizing the peasantry: Anthropology in global perspective.*
        Boulder, CO: Westview Press.
1998.   Transnationalism in California and Mexico at the end of empire.
        In *Border identities: Nation and state at international frontiers,* ed.
        Thomas M. Wilson and Hastings Donnan, 117–41. Cambridge:
        Cambridge University Press.

Keith, Michael, and Steve Pile, eds.
1993.   *Place and the politics of identity.* London: Routledge.

Kendall, Carl, John Hawkins, and Laurel Bossen, eds.
1983.   *Heritage of conquest thirty years later.* Albuquerque: University of New
        Mexico Press.

Kinzer, Stephen.
2001.   Guatemala: The unfinished peace. *New York Review of Books,* June.

Kleinman, Arthur, Veena Das, and Margaret Lock, eds.
1997.   *Social suffering.* Berkeley and Los Angeles: University of California
        Press.

Kobrak, Paul.
1997.   Village troubles: The civil patrols in Aguacatán, Guatemala. Ph.D.
        dissertation, University of Michigan.

LaFarge, Oliver, and Douglas Byers.
1931.   *The year bearer's people.* Middle American Research Institute,
        Publication No. 3. New Orleans: Tulane University.

Lamphere, Louise, ed.
1992.   *Structuring diversity: Ethnographic perspectives on the new
        immigration.* Chicago: University of Chicago Press.

Lartigue, François.
1983.   L'Organisation communautaire d'un village Quiché: Les politiques
        d'une réserve de main-d'œvre Indienne. In *San Andrés Sajcabajá:
        peuplement, organisation sociale et encadrement d'une population dans
        les hautes terres de Guatemala,* ed. Henri Lehmann, 103–13. Paris:
        Centre d'Études Mexicaines et Centraméricaines.
1991.   Éloge d'un mort et trace dans la cendre. In *Mayas: La passion des
        ancêtres, le desir de durer,* ed. A. Breton and J. Araud, 276–82. Paris:
        Autrement.

Le Bot, Yvon.
    1992.   *La guerre en terre Maya: Communauté, violence et modernité au Guatemala.* Paris: Éditions Karthala.

Le Bot, Yvon, and Cécile Rousseau.
    2000.   Du bon usage des autobiographies . . . et de leurs critiques: À propos de l'affaire Rigoberta Menchú. *Critique Internationale* 6: 57–66.

León-Portilla, Miguel.
    1986.   *Tiempo y realidad en el pensamiento maya.* Serie de cultura mesoamericana 2. Mexico City: Universidad Autónoma de México, Instituto de investigaciones históricas.

Levitt, Peggy.
    2001.   *The transnational villagers.* Berkeley: University of California Press.

Levitt, Peggy, Josh de Wind, and Steven Vertovec.
    2003.   International perspectives on transnational migration: An introduction. *International Migration Review* 37 (3): 565–75.

Levitt, Peggy, and Nina Glick Schiller.
    2004.   Conceptualizing simultaneity: A transnational social field perspective on society. *International Migration Review* 38 (3): 1002–39.

Lira, E.
    1997.   Remembering: Passing back through the heart. In *Collective memory of political events: Social psychological perspectives*, ed. J. W. Pennebaker, D. Paez, and B Rimé, 223–52. Mahwah, NJ: Erlbaum.

Loucky, James.
    2000.   Maya in a modern metropolis: Establishing new lives and livelihoods in Los Angeles. In *The Maya diaspora: Guatemalan roots, new American lives*, ed. James Loucky and Marilyn M. Moors. Philadelphia: Temple University Press.

Loucky, James, and Marilyn M. Moors, eds.
    2000.   *The Maya diaspora: Guatemalan roots, new American lives.* Philadelphia: Temple University Press.

Lovell, W. George.
    1985.   *Conquest and survival in colonial Guatemala: A historical geography of the Cuchumatan highlands, 1500–1821.* Kingston: McGill-Queen's University Press.
    1988.   Surviving conquest: The Maya of Guatemala in historical perspective. *Latin American Research Review* 23 (2): 25–57.
    1995.   *A beauty that hurts: Life and death in Guatemala.* Toronto, ON: Between the Lines.
    1999.   Land and peace: Two points of view. In *Journeys of fear: Refugee return and national transformation in Guatemala*, ed. Liisa L. North and Alan B. Simmons. Montreal: McGill-Queen's University Press.

Lovell, W. George, and Christopher H. Lutz.
1994.   Conquest and population: Maya demography in historical perspective. *Latin American Research Review* 29 (2): 133–41.
2001.   The primacy of larger truths: Rigoberta Menchú and the tradition of native testimony in Guatemala. In *The Riboberta Menchú controversy*, ed. Arturo Arias, with a response by David Stoll. Minneapolis: University of Minnesota Press.

Lutz, Christopher H., and W. George Lovell.
1990.   Core and periphery in colonial Guatemala. In *Guatemalan Indians and the State: 1540 to 1988*, ed. C. Smith, with the assistance of Marilyn N. Moors, 35–51. Austin: University of Texas Press.
2000.   Survivors on the move: Maya migration in time and space. In *The Mayan diaspora: Guatemalan roots, new American lives*, ed. James Loucky and Marilyn M. Moors. Philadelphia: Temple University Press.

Lykes, M. Brinton, Mary M. Brabeck, Theresa Ferns, and Angela Radan.
1993.   Human rights and mental health among Latin American women in situations of state-sponsored violence. *Psychology of Women Quarterly* 17: 525–44.

Mahler, Sarah J.
1998.   *American dreaming: Immigrant life on the margins*. Princeton, NJ: Princeton University Press.

Malkki, Liisa.
1992.   National geographic: The rooting of peoples and the territorialization of national identity among scholars and refugees. *Cultural Anthropology* 7 (1): 24–44.
1995.   *Purity and exile: Violence, memory, and national cosmology among Hutu refugees in Tanzania*. Chicago: University of Chicago Press.

Manz, Beatriz.
1988.   *Refugees of a hidden war: The aftermath of counter-insurgency in Guatemala*. New York: State University of New York Press.

Marcus, George E.
1995.   Ethnography in/of the world system: The emergence of multi-sited ethnography. *Annual Review of Anthropology* 24: 95–117.

Martín-Baró, Ignacio.
1996.   *Writings for a liberation psychology*. Reprint ed. Boston: Harvard University Press.

Martínez Peláez, Severo.
1971.   *La patria del criollo: Ensayo de interpretación de la realidad colonial guatemalteca*. Reprint ed. Guatemala: Editorial Universitaria.

Massey, Douglas S., Joaquín Arango, Graeme Hugo, Ali Kouaouci, Adela
        Pellegrino, and J. Edward Taylor.
    1994.   An evaluation of international migration theory: The North American
        case. *Population and Development Review* 20 (4): 699–751.

McAllister, Carlota.
    2000.   Good people: Violence and responsibility in a post-revolutionary
        Guatemalan village. Ph.D. dissertation, Johns Hopkins University.

McCleary, Rachel.
    1997.   Guatemala's postwar prospects. *Journal of Democracy* 8 (2): 129–43.

McCreery, David.
    1983.   Debt servitude in rural Guatemala, 1876–1936. *Hispanic American
        Historical Review* 63 (4): 735–59.
    1990.   State power, indigenous communities, and land in nineteenth-century
        Guatemala. In *Guatemalan Indians and the state: 1540 to 1988*, ed.
        C. Smith, with the assistance of Marilyn N. Moors, 96–115. Austin:
        University of Texas Press.
    1994.   *Rural Guatemala: 1760–1940*. Stanford, CA: Stanford University Press.

Messer, Ellen.
    1995.   Anthropology and human rights in Latin America. *Journal of Latin
        American Anthropology* 1 (1).

MINUGUA.
    2000.   Undécimo informe sobre derechos humanos de la misión de
        verificación de las naciones unidas en Guatemala. Guatemala,
        September.

Monaghan, John.
    1995.   *The covenants with earth and rain: Exchange, sacrifice, and revelation
        in Mixtec sociality.* Norman: University of Oklahoma Press.

Montejo, Víctor D.
    1987.   *Testimonio: Muerte de una comunidad indígena en Guatemala.*
        Editorial Universitaria, Coleccion 500 anos, vol. 2. Universidad de
        San Carlos de Guatemala.
    1993.   The dynamics of cultural resistance and transformations: The case
        of Guatemalan-Mayan refugees in Mexico. Ph.D. Dissertation,
        University of Connecticut.
    1999.   Tied to the land: Maya migration, exile, and transnationalism. In
        *Identities on the move: Transnational processes in North America and
        the Caribbean basin*, ed. Liliana R. Goldin, 185–202. Albany, NY:
        Institute for Mesoamerican Studies, State University of New York.

Morris, David B.
    1997.   About suffering: Voice, genre, and moral community. In *Social*

suffering, ed. Arthur Kleinman, Veena Das, and Margaret Lock. Berkeley and Los Angeles: University of California Press.

Nash, Manning.
1989.   *The cauldron of ethnicity in the modern world*. Chicago: University of Chicago Press.

Nell, Liza.
2004.   Conceptualizing the emergence of immigrants' transnational communities. *Migration Letters* 1 (1): 50–56.

Nelson, Diane M.
1999a.   *A finger in the wound: Body politics in quincentennial Guatemala*. Berkeley and Los Angeles: University of California Press.
1999b.   *Rigoberta Menchù, is truth stranger than testimonial?* Guatemala: Guatemala Scholars Network.

Nolin Hanlon, Catherine L.
1995.   Flight, exile and return: Place and identity among Guatemalan Maya refugees. Master's thesis, Queen's University, Kingston, Ontario.
2000.   Transnational ruptures: Political violence and refugee and (im)migrant experiences in Guatemala and Canada. Ph.D. dissertation, Department of Geography, Queens University.

Nonini, Donald M., and Aihwa Ong, eds.
1997.   *Undergrounded empires: The cultural politics of modern Chinese transnationalism*. New York: Routledge.

North, Liisa L., and Alan B. Simmons.
1999.   Fear and hope: Return and transformation in historical perspective. In *Journeys of fear: Refugee return and national transformation in Guatemala*, ed. Liisa L. North and Alan B. Simmons, 3–30. Montreal: McGill-Queen's University Press.

Oakes, Maud.
1951.   *The two crosses of Todos Santos: Survivals of Mayan religious ritual*. Princeton, NJ: Princeton University Press.

ODHAG (Oficina de Derechos Humanos del Arzobispado de Guatemala).
1997.   *Informe Anual 1996*. www.odhag.org.gt. Guatemala City: ODHAG.
1998a.   *Informe Anual 1997*. Guatemala City: ODHAG.
1998b.   *Guatemala: Nunca más. Informe proyecto interdiocesano de recuperación de la memoria histórica*. Guatemala City: ODHAG.

Olmos, Miguel Aguilera.
2001.   Fronteras imaginadas. Paper presented at Conference ACELAC/ CALACS. Antigua, Guatemala, February 22–24, 2001.

Olwig, Karen Fog, and Kirsten Hastrup, eds.
1997.   *Siting culture: The shifting anthropological object*. London: Routledge.

Ong, Aihwa.
  1999.   *Flexible citizenship: The cultural logics of transnationality*. Durham,
          NC: Duke University Press.

Oxfam.
  1982.   *Witness to political violence in Guatemala*. New York: Oxfam America.

Payeras, Mario.
  1983.   *Days of the jungle*. New York: Monthly Review Press.

Pellizzi, Francesco.
  1988.   To seek refuge: Nation and ethnicity in exile. In *Ethnicities and
          nations: processes of interethnic relations in Latin America, Southeast
          Asia, and the Pacific*, ed. R. Guidieri, F. Pellizzi, and S. Tambiah.
          Austin: University of Texas Press.

Peñalosa, Fernando.
  1996.   *The Mayan folktale: An introduction*. Rancho Palos Verdes, CA: Yax
          Te' Press.

Perera, Victor.
  1993.   *Unfinished conquest: The Guatemalan tragedy*. Berkeley and Los
          Angeles: University of California Press.

Pessar, Patricia R.
  1988.   Introduction: Migration myths and new realities. In *When borders
          don't divide: Labour migration and refugee movements in the Americas*,
          ed. Patricia Pessar. New York: Center for Migration Studies.

Pœrregaard, Karsten.
  1997.   Imagining a place in the Andes: In the borderland of lived, invented,
          and analyzed culture. In *Siting culture: The shifting anthropological
          object*, ed. Daren Fog Olwig and Kirsten Hastrup. New York:
          Routledge.

Popkin, Eric.
  1999.   Guatemalan Mayan migration to Los Angeles: Constructing
          transnational linkages in the context of the settlement process. *Ethnic
          and Racial Studies* 22 (2): 267–89.

Portes, Alejandro.
  2003.   Conclusion: Theoretical convergencies and empirical evidence in the
          study of immigrant transnationalism. *International Migration Review*.
          37 (3): 874–92.

Portes, Alejandro, and Rubén G. Rumbaut.
  1996.   *Immigrant America: A portrait*. Berkeley: University of California
          Press.

Portes, Alejandro, Luis E. Guarnizo, and Patricia Landolt.
    1999.   The study of transnationalism: Pitfalls and promise of an emergent
             research field. *Ethnic and Racial Studies* 22 (2): 217–37.

Rajchman, John, ed.
    1995.   *The identity in question.* New York: Routledge.

Remijnse, Simone.
    2002.   *Memories of violence: Civil patrols and the legacy of conflict in Joyabaj,
             Guatemala.* Amsterdam: Rozenberg Publishers.

Ricoeur, Paul.
    1976.   *Interpretation theory: Discourse and the surplus of meaning.* Fort
             Worth: Texas Christian University Press.
    1984.   *Time and narrative.* Vol. 3. Chicago: University of Chicago Press.

Rouse, Roger Christopher.
    1989.   Mexican migration to the United States: Family relations in the
             development of a transnational migrant circuit. Ph.D. dissertation,
             Stanford University, California.
    1991.   Mexican migration and the social space of postmodernism. *Diaspora*
             1 (1): 8–23.
    1992.   Making sense of settlement: Class transformation, cultural struggle,
             and transnationalism among Mexican migrants in the United States.
             In *Towards a transnational perspective on migration: Race, class,
             ethnicity, and nationalism reconsidered,* ed. Nina Glick Schiller et al.,
             25–52. Annals of the New York Academy of Sciences, vol. 645. New
             York: New York Academy of Sciences.

Rousseau, Cécile, Maria Morales, and Patricia Foxen.
    2001.   Going home: Giving voice to memory strategies of young Mayan
             refugees who returned to Guatemala as a community. *Culture,
             Medicine and Psychiatry* 25: 135–68.

Rushdie, Salman.
    1991.   *Imaginary homelands: Essays and criticism 1981–1991.* London:
             Granta Books.

Sanford, Victoria.
    2003.   *Buried secrets: Truth and human rights in Guatemala.* New York:
             Palgrave Macmillan.

Sassen, Saskia.
    1999.   *Guests and aliens.* New York: New Press.

Sayad, Abdelmalek.
    1999.   *La double abscence: Des illusions de l'émigré aux souffrances de
             l'immigré.* Collection Liber. Paris: Seuil.

Scarry, Elaine.
  1985.   *The body in pain: The making and unmaking of the world.* New York:
          Oxford University Press.

Schirmer, Jennifer.
  1998.   *The Guatemalan military project: A violence called democracy.*
          Philadelphia: University of Pennsylvania Press.
  2003.   Whose testimony? Whose truth? Where are the armed actors in the
          Stoll-Menchú controversy? *Human Rights Quarterly* (25) 1: 60–73.

Schlesinger, Stephen, and Stephen Kinzer.
  1982.   *Bitter fruit: The untold story of the American coup in Guatemala.* 1st
          ed. Garden City, NY: Doubleday.

Sexton, James D., ed.
  1981.   *Son of Tecún Umán: A Mayan Indian tells his life story.* Tucson:
          University of Arizona Press.
  1985.   *Campesino: The diary of a Guatemalan Indian.* Tucson: University of
          Arizona Press.
  1992.   *Ignacio: The diary of a Mayan Indian of Guatemala.* Philadelphia:
          University of Pennsylvania Press.

Simon, Jean-Marie.
  1987.   *Guatemala: Eternal spring, eternal tyranny.* New York: W. W. Norton.

Smith, Carol A.
  1988.   Destruction of the material bases for Indian culture: Economic
          changes in Totonicapán. In *Harvest of violence: The Maya Indians
          and the Guatemalan crisis,* ed. Robert M. Carmack, 206–34. Norman:
          University of Oklahoma Press.
  1990a. Introduction: Social relations in Guatemala over time and space. In
          Guatemalan Indians and the state: 1540 to 1988, ed. C. Smith, with
          the assistance of Marilyn N. Moors, 1–34. Austin: University of Texas
          Press.
  1990b. Origins of the national question in Guatemala: A hypothesis. In
          Guatemalan Indians and the state: 1540 to 1988, ed. C. Smith, with
          the assistance of Marilyn N. Moors, 72–95. Austin: University of
          Texas Press.
  1990c. Class position and class consciousness in an Indian community:
          Totonicapan in the 1970s. In *Guatemalan Indians and the state:
          1540 to 1988,* ed. C. Smith, with the assistance of Marilyn N. Moors,
          205–29. Austin: University of Texas Press.
  1990d. Failed nationalist movements in 19th century Guatemala: A parable
          for the third world. In *Nationalist ideologies and the production
          of national cultures,* ed. R. G. Fox. American Ethnological
          Society Monograph Series, No. 2. Washington, DC: American
          Anthropological Society.

1991.   Maya nationalism. *NACLA Report on the Americas* 25 (3): 29–33.

1993.   Local history in global context: Social and economic transitions
        in western Guatemala. In *Constructing culture and power in Latin
        America,* ed. D. H. Levine. Ann Arbor: University of Michigan Press.

Smith, Carol A., ed., with the assistance of Marilyn Moors.

1990.   *Guatemalan Indians and the state: 1540 to 1988.* Austin: University of
        Texas Press.

Smith, Waldemar R.

1977.   *The fiesta system and economic change.* New York: Columbia
        University Press.

Stavenhagen, Rodolfo.

1975.   *Social classes in agrarian societies.* Garden City, NY: Doubleday.

Stepputat, Finn.

1994.   The imagined return community of Guatemalan refugees. *Refuge* 13
        (10): 13–15.

1995.   Repatriation and the politics of space: The case of the Mayan diaspora
        and return movement. *Journal of Refugee Studies* 7 (2–3): 175–85.

Stoll, David.

1993.   *Between two armies in the Ixil towns of Guatemala.* New York:
        Columbia University Press.

1997.   To whom should we listen? Human rights activism in two
        Guatemalan land disputes. In *Human rights, culture, and context:
        Anthropological perspectives,* ed. Richard A. Wilson, 187–215.
        Chicago: Pluto Press.

1999.   *Rigoberta Menchú and the story of all poor Guatemalans.* Boulder, CO:
        Westview Press.

Strathern, Marilyn.

1995.   Nostalgia and the new genetics. In *Rhetorics of self-making,* ed. D.
        Battaglia. Berkeley and Los Angeles: University of California Press.

Suarez-Orozco, Marcelo M.

1990.   Speaking the unspeakable: Toward a psychological understanding of
        responses to terror. *Ethos* 18 (3): 353–83.

Summerfield, Derek.

1998.   The social experience of war and some issues for the humanitarian
        field. In *Rethinking the trauma of war,* ed. P. J. Bracken and C. Petty,
        9–37. London: Free Association Books.

Swetnam, John.

1989.   What else did Indians have to do with their time? Alternatives
        to labor migration in pre-revolutionary Guatemala. *Economic
        Development and Cultural Change* 38: 89–112.

Taussig, Michael.
   1987.   *Shamanism, colonialism, and the wild man: A study in terror and healing.* Chicago: University of Chicago Press.

Tax, Sol.
   1937.   The municipios of the midwestern highlands of Guatemala. *American Anthropologist* 39 (3): 423–44.
   1953.   *Penny capitalism: A Guatemalan Indian economy.* Chicago: University of Chicago Press.

Tedlock, Barbara.
   1982.   *Time and the highland Maya.* Albuquerque: University of New Mexico Press.

Tedlock, Dennis, translator.
   1996.   *Popol Vuh: The definitive edition of the Maya book of the dawn of life and the glories of gods and kings.* New York: Simon and Schuster.

Thelen, David.
   1989.   Memory and American history. *Journal of American History* 75 (4).

Thomas-Hope, E. M.
   1985.   Return migration and its implications for Caribbean development: The unexplored connection. In *Migration and development in the Caribbean: The unexplored connection,* ed. M. Kritz, L. Lim, and H. Zlotnik. New York: Oxford University Press.

Todorov, Tzvetan.
   1984.   *The conquest of America.* New York: Harper Collins.

Trouillot, Michel-Rolph.
   1991.   Anthropology and the savage slot: The poetics and politics of otherness. In *Recapturing anthropology: Working in the present,* ed. R. Fox. Santa Fe, NM: School of American Research.

Trudeau, Robert H.
   1993.   Understanding transitions to democracy: Recent work on Guatemala. *Latin American Research Review* 28 (1): 235–47.

Tsing, Anna Lowenhaupt.
   1994.   From the margins. *Cultural Anthropology* 9 (3): 279–97.

UNDP.
   2000.   *Human Development Report 2000.* Published for the United Nations Development Programme. New York: Oxford University Press.

U.S. Census Bureau.
   2003   *The Hispanic population in the United States: March 2002.* www.census.gov/prod/2003pubs/p20-545.pdf.

Van Gennep, Arnold.
  1960.   *The rites of passage.* Translated by Monika B. Vizedom and Gabrielle
          L. Caffe. Introduction by Solon T. Kimball. Chicago: University of
          Chicago Press.

Varese, Stefano.
  1997.   Identidad y destierro: Los pueblos indígenas ante la globalización.
          Revista de Critica Literaria Latinoamericana 23 (46): 19–35.

Vertovec, Steven.
  1999.   Conceiving and researching transnationalism. *Ethnic and Racial
          Studies* 22 (2): 447–62.

Wagley, Charles.
  1941.   *Economics of a Guatemalan village.* Memoirs of the American
          Anthropological Association 58. Menasha, WI: American
          Anthropological Association. .
  1949.   *The social and religious life of a Guatemalan village.* Memoirs of the
          American Anthropological Association 71. Menasha, WI: American
          Anthropological Association.

Warren, Kay B.
  1978.   *The symbolism of subordination: Indian identity in a Guatemalan
          town.* Austin: University of Texas Press.
  1992.   Transforming memories and histories: The meanings of ethnic
          resurgence for Mayan Indians. In *Americas: New interpretive essays,*
          ed. Alfred Stepan. New York: Oxford University Press. .
  1993.   Interpreting *la violencia* in Guatemala: Shapes of Mayan silence and
          resistance. In *The violence within: Cultural and political opposition in
          divided nations,* ed. K. B. Warren. Boulder, CO: Westview Press.
  1998.   *Indigenous movements and their critics: Pan-Maya activism in
          Guatemala.* Princeton, NJ: Princeton University Press.

Watanabe, John M.
  1990.   Enduring yet ineffable community in the western periphery of
          Guatemala. In *Guatemalan Indians and the state: 1540 to 1988,* ed.
          C. Smith, with the assistance of Marilyn N. Moors, 183–204. Austin:
          University of Texas Press.
  1992.   *Maya saints and souls in a changing world.* Austin: University of Texas
          Press.

Wasserstrom, Robert.
  1975.   Revolution in Guatemala: Peasants and politics under the Arbenz
          government. *Comparative Studies in Society and History* 17: 443–78.

Wearne, Phillip, and Peter Calvert.
  1989.   *The Maya of Guatemala.* Report (Minority Rights Group) No. 62.
          London: Minority Rights Group.

Weber, Max.
   1997.   What is an ethnic group? In *The ethnicity reader: Nationalism, multiculturalism, and migration*, ed. M. Guibernau and J. Rex, 15–16. Cambridge: Polity Press.

Weissert, Will.
   2000.   Guatemala vigilante killings common. Associated Press, *New York Times*, July 11, 2000.

Wellmeier, Nancy.
   1994.   Rituals of resettlement: Identity and resistance among Maya refugees. In *Selected papers on refugee issues: III*, ed. J. L. Macdonald and A. Zaharalick. Committee on Refugee Issues, American Anthropological Association. Washington DC: American Anthropological Association.
   1998.   *Ritual, identity, and the Mayan diaspora*. New York: Garland Publishers.

Wilkinson, Daniel.
   2002.   *Silence on the mountain: Stories of terror, betrayal, and forgetting in Guatemala*. New York: Houghton Mifflin.

Williams, Braquette F.
   1989.   A class act: Anthropology and the race to nation across ethnic terrain. *Annual Review of Anthropology* 18: 401–44.

Wilson, Thomas M., and Hastings Donnan, eds.
   1998.   *Border identities: Nation and state at international frontiers*. Cambridge: Cambridge University Press.

Wilson, Richard.
   1991.   Machine guns and mountain spirits: The cultural effects of state repression among the Q'eqchi' of Guatemala. *Critique of Anthropology* 11 (1): 33–61.
   1995.   *Maya resurgence in Guatemala: Q'eqchi' experiences*. Norman: University of Oklahoma Press.
   1997a.   Comment: Consciousness, violence, and the politics of memory in Guatemala. *Current Anthropology* 38 (5): 832–35.

Wilson, Richard, ed.
   1997b.   *Human rights, culture, and Context*. London: Pluto Press.

Wolf, Eric.
   1957.   Closed corporate peasant communities in Mesoamerica and central Java. *Southwestern Journal of Anthropology* 13 (1): 1–18.

Wolfensohn, Galit.
   2001.   Refugees and collective action: A case study of the association of dispersed Guatemalan refugees. *Refuge* 19 (3): 25–31.

Woodward, Ralf Lee, Jr.
  1976.   *Central America: A nation divided.* New York: Oxford University
           Press.
  1990.   Changes in nineteenth-century Guatemalan state and its Indian
           policies. In *Guatemalan Indians and the state: 1540 to 1988,* ed. C.
           Smith, with the assistance of Marilyn N. Moors, 52–71. Austin:
           University of Texas Press.

Young, Allan.
  1995.   *The harmony of illusions: Inventing post-traumatic stress disorder.*
           Princeton, NJ: Princeton University Press.

Zarowsky, Christina.
  2004.   Writing trauma: Emotion, ethnography, and the politics of suffering
           among Somali returnees in Ethiopia. *Culture, Medicine and Psychiatry*
           28 (2): 189–209.

Zur, Judith N.
  1998.   *Violent memories: Mayan war widows in Guatemala.* Boulder, CO:
           Westview Press.

INDEX

Numbers in parentheses following notes indicate main text page with references to those notes.

family members left behind for, 127, 137, 139, 140, 218

hired workers for, 72, 96, 129–30

knowledge not passed on for, 96, 142, 143, 144

maintenance of, remittances for, 96, 129–30

overview of, 69–70

photographs of, 175

by PLANTAS leaders, 163

on rented land, 256, 257

by urbanized K'iche's, 72

wage labor in addition to, 64, 77

wartime disruption of, 89

milpa (defined), 254

milpa products, commodification of, 43

Mingo, Don (elderly father of transmigrants), 137

MINUGUAs (term), 20, 271n33

MINUGUA (United Nations Human Rights Mission)

departure, aftermath of, 252

as *Derechos Humanos* concept personified, 296n11 (209)

indigenous rights promoted by, 169

Mayan ceremony, presence at, 167

peace process, participation in, 10, 21

postwar human rights monitoring of, 55, 57

purpose and activities of, 53–54, 280–81nn60–62, 281n64

mirror, broken, memory as, 295n3 (204)

missionaries, impact of, 46

MLN (Movimiento de Liberación Nacional), 81

mobility, meanings, collective of, 65, 66, 152

mobility, types of, 78

mob vigilante justice, 54–55, 281n66

model villages, 50, 52, 278n50

modernization impact on indigenous identity, 24

mojados

defined, 2, 254, 268n4

essentialized, 194–97

identification as, 171

identity of, 153

music on experiences of, 4, 268n6

Momostenango, Indian uprising at, 31, 274n18 (32)

money, sending home. *See* remittances

money, transporting, 19, 20, 101, 128

monolingualism (term), xx, 266n33

monte, el

defined, 268n5 (2)

Indianness, attitudes toward, 176

living conditions in, 234

migration from, 103

remittances to, 129

residents, social status of, 78

Montreal, Canada, Central American refugee community in, xiv

"moral community of forgetting," 205, 220–22

Morales, Inocente, 96–97, 123–24, 148, 170–71, 173–74, 177, 188, 190–91, 251, 252, 256–57, 258

morality, 69, 70, 72

moral notions, shared, 203

multicultural model, 24

multiple identities, 194, 200–201, 249–50, 293n8 (159)

multiplicity of migration strategies and options, 78, 79, 126, 127, 197, 234, 283n79 (60)

multiplicity of references, 172

multisite research, strengths of, 21

municipios

creation of, 26

economic interdependence of, 35

ethnic self-categorization in, 35, 36

external influences resisted by, 33

forced labor impact on, 32

heterogeneous, 23

land conflicts between, 31, 40

organization, changes in, 81

party politics in, 39

postwar conditions in, 58

music on transnational experience, 4, 268n6

mutual aid and support, 122, 132

"myth of return," 232

narrativity, meaning, creating through, 295n2 (203)

Natalia, Doña (grandmother), 143

Natalia, Doña (grandmother), family of, 255–56

National Civil Police Force, 54

National Congress of Guatemalan Organizations (Congreso Nacional de Organizaciones Guatemaltecos), 291n29 (118)

National Coordinating Committee of Guatemalan Widows (CONAVIGUA), 155